D1557415

CULTURES OF COMMERCE

Cultures of Commerce

Representation and American Business Culture, 1877–1960

Edited by
Elspeth H. Brown,
Catherine Gudis,
and
Marina Moskowitz

CULTURES OF COMMERCE
© Elspeth H. Brown, Catherine Gudis, and Marina Moskowitz, 2006.

First published in 2006 by
PALGRAVE MACMILLAN™
175 Fifth Avenue, New York, N.Y. 10010 and
Houndmills, Basingstoke, Hampshire, England RG21 6XS
Companies and representatives throughout the world.

PALGRAVE MACMILLAN is the global academic imprint of the Palgrave Macmillan division of St. Martin's Press, LLC and of Palgrave Macmillan Ltd. Macmillan® is a registered trademark in the United States, United Kingdom and other countries. Palgrave is a registered trademark in the European Union and other countries.

ISBN-13: 978–1–4039–7050–3
ISBN-10: 1–4039–7050–5

Library of Congress Cataloging-in-Publication Data

Cultures of commerce : representation and American business culture, 1877–1960 / edited by Elspeth H. Brown, Catherine Gudis, and Marina Moskowitz.
    p. cm.
Includes bibliographical references.
ISBN 1–4039–7050–5 (alk. paper)
    1. Corporate culture—United States—History. 2. Consumption (Economics)—Social aspects. 3. Advertising—United States—History. 4. Public relations—United States—History. I. Brown, Elspeth H., 1961– II. Gudis, Catherine. III. Moskowitz, Marina, 1968–

HM791.C844 2006
302.3'50973—dc22   2005056289

A catalogue record for this book is available from the British Library.

Design by Newgen Imaging Systems (P) Ltd., Chennai, India.

First edition: May 2006

10 9 8 7 6 5 4 3 2 1

Printed in the United States of America.

In memory of
Clark Davis
(1966–2003)

Contents

List of Illustrations   ix

Contributors   xi

Introduction   1
Elspeth H. Brown, Catherine Gudis, and Marina Moskowitz

Part I   Designing Markets

1   Broadcasting Seeds on the American Landscape   9
    Marina Moskowitz

2   The Importance of Being True Blue: The Du Pont
    Company and the Color Revolution   27
    Regina Lee Blaszczyk

3   The Popular Front and the Corporate Appropriation
    of Modernism   51
    Shannan Clark

4   Rationalizing Consumption: Lejaren à Hiller and the
    Origins of American Advertising Photography, 1913–1924   75
    Elspeth H. Brown

5   Art and Commerce: The Challenge of Modernist
    Advertising Photography   91
    Patricia Johnston

Part II   Business and the Politics of Difference, 1900–1930

6   "New York is Not America": Immigrants and Tourists in
    Post–World War I New York   117
    Angela M. Blake

7 "The First Thing Every Negro Girl Does": Black Beauty Culture,
Racial Politics, and the Construction of Modern Black
Womanhood, 1905–1925   143
Tiffany M. Gill

8 The Sentimental Work of Play: Manhood and the American
Toy Industry, 1900–1930   171
Woody Register

Part III   Commerce and the
Built Environment, 1900–1940

9 The Metropolitan Life Tower: Architecture and Ideology
in the Life Insurance Enterprise   199
Roberta Moudry

10 Architectures of Seduction: Intimate Apparel Trade Shows and
Retail Department Design, 1920–1940   229
Jill Fields

11 The Architecture of Mobility: Outdoor Advertising and
the Birth of the Strip   251
Catherine Gudis

Part IV   Representation and Organizational
Culture in Post–World War II United States

12 Postwar Sign, Symbol, and Symptom:
"The Man in the Gray Flannel Suit"   277
Anna Creadick

13 "Girls in Gray Flannel Suits": White Career Women in
Postwar American Culture   295
Clark Davis

14 Ayn Rand and the Politics of Property   321
Andrew Hoberek

Afterword

15 Advertisements for Ourselves: Being and Time in a
Promotional Economy   343
Jean-Christophe Agnew

Index   365

List of Illustrations

1.1 The "Boston" Small Pea Bean, marketed by Briggs Brothers and Company, of Rochester, New York, in their 1890 catalogue, *Flower, Garden, and Field Seeds*   12

1.2 Six varieties of sugar corn, marketed by the W. Atlee Burpee Company in its 1885 catalogue   14

1.3 The physical plants of the Robert Buist Company, encompassing both growing fields and a busy warehouse scene   20

2.1 The True Blue Oakland was the automotive sensation of 1924. Oakland Motor Car Company, advertisement in *Motor*, January 1924   30

2.2 A lesson in color harmony, Murphy Varnish Company, advertisement in *Autobody*, January 1924   33

2.3 Captain H. Ledyard Towle at the Duco Color Advisory Service in New York. *Du Pont Magazine*, May 1926   35

3.1 Students at the Design Laboratory School made these clocks in 1936 as part of their introductory coursework   55

3.2 The influence of Bauhaus graphic design is readily apparent in this illustration from the cover of pamphlet made in 1939 by the New York Joint Council of the United Office and Professional Workers of America to promote its new group health insurance for its members   62

3.3 A surrealist photomontage created in early 1941 by a student in Herbert Bayer's class for the American Advertising Guild in response to one of his assignments on developing technique   64

4.1 The photographic medium connoted the modern efficiency of American business culture and was used extensively in advertisements based on the rational appeals of "reason why" copy   78

4.2 Hiller's experience in illustrating the subjective became relevant for his later work in advertising. Ad for the Aeolian Company, Lejaren à Hiller, photographer. *The Saturday Evening Post* (November 24, 1917), 46   83

4.3   As Hiller's advertising work progressed, he relied
      increasingly on set design and lighting rather than on
      combination printing to achieve his effects. Ad for the
      Aeolian Company, Lejaren à Hiller, photographer
      The Saturday Evening Post (September 22, 1917), 78   85

5.1   Advertisement for Ide collars, *Vanity Fair,*
      November 1922, p. 5. Paul Outerbridge, Jr., photographer   96

5.2   Photograph for Ford Motor Company, River Rouge Plant,
      "Criss-Crossed Conveyors," 1927   98

5.3   Advertisement for Cannon towels, *Vogue,*
      June 15, 1936, inside cover   105

6.1   This image, accompanying an article by well-known
      government propagandist George Creel, entitled
      "Meeting Pot or Dumping?" appeared in *Collier's*
      magazine, September 3, 1921   128

8.1   Far-seeing businessmen, this illustration from a
      1917 issue of *Playthings* contends, were finally appreciating
      toys as serious business and looking for managers who
      were man enough to lead it out of the "Christmas
      tree class" of seasonal sale   172

8.2   A commonly used strategy for disguising the transparent
      commercialism of toy-selling with the "hearty spirit of
      childhood" was to integrate sales clerks into the commodities
      they sold   180

8.3   Toy men praised Marshall Field's "Inspiration" ad, with
      its civilization-building boy at play and doll-playing
      girl at his knee, for its success in expressing the vital
      necessity of toys as tools for hardy growth, instead of
      gewgaws for mere amusement   185

9.1   Metropolitan Life Insurance Company Home Office, ca. 1909   200

9.2   "A Twentieth Century Campanile in New York" Cover,
      Scientific American, March 30, 1907   207

9.3   Hygienic Drinking Cup, ca. 1920   211

10.1 Marshall Field department store, *Women's &*
      Infants' Furnisher, July 1921, p. 29   236

10.2 Corset fashion show of figure types organized by
      Miss MacKenzie, corset buyer for Gates Dry Goods
      Co., Fort Dodge, Iowa. *Corsets & Brassieres,*
      November 1935, p. 51   242

10.3 This award winning window design at
      Kerr Dry Goods Company, Oklahoma City, Oklahoma
      effectively plays upon themes of female spectatorship,
      undergarments' status as both seen and hidden, and
      women's self-display as "to-be-looked-at."
      Corsets & Brassiers, July 1930, p. 49   245

Contributors

Jean-Christophe Agnew is Professor of American Studies and History at Yale University. He is the author of *Worlds Apart: The Market and the Theater in Anglo-American Thought, 1550–1750* (1986) and numerous articles on consumer culture and cultural history. Most recently he co-edited with Roy Rosenzweig *A Companion to Post-1945 America* (2002).

Angela M. Blake is an Assistant Professor in the Department of Communication and the Program in American Studies at Miami University, Ohio. She teaches courses in media history, sound studies, and urban culture. She is the author of *Spin City: How New York Became American, 1890–1924* (Johns Hopkins University Press, 2006) and has held fellowships at Dumbarton Oaks, the Smithsonian Institution, and the Library of Congress.

Regina Lee Blaszczyk is a visiting scholar in the Department of the History and Sociology of Science at the University of Pennsylvania and a senior research associate at the Hagley Museum and Library. Her books include *Imagining Consumers: Design and Innovation from Wedgwood to Corning* (2000), *Partners in Innovation: Science Education and the Science Workforce* (edited, 2005), and *Major Problems in American Business History: Documents and Essays* (co-edited, 2006).

Elspeth H. Brown is an Assistant Professor of History and American Studies at Miami University, Ohio. She is the author of *The Corporate Eye: Photography and the Rationalization of American Commercial Culture, 1884–1929* (Johns Hopkins University Press, 2005), and has held fellowships at the Smithsonian Institution, the John W. Kluge Center at the Library of Congress, and the Getty Research Institute.

Shannan Clark teaches Contemporary Civilization at Columbia University, where he is completing a dissertation on design, advertising, and publishing in the United States during the middle decades of the twentieth century.

Anna Creadick is Assistant Professor of English and American Studies at Hobart and William Smith Colleges in Geneva, New York. She is currently working on a book-length manuscript about the pursuit of "normality" in post–World War II America.

Clark Davis was Associate Professor of History at CSU Fullerton. He was the author of *Company Men* (JHU Press, 2000), as well as numerous articles.

When he died suddenly in 2003, he was writing a monograph on visions of occupational success in postwar America. This essay stems from that project and is dedicated to his son, Jackson Patrick Koos Davis.

Jill Fields is an Associate Professor of History at California State University, Fresno, where she teaches courses in U.S. social, cultural, and women's history. Her book on the history and meaning of intimate apparel in modern America is being published by the University of California Press in 2006.

Tiffany M. Gill is an Assistant Professor in the Department of History and the Center for African and African American Studies at the University of Texas at Austin. Her dissertation was awarded the Herman E. Krooss Prize for best dissertation in business history at the Business History Conference's (BHC) annual meeting in 2004. *Civic Beauty: Beauty Culturists and the Politics of African American Female Entrepreneurship in the Twentieth Century*, her forthcoming book, will be published by the University of Illinois Press.

Catherine Gudis is Assistant Professor of History at the University of California, Riverside. She is the author of *Buyways: Billboards, Automobiles, and the American Landscape* (New York and London: Routledge, 2004) and recently completed a large-scale, multimedia project on the history of Wilshire Boulevard for the Los Angeles Conservancy.

Andrew Hoberek is Associate Professor of English and Peace Studies at the University of Missouri-Columbia and the author of *The Twilight of the Middle Class: Post-World War II American Fiction and White-Collar Work* (Princeton, 2005).

Patricia Johnston, Professor of Art History at Salem State College, is author of the award-winning book *Real Fantasies: Edward Steichen's Advertising Photography* (University of California Press, 1997) and editor of *Seeing High and Low: Representing Social Conflict in American Visual Culture* (University of California Press, 2006). She has held fellowships from the National Endowment for the Humanities and the Charles Warren Center for Studies in American History at Harvard University.

Roberta Moudry is an architectural and urban historian. She has taught architectural and urban history at Cornell University, and has received research grants from the National Endowment for the Humanities, the Getty Grant Program, the Architectural History Foundation, the Graham Foundation for Advanced Study in the Fine Arts, and the Gilder Lehrman Institute of American History. She is the editor of *The American Skyscraper: Cultural Histories* (Cambridge University Press, 2005).

Marina Moskowitz is a Senior Lecturer in History and American Studies at the University of Glasgow. She is the author of *Standard of Living: The Measure of the Middle Class in Modern America* (Johns Hopkins University Press, 2004) and has held fellowships at the Smithsonian Institution and the Charles Warren Center at Harvard University.

Woody Register teaches U.S. history and American Studies at Sewanee: The University of the South. He is the author of *The Kid of Coney Island: Fred Thompson and the Rise of American Amusements* (Oxford University Press, 2001).

Introduction

*Elspeth H. Brown, Catherine Gudis, and
Marina Moskowitz*

Toward the end of the nineteenth century, the United States experienced the birth of a nationally integrated business culture. Through both horizontal and vertical integration, as well as the development of the modern corporation, the size of many manufacturing companies increased dramatically. As the second industrial revolution ushered in an era of mass production, modern practices of sales and distribution were developed to stimulate consumption, generating new tiers of managerial, clerical, and sales staff.

These newly minted businessmen and -women turned to cultural forms as a means to enhance the market. A generation of applied psychologists had successfully shown that both workers and consumers were motivated as much by subjective desires and inchoate emotional longings as by rational appeals. If this was the case, how might managers, art directors, retail architects, and other business brokers best reach and persuade the workers and consumers upon which the economy depended? Culture emerged as a key aspect of business strategy in boosting production, planning distribution, and ensuring sales.

While many Americans learned of this new market culture by taking part in it, an even larger sector became familiar with the new force in the American economy through its reflection in a variety of cultural productions. Short stories set in businesses appeared in popular magazines; comic strips of office life played out in the daily newspapers; films and photographs portrayed an emerging corporate culture. The second industrial revolution dovetailed with an emerging mass culture to join mass production and cultural production. The image of American commerce, as well as its participants, the businessman and "office girl," took hold in everyday life.

The editors of this book use the term "culture" to refer to the innumerable productions that a group creates to express and recognize itself, its values, its aesthetics, and its organizing principles. In the case of this book, these productions include dress, film, fiction, printed matter, graphic and product design, and the built environment. Of these many possible components of culture, those characterized by representations are at the core of this book. The term "representation" connotes both the sensory form (the end product if you will) as well as the active process of re-presenting the material world through a set of semiotic conventions denoting, say, socioeconomic distinctions, or those of race, ethnicity, religion, or gender. This volume examines the ways in which cultural representations are harnessed, often deliberately but sometimes unwittingly, to promote business as a fundamental American concern.

Buyers, sellers, and those who mediated between them used these representative mechanisms to draw attention to, understand, and ultimately agree upon the value (economic and otherwise) of particular commodities. When the daily exchange of goods and services became no longer based on a personal agreement of value and the terms of trade, market relations grew increasingly mediated by mass culture, including massively distributed representations. While industrial production continued to accrue the benefits of improved technology and newly designed organizational and managerial systems, these developments were matched by innovations in distribution and marketing. Those who conceived of, designed, depicted, promoted, and sold commodities and professional services made up a burgeoning sector of the white-collar American workforce. American consumers, whose ranks crossed all classes and grew immeasurably in the middle, in turn had widening choices in the ways in which they could engage in the market.

While there is a strong tradition of historical scholarship on the structural changes in American business and their impact on workers and consumers, the broader impact of business on other cultural forms, and vice versa, is a burgeoning field of study. Historians of American culture have increasingly explored the role of commerce in late-nineteenth and twentieth-century history; historians of business are increasingly turning to the realm of culture to explore the fuller influences on and implications of decisions made within the business community. On the first of these two axes, *Cultures of Commerce* builds on the growing literature that explores commerce and consumption as one thread in the creation of a modern American culture. On the second axis, the current generation of business historians is answering recent challenges to incorporate broader cultural perspectives into their studies.

The following essays are linked by the argument that the structures and perspectives of American business both influenced and reflected American culture during the country's shift to mass production and consumption at the end of the nineteenth century through the postwar economic boom of the 1950s. Images of production processes, consumer goods, or the workers and managers who created these goods, whether in fiction, photographs, architecture, art, or film, reflected the tensions of American attitudes toward business, as the impulse toward economic and technological "progress" clashed with an older set of American ideals based on financial independence and individual freedom. By looking at the broader meanings of these business representations, as well as the mechanisms by which these images were produced, distributed, and often sold, this collection explores both the culture of the market and the marketplace of culture.

The essays presented in this book focus on the intersection of culture with modern market relations, with a focus on the late nineteenth- and twentieth-century United States. The chapters overall raise themes such as the relationship between commerce and culture; the role of design and aesthetics in the production and distribution of goods; how ethnic, gender, and racial difference intersect with market economies; the design of the built environment in relationship to both production and retail sites; and the representation of postwar organizational culture. The essays overall stress the centrality of culture in structuring modern market relations.

The volume is divided into four parts that are organized chronologically and thematically. Part I, "Designing Markets," explores how culture brokers central to the creation and distribution of commercial aesthetics, such as art directors, photographers, and color consultants, drew upon design principles to build markets for commodities.

Marina Moskowitz's "Broadcasting Seeds on the American Landscape" analyzes marketing material relating to the nineteenth-century seed trade, which produced a visual culture inspired by botanical illustration in the natural sciences, still-life painting in art, and advertising ephemera in commerce. These visual representations reinforced the promise of the variety and abundance of the American landscape, while also depicting the increasing industrialization of the trade itself, through commercial "self-portraits" of warehouses and factory-like spaces devoted to packaging and exchange.

Regina Lee Blaszczyk's "The Importance of Being True Blue: The Du Pont Company and the Color Revolution" examines the use of color styling (a precursor to industrial design) as a prime marketing effort of the 1920s. In doing so, Blaszczyk considers the product itself as a marketing tool. In "The Popular Front and the Corporate Appropriation of Modernism," Shannon Clark explores a range of ambitious cultural initiatives conducted by members of the leftist avant-garde in the 1930s to promote visual modernism as a means of furthering radical social transformation, including collaborations with liberal allies at the sites of mass cultural production. He finds that these collaborations unintentionally abetted the assimilation and appropriation of modernist aesthetics by business in order to legitimate corporate capitalism.

Two of the essays in "Designing Markets" focus on early twentieth-century commercial photography. Elspeth H. Brown's "Rationalizing Consumption: Photography and Commercial Illustration, 1913–1919," investigates early commercial photographic practice in order to understand the role of photography in negotiating the implicit cultural tension caused by increased rationalization of work, the standardization of consumer goods, and the psychology of "individual" desire. The major figure for this essay is Lejaren à Hiller, a photographic illustrator who, in the World War I years, invented photographic illustration for print advertising in its modern form. Patricia Johnston's essay "Art and Commerce: The Challenge of Modernist Advertising Photography" demonstrates how the conceptualization by modernist theory of art and commerce as separate enterprises obfuscated a more complex historical record. While modernist theory tried to draw clear lines between fine and applied arts (and between culture and commerce), interwar advertising and high culture practices blurred and overlapped the boundaries of artistic and commercial photography.

The essays in Part II, "Business and the Politics of Difference," show how gender, racial, and ethnic differences have been depicted and deployed by business boosters and entrepreneurs to further a range of social, political, and economic goals. In " 'New York is Not America': Immigrants and Tourists in Post–World War I New York," Angela Blake examines urban tourism in postwar New York City, when the city's large immigrant population presented a challenge to city boosters, who still struggled with ongoing perceptions that New York was not "America." By the 1920s, boosters and tourism promoters used the image of the city's diversity for their own purposes, transforming an older fashion for "slumming" in the city's "foreign" quarters to attract middle-class tourists.

Tiffany M. Gill's " 'The First Thing Every Negro Girl Does': Black Beauty Culture, Racial Politics, and the Construction of Modern Black Womanhood, 1905–1925" shows how black beauty culturists found financial stability as entrepreneurs, as well as means of personal expression. Gill also illuminates how the industry allowed its practitioners entry into the arena of Post–World War I racial politics. Woody Register's "The Sentimental Work of Play: Manhood and the American Toy Industry, 1900–1930" considers the marketing schemes of men in the American toy business who were faced with the problem of how to present their own work as constructive and masculine while marketing their products as suitable for play. Their work helped broaden the leisure class.

Part III, "Commerce and the Built Environment, 1900–1940," focuses on the implications of the market on architecture and the built environment, as well as the influence of the increasingly conquered American landscape on the market. Roberta Moudry's "The Metropolitan Life Tower: Architecture and Ideology in the Life Insurance Enterprise" examines the Metropolitan Life Insurance Company and their building program in New York City in the first half of the twentieth century. Moudry's study of the Met Life building traces the three-dimensional impact of a corporation and its culture on the spaces of the city. Jill Fields' essay, "Architectures of Seduction: Intimate Apparel Trade Shows and Retail Department Design, 1920–1940," explores retail interior design and wholesale promotions concerning the merchandizing of corsets in the interwar period. The essay argues that corset merchandizers relied upon idealized associations with feminine elegance, romance, and heterosexuality to promote shopping and commerce itself as a sexually alluring, yet respectable, activity. Catherine Gudis' essay, "The Architecture of Mobility: Outdoor Advertising and the Birth of the Strip," examines how the desire of advertisers to address mobile audiences fostered new architectural types, urban decentralization, and an increasing sense of placelessness, while it unhinged the market from geographic borders.

Part IV, "Representation and Organizational Culture in Post–World War II United States," concerns the fictional representations and material culture of postwar corporate America. In "Postwar Sign, Symbol, and Symptom: 'The Man in the Gray Flannel Suit'," Anna Creadick analyzes the material culture of the icon of the twentieth-century business world: the gray flannel suit. Drawing on fashion journalism, popular literature, and film, Creadick traces the rise of the business dress in the twentieth century. In his essay " 'Girls in Gray Flannel Suits': White Career Women in Postwar American Culture," Clark Davis questions the myth of the suburban housewife in postwar America by exploring the increase in paid work for middle-class white women. Davis juxtaposes an economic history of the female labor force with the representation of the working woman in postwar American film.

Andrew Hoberek's essay "Ayn Rand and the Politics of Property" analyzes the author and philosopher Ayn Rand's 1957 novel *Atlas Shrugged* (1957) in relation to contemporary critiques of conformist culture. Hoberek argues that Rand's portrayal of heroic owner-operators served to conserve a middle-class agency in a period when entrepreneurial autonomy had given way to a new definition of the middle class based on white-collar, managerial employment.

The volume's concluding essay is Jean-Christophe Agnew's "Advertisements for Ourselves: Being and Time in a Promotional Economy," a meditation on the history and historiography of commercial culture. Agnew traces the increased diffusion of promotional culture over the course of the twentieth century and the ways in which the acts of buying and selling have become harder to separate into discrete practices. Agnew suggests that looking to the cultural form itself may help provide some interpretive cohesion to the difficult range of phenomena that comprise the contemporary market.

Although all of the essays touch on different aspects of the intersection of culture and commerce, a number of topics and concepts appear and reappear throughout the essays. A prominent thread is the centrality of design, in both two and three dimensions, whether in product advertising, color forecasting, or corporate and commercial architecture. The essays also seek to bring into dialogue relations of production, distribution, and consumption—aspects of market economies that historians often treat separately. These essays demonstrate the importance of considering the market cohesively, in which individuals play different roles: we are each of us producers, distributors, and consumers, sometimes at different times, sometimes simultaneously. As a whole, the authors interrogate the relationship between markets and cultures, emphasizing the use of representation both in organizing business and in training Americans for this range of overlapping roles.

As a final word, the editors hope that the historical moments explored by this scholarship will provide enough clarity of distance to enable readers to fathom our own times.

Part I

Designing Markets

Chapter 1

Broadcasting Seeds on the American Landscape

Marina Moskowitz[1]

Prior to the nineteenth century, whatever planting was done by Americans (first colonists and then citizens) originated with seeds that were saved from previous plantings, traded informally both on the North American continent and across the Atlantic, or received as small gifts. By the end of the nineteenth century, over 800 companies had been formed (and some had already disbanded and merged into larger ones) to supply growers of all sorts with seeds.[2] What changed? How did an object that farmers and gardeners could well produce themselves from year to year by letting a few plants reach maturity become a commodity? The answer to this question was, of course, a multifaceted narrative, but at the heart of that narrative were not words, but images. The prolific illustrated broadcasts of the seed trade were central to this complex process of commodification.

While it could be argued that all businesses benefited from developments in print technology over the course of the nineteenth century, there does seem to have been a special relationship between, or even overlap of, seed sellers and the printing trade.[3] Several early American seed sellers were also trained as printers and published their own catalogues, while the larger seed companies that flourished in the late-nineteenth century often included on-site printing works to produce their marketing materials. Over time, this printed matter incorporated copious illustrations, from wood engravings to chromolithographs and electrotypes. Covers of seed catalogues and the color plates tipped in between their pages, seed packages, trade cards, and other promotional materials proliferated over the course of the nineteenth century. Still, many industries produced the volume of printing that the seed trade did, and in similar forms of ephemera. What set the seed trade apart from other businesses was not the medium but the content of their promotional materials.

The seed trade offered more individual items for sale than perhaps any other industry, packaging the variety of nature enhanced by the science of hybridization. Each new plant strain or species, whether found or created, was an opportunity for illustration, and the possible combinations of these specimens were, literally, countless. More unusually, in the seed industry, illustrations in advertisements, catalogues, or on packages did not represent the actual object sold. Seeds themselves were not depicted, but rather the promise of what those seeds might produce. This may seem quite an obvious point, but it set the seed trade apart from many other businesses that employed various forms of printmaking, and later photography, to represent their merchandise. Seed companies did not represent what they themselves produced, but rather what purchasers of their seeds could produce. While concerns with accuracy of representation did still come into play, this one step remove from the product sold allowed for greater artistic license to depict the ideal outcome of planting. Even if the companies claimed that a given image was accurately based on an actual specimen grown from a particular type of seed, the temporal, perishable quality of the plants made that accuracy impossible to measure. It is both this abundance of possible images and the ability to paint and print them in creative ways that lent visual culture its particular importance to the seed trade.

The pictorial tradition of the seed trade both documented and itself helped constitute the process of commodification that allowed for such rapid growth of commercial exchange. The graphic materials allowed potential purchasers to envision the end results of consumer goods that were, in their own right, difficult to evaluate. Seeds became saleable in part because of the visual identifications offered by companies for flowers and produce. Whether the graphics depicted newly developed strains that literally had not been seen before, or served as reminders of what the best culture of common varieties could produce, they were increasingly considered a necessary component of the description of a firm's seed list to the point where many seed catalogues contained illustrations of every flower and most vegetable seeds for sale. While verbal descriptions were still useful for quantitative information, such as the length of time to the bearing of fruit or flowers, their communication of more qualitative information—what a flower looked like or what size a specimen of vegetable was—often depended on comparison to other plants, relying on some degree of horticultural literacy. Graphics made such information more easily accessible to a wider potential market by not requiring specialized information and by tapping into familiar visual conventions of the time. The vibrant horticultural imagery, and the processes by which they were produced, sat at the intersection of a number of trajectories, including still-life painting in fine art; botanical illustration in the natural sciences; and advertising ephemera in the realm of commerce.

Representation

There is no question that the commercial engravers who contributed to the depiction of horticultural commodities were familiar with the artistic currents of their day. The broad range of their subjects, and especially the varied settings of farms, gardens, and domestic interiors in which they situated the plants, allowed for numerous approaches to the art of illustration. Particularly in the lush chromolithographs of American landscapes, first offered as premiums or tipped into catalogues and later incorporated into designs for catalogue covers, artists and the managers for whom they worked had great leeway in determining how best to reach the ever-widening market for seeds.

For example, those charged with producing specifically agrarian images may have been particularly drawn to the work of the Barbizon School, mid-nineteenth-century French landscape painters such as Jean Francois Millet and Theodore Rousseau. The cover of the Spring 1907 catalogue of the Farmer Seed Company, of Faribault, Minnesota, featured a direct copy of Millet's 1857 painting, *The Gleaners*, a well-known image in the United States by that time.[4] At the same time, artists such as James McNeil Whistler, Edgar Degas, and Claude Monet passed along to others on both sides of the Atlantic their fascination with Japanese art, particularly wood block prints; the popularity of *Japonisme* extended as far as garden design, with the introduction of what was deemed appropriate plant material for Japanese style gardens, such as lily bulbs, as well as the stylized depiction of such plants. Because much of commercial illustration relied on printmaking, this influence of Japanese wood block prints had more prosaic applications as well, such as the Rochester-based firm Briggs Brothers and Company's illustration of the Boston small pea bean from an 1890 catalogue (figure 1.1).[5]

While these images show an awareness of specific artistic schools or styles, the ephemera of the seed industry is perhaps most closely related to a specific genre, that of still-life painting. While catalogues did contain numerous images of isolated plants, they also suggested how those plants might be incorporated into domestic settings, such as a vase of flowers or bowl of fruit on a sideboard with domestic furnishings in view. They also showed arrangements of plant material, carefully composed as one might find with other inanimate objects.[6] However, if the overall effect of these illustrations called to mind contemporary still lifes, the process of producing the images might be quite different from the tradition in the fine arts. It is clear from correspondence between the companies and their engravers that issues of composition or arrangement of the specimen to be depicted were carefully negotiated and the final image did not result from the artistic exercise of capturing a small scene in its entirety.

In fact, the commercial still life was often as much of a hybrid as its subjects might be. In some instances, artists were asked to paint specific elements separately, and the elements were even gathered from different sources, and then composed together on the final printing plate. In one instance, a company commissioned representations of three different flowers, explaining, "We expect to make up the flower plate of these three subjects together with a pansy the painting of which was made in Germany."[7] On another occasion a company manager wrote to an artist, "our idea is to have the colored plate of flowers represent one or two of our large Petunias with 3 or 4 of these Balsams and if possible to work in the flower of the canna."[8]

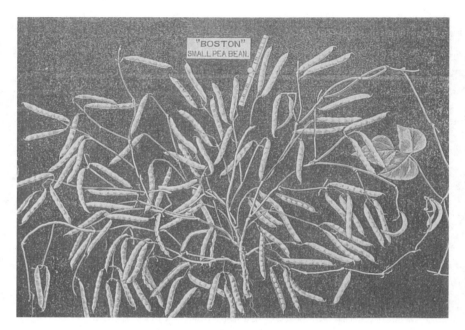

Figure 1.1 The "Boston" Small Pea Bean, marketed by Briggs Brothers and Company, of Rochester, New York, in their 1890 catalogue, *Flower, Garden, and Field Seeds.* The illustration suggests the artist's familiarity with Japanese wood block prints, while also incorporating horticultural information about the states of the bean's growth and the size of pods and individual beans

Source: Warshaw Collection of Business Americana, Archives Center, National Museum of American History, Smithsonian Institution.

These commercial still-life images emphasized both the perfection of particular specimen (and hence the perfection of the seeds on offer) and an overall sense of abundance.

Similarly, the graphics produced by the seed trade were reminiscent of the traditions of botanical illustration, but were sometimes achieved by quite different processes than the direct observation of specimen expected of natural scientists. One of the common tropes of botanical instruction, translated into horticultural tuition by the seed companies, was to show the different states of a particular plant within one image. Hence, flowers were often depicted on stems going all the way down to their roots, and with blossoms in bud, perfectly open, and already dried and containing seeds. For produce, plants might be depicted showing blossoms, the fruit or vegetable, and the seeds that it contained.[9] Both artists and companies seemed aware of these conventions of botanical illustration, and offered their catalogues as a means of both consumer and horticultural instruction. A representative of the Burpee company, founded in 1876 outside of Philadelphia, issued engraver A. Blanc instructions for catalogue illustrations, writing "Please select the best spray of Dolichos and draw it showing 3 or 4 open flowers, a few buds and 3 or 4 of the small seed pods as per specimens."[10] Showing the varied states of growth might be all the more important with vegetables, where at least for peas and beans, the seed pods were also the crop to be physically consumed. The Burpee company directed the artist W.M. Momberger, in painting a new species of pole bean, to "show the distinct character of the leaf, the prolific habit of bearing which you will notice by examining the cluster sent you, and a natural size pod showing size of beans and for this purpose we placed in basket enclosed in an envelope a very good pod."[11] Indeed, peas and beans were often shown as a cutaway drawing, depicting the pod with part of one side torn away to expose the bean.

Companies instructed their customers not only on states of cultivation, but also plant variety, either between or within specie. Illustrations could show the many different types of any given product; for example, catalogues might feature up to thirty varieties of pea, or even one hundred varieties of popular flowers such as sweet peas and pansies. Companies might also wish to show the variety available even to those purchasing one type of seed. Issues of variety were instructed through visual means more easily than verbal descriptions would allow; the artist Momberger was asked to paint a few Balsam flowers all from the same species but with noticeably different markings; his contact at the Burpee company said to him, in a statement that might apply all the more to the potential consumer, "it will no doubt surprise you when we state it is not an unusual thing to find on one plant as many different marked flowers as we have sent you" (figure 1.2).[12]

Although the end result of the illustrations might have been informed by these botanical traditions, the processes of observation were often quite different. The images found in catalogues and chromolithographs were often manufactured; not only depictions of arrangements, but even an image of a single plant might be drawn as a composite of a number of specimens. In 1891, Howard Earl of the Burpee company wrote to the Stecher Lithographic company of Rochester, New York about some plants they had sent for illustration: samples of platycodon, mignonette, and petunia. Of the platycodon, Earl requested an image twice the size of the flower sent; for the mignonette, he requested an image of "a first class Mignonette of great substance with bright red individual flowers," adding the instructions "where the seed pods occur in specimens please fill in with florets." A few days later, Earl sent one beet specimen each to a few different artists; to each one he wrote that the sample "remained in the ground too long and has lost its evenness of form so you will please bear this in mind when painting same."[13] Frequently, the company would send photographs and specimen together, suggesting that an artist, for example, copy the shape of a cabbage depicted in a photograph, using a real cabbage as a guide to color. Despite these manipulations, the companies might also ask engravers to add the words "Painted from Nature" to their plates. Liberties could be taken with the representation of a product's end result, because that image could not be expected to be exactly reproducible—no two plants are ever exactly alike. This natural variety was a benefit, allowing companies to depict

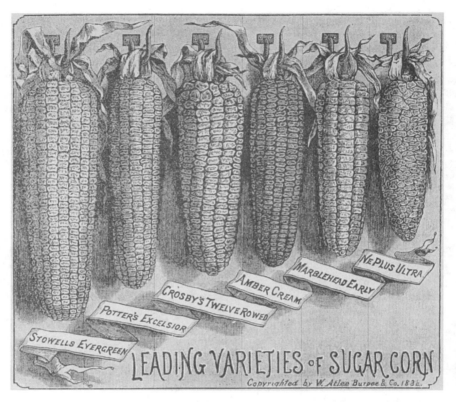

Figure 1.2 Six varieties of sugar corn, marketed by the W. Atlee Burpee Company in its 1885 catalogue. The image introduces the varieties' common names as well as horticultural features such as relative size of ears and kernels

Source: Warshaw Collection of Business Americana, Archives Center, National Museum of American History, Smithsonian Institution.

idealized plants that would inspire potential consumers to try their hands at growing them.

Reproduction

At the heart of the seed trade lay a tension between the variety of nature and the need for reliable—if not reproducible—products to sell. The seed trade was an early and widespread business in the United States, and yet one that defies what are now stereotypical notions of factories and industrial work. While many nineteenth-century entrepreneurs turned to mechanized processes in order to produce uniform goods, the seed trade still had (at least) one foot planted firmly in the soil, and could not seek to overcome the rhythms and range of the natural world. The vibrant horticultural imagery distributed by the trade was used to temper this tension: to promote the natural abundance available from any given company while also assuring consumers of the ideal that could potentially be grown from the product on offer. The relationship between the unique design of nature and the large-scale horticultural production that enables its broad dissemination is paralleled by the unique design of the artist and the mechanical reproduction that allows that design widespread circulation.

The issue of reproducibility, in this case not of consumer goods, but of the illustrations that hold the promise of those goods, was recognized by the trade and addressed in several different ways. "The first natural inquiry is, what in the world does electrotyping have to do with the seed trade?" Briggs and Brother, a seed company based in Rochester, New York, posed this rhetorical question to readers of their 1875 promotional series, *Briggs' Quarterly Floral Work*. Here, they raised a technical question: what form of printmaking was most suited to the scale of the market that the company sought to address? As Briggs and Brother answered the question they had raised: "The engravings are made on wood, and labels cannot be printed from the wood by thousands, so a cast is made from a block and the surface is then plated with copper, ready to go to the press."[14] Briggs outlined the primary use of electrotypography for catalogue illustrations and seed packet labels by the last quarter of the nineteenth century, although chromolithography was used extensively for color plates and catalogue covers.

Seed companies put advancing print technology to good use, seeking to win over not only the ultimate retail consumer but also whatever wholesale mediator might lie in between. Providing eye-catching marketing materials, as well as reliable seeds, was an essential part of the business. In 1895, the Burpee company advertised for agents to sell collections of their flower seeds; they offered as part of their promotional kits what they called an "elegant lithographed hanger, painted in fourteen colors," stating that with such striking advertising matter, the collections would be "easy to sell."[15] Similarly, several companies promoted their decorative seed packets, as well as the seeds within them, essentially advertising their advertisements. Competition over the best seeds might be played out through competition over the best illustrations. The Burpee company gave one commercial artist the direction, "We . . . send you one spike Canna Emile le Clerc of which we want you to paint one of the best single flowers and please try to improve upon the painting which is on the front of Henderson's catalogue for 1890," suggesting that even the choice of flower to paint was influenced by the competition between companies.[16]

Commercial artists clearly played an important role in creating and projecting the image of the trade, but interestingly, despite the intense competition between firms, this image could be a collective one. While catalogue covers and tipped in color prints were clearly points of pride, many companies used identical engravings in the interior pages of their catalogues. Of course, there was a tradition of the use of stock images in advertising materials, growing out of the incorporation of certain visual symbols in newspaper advertisements. But this practice of reproducing illustrations not just from one catalogue to another, but from one firm to another, raises the question of who actually distributed the graphics: individual artists, engraving companies, or the seed companies themselves. Copyright information, if it appears on the illustrations, is inconclusive, because it can appear under a variety of individual and corporate names; rather, one must rely on correspondence, printed discussions of the illustrations, and indeed, the patterns in which they appear. Relationships between companies and artists were fluid, and took on a variety of forms. What is clear is that some commercial artists and engravers specialized in the horticultural drawings valued by the seed and nursery trade.

One model of commercial relations was the artist working independently for a variety of companies, perhaps sparking competition between them. An obvious example for the student of the trade in the 1880s and 1890s is an artist whose signature "A. Blanc" jumps out from page after page of seed trade catalogues. Blanc was based in Philadelphia and it does appear that his or her earliest images were commissioned by the W. Atlee Burpee Company. Other companies based in Philadelphia also used Blanc as a supplier of images, as did some of the concentration of firms centered on Rochester, New York; specific images of plants were used continually over a couple of decades from about 1885 to 1905. In the middle of this time span, Blanc issued catalogues of horticultural engravings, and became one of the world's experts on cactus plants, owning one of the largest American collections of cacti. Whether horticultural interest led to a specialization in horticultural printmaking, or vice versa, is unclear, but Blanc's work certainly adds to our knowledge of how information was disseminated by visual means. Blanc apparently tried to retain the engravings used by the Burpee Company, perhaps to promote and re-sell; the company offered to sell Blanc back the original woodcuts at 75 cents per square inch. This exchange occurred just at the time that Blanc issued a new series of catalogues in 1895 and 1896.[17] Whether purchasing images from stock catalogues or not, seed firms would certainly have had enough familiarity with one another's catalogues to recognize Blanc's images; the illustrations were valued highly enough that firms were willing to reproduce them, even if it meant sharing with competitors.

While Blanc was selling engravings to different companies, clearly companies were also selling them from one to another. When companies developed new hybrids, they would generally sell them to other distributors, looking for the widest possible access. The Burpee company might retail the Bliss company's Abundance Pea, quite a different idea from the exclusivity of brand-name products that we might think of as the norm today. Distributing electrotypes was clearly part of this process of dissemination. An advertising leaflet for the new Cupid sweet pea flower developed by the Burpee company was geared to the seed trade, and offered "electrotypes of any of the illustrations" shown in the leaflet to any company that wanted to incorporate the new species into their own catalogues. Often these engravings included the name of the plant, which in turn often included the company's name, so offering these engravings was also a means of maintaining credit for new hybrids.[18]

In addition to the same image being used by different firms, there are also instances of almost, but not quite, identical, images appearing, suggesting that engravers noted one another's work, or were encouraged to do so by their sponsoring firms. The seed companies clearly fostered competition between various artists. Artists were pitted against one another, perhaps unknowingly; records of the Burpee company show numerous instances of the farm manager sending out identical sets of specimen to different lithographers at the same time, asking for images, clearly to choose the best one upon their return. At a time when the Burpee Company had been commissioning the engraver W.M. Momberger, based in New York City, on a regular basis, they sent balsam samples to both Momberger and George Browne of Rochester, New York. The manager later evaluated that the Browne drawings were "fair but I don't think they are anything extra as the coloring on most of them is quite poor" and continued requesting illustrations from Momberger. A similar competition ensued over a color plate of sweet peas.[19] The Burpee company was developing a reputation for the popular plant, and the farm manager wanted to foster this specialty through a decorative color plate showing several varieties; due perhaps to the skepticism of his boss Burpee, who did not believe that a resemblance to nature could be achieved, Earl approached at least three different commercial artists for their work.[20]

Other firms did seek unique representations of their wares, employing engravers to work full time for them exclusively, for both financial and promotional reasons. After explaining their use of electrotypes, as quoted above, a Briggs and Brother pamphlet continued the Socratic dialogue: "The next question would naturally be, why is not this work sent to a regular electrotyping establishment to be done? This is easily answered. We have enough work of this kind to keep two men busy, and find that it pays better to do our own electrotyping as we want it and when we want it. We have facilities that few electrotypers have."[21]

In another promotional pamphlet, Briggs and Brother advertised not only seeds but also the decorative chromolithographs of the flowers they sold and gave away as premiums. They touted their design team: "Mr. Lockhart devotes his entire time to putting upon canvas the many beautiful flowers grown by Briggs and Brother, and his sanctum in one corner of our Seed Establishment is filled with rare copies . . . Mr. Leadley has charge of Engraving for this house, and his work bespeaks his skill."[22] In a later publication, Briggs and Brother even visually depicted these artists at work, in what might be considered a self-portrait:

As a center piece of this engraving will be found our artist, copying flowers upon the canvas which he has arranged upon his easel. All of the floral chromos we issue are painted by one of the best artists in this peculiar line in the country, and from flowers grown in our own gardens. His duties are confined to sketching and copying flowers or vegetables from nature, designing and painting the original for the chromo, and designing the ornamental labels and show cards, millions of which we print annually, and in furnishing the designs for the

engravings that adorn the various publications of the house of Briggs and
Brother. The design is transferred to box wood and the engravers ply their tools
until the engraving is perfected. Two men are constantly employed at this work
the year round.[23]

This artist's self-portrait was only one of the many instances in which the seed
trade promoted not only its products but also its processes through visual
culture.

Commodification

The tradition of heavily illustrated marketing materials meant that engravers
and writers of advertising copy were on hand to depict not only the botanical plants that grew from seeds, but also the physical plants in which the seeds
were grown and from where they were distributed. The artists employed by
the seed trade drew not only portraits of themselves at work, but also what
might be considered commercial self-portraits of the firms, documenting the
trade's work throughout the phases of production, or planting, and distribution. The trade took the seeds from their growing fields and added value to
them by preparing, packaging, and distributing them. In the varied facets of
its production processes, the seed trade bridged the distinctions between
agricultural and industrial settings, rural and urban work sites, and even,
though to a lesser degree, manual and mechanized labor. These processes of
commodification were captured in print and publicized along with the commodities themselves.

Many nineteenth-century industries developed mechanized production
processes that, while replicating and replacing earlier craft-based work, could
not themselves be replicated on a domestic scale or without significant
capital investment. Seed growers, however, shared their work processes with
the farmers and gardeners who would eventually buy their goods. Though
the scale of seed growing might be considered typical of the industrial
realm, the methods of tending plants were not. Farmers and gardeners
needed to be persuaded that it was worthwhile to buy seeds, when they could
harvest them from their own fields and plots. In their attempt to influence
the hard-fought debate between seed saving and seed buying that played out
in the agricultural and horticultural press, the seed trade capitalized on the
processes that separated them from the home or farm grower. Natural products were transformed into commercial products by sorting, categorizing,
storing, weighing, packaging, mailing, and offering of advice, all of which
made seeds sold by firms more convenient, and perhaps even more valuable,
than those saved from last year's plants. If seeds were produced in the fields,
they were manufactured, and commodified, in the warehouses where these
ancillary activities took place.

All of these work sites appeared in seed trade ephemera, although they
were portrayed in somewhat different ways. The agricultural and horticultural
fields in which plants were allowed to "go to seed" (in this case connoting

productivity rather than decline) might be considered the primary sites of production in the trade, but the structure of the trade was such that these fields might not be owned by or associated in any way with the firm eventually selling the seeds. The companies that sold seeds to the retail and wholesale market varied in how they themselves obtained the seeds they sold. Small firms might act solely as distributors, of seeds bought from other firms or from growers, while the larger firms did grow some of their own stock, while also buying from both American and European growers. The larger firms also held extensive testing grounds, where they ensured the quality of the seeds they had not grown themselves. No firm grew all the seeds it sold, as, in the words of the Burpee Company, "this would be a physical impossibility."[24] Whether because these fields were not the best emblem of a firm's contribution, or because of the consumer's familiarity with this phase of the production cycle, depictions of growing fields tended to be somewhat generic landscape images, with little or no sign of human endeavour.[25] Even sites that were strongly associated with specific companies, such as the Burpee Company's Fordhook Farm in Doylestown, Pennsylvania, might stress the plants rather than active engagement with them. A verbal description of the Farm from the 1890s relates the almost passive quality with which the work there is presented: "The Farm Annual is written at Fordhook Farm, where we live among our growing crops and have thousands of field trials under our daily observation."[26] Graphic depictions of Fordhook Farm, first in prints and later in photographs, often showed the growing fields themselves, with no humans among the plants, or just a few doing unspecified tasks.

If the landscapes where seeds were grown and tested were often depicted as rural idylls, by contrast, the interior sites of processing were portrayed as busy hives of work (figure 1.3). The emphasis on these spaces of sorting, storing, and sending, which mediated between the producers' and consumers' fields, showed the processes of distribution to be as significant to the growth of the seed industry as those of production. Trade catalogues, themselves symbols of the act of distribution, might devote several pages to the different sectors of the interior workspaces, both graphically and verbally depicting the work that occurred within them—ranging from opening mail, sorting seeds, designing and printing marketing materials, packaging, and mailing.[27] The companies used these representations to give a sense for the scale of their business, in terms of both production and consumption. In narrative descriptions of their physical plants, they enumerated the vast quantities of exchange: the millions of seed packets stored; the millions of paper bags cut and sealed; the thousands of letters bringing orders each day. The accompanying engravings also showed the increasing magnitude of trade, by illustrating the increasing numbers of both workers and products within the warehouses. These portrayals of work in the seed trade echoed representations of other, usually more mechanized, industries, commonly found in nineteenth-century business ephemera and also popular periodicals such as *Scientific American* or *Appleton's Journal*.

Figure 1.3 The physical plants of the Robert Buist Company, encompassing both growing fields and a busy warehouse scene. While both illustrations demonstrate the scale of Buist's business, the representation of the wholesale order department shows more clearly and at closer range the work involved in preparing seeds for market

Source: Warshaw Collection of Business Americana, Achieves Center, National Museum of American History, Smithsonian Institution.

The purpose-built structures in which this work took place were more frequently promoted and identified with specific firms. The buildings themselves, with elegant facades and highly visible company names, constituted a form of advertising in a local community, but the representation of these sites in graphic form allowed that advertising to be widely disseminated. If the word industrial suggests a highly organized or systematized form of work, it also connotes "scale and scope" (to borrow from the business historian Alfred Chandler), not only in production but also in potential markets.[28] The urban warehouses of the seed trade symbolized in built form the breadth of the consumer base. In 1867, the *American Agriculturalist* commended B.K. Bliss as a leader in the seed trade by writing, "By liberal advertising, thorough system, and indefatigible attention to the details of his work, he has built up a business extending all over the United States, and demanding larger facilities."[29] The facilities in question, however, were not at the firm's growing fields in Springfield, Massachusetts, but rather their new warehouse building in New York City, through which all orders were handled. Promotional materials of the latter half of the nineteenth century frequently included engravings of these grand warehouse buildings, whether incorporated into a billhead or gracing the last page or back cover of a trade catalogue.[30] The practice of displaying commercial and industrial buildings to identify a firm was widely shared throughout American business ephemera. Still, the seed trade adapted these graphic conventions of the day to sites of distribution; the sites of production were depicted in more romantic, pastoral views. The physical plants of the seed trade were indeed hybrids of agricultural and industrial labor. Portrayals of these workspaces demonstrated not only the ways in which natural products were commodified but the progression of seeds from field to market, from where they would return to the landscape, planted by the consumer.

Replication

In presenting itself as resident in the borderland between agriculture and industry, the seed trade recognized that its market was a hybrid as well. The American consumer market for seeds was vast, in both geographic and socioeconomic terms. While the start of a demographic shift from rural to urban areas certainly did begin in the nineteenth century, that shift did not imply a decline in planting, but rather, a greater variety of markets; the rise in urban populations led to growth in market gardens, cottage kitchen gardens, leisure-time flower gardens, and garden suburbs with vast lawns. Seed companies catered indiscriminately to those who planted for sustenance, economic pursuit, or leisure, and the copious illustrations in their printed matter were designed to appeal to the broad range of potential consumers.

The investment in printing equipment was seen to have a direct return in sales figures, by nurturing the growing market for seeds. The combination of art and commerce is perhaps best summed up by a complimentary letter sent from the Burpee company farm manager to one of the artists who worked for them, commenting on a color plate showing new vegetable strains, to be inserted in a new catalogue: "The vegetable sketch came to hand yesterday and Mr. Burpee is more than pleased with it and told me to compliment you when writing both for the arrangement and work. You have certainly made an excellent plate and I have great hopes that it will please our customers and sell lots of seed."[31] Such a sentiment was not restricted to private correspondence, but might be shared with consumers, thinly veiling sales strategy with the idea that the prints were given as gifts; even when a small fee was charged, this price was generally lower than what commercial lithographers would have commanded. Briggs and Brother published in their 1875 catalogue a description of their annual chromolithograph, stating boldly, "We do not care to make money on them, but issue them at nearly or quite cost, knowing that their dissemination creates increased interest in flowers and results in still greater sale of seeds."[32] Although they worked to commodify their product, the seed trade continued to draw on the tradition of gift exchange, through which seeds had been transferred from person to person, and place to place, for generations, or indeed centuries.

Seed companies recognized the important bond between the seller and the buyer in a trade where the commodity sold was difficult to judge or value before its use. As the Burpee Company wrote in their 1872 catalogue: "The relations of the Planter to his trusted Seedsman are more intimate than those of the buyer and seller in any other line of business; with other goods the buyer can largely judge of the quality and value by the sample, while with seeds the purchase is altogether a matter of confidence. To merit and maintain this confidence is the constant aim of the conscientious Seedsman."[33] Of course, firms strove to sell reliable and productive seeds as the first priority in "maintaining this confidence." But they also used other approaches, such as offering copious horticultural advice in catalogues and other publications; friendly counsel on the planning, sowing, tending, and harvesting of fields, gardens, lawns and other planted landscapes helped retain personal touch in what was an increasingly far-flung business. The gift (or low-cost treat) of vibrant visual imagery was just one of the many measures that seed companies took to gain and maintain their customer's trust.

The illustrations, particularly chromolithographs, offered by the trade were facets of the "intimate relations" between seed sellers and consumers because they were designed to be incorporated into consumers' homes as constant reminders of the products on offer. Chromolithographs were popular nineteenth-century ornament for the middle-class American home, and, while selling their seeds, companies contributed to this home décor; the nineteenth-century middle-class home was not a haven from the commercial world, but rather a host to it.[34] Seed companies held an advantage over other types of firms who might also seek to influence home design in that their own commodities, particularly flowers but also picturesque fruits and vegetables, arranged into still-life displays, were among the subjects frequently recommended for domestic design. The companies certainly presented the color plates, whether tipped into their catalogues or offered as separate sheets, as potential artwork for the home. For an 1895 color plate of sweet peas, the Burpee Company requested their lithographers to add that the images were "painted from nature at Fordhook Farm," both associating the image with their own fields and vouching for its authenticity, but they made clear that this information should not detract from the decorative possibilities. The company manager wrote, "The printing to go on the sketch you will understand is to go at the extreme bottom and to be such as can be easily covered by the wood of a frame."[35] The color plate, no matter how commercial in origin, was indeed suitable for framing, and could provide an addition to any family home. Briggs and Brother advertised that their own color plates of flowers, available for either $1 plain or $1.50 varnished and mounted and with frame options ranging from 70 cents to $1.40, were "acknowledged to be the finest flower pieces extant, and are in all respects equal to the highest priced chromos sold."[36] In fact, Briggs advised on the placement of horticultural artwork within the home, writing that their illustrations were "fit ornaments for any parlor, or, as we prefer them, for the dining or sitting room," guidance that echoed domestic advice literature of the day.[37]

The visual culture of the seed trade not only brought natural motifs into the home, but also might inspire particular plant use and garden designs; the images were both ornaments for the interior and models for the landscape. The ideals of perfection and abundance in nature captured in the prints applied not only to the individual plants grown from particular seeds, but also to the landscapes created by cultivating groups of seeds. Grass seeds were advertised with drawings of lush lawns surrounding picturesque houses; grain seeds with seemingly endless fields of productive farmland; or flower seeds with intricately planted pleasure gardens. That these images were prescriptive, as well as descriptive, was noted by the companies themselves. Briggs and Brother suggested the extent to which they hoped their annual color print would inspire gardeners, writing "There is not a flower in the chromo that even an amateur cannot successfully grow, especially after consulting the various publications we issue."[38] Images that began as representations of natural commodities became the bases for consumers to replicate in their own gardens.

In fact, the idea of painting from nature may have been less important to the seed companies as the idea that nature should follow the lines of their paintings and drawings. In 1896, the Burpee Company invited the French painter Paul de Longpre to visit their fields at Fordhook Farm. De Longpre would soon move to the United States and cultivate not only an elaborate garden in Los Angeles, but also an American market for his Victorian flower paintings; he was beginning to make his mark with such projects as the illustrations for an edition of William Cullen Bryant's *Poems of Nature*.[39] At Fordhook Farm, de Longpre painted a bouquet of fifteen varieties of sweet peas, in fact a small selection of the hundred or so varieties on sale that year. The company then commissioned a lithograph in 14 colors, reproducing for a large audience for 10 cents a copy the painting they valued at $250. But the connection between art and nature went beyond the representation of the latter. The company suggested that gardeners might want to replicate the work of art in the nature of their garden, reversing the process that de Longpre had followed. On offer for 1896 was the "Artist's Blend" of sweet pea seeds, with the explanation, "Everyone who sees the beautiful painting . . . will want a bouquet of Sweet Peas for household decoration, *to equal in nature* the charming effect of the artist's brush. Therefore we have blended in proper proportions seed of the choice new sorts selected by Mr. De Longpre for his painting."[40] Thus, the visual culture of the seed trade might do more than generally attract customers to a particular company's wares; they might in fact guide the selection and arrangement of those wares, making nature reflect art, as well as the reverse. This cycle of representation, reproduction, and replication illustrates how central horticultural imagery was to the cultivation of seeds as consumer goods.

Notes

1. This essay was written as part of the project "Seed Money: The Economies of Horticulture in Nineteenth-Century America," generously supported by the AHRC/ESRC Cultures of Consumption Programme, Reference No. RES-154-25-0001. Research support for the early phases of the project was granted by the Smithsonian Institution, the Dumbarton Oaks Research Center and Library, and the Charles Warren Center for American History at Harvard University. Early versions of this essay were delivered at the American History Seminar at the Institute for Historical Research, October 2003; The Character of Nineteenth-Century Visual Culture, Amsterdam, Netherlands, November 2002; and Art and Agriculture, a symposium of the Agricultural History Society, Dearborn, Michigan, June 2005. The author would like to thank the audiences at these seminars for helpful feedback.
2. David M. Tucker, *Kitchen Gardening in America: A History* (Ames, Iowa: Iowa State University Press, 1993) 84.
3. Sandra Markham has explored this relationship in the Rochester, New York area in her excellent article, "Living Preachers, Through Voiceless Lips: Printing for the Nursery Industry, 1840–1920," *Ephemera Journal*, Vol. 9 (2001) 13–30. For more general discussion of the use of business ephemera in the nineteenth century, see Kenneth Ames, "Trade Catalogues and the Study of History," *Accumulation and Display: Mass Marketing Household Goods in America, 1880–1920* (Winterthur: Henry Francis DuPont Winterthur Museum, 1986) 7–14 and Robert Jay, *The Trade Card in Nineteenth-Century America* (Columbia: University of Missouri Press, 1987).
4. A copy of the catalogue is held in the Henry G. Gilbert Nursery and Seed Trade Catalog Collection of the National Agricultural Library, Beltsville, Maryland. Examples from the collection may be viewed on: http://www.nal.usda.gov/speccoll/collect/nursery/nursery.html. For general background on the Barbizon school of landscape painters, see Steven Adams, *The Barbizon School and the Origins of Impressionism* (London: Phaidon Press, 1994); for links between the Barbizon painters and the United States, see Laura Lee Meixner, "Jean-Francois Millet: His American Students and Influences," PhD Dissertation, Ohio State University, 1979.

5. Briggs Brothers and Co., *Flower, Garden, and Field Seeds* (Rochester: Briggs Brothers and Co., 1890) inside back cover; the illustration is unsigned but the majority of graphics in the catalogue were produced by A. Blanc, so it is possible that this image is Blanc's work as well. For background on the influence of Japonisme in the United States, see Julia Meech and Gabriel Weisberg, *Japonisme Comes to America: The Japanese Impact on the Graphic Arts, 1876–1925* (New York: H.N. Abrams, 1990).

6. The prolific William H. Gerdts has written extensively on American still-life paintings; see *Painters of the Humble Truth: Masterpieces of American Still Life, 1801–1839* (Columbia, MO: University of Missouri Press, 1981) for coverage of nineteenth-century artists who influenced commercial graphic design. For particular discussion of botanical and horticultural subjects, see also, John Brindle and Sally Secrist, *American Cornucopia: Nineteenth-Century Still Lifes and Studies* (Pittsburgh: Hunt Institute for Botanical Documentation, 1976).

7. Letter, Earl to Stecher Lithographic Co., 1 September 1891, Copy Book 3, Box 128, W. Atlee Burpee Collection, Archives of American Gardens, Division of Horticulture, Smithsonian Institution, Washington DC. (All further references to this archival collection will be designated "Burpee Coll." with appropriate locating information).

8. Letter, Earl to Momberger, August 5, 1890, Copy Book 3, Box 128, Burpee Coll.

9. For background on botanical illustration, see Martyn Rix, *The Art of the Plant World: The Great Botanical Illustrators and their Work* (Woodstock, NY: Overlook Press, 1981) and Gill Saunders, *Picturing Plants: An Analytical History of Botanical Illustration* (London: Zwemmer, 1995).

10. Letter, W. Atlee Burpee Co. to A. Blanc, September 30, 1893, Copy Book 1, Box 127, Burpee Coll.

11. Letter, Earl to Momberger, September 29, 1890, Copy Book 3, Box 128, Burpee Coll.

12. Letter, Earl to Momberger, September 29, 1890, Copy Book 3, Box 128, Burpee Coll.

13. Letter, Earl to Stecher, September 7, 1891; Earl to Momberger, 7 September 1891; both letters located in Copy Book 3, Box 128, Burpee Coll.

14. Briggs and Bro., *Briggs' Quarterly Floral Work* (Rochester, NY: Briggs and Bro., April 1875) 12.

15. Flyer for flower seeds, 1895, Folder 1, Box 380, Burpee Coll.; A. Blanc, *Electrotypes of Flowers, Plants and Shrubs* (Philadelphia: 1895).

16. Letter, Earl to Momberger, August 5, 1890, Copy Book 3, Box 128, Burpee Coll.

17. Letter, Earl to Blanc, June 27, 1895, in Copy Book 2, Box 127, Burpee Coll.

18. "Cupid," pamphlet, 1896, Folder 2, Box 380, Burpee Coll.

19. Letter, Earl to Burpee, August 18, 1890, Copy Book 3, Box 128, Burpee Coll.

20. Letter, Earl to Browne, July 7, 1892, Copy Book 3, Box 128, Burpee Coll.

21. Briggs and Bro., *Briggs' Quarterly Floral Work*, 12.

22. Briggs and Bro., *Advance Retail Price List* (Rochester, NY: Briggs and Bro.,1873) inside back cover.

23. Briggs and Bro., *Briggs' Quarterly Floral Work*, 12.

24. W. Atlee Burpee and Company, *Burpee's Select List of Novelties and Specialties in Seeds* (Philadelphia: Burpee and Co., 1889) 3.
25. See, for example, Robert Buist, Jr., *Buist's Garden Guide* (Philadelphia: Robert Buist, Jr., 1889) 2, 4; W. Atlee Burpee and Company, "Burpee's Select List of Novelties and Specialties in Seeds" (Philadelphia: Burpee and Co., 1889) 4–5.
26. W. Atlee Burpee and Company, *Burpee's Farm Annual* (Philadelphia: Burpee and Co., 1897) 1.
27. See, for example, B.L. Bragg and Co., *Agricultural Warehouse and Seed Store* (Springfield, MA: B.L. Bragg and Co., 1889) 1; Buist, *Buist's Garden Guide*, inside front cover; and W. Atlee Burpee and Company, *Burpee's Farm Annual* (Philadelphia: Burpee and Co., 1887) 14–15.
28. Alfred Chandler, *Scale and Scope: The Dynamics of Industrial Capitalism* (Cambridge, MA: Belknap Press, 1990).
29. Testimonial letter from the *American Agriculturalist*, October 1867, quoted in, B.K. Bliss and Son, *Spring Catalogue and Amateur's Guide* (New York: Bliss and Son, 1868) inside front cover.
30. See, for example, B.L. Bragg, *Agricultural Warehouse and Seed Store*, back cover; Briggs and Bro., *Briggs' Quarterly Floral Work*, 8; W. Atlee Burpee and Company, *Burpee's Farm Annual* (Philadelphia: Burpee and Co., 1883) back cover.
31. Letter, Earl to Schlitzer, October 1, 1895, Copy Book 3, Box 128, Burpee Coll.
32. Briggs and Bro., *Briggs' Quarterly Floral Work*, 3.
33. *Burpee's Farm Annual* (Philadelphia: W. Atlee Burpee and Co., 1892) 17.
34. On chromolithography and domestic décor, see Lori Rotskoff, "Decorating the Dining-Room: Still-Life Chromolithographs and Domestic Ideology in Nineteenth-Century America," *Journal of American Studies* Vol. 31, No. 1 (April 1997): 19–42; for further discussion of the nexus of the domestic and the commercial, see Elizabeth White Nelson, *Market Sentiments: Middle-Class Market Culture in Nineteenth-Century America* (Washington DC: Smithsonian Books, 2004).
35. Letter, Earl to Brett Lithographic Co., September 21, 1895, Copy book 3, Box 128, Burpee Coll.
36. Briggs and Bro., *Advance Retail Price List*, inside back cover.
37. Briggs and Bro., *Briggs' Quarterly Floral Work*, 3; Rotskoff, "Decorating the Dining Room."
38. Briggs and Bro., *Briggs' Quarterly Floral Work*, 3.
39. W. Atlee Burpee and Company, *Burpee's Farm Annual* (Philadelphia: Burpee and Co., 1896). 11. For further background on de Longpre, see Nancy C. Hall, *The Life and Art of Paul de Longpre* (Irvine, CA: Irvine Museum, 2001).
40. W. Atlee Burpee Co., Sweet pea brochure, Folder 3, Box 3, Seed and Nursery Trade, Warshaw Collection of Business Americana, Archives Center, Smithsonian Institution.

Chapter 2

The Importance of Being True Blue: The Du Pont Company and the Color Revolution

Regina Lee Blaszczyk

In August 1926, Irénée du Pont, vice chairman at E. I. du Pont de Nemours & Company, wrote to Henry H. Bassett, general manager of the Buick division at General Motors Corporation (GM). During the early 1920s Du Pont and GM, both under the leadership of Pierre S. du Pont, had collaborated to develop Duco Finish—a type of quick-drying, durable, inexpensive, and colorful automotive lacquer. More recently, Du Pont's corporate colorists had created a distinctive palette for GM. Now the automotive giant, which used Duco on many of its cars, was trying to lure Du Pont's premier colorist, H. Ledyard Towle, to its Fisher Body division. Irénée du Pont objected.[1]

Towle ran the Du Pont Company's Duco Color Advisory Service in New York, taking orders from automobile companies and advising them on style and color. In the process Towle developed an insider's view of automobile finishing. The Duco Color Advisory Service enhanced Du Pont's reputation as a trustworthy firm that responded to its customers' needs while safeguarding their aesthetic decisions. If Towle were to leave for GM, accounts with other automakers might be jeopardized. Irénée du Pont cautioned Bassett: "Many of the customers for Duco would properly feel that some of their confidences had been violated." It was imperative that Towle—and Detroit's trade secrets about color—remain at Du Pont.[2]

The Du Pont-GM deliberations over Towle coincided with major shifts in business practice during the 1920s. Companies making all types of products, from pots and pans to airplanes and automobiles, experimented with ways to increase sales, including mass advertising, installment selling, model changes—and color merchandising. The popularity of color as a business tool led *Fortune*, the nation's new corporate magazine, to publish a 1930 feature on "Color in Industry," describing a "suddenly kaleidoscopic world," in which color served as "a master salesman, a distributor extraordinary." The market was flooded with blue beds, mauve mops, and apricot autos. Long before the flashy Harley Earl put streamlining in the spotlight, GM and other automakers depended on colorists for body designs, accessory choices, and paint schemes. *Fortune* gave a catchy name to this monumental change: "the color revolution."[3]

The color revolution owed much to corporate experts like Towle, praised by *Fortune* as "one of industry's most ardent colorists." Towle and other industrial colorists belonged to a group of creative people that I have elsewhere called "fashion intermediaries." These business professionals emerged as industrializing economies placed greater emphasis on the diversified mass market. Fashion intermediaries wore any number of hats, working as retail managers, department store buyers, company art directors, consultant designers, business home economists, salesmen, market researchers, advertising executives, and color experts. As go-betweens, they helped business to target the right consumers, envision their expectations, and design products that met their demands. Many specialized in art and design, advising business on the tricky job of managing aesthetic risk. They understood the vocabulary of visual and material life, explaining style, fashion, and taste to puzzled executives. They were especially important in periods of great economic change, at moments when manufacturers and retailers grappled with new markets and new market segments.[4]

Fashion intermediaries played a conspicuous role in American commercial culture during the style-conscious 1920s. Then, industries wrestled with a "buyers' market," in which "numerous and insistent" shoppers called the shots. Productive capacity outstripped demand, forcing factories into bitter fights for retail dollars. "Consumers have crowded about producers with outstretched hands full of purchasing power," reported *Automotive Industries* in 1922. They begged for something to "wear, eat, drink, parade before . . . friends, or otherwise enjoy." Ascribing to the adage that "the consumer is king," companies could not "afford to misjudge demand, either with respect to what it wants, how much of that it wants, or what share of it competitors will permit." The buyers' market dictated that producers "search out the consumer and sell him," often in brutal showdowns with the competition. Manufacturers and retailers had to shape up or ship out. Many bit the bullet and paid fashion intermediaries for their aesthetic assistance.[5]

Du Pont desperately needed the color smarts of fashion intermediaries. During the early twentieth century, the explosives company had diversified into chemicals—plastics, paints, and dyes—without knowing much about those businesses. Du Pont grew rapidly, restructuring itself several times before finding an organizational chart that fit. When Du Pont's laboratories discovered ways to improve basic chemicals, managers realized that the company's future lay in synthesizing new materials for sale to fabricators who would turn them into consumer goods. They also found that this product portfolio increased managerial headaches. Duco finishes, for example, outperformed other lacquers, but the novelty befuddled users. When customers asked questions about technology and aesthetics, Du Pont hired sales engineers to provide answers. The Duco Color Advisory Service was part of this technical service network.[6]

Du Pont's color intermediaries straddled the spheres of sales, design, and technology to help the firm gain competitive advantage in the finishes market. To achieve this end they compromised. By tradition, clothing set the style trends, and other industries followed. In automobile paints corporate colorists had to temper the sometimes outrageous hues generated by Paris couture houses and Modernist painters to suit the American context, with its casual lifestyles and varied tastes. Another constraint came from the factories, which demanded cost-effectiveness. Producers were caught between the efficiencies of black and the uncontrolled, expensive explosion of color. Finally, the rule of averages dominated the great middlebrow market, the major audience for colorful cars. In the middle there was a certain degree of homogeneity, but there also was a great deal of difference. Middle Americans shared the desire for higher living standards, while they divided by income, education, ethnicity, and social class. Commercial color became a tool for expressing this subtle tension; Du Pont's corporate colorists were the men who mediated the terrain.[7]

Duco Innovation

Duco lacquer is often remembered for its role in the struggle between General Motors and the Ford Motor Company over the rapidly expanding auto market. During 1918–1919, Du Pont invested 30 percent of its capital into GM stock, hoping to profit from the growing automotive trade and to secure the car manufacturer's business in fabrics, plastics, paint, and varnish. Pierre S. du Pont took over the GM presidency from founder William C. Durant in 1920 and, with the help of vice president Alfred P. Sloan Jr., restructured the ailing automaker. The GM-Du Pont pipeline channeled managerial, engineering, and scientific talent between the two companies. By early 1922, the firms started to adapt Viscolac, a Du Pont nitrocellulose lacquer used for painting pencils, to automobile finishes.[8]

Those experiments eventually produced the first Duco colors, which GM used on the True Blue Oakland in late 1923. During the early 1920s, the only durable, inexpensive automotive finish was the famous high-temperature baked black enamel that Henry Ford used on his Model T. Luxury cars such as the Cadillac and Rolls Royce came in a range of hand-painted colors, but even those varnishes faded, chipped, and scratched. The owners of luxury vehicles garaged their cars from the weather and expected to pay for new paint jobs in due course. Sloan, who had become GM president in May 1923, believed that consumers buying lower-priced cars would appreciate a range of color choices, particularly if the paints lasted. As the GM and Du Pont laboratories wrapped up their tests on nitrocellulose lacquers, the automaker's Buick and Oakland divisions took up the new finish. In 1923, the Oakland Motor Car Company decided to paint all seven of its 1924 touring cars with Duco: two shades of blue, with accent stripes of red or orange. When the True Blue Oaklands debuted at the New York Automobile Show in December 1923, dealers and consumers responded to the new aesthetic dimension and

Figure 2.1 The True Blue Oakland was the automotive sensation of 1924. Oakland Motor Car Company, advertisement in *Motor*, January 1924

the promise of improved technical performance (figure 2.1). By early 1924, orders poured into GM showrooms; "Duco has become so popular," reported one executive, "that customers are now demanding it." Sloan recognized that Duco was a sensation, and he recommended that GM adopt it for all models. By mid-1925 GM's divisional managers, from Chevrolet to Cadillac, were putting aside tried-and-true varnishes and high-temperature enamels in favor of Duco.[9]

Duco had several advantages over traditional coatings. Older varnishes were brushed on in more than a dozen steps and needed lengthy drying periods between coats. Quick-drying, spray-on Duco reduced the stages, drying time, labor costs, and storage space. Traditional varnishes chipped, cracked, crazed, and faded; Duco lacquer was almost invincible. It tolerated air, sun, rain, mud, dampness, heat, cold, salt water, bacteria, perspiration, dirt, soaps, and detergents. Most low-end finishes came in few colors; Duco, a rainbow of hues. Along with the annual model change and installment buying, the new finish added value to GM's automotive line.[10]

Detroit Meets the Color Revolution

Duco was a marvelous miracle material—and much more. It served as a focusing device that compelled Detroit to give due consideration to the suppositions and strategies of the style industries. In short, the True Blue Oakland, the first successful application of Duco, made the automotive and chemical industries sit up and take aesthetics seriously.

The color revolution that swept across America in the 1920s built on transitions that had been underway for seventy-five years. During the Gilded Age, English and German chemical companies made new synthetic dyes that American mills used to make fabrics, draperies, carpets, and other textiles in a variety of bright, permanent hues. Printers used chromolithography to generate colorful trade cards for advertisers and decorative pictures for houses, clubs, churches, and offices. Even the commercial streets touted new hues, as the A&P and Woolworth adopted bright red storefronts as part of chain-store branding. These things sharpened the eye and whetted the appetite for color.[11]

In the art world, painters experimented with expressive modes that depended heavily on color theories developed in the nineteenth century. European painters pioneering in Impressionism, Cubism, and other revolutionary modes engaged color's emotive and expressive qualities, using new oil paints in brilliant hues. In Paris after 1900, the young Americans Stanton MacDonald-Wright and Morgan Russell created a movement known as Synchromism, meaning simply "with color." Afterwards New York painters followed suit to pioneer American Modernism. At design schools teachers explored color's mystique. As principal of the Massachusetts Normal Art School, Albert H. Munsell dedicated his career to creating a color system accessible to students training for jobs as artists and designers in New England industries. Munsell's patented photometer enabled him to determine the light values of colors. His 1905 book, *A Color Notation*, which outlined his methods for identifying and describing color, received critical acclaim in scientific circles, where measurement was still in its infancy. After his death in 1918 Munsell's followers refined the system and aggressively promoted it to schools and businesses.[12]

By the early 1920s, American popular culture fomented a heightened interest in color psychology. Practitioners from several professions—interior decoration, fine art, advertising, and education–rushed to press with how-to books. Everyone talked about color as the next big thing, as a tool for tapping into human emotions and improving material circumstances of the human condition. Even big business embraced the trend. In 1923, General Electric physicist Matthew Luckiesh, a prolific writer on lighting, optics, and vision, published *Light and Color in Advertising and Merchandising*, which helped to legitimatize color in the eyes of the nation's top executives.[13]

The strongest endorsement of color as a merchandising tool came from the industrial arts, where color forecasting had emerged as a cutting-edge practice in textiles and ready-to-wear. World War I severed supplies of German dyes and French fashion predictions, forcing Americans to create their own. In 1914, New York's garment trade established the Textile Color Card Association (TCCA), where managing director Margaret Hayden

Rorke issued forecasts for mass-market textile mills and ready-to-wear manufacturers. One upscale fabric mill, the Cheney Brothers Silk Manufacturing
Company, created its own color cards. The factory's art director, advertising
agency, and public relations counsel collaborated to create signature hues
for Cheney Silks. In the industrial arts, there was plenty of room for diversity.
Rorke aimed to please the masses; Cheney catered to consumers who
followed high fashion. Nothing more clearly spoke to color's versatility in
marketing.[14]

Astute onlookers noted consumers' dissatisfaction with Detroit's dull
designs and nudged automakers toward the industrial arts. The fashionable
French joked about Detroit's undeveloped chromatic sensibilities, calling
"American automobiles funeral cars because so many of them are black."
Back home editors at the trade journal *Automotive Industries* urged car makers in April 1923 to "develop other colors which can compete with black in
cheapness and durability." As fashion intermediaries salesmen joined the
chorus for more colorful cars. In Cleveland, Edward Patton drew on years of
experience at the Franklin Motor Car Company to differentiate regional
color preferences: many city dwellers turned up their noses at the fancy paint
jobs that rural and small-town folks loved. Occupation, ethnicity, and social
class complicated the mix: in upstate New York, for example, lumbermen
liked green, small-town conservatives bought blue, and one Italian bootleg-
ger went for "a vivid green car with brilliant red wheels." Salesman Wheeler
Earl, who ran a Hupmobile showroom on Broadway, explained how gender
fit. "Women, I find, are the biggest factors in deciding sales," Earl reported.
"They must be perfectly satisfied about the appearance and comfort of the
car." In Manhattan, stylish women picked the cars, and color figured into
their decisions.[15]

Even before True Blue's debut, then, observers with their fingers on the
pulse of the buyers' market called for colorful, mass-market cars that matched
consumer tastes. The True Blue Oakland's success in winter 1923–1924
pressed Detroit into action. Paint makers determined not to be outdone by
Du Pont introduced their own colorful paints, varnishes, and lacquers. The
Egyptian Lacquer Manufacturing Company, John L. Armitage & Company,
the Hilo Varnish Company, and Valentine & Company all jumped into the
fast-drying finish market.[16]

Customers for quick-drying colored lacquers included both auto manufacturers and local custom-shop painters, which refinished cars. This niche
business blossomed as repainting got easier with nitrocellulose finishes. The
Murphy Varnish Company and the Ditzler Color Company developed
chromatic aids to help custom painters understand the mysteries of color
(figure 2.2). Devices that simplified color selection democratized aesthetic
decisions, which had long been the purview of artists and homemakers. They
showed men, from top executives to shop mechanics, exactly what beauty
could do for commerce, and how its proper management could stimulate
sales in the segmented automobile market.[17]

Figure 2.2 A lesson in color harmony, Murphy Varnish Company, advertisement in *Autobody*, January 1924

Establishing the Duco Color Advisory Service

At first Du Pont kept ahead by selling Duco to evermore car manufacturers and refinishing garages. By early 1925, its customers included five General Motors divisions and fourteen other automakers. That year Du Pont sold more than a million gallons of Duco at $5 each. Technically, Duco outstripped the competition, and the future looked bright. Yet those who knew something about color felt uneasy. They realized that Du Pont had to catch up with consumers' growing sophistication about color.[18]

In January 1925, two Du Pont managers discussed the company's need for "practical advice" on "the psychology of colors." As general manager of Du Pont's plastics department, F. B. Davis confided his ideas about Pyralin Toilet Ware, a line of celluloid boudoir accessories that needed updating, to the head of Du Pont's development department, Fin Sparre. So far Du Pont plastics had kept up with feminine color preferences by tracking sales statistics and reacting to blips in purchasing patterns. The chief salesman studied the figures, ingested what he saw, and ventured an educated guess about color trends. Davis thought that a trained color expert could do better. Drawing on art theories, he or she could work with technicians on new hues that were aesthetically sound—and enduring. With expertise in fashion and scientific management, he could also anticipate a major fad, allowing Du Pont to capitalize on "its popularity for at least one season before other manufacturers come into competition on the same color." Color management, Davis told Sparre, was all about using style to raise profits. Professional colorists would definitely help the Pyralin department meet the bottom line and, along the way, attend to the chromatic woes of other Du Pont products— including Duco automotive finishes.[19]

Du Pont took the chromatic leap in October 1925 when it hired Towle and created the Duco Color Advisory Service to design the "latest and most desirable color combinations" for the auto industry (figure 2.3). Born in Brooklyn, Towle had studied landscape and portrait painting at the Pratt Institute and the Art Students League under Frank Vincent Dumond and William M. Chase. During World War I, Towle put his art training to good use as a member of the U.S. Army's celebrated Camouflage Corps. Afterwards he adapted to the burgeoning world of advertising, working sequentially as art director for three New York agencies: H. K. McCann, Frank Seaman Inc., and Campbell-Ewald Company. At Seaman he also served as the executive in charge of the Du Pont account and as copy executive for several GM divisions: Cadillac, Oldsmobile, La Salle, and Pontiac.[20]

In the 1920s, large New York agencies like Seaman billed themselves as full-service companies prepared to help clients conceptualize campaigns, write copy, create artwork, design products, stimulate publicity, and conduct consumer research. Their art departments showed clients how to capitalize on color's eye appeal in print advertisements and product designs. In this capacity Towle "first worked on color with the automotive industry back in 1924," when he was "the only color engineer calling on the automobile

Reproducing the colors of silks, fresh from Paris, in Duco

Figure 2.3   Captain H. Ledyard Towle at the Duco Color Advisory Service in New York. *Du Pont Magazine*, May 1926. Hagley Museum and Library

trade." The painter turned art director—versed in advertising, aesthetics, and autos—seemed like the perfect fit with Du Pont's plans to rationalize the inchoate sphere of color.[21]

Shortly after his arrival at Du Pont, Towle devised a color styling program to augment Duco's prestige among automakers, refinishing garages, and car buyers. Du Pont's auto customers manufactured models at different price points in the middle ground. To meet the desires of middlebrow consumers Towle pointed them toward color combinations "known to please the average," which his "staff of color experts" knew "how to choose with certainty." This meant tying Du Pont finishes to European fashion trends, keeping Duco abreast of changing tastes, and designing paint schemes that enhanced automotive shapes. These measures patterned the Duco Color Advisory Service after precedents in the industrial arts.[22]

To advance the first mission Towle sailed to Europe every fall, where he visited the Olympia Show in London and the Automobile Salon in Paris. There he studied the new cars and the smartly dressed people and cabled reports to the Duco Color Advisory Service, which repackaged them as press releases. Towle's color message circulated through American popular culture as newspapers from New York to New Orleans published his lively, engaging descriptions. "All Paris is color mad!" Towle declared in the *Providence*

Tribune in late 1926, describing beautiful objects and elegant people. The Grand Palais, which hosted the automobile salon, seemed aflame in warm maroons and burnt oranges. On snappy boulevards autos of the "haute monde and the demi-monde" whirled by in "squadrons of satisfying color . . . like a flashing mountain torrent at the end of a rainbow." During the evening the audience at the Paris Opera House bowed to the chromatic gods. "The boxes looked like veritable baskets of flowers hung along the walls," Towle marveled. "So filled were they with beautiful women, their gowns of orchid, peach, Rose de Versailles, Saint Germaine green, glacier or cloth of gold." Towle saw color nuance everywhere; he understood its place in the fashion system, and he sought to explain its significance.[23]

These European reports conveyed different messages to different audiences. The rich descriptions demonstrated Towle's visual and verbal acumen and his acute powers of observation and articulation. He carefully distinguished between the "myriad golden browns and copper-reds and brown-yellows." Each autumnal hue painted on a French show car conveyed a unique mood or feeling, and Towle captured that distinctiveness by cataloguing all the colors. His hurried cadence expressed the excitement that distinguished the world of fashion, sweeping up readers in the glamour of metropolitan Paris at the height of the season. To Du Pont managers, concerned mostly with balance sheets and organizational charts, Towle's artistic language testified to his cultural capital, to his value as an aesthete with access to the elite Paris salons. To readers of America's daily newspapers, Towle depicted a fantastic faraway land, where luxury reigned supreme and color-coordinated possessions signaled belonging.[24]

While Towle's grand tours exposed him to continental color *au courant*, they also provided him with the chance to hobnob with designers in London and Paris, the fashion capitals of Europe. Sometimes he simply shopped, taking notes at runway shows for trade articles on high-fashion fabrics. In the fall of 1926, he solicited automotive paint schemes from the major Paris couture houses: Lanvin, Philippe & Gaston, Lucien Lelong, Premet, Drecoll, Jenny, Callor Soeurs, Madeleine Vionnet, Paul Pioret, and Patou. Lelong daringly combined green and peach tones on a roadster while blending royal purple and silver for a town car. Vionnet's flare for sports cars led him to create a scheme for one in "tones of Dekkan Brown and London Smoke." The list went on as the "Paris creators of style" did their magic to glamorize American cars.[25]

Around the winter holidays Towle returned to New York for the Automobile Salon and the National Automobile Show, where American car makers exhibited the latest engineering features, accessories, upholstery, and color schemes. By the mid-twenties brilliant hues were all the rage. Like the no-frills Model T, funereal tints faced extinction. At the January 1926 National Show colors trumped black, which appeared on only 7.4 percent of the cars. Gray accounted for 30.9 percent, blue 25.6, green 14, cream and yellow 9.3, olive and tan 5.6, brown 3.3, and red .9. Among the show stoppers were twelve Lincolns decorated in spectacular hues "adapted from the plumage of rare American and tropical birds": Ecuador's Green Tanager, Haiti's Lizard-Cuckoo, Venezuela's Yellow Woodpecker, and more. One year later the display was even more stupendous. The "mass production man," Towle reported in the *Brooklyn Standard Union* and the *Pittsburgh Gazette-Times*, had caught on to the fact that "the whole country is becoming more fond of the use of color." Auto plants expertly wielded paintbrushes, showing cars with two-tone schemes in "warm, appealing beautiful harmonies." They made fenders, window brackets, rear tire covers, and upholstery to match the rest of the car. With satisfaction Towle described the 1927 National show as "the high water mark in color harmony."[26]

This color explosion embodied the essence of modernity, and professional colorists like Towle, who managed the phenomenon, were counted among the most modern of men. As consumer demand drove the color revolution, fashion intermediaries responded on behalf of the car industry. The "wealth of color application" at the National, Towle wrote, owed much to "the brains and experience of men who have made a lifelong study of color." While tooting his own horn, Towle praised others, including the Paris dressmakers, who had created the show's stupendous color harmonies. He understood cross-disciplinary fertilization as integral to colors that resonated among the great middle ground. Envisioning an alchemy of color, he urged automakers to heed the messages of those who selected hues "for the leading fashions in the silk, hosiery and shoe trades." These people valued the fusion of nature and culture, art and industry. The resolution that experts could collaborate to harness color for economic gain marked Towle and his contemporaries as modern.[27]

Towle's holistic modernism influenced his "form follows function" approach to color styling. He believed that a color scheme should bear some relationship to the car's shape. With the new nitrocellulose varnishes, some automakers went wild with color, ruining good models with injudicious paint jobs. One company entirely painted a 1926 roadster with a brilliant paint intended for stripes only. Towle was in his element with these problems. His artistic eye zoomed in, and his brain went into marketing gear. The best paint jobs, he wrote, accentuated the machine's form and hid its figure flaws. "Long vigorous stripes along the lower band molding" made a model "look longer." Why not, Towle posited, wrap the stripe around the car's front? People touring the 1927 National marveled at the new multicolored wheels, suggesting they might like the polychrome effects that accentuated the car's form. Why not put intricate motifs all over some models? The results would delight the eye, feed the senses, and advance the nation's aesthetic health. Like other modernists, Towle envisioned a world improved by experts wielding special know-how for the greater good. He was an aesthetic doctor with a stethoscope and a prescription pad. His patient was the visually naive auto industry; his medicine, judiciously applied color.[28]

Taking Charge of Color at GM

Between 1925 and 1928 Towle worked hard to put the Duco Color Advisory Service on a solid footing. He stuck with Du Pont in 1926, despite GM's overtures. By July 1928, however, he accepted the lead automaker's offer and moved to Michigan. There he worked as GM's first color engineer and co-founded its Art and Colour Section with the flamboyant Hollywood custom builder, Harley Earl.[29]

While at Du Pont, Towle routinely visited Detroit to meet Duco clients at their factories or his company's offices in the General Motors Building. He also saw GM executives when summoned, sometimes joining the General Technical Committee at the General Motors Proving Ground. In June 1927, he talked to this group of high flyers, including Sloan, research chief Charles F. Kettering, and top dogs from the Oakland and Chevrolet divisions, about "the influence of color on beauty and sales." He provided a forceful object lesson: three pairs of Chevrolets in two-tone paint schemes that made some of them look long, others high, and still others squat. When GM big shots thought they saw cars of different sizes, Towle enjoyed the victory. He had demonstrated how carefully managed color could influence visual perception; he later referred to the two-tone trick as "reverse camouflage." Ahead of the curve Sloan announced GM's plans to set up an "Art and Colour Section for the purpose of developing outlines and colors for the various cars in the Corporation." The new office would cooperate with all of the GM car divisions, Sloan said, to provide "attractive color combinations for our product."[30]

As the quintessential big business executive, Sloan must have savored the idea of integrating color merchandising into GM's organizational chart. The move fit with the sophisticated system of statistical and financial controls established by his corporation in the early 1920s. Forecasting was already part of GM's operations. Every ten days GM dealers sent sales updates to headquarters, where accountants analyzed the reports for the sake of inventory control. Their forecasts became the basis for efficient inter-divisional administration, enabling GM to anticipate the demand for steel, tires, and car models. Applying this rational technique to aesthetics—dissecting consumer preferences for body types, paint jobs, upholstery fabrics, hood ornaments, and the like—seemed like the right step. The automaker's Art and Colour Section was established to manage aesthetic risk and to interface with GM's advertising people to promote the stylish new cars. Sloan believed that GM, with its own in-house color experts, could "deal with color on a scientific basis."[31]

At the Art and Colour Section Towle continued his work as a stylist and stretched into forecasting, grafting methods from the industrial arts on to the GM model. Color forecasters, he explained, were like meteorologists. Practitioners studied evidence from around the country and used their knowledge of historical patterns to make predictions. "The only way to make cars in colors that will sell well to the public," Towle stated, "is to have the manufacturer's dealers gather definite information as to colors that the public prefers." If one dealer "says that blue is popular, you are not sure," he continued. "If another dealer somewhere else also says that blue is popular, you begin to think it may be so; and if the same news come from all over, you are very sure that blue should be the color of your coaches and sedans." Always skeptical Towle checked dealers' input against public taste as "revealed in the periodicals, in newspapers and over the radio as regards clothing, house furnishings and other articles." His fashion antennae were always tuned to the consumer channel. Much about Towle's method drew on hard facts, but much also depended on experience, intuition, and common sense.[32]

As GM's head colorist Towle issued a monthly forecast comprised of a lively circular on general style trends and a statistical appendix listing car sales by color. In the circular for June 1929, he spoke generally about the powerful legacy of True Blue. Dealer feedback for May had revealed that multiple shades, including Duco's Jefferson Blue, Briton Blue, Calumet Blue, Cadillac Blue, and Bonneville Blue, appeared on top-selling cars. At first glance this information seemed like a simple testament to blue's sustained popularity. But Towle dug deeper; his detailed tabulations showed that consumer choices varied from region to region and from model to model. In the Pacific Northwest, 87 percent of Pontiac buyers preferred shades of blue; 5 brown, 5 green, and 3 cream. In the Northeast, only 17 percent of Buick buyers liked blue, 30 green, 22 beige, 14 black, 3 grey, and 2 brown. The comparisons went on. Although it was possible to follow national trends, over-generalizations could be dangerous. Consumer longing for individualization always threw a monkey wrench into the mix.[33]

Towle's forecasts showed GM how to get a handle on the slippery matters of style, fashion, and taste. His predictions echoed the voices of earlier intermediaries such as Edward Patton and Wheeler Earl, who in 1923 had told automakers to watch the consumer. His published reports emulated those of Margaret Hayden Rorke, forecaster extraordinaire for mass-market clothing; and his aesthetics resembled those of Hazel H. Adler, a prominent consultant who used color harmonies based on Modernist painting. When faced with growing business enthusiasm for the Munsell system, Towle criticized its constraints on creativity. Munsell's followers used rules of complementarity to devise color combinations; Towle preferred to mix and match until the right ensemble caught his eye. Serendipity had a place; the best color harmonies erupted from "accidents" in the design studio. All of this meant that "style setting" was a "risky business." Towle knew that it would never be possible to get inside the car buyer's head; it was the nature of the beast. Culture was ever changing, consumer tastes evanescent. His forecasts finessed the issue, as much as it was humanly possible.[34]

In 1930, Towle left GM to work for the Campbell-Ewald agency in Detroit, where he specialized in outdoor advertising, including billboards and posters. We may never know why Towle departed, but he may have felt smothered next to the domineering Harley Earl. In a memo to Kettering he hinted at discord, referring to GM's color section as a "vale of tears." After a brief stint at Campbell-Ewald Towle moved on again. He was happiest bridging color, design, and advertising. In 1934, he became founding director of the Division of Creative Design and Color at Pittsburgh Plate Glass, which did color schemes for appliances, layouts for showrooms and storefronts, new hues for paints and varnishes, and company advertising. He remained an important figure in the color revolution, extending its influence with his designs for industry, commerce, and architecture.[35]

Duco Simplified

Towle's successor at the Duco Color Advisory Service was another adman turned colorist, Howard Ketcham. A member of New York high society, Ketcham grew up in Manhattan and Long Island and attended prestigious schools: St. Paul's and Amherst College. From 1925 to 1927 he followed in Towle's footsteps, working as art director for H. K. McCann while studying at the New York School of Design. In 1927, he joined the Duco office where he worked until 1935, when he established Howard Ketcham Inc., a color consultancy in Rockefeller Center.[36]

Ketcham inherited from Towle a color service that stressed the market value of beauty as practiced in the industrial arts. Initially, Ketcham continued these efforts through a joint project with Cheney Brothers, the silk mill that understood how consumer choice drove the fashion system. "Many persons believe that fashions are set by the manufacturer and thrust upon a sheeplike people," explained Cheney sales director Paul Thomas. "We hear that women are slaves of fashion and are being exploited by the great dressmakers." Nothing could have been farther from the truth: "The dressmakers are slaves to women and have nervous breakdowns trying to find the thing that fits into the mental attitude of the female of the human species." In the battle against rayon Cheney had put forth an aggressive marketing plan that included mass advertising, celebrity promotions, and color forecasting. "To anticipate the demand seems dangerous," wrote Cheney art director Henry Creange, "to await it, and then try to serve an impatient public, is fatal." With Creange's guidance Cheney had evolved a distinctive approach to the "mass production of style goods." The strategy revolved around a three-tiered portfolio: "novelties" or new seasonal items, "second-season" lines, and "staples." The high-fashion novelties, spun off Creange's color forecasts, yielded most of the profits. Over the years Thomas had been "very friendly to du Pont interests," supplying the firm with Cheney forecasts. Now he hoped that a tie-in with Du Pont would clinch its status as a technological leader. The Duco Color Advisory Service, in turn, expected to learn something about top-cabin design and marketing.[37]

In late 1928, Du Pont announced a set of Duco car colors based on Cheney's forecast for next fall. It included Red Shadow Red, "a yellow red suitable for use with brown or beige, as a wire-wheel color or for striping," Sea Bubble, "a natural beige first developed by the silk industry which has received wide acceptance in the textile trade as well as in the automotive industry," and Rich Loam, "a rich gray brown developed to duplicate the appearance of freshly turned earth." There were also Pewter Pot, Blu-Gray, Gray Gull, Bay Tree, Verdancia, Water Glo, and Lei orange. The Cheney-Du Pont palette continued Towle's mission to augment Du Pont's cultural capital with high-class lines.[38]

Although Ketcham recognized the importance of the industrial arts, this colorist, who was later called the father of color engineering, marched to a different drummer. Convinced that nitrocellulose lacquer production should be more efficient, Ketcham made simplification the raison d'etre of the Duco Color Advisory Service. In this regard he embraced the practices of the engineering profession, which since the Progressive era had labored to better American living standards through incremental improvements in material life. As secretary of commerce, engineer Herbert C. Hoover sanctioned this with public projects that standardized and simplified everything from lumber to roofing tiles. Instead of fifty-five sizes of paving brick, the construction trade now had eleven. "We do not by this process propose to abolish Easter bonnets," Hoover's department explained, "we propose more bonnets for the same money and efforts." At the Duco Color Advisory Service Ketcham had a similar goal: drastically reduce Du Pont's portfolio of 7,500 colors while increasing sales of Duco finishes. The trick lay in determining which colors resonated in the great middle ground. In his eight years as director Ketcham's simplification initiative pivoted on two tactics: the rationalization of color forecasts and the radical reduction of the Duco palette.[39]

Ketcham's first step was to create the Automobile Color Index, a monthly quantitative analysis of Duco sales. This hybrid forecasting tool owed its analytical rigor to GM, and its respect for fashion to Cheney. In emulation of the silk maker Ketcham divided Duco colors into three groups, à la Creange. In Du Pont's system "standard" colors were the old standbys; they were always in production, regardless of fads. "Style" colors were trendy; they reflected the latest fashions in textiles and automobiles. "Staple" colors fell in the middle. They embellished bumpers, trim, or wheels and were made in small quantities. Beginning in summer 1929, Ketcham tracked these color groups and measured the rise and fall of color families, such as reds, browns, and yellows. Keeping tabs on major colors, the index showed how the Great Depression affected consumers' buying habits. By 1933, black was back in business, a major challenger to blue. The Automobile Color Index reported these trends in elaborate charts and graphs that demonstrated the statistical expertise of Du Pont's new chief colorist.[40]

The Duco Color Advisory Service balanced this quantitative data with observations of fashion trends in style centers like London, Paris, and Vienna. From late 1929 the color bureau issued monthly forecasts, published by newspapers such as the *New York Times* and trade journals such as *Autobody*. Under Ketcham's watch automotive color forecasting assumed statistical rigor and punctual regularity while maintaining a high degree of aesthetic sophistication.[41]

In 1932, Ketcham unveiled Du Pont's full-fledged tribute to color engineering: Duco Calibrated Colors, a series of 290 tints based on the Munsell system. By then American paint companies had 11,500 different automotive colors in their inventories. There was no logic behind this enormous selection; it stemmed not from the multiplicity of consumer tastes but from a lack of planning. Since World War I the palette had grown at the rate of 800 colors per year. Many lacquer makers carried colors that no one had ordered for several years. But the bigger problem lay in manufacturing practice. Some producers found it difficult to control chemical reactions in their factories, generating "as many as 80 variations of one original color." When harried automakers accepted the off-color releases, they exacerbated the problem. Things got worse when car companies switched paint suppliers, which unsuccessfully tried to match competitors' colors. The end result was an increasing number of mismatches.[42]

The basic color aids introduced in the mid-1920s by paint makers like Murphy and Ditzler had outrun their usefulness. Ketcham reported that most paint salesrooms no longer carried samples; it was impossible to display thousands of color chips. The Duco Color Advisory Service wrestled with the excess; the objective was to eradicate waste so as to enhance the freedom of choice for clients and consumers. Ketcham's staff studied several color systems before selecting Munsell as the Du Pont standard. Whether the product was food or paint, the Munsell method provided a uniform way of measuring and describing color. Ketcham found it ideal for his simplification project. The Duco office, collaborating with eighteen firms in the auto industry, used the Munsell system to pick the three hundred colors most often used by body builders and refinishing shops.[43]

To explain Duco Calibrated Colors Ketcham relied on the scientific language of Munsell measurement, which stood in sharp contrast to the rhetoric of fashion forecasting. Whereas Towle had exuded emotion, Ketcham stressed hard facts. He dispassionately talked about color's physical dimensions: hue, value, and chroma. Writing for the refinishing trade, he described one two-toned harmony simply and directly: "Allover color a light maroon. The character of such a maroon can be improved through the use of light, bright blue green as a striping accent. Maroon is in reality a low value of red. Blue green is the complement of red. The use of a color with its complement tends to intensify both colors." The language of efficiency had market value. The Munsell lingo reflected Duco's newfound awareness of color as something that could be tamed, controlled, and packaged.[44]

Ironically Ketcham's simplification plan sat squarely in industrial arts, where Albert H. Munsell did his pioneering research. During the 1920s, the Munsell Research Laboratory and the Munsell Color Company carried his torch by pursuing photometric research with the Bureau of Standards and publicizing the system among schools and businesses. Between 1928 and 1930 Walter M. Scott, the former chief chemist for Cheney, worked as service director for the Munsell Color Company. At the silk mill Scott had used the Munsell system, and this provided the basis for his enthusiastic promotion of it as an aesthetic tool for business. By the early 1930s, Munsell's practical method of color measurement was fast becoming the accepted standard in the industrial arts.[45]

After leaving Du Pont Ketcham continued to balance commitments to art, technology, science, and commerce. In 1937, he reflected on color's recent achievements and challenges. Consumer surveys proliferated as more self-styled experts entered the marketing arena. Ketcham believed that the new-comers missed the beat on color. Some market researchers simply drew parallels between income and color choices: people earning $2,500 or less liked blue on small household gadgets; the $2,500 to $5,000 crowd bought green; and the $10,000-plus folks preferred gray. These simple correlations masked nuances. "The consumer jury," Ketcham explained, "is hypercritical. They know that there are many blue hues. Blue to them may mean greenish blues, purplish blues and pure blues." Consumers were picky, but color engi-neers versed in Munsell theory could home in on people's choices in a scien-tific way. "Each hue has high, middle, and low values," he wrote, "and weak, moderate and strong chroma variations." Any color market analysis worth its salt "must determine the exact hue and chroma desired." The color prefer-ences of the man and woman on the street were complex. Ketcham's air of rationality legitimized his continued emphasis on the value of difference.[46]

In the ten years between the arrival of Towle and the departure of Ketcham, Du Pont experienced a remarkable transformation in color practice. The company's first colorist stressed aesthetic excellence; the second thrived on science and technology. Their temperaments, assumptions, and techniques differed, but their goals were the same. Both men understood the fundamen-tal responsibility of the colorist in the buyers' market. "It is just as costly to be too far ahead of the color trend as it is unprofitable to lag behind it," wrote Ketcham, echoing Henry Creange. "So, the manufacturer or dealer who wishes to meet markets when they arrive does well to determine in advance the public choice in colors." How was this feat accomplished? Seasoned col-orists took their lessons from the marketplace, whether watching the ladies ogle Paris gowns or analyzing the sales of blue Buicks. They were, in short, "obliged to keep abreast of the consciousness of the color consumer."[47]

Why True Blue Mattered

This vignette about Du Pont and the color revolution tells us much about the inner workings of the fashion system during the modern era. In many respects Du Pont's venture into color styling and engineering testifies to the symbiosis of two economic spheres: the center economy dominated by high-technology firms and the periphery where creativity flourishes. In other ways it reveals a great deal about the management of aesthetic risk at Du Pont and GM. Moving beyond trickle-down theories and generaliza-tions about corporate manipulation, it shows precisely how fashion colors were produced and how they traveled the highways and byways of American business culture.

Du Pont discovered that there was nothing easy about the business of fashion. Men in the paint trade found it tough to pin down the consumer: she was female, feisty, and fickle. Admitting ignorance, the chemical works hired fashion intermediaries who could help. If it were to compete in consumer markets, big business had to emulate small business. In the end Du Pont followed the textile trade, which, like other batch production industries, had perfected a system of consumer mediation. The growing chemical behemoth even adopted the color system most favored by the industrial arts.

As Du Pont standardized the Duco palette, the company helped to establish new ground rules for design and innovation in consumer durables. By the mid-1930s Duco color choices embodied tastes in the great imagined middle ground, the mass market. At the same time the Du Pont paint portfolio allowed for deviation. Blue appealed to conservatives, but the nation's George Babbitts came in many different stripes. Besides True Blue there were hundreds of other blues, all geared toward the range of middlebrow tastes. The county judge could drive a navy Cadillac sedan, and the first-generation college student could have an electric blue Chevrolet roadster. To those atop the middle class and those just entering, blue bespoke their affinity with the comfortable conservatism of Babbitt's America. But the tremendous range of blue hues allowed these middle sorts to signal differences.

The proliferation of forecasting systems gets to the crux of the matter. There was no "one best way" to predict colors precisely because there was no single taste and no single category of products. In textiles the TCCA sat squarely in the mass market, while Cheney reached for the mountaintop. In paints Du Pont wanted it all and found compromise with Munsell measurements. Yet these forecasting systems had commonalities. Whether in textiles or automobiles, the palette as a whole had mass appeal; individual colors, a tad of distinctiveness. Each was designed to work with a specific line of products. A woman might wear a suit in Elsa Schiaparelli's Shocking Pink for decades, but a Fire Red car got tiresome pretty soon. Exact copies of couture colors looked strange on fenders, doors, and upholstery. Men like Towle and Ketcham explained why.

As they labored over forecasts corporate colorists of the interwar years gave full expression to "form follows function," the prescient Victorian shibboleth that became the Modernist mantle. Towle promoted this concept when he explained how a two-tone paint job could alter a car's silhouette. Ketcham helped it along by simplifying selection with Duco Calibrated Colors. Without the confusion of too much choice, automakers were free to concentrate on matching color variations to body styles. At GM Harley Earl built on this foundation when he put streamlining at the center of design practice in the 1930s. In a backhanded way, then, Du Pont's early colorists counted among the pioneers of modern design.

Back in 1926, Irénée du Pont had castigated GM's Buick division for making overtures to Du Pont's head colorist. His concern revealed a remarkable confidence about the importance of color to modern merchandising.

In the long run, however, the preservation of trade secrets mattered less than the dissemination of color theory. Stylists like Towle and Ketcham understood these fashion basics, and they labored to carve a place for their emerging profession in American industry. During their Du Pont years color authority moved from periphery to center as a marketing value. When industrial colorists spoke, corporations listened. By the mid-1930s color experts had a toehold in American business culture.

Notes

1. Irénée du Pont, Wilmington, Del., to Harry Bassett, Flint, Mich., August 17, 1926, folder: VC 24, General Motors, box 33, acc. 228: Papers of Irénée du Pont, Hagley Museum and Library, Wilmington, Del; Arthur Lloyd Welsh, "The Du Pont-General Motors Case" (Ph.D. diss., University of Illinois, 1963), ch. 5.
2. Irénée du Pont to Harry Bassett ("violated"). The Duco Color Advisory Service was part of Du Pont's Paint, Lacquer, and Chemicals Department, renamed the Fabrics and Finishes Department in 1929. See William M. Zintl, "History of the Du Pont Paint Business," 1947, pp. [83C], 84, acc. 1850: R&D History Project Files, Hagley Museum and Library, Wilmington, Del. [hereafter cited as "R&D-Du Pont"].
3. "Color in Industry," *Fortune* 1 (1930): 85–94 (90, "master"; 92, "color revolution"). Most scholars have credited Harley Earl and Henry G. Weaver with GM's aesthetic innovations without due consideration of Towle and other colorists. For example, see Stephen Bayley, *Harley Earl and the Dream Machine* (New York: Knopf, 1983); David Gartman, *Auto Opium: A Social History of American Automobile Design* (London: Routledge, 1994); Sally Clarke, "Consumers, Information, and Marketing Efficiency at GM," *Business and Economic History* 25 (autumn 1996): 186–195; Sally Clarke, "Managing Design: The Art and Colour Section at General Motors, 1927–1941," *Journal of Design History* 12 (1999): 65–79.
4. "Color in Industry," 90 ("ardent"). On fashion intermediaries, see Regina Lee Blaszczyk, *Imagining Consumers: Design and Innovation from Wedgwood to Corning* (Baltimore: Johns Hopkins University Press, 2000). On aesthetic risk, see ibid., and Regina Lee Blaszczyk, "The Aesthetic Moment: China Decorating, Consumer Demand, and Technological Change in the American Pottery Industry, 1865–1900, *Winterthur Portfolio: A Journal of American Material Culture* 29 (summer/autumn 1994): 121–153.
5. H. S. Person, "Management Must Be Made to Fit Dominant Buyers' Market," *Automotive Industries* 47 (November 30, 1922): 1059–1062 (1060, "parade"; 1062, "king," "numerous," "search").
6. David A. Hounshell and John Kenly Smith Jr., *Science and Corporate Strategy: Du Pont R&D, 1902–1980* (New York: Cambridge University Press, 1988), part II and ch. 6. On finishing engineers, see E. I. du Pont de Nemours & Company, ". . . but what would both, *together*, think of your finishing system," advertisement from *Nation's Business*, October 1926, and "What we need," advertisement from *Nation's Business*, November 1926, both in folder 2: Duco advertisements, box 36, acc. 1803: Papers of the Advertising Department, E. I. du Pont de Nemours & Company, Hagley Museum and Library, Wilmington, Del [hereafter cited as "AD-DuPont"].

7. On living standards and middle-class taste, see Shelley Kaplan Nickles, "Object Lessons: Household Appliance Design and the American Middle Class, 1920–1960" (Ph.D. diss., University of Virginia, 1999); Regina Lee Blaszczyk, "No Place Like Home: Herbert Hoover and the American Standard of Living," pp. 113–135, in *Uncommon Americans: The Lives and Legacies of Herbert and Lou Henry Hoover* (Westport, Conn.: Praeger, 2003); Marina Moskowitz, *Standard of Living: The Measure of the Middle Class in Modern America* (Baltimore: Johns Hopkins University Press, 2004); Kristina Wilson, *Liveable Modernism: Interior Decorating and Design in the Great Depression* (New Haven: Yale University Press, 2004).

8. Alfred P. Sloan Jr., *My Years with General Motors* (New York: Doubleday, 1964); Alfred D. Chandler Jr. and Stephen Salisbury, *Pierre S. du Pont and the Making of the Modern Corporation* (New York: Harper & Row, 1978), ch. 17–21; Richard S. Tedlow, *New and Improved: The Story of Mass Marketing in America* (New York: Basic Books, 1990), ch. 3; David Farber, *Sloan Rules: Alfred P. Sloan and the Triumph of General Motors* (Chicago: University of Chicago Press, 2002), ch. 3; Adrian Kinnane, *DuPont: From the Banks of the Brandywine to Miracles of Science* (Wilmington, Del.: E. I. du Pont de Nemours and Company, 2002), ch. 4.

9. Hounshell and Smith, *Science and Corporate Strategy*, pp. 141–144; F. H. Kane, "1924 Oaklands Finished in Duco," *Du Pont Magazine* 18 (April 1924): 6–8; L. R. Beardslee, GM, New York, to J. J. Moosman, Du Pont Company, Parlin, N. J., February 14, 1924 ("customers"), R&D-Du Pont.

10. Herbert Chase, "Exceptional Durability Is Claimed for New Body Finish," *Automotive Industries* 49 (July 26, 1923): 158–159; W. L. Carver, "Labor Costs Halved by Use of Duco in Finishing Oakland Bodies," *Automotive Industries* 49 (September 13, 1923): 524–526; George Rice, "Why Colors of Automobile Finishes Sometimes Fail," *Motor Vehicle Monthly* 64 (January 1927): 58.

11. Kathryn Steen, "Wartime Catalyst and Postwar Reaction: The Making of the U.S. Synthetic Organic Chemicals Industry, 1910–1930" (Ph.D. diss., University of Delaware, 1995); Anthony S. Travis, *Dyes Made in America, 1915–1980: The Calco Chemical Company, American Cyanamid, and the Raritan River* (Jerusalem: Hexagon Press, 2004); P. J. Wingate, *The Colorful Du Pont Company* (Wilmington, Del.: Serendipity Press, 1983); Pamela Walker Laird, *Advertising Progress: American Business and the Rise of Consumer Marketing* (Baltimore: Johns Hopkins University Press, 1998); Bernice L. Thomas, *America's 5 & 10 Cent Stores: The Kress Legacy* (New York: John Wiley & Sons, 1997).

12. Will South, *Color, Myth, and Music: Stanton MacDonald-Wright and Synchromism* (Raleigh, North Carolina: North Carolina Museum of Art, 2001); Dorothy Nickerson, "History of the Munsell Color System," *Color Engineering* 7 (September–October 1969): 42–51.

13. For the 1920s interest in color, see Agnes Rowe Fairman, *Color Harmony in Window Draperies* (New York: Orinoko Mills, 1921); Adolph Judah Snow, *The Book of Happiness: Predicated upon the Scientific Selection of Colors for Interior and Exterior Decoration* (Philadelphia: John Lucas & Co., 1922); Millicent Melrose, *Color Harmony and Design in Dress* (New York: Social Mentor Publications, 1922); International Correspondence Schools, *Show-card and Color Schemes* (Scranton, Penn.: International Textbook Company,

1923); Matthew Luckiesh, *Light and Color in Advertising and Merchandising* (New York: D. Van Nostrand, 1923).

14. "Progress in Color Standardization," *American Silk Journal* 41 (April 1921): 66; *National Cyclopedia of American Biography*, s.v., "Rorke, Margaret Hayden"; Regina Lee Blaszczyk, "The Colors of Modernism: Georgia O'Keeffe, Cheney Brothers, and the Relationship Between Art and Industry in the 1920s," in *Seeing High and Low: Representing Social Conflict in American Visual Culture*, edited by Patricia Johnston (Berkeley: University of California Press, 2006). Throughout this essay, I use the term "industrial arts" to describe the intricate web of manufacturers, retailers, museums, and design schools that generated and promoted the bulk of mass-market consumer goods from the mid-1800s to World War II. Historians have not fully studied the industrial arts, which have been overshadowed in the scholarly literature by reform efforts, including the Aesthetic Movement, the Arts and Crafts Movement, and consultant industrial design. For case studies of several industrial arts firms, see Blaszczyk, *Imagining Consumers*.

15. "Why Paint Them Black?" *Automotive Industries* 48 (April 26, 1923): 938 ("funeral"; "cheapness"); "Let's Have More Cars in Color," *Motor* 40 (July 1923): 42, 84 (42, "vivid green"); Clifford B. Knight, "The Women Decide," *Motor* 40 (October 1923): 56, 96 (96, "women").

16. Herbert Chase, "Egyptian Lacquer Develops New Nitro Cellulose Automobile Finish," *Automotive Industries* 50 (April 10, 1924): 828–829; "Armocote Baking Enamel Now Being Made in Limited Number of Colors," *Automotive Industries* 50 (April 17, 1924): 859; "Crystallizing Lacquer has Many Uses," *Automotive Industries* 50 (April 24, 1924): 935; "New Valentine Varnish System Said to Double Life of Finish," *Automotive Industries* 50 (May 1, 1924): 968–969.

17. On Murphy, see Isolde J. Ketterer, "Motor Cars are Going in for Brighter Hues," *Motor* 41 (June 1924): 41, 58, 72. On Ditzler, see "Egyptian Colors Introduced for Automobiles," *Motor Vehicle Monthly* 59 (February 1924): 34; Ditzler Color Company, "The Sales Appeal of Color to the Fore," advertisement in *Automotive Industries* 51 (September 4, 1924): 1.

18. Du Pont Company, "Every Automobile Show is a DUCO Exposition!" advertisement in *Motor* 43 (January 1925): 293; Herbert Chase, "Finishing and Refinishing Approaching High Engineering Standard," *Automotive Industries* 50 (May 22, 1924): 1134–1137; J. J. Riley, "Recommendations for Refinishing with Pyroxylin," *Motor Vehicle Monthly* 61 (October 1925): 44, 46, 65. Du Pont also sold nitrocellulose lacquers to factories making furniture, office equipment, appliances, piano components, railroad locomotives and cars, umbrellas, radios, gasoline pumps, typewriters, and vacuum cleaners. See E. I. Du Pont de Nemours & Company, "Chariots of Content," advertisement from *Saturday Evening Post*, October 11, 1924, folder 4: Advertising tearsheets, 1924, box 43, AD-Du Pont. In 1926, Du Pont introduced Brush Duco for household use; although widely advertised, sales lagged until Du Pont resolved technical complications. See Zintl, "History of the Du Pont Paint Business," pp. 84–87.

19. F. B. Davis to Fin Sparre, color letter, January 8, 1925, folder: Plastics Dept., October 1921–August 1928 ("practical advice"), box 62, acc. 1662: Administrative Papers of the Office of the President, E I. du Pont de Nemours & Company, Hagley Museum and Library, Wilmington, Del. [hereafter cited as "PP-DuPont"].

20. "Activities in the Motor Trade," *New York Times*, October 4, 1925, XX10 ("latest"); *Who Was Who in American Art*, s.v. "Towle, H. Ledyard"; "Towle-Smith Wedding on June 18," *New York Times*, June 14, 1912, 11; "Towle Joins General Motors," *Motor Vehicle Monthly* 64 (July 1928): 52. On Towle at Seaman, see "H. Ledyard Towle . . . Will Speak on Color," Announcement for lecture to the Pittsburgh Advertising Club on January 21, 1941, acc. 2191, H. Ledyard Towle Papers, Hagley Museum and Library, Wilmington, Del. [hereafter cited as TP].

21. Roland Marchand, *Advertising the American Dream: Making Way for Modernity, 1920–1940* (Berkeley: University of California Press, 1984); Towle, *Second Annual Report, Division of Creative Design and Color, 1936–1937* [Pittsburgh: Studio of Creative Design, Pittsburgh Plate Glass Company, 1937], p. 4 ("color engineer"), TP.

22. Du Pont Company, "Duco Color Advisory Service," advertisement in *Autobody* 8 (November 1925): 205 ("average"; "experts"; "certainty").

23. Towle, "Paris Ablaze with Color! Motor Cars Express Individuality," *Providence Tribune*, November 21, 1926 ("mad"; "rainbow," "boxes"); "Duco Colors Are Revealed," *News* (Cleveland, Ohio), date illegible [October 1926]; Towle, "Duco Expert Sees Colors of Paris in Bright Array," *New Orleans Times-Picayune*, November 21, 1926, all in TP.

24. Towle, "Paris Ablaze with Color!" ("myriad").

25. Towle, "Color Trends in Paris," *American Silk Journal* 47 (February 1928): 49; [Towle, "The Motor Car Show at Olympia Is Filled with Color"], October 26, [1926] (quotations); "Duco Colors Are Revealed," *(Cleveland) News*, [1926], TP. For next year's European trip, see "Bright Color Now Mark Foreign Autos," *New York Times*, October 17, 1927, 31; Towle, "Color Effects at the Olympia Show," *Autobody* 11 (November 1927): 156. On the Paris fashion houses in this period, see Nancy J. Troy, *Couture Culture: A Study in Modern Art and Fashion* (Cambridge, Mass.: MIT Press, 2003), and Dilys E. Blum, *Shocking! The Art and Fashion of Elsa Schiaparelli* (Philadelphia: Philadelphia Museum of Art, 2003).

26. "Body Colors at the Show," *Automotive Industries* 54 (January 14, 1926): 57. For "plumage" see "As Others Saw Us," *Motor* 45 (January–February 1926): 19. For the "harmonies" and the "mass-production man" see Towle, "As Many as Six Hues Found in One Machine: Black Is Out of Vogue," *Brooklyn Standard Union*, January 23, 1927; Towle, "Motor Industry Answering Demand of Public for Color," *Gazette-Times* (Pittsburgh), March 6, 1927, both in TP. On the "high water mark," see "Finds Auto Show Blaze of Beauty: Capt. H.L. Towle, Artist, Says It Surpasses All Predecessors in Colors and in Lines," *New York Times*, January 14, 1927, p. 21.

27. Towle, "As Many as Six Hues Found in One Machine," ("wealth"; "brains"; "shoe trades"). Trade observers concurred that "the color experts of our paint manufacturers" made an impact. See "Reflections of the National Show," *Autobody* 11 (February 1927): 48.

28. Towle, "As Many as Six Hues Found in One Machine," ("stripes"); "Color Appeal," *Autobody* 12 (September 1927): 89.

29. "Towle Joins General Motors"; Morris Midkiff, "$25,000 in Exhibits Placed on Display as Architects Meet,"*Austin Statesman*, September 26, 1940, TP.

30. Minutes of the General Technical Committee, General Motors Proving Ground, June 8, 1927 ("beauty and sales"; "various cars"; "attractive"), file 87–11.9–1, Charles F. Kettering Papers, Kettering/GMI Alumni Foundation Collection of Industrial History, Flint, Mich. [hereafter cited as KP]. For Towle's account of the two-tone Chevrolet demonstration, see Towle, "Projecting the Automobile into the Future," *SAE Journal* 29 (July 1931): 33–39, 44 (38, Chevrolet); Towle, "Art and Color in Body Design," Presentation before the Society of Automotive Engineers, Detroit Section, February 3, 1941, pp. 12–14, TP; Towle, "Color Dynamics Presentation to Architects," [1940s], [2, "reverse camouflage"], TP.

31. Minutes of the General Technical Committee, June 8, 1927; Alfred D. Chandler Jr., *Strategy and Structure: Chapters in the History of the American Industrial Enterprise* (Cambridge, Mass.: MIT Press, 1962), pp. 145–153. Sloan's account of Art and Colour Section's early years focuses on Earl; see *My Years with General Motors*, ch. 15.

32. Towle, "Projecting the Automobile into the Future," pp. 35–36 ("blue").

33. [Towle, Art and Colour Section, General Motors Corporation], "Forecast with Colour News and Notes," June 1929, p. 4, and appendix, pp. [4, 6], file 87–11.4–3, KP.

34. Hazel H. Adler, "Capitalizing on Color," *American Dyestuffs Reporter* 14 (December 14, 1925): 819–820; "Color Expert Explains How to Get Harmonious Combinations," *Automotive Industries* 56 (February 5, 1927): 152–153 (152, "accidents"); [Towle, Art and Colour Section, General Motors Corporation], "Forecast with Colour News and Notes," May 1929, p. 4 ("risky"), file 87–11.4–3, KP.

35. Towle to Charles F. Kettering, June 19, 1929, ("vale of tears"), file 87–11.4.3, KP; Towle to G. D. Crain Jr., Advertising Publications, Chicago, December 5, 1952, TP.

36. "Howard Ketcham, Authority on Color Use to Corporations," *New York Times*, May 7, 1982, D-19; "Industrial Color Expert Opens New York Office," *Industrial Finishing* 11 (February 1935): 49–50.

37. Paul Thomas, "The Secrets of Fashion and Art Appeal in the Automobile," *SAE Journal* 23 (December 1928): 595–601 (596, "sheeplike"); Blaszczyk, "No Place Like Home," p. 126 ("bonnets"); Mr. Price, Duco Color Advisory Service, N.Y., to W. A. Hart, Director of Advertising, October 20, 1928; Matt Denning, Assistant Director of Advertising, to Lammont du Pont, President, October 24, 1928, both in box 3, PP-Du Pont.

38. "New Duco Colors Developed," *Motor Vehicle Monthly* 64 (December 1928): 60 (quotations); Duco Information Service, "Bulletin," October 17, 1928, box 3, PP-Du Pont.

39. Blaszczyk, "No Place Like Home," p. 126 ("bonnets").

40. "Automobile Color Index," *Autobody* 16 (July 1929): 12–13; "Colors in the Automobile Industry: The Work of the Duco Color Advisory Service," *Authorized Duco Refinisher News* 9 (February 1931): 14–15; Howard Ketcham, "Fashion Factors in Automobile Colors," *Du Pont Magazine* 37 (September–October 1933): 15, 17.

41. James Spearing, "At the Wheel," *New York Times*, June 16, 1929, XX16; P. H. Chase, "Color at the Paris and London Shows," *Autobody* 14 (November 1928): 170–171; "Blue Now Leads Automobile Colors," *Motor Body, Paint and Trim* 66 (June 1930): 40.

42. Ketcham, "Calibrated Colors I," *Industrial Finishing* 9 (November 1932): 26–30 (25, "80 variations"); Ketcham, "Calibrated Colors II," *Industrial Finishing* 10 (December 1932): 34–36.
43. Nickerson, "History of the Munsell Color System."
44. Ketcham, "Selection of Colors I," *Industrial Finishing* 9 (January 1933): 14–16, 18; Ketcham, "Selection of Colors II," *Industrial Finishing* 9 (February 1933): 24, 26–27; Ketcham, "Color Schemes for Autos," *Industrial Finishing* 9 (June 1933): 12–15 (12, "light maroon").
45. Nickerson, "History of the Munsell Color System."
46. Ketcham, "Choosing Product Colors," *Industrial Finishing* 14 (December 1937): 16–19 (19, quotations).
47. Ibid.

Chapter 3

The Popular Front and the Corporate Appropriation of Modernism

Shannan Clark

During the 1930s and 1940s, artists and designers in the United States with leftist political sympathies embarked upon a range of ambitious cultural initiatives to promote modernist aesthetics. By harnessing the symbolic power of a range of modernist styles, including functionalism, abstraction, and surrealism, these activists hoped to further their efforts to cultivate class-consciousness among the creative workers whose mental labor enabled the culture industries to function. Yet, rather than creating conditions that challenged corporate hegemony over the systems of mass culture production, the initiatives launched by the radical partisans of the Popular Front ultimately abetted the assimilation and appropriation of modernism by corporate capitalism. Instead of fostering an enlarged conception of the working class that included artists, professionals, and other white-collar workers, they inadvertently helped to furnish corporate America with mastery of a new set of visual idioms with which to represent its resurgence and revitalization after the crisis of the Depression.

The cultural activists of the Popular Front sought to achieve their objectives in several ways. When feasible, they sought to develop autonomous institutions that were largely independent of direct corporate control. Their most successful effort along these lines was the Design Laboratory, which was the first comprehensive school of modernist design in the United States. Established in New York City in 1935 as part of the Federal Art Project (FAP), the school was reorganized two years later, after the elimination of its government funding, as a cooperative under the auspices of the Federation of Architects, Engineers, Chemists and Technicians (FAECT), a left-led union affiliated with the Congress of Industrial Organizations (CIO). In 1938, the school reorganized again as the completely independent Laboratory School of Industrial Design and entered perhaps its most dynamic and productive phase before its chronic financial woes finally forced it to close its doors for good in 1940. In addition to independent ventures like the Laboratory, the CIO's left-led unions of culture workers, such as the FAECT, the New York

Newspaper Guild, the Book and Magazine Guild, the American Advertising Guild, and the United American Artists also themselves constituted a kind of adversarial subculture within the business-oriented mainstream of mass culture production. Through their organizing activities in publishing houses, advertising agencies, and design studios, these unions served as an important means for the transmission of modernist styles and techniques to ordinary workers. In examining the possibilities and limitations of both of these tactical approaches employed by Popular Front activists to promote modernism as a means of representing radical political connotations, this essay will elucidate how the Left's plans to subvert the apparatus of mass culture came in turn to be subverted.

By focusing on these Popular Front cultural initiatives, the analysis offered here departs from many conventional narratives of American modernism, in which the role of the indigenous American modernist avant-garde and its organic connections with the American political left has been downplayed or overlooked. Until recently, many historians and cultural critics have tended to portray modernism primarily as a European import. While acknowledging the vaguely leftist political affinities of influential early founts of modernist design like the legendary German Bauhaus, scholars and commentators have typically assumed that modernist representational strategies and visual idioms were stripped of whatever political connotations they might have had upon their arrival on American shores. In part, this reflects the emphasis in their cultural narratives on the role of institutions like the Museum of Modern Art, and the efforts of enlightened business executives such as Walter Paepcke of the Container Corporation of America who patronized modern art and design. It also reflects the ideological pressures of the Cold War and the largely successful campaign by many Cold-War liberal intellectuals to recast the cultural agenda of the Depression-Era left as fundamentally anti-modernist. Long after the demise of the Popular Front, its opponents continued to defame its cultural endeavors as nothing more than kitschy realism suited only for crude Stalinist philistines. Over time, they succeeded in nearly expunging the Popular Front left from the story of American modernism.[1]

In fact, the cultural politics of the Popular Front were much more complex, as radical artists employed diverse aesthetic strategies to represent a class-conscious view of the world. To be sure, numerous artists on the Left, such as William Gropper and Philip Evergood, embraced an aesthetic of "social realism" in their work. But while the Popular Front's social realists sought to represent traditional categories of manual labor, its modernists sought to use their innovative and experimental approaches to art and design as a pragmatist exercise to provoke a reconsideration of class identity on the part of those engaged in mental labor. The ensuing aesthetic heterodoxy perhaps dissipated the symbolic power of modernism as a bearer of radical political connotations, and contributed in part to the inability of Popular Front activists to control effectively the uses of modernism or to ward off competing claims for its significance. By the late 1940s, the pragmatist conception of modernist aesthetics espoused by Popular Front activists had become marginalized. Cultural elites succeeded in constructing a modernist hierarchy of taste that defined formally correct examples of Modern art and design as depoliticized high art to be defended against the rising tide of what critic Dwight Macdonald disdainfully labeled as "masscult." Popularization of modernism in business culture and mass consumer culture tended not to be seen as laudable attempts to apply practically advanced styles and techniques, but rather as threats to the capacity of high modernism to signify refinement. Even those members of the new postwar American avant-garde who continued to employ modernism pragmatically rather than formally envisioned their artistic expression as a catalyst for personal liberation rather than heightened class-consciousness.[2]

Yet the styles and techniques promoted through the Design Laboratory as well as through the organizing and the extension programs of the CIO's left-led unions of culture workers were not ideologically neutral forms that could be simply and easily appropriated without contest by agents of business culture or high culture. Only after years of collaborations and compromises with Popular Front activists that attested to their influence from the early 1930s until the late 1940s, and the subsequent defeat of the left's political and cultural networks with the onset of the Cold War, could modernist art and design finally be unequivocally utilized—either directly by executives and managers as they attempted to cultivate an enlightened image of business as an institution or indirectly by the museums and universities that captains of industry patronized and endowed—to legitimate corporate capitalism. Omitted from most accounts of the ascendancy of modernism in the United States, the Popular Front nonetheless was a crucial part of the context in which modernist aesthetics evolved. Recovering and reassessing the legacy of the modernist initiatives of the Popular Front gives us a more complete perspective on American culture in this pivotal period.[3]

The Design Laboratory was the most promising training ground for the new type of class-conscious culture worker touted by the Popular Front. The school furnished a vital point of contact between the business culture of commercial design, the experimental modernism of the Depression-Era avant-garde, an unprecedented governmental arts bureaucracy, and the militant unionism of the CIO. According to the FAP, the school had been "created to supply unfulfilled and pressing need in America" by providing comprehensive training that "emphasizes coordination in the study of aesthetics, industrial products, machine fabrication and merchandising." Its goal was "to train designers, not specialized craftsmen, by correlating through instruction the general principles of design and fine arts with shop practice." When it opened its doors, more than 600 people attempted to register in the first several weeks. But the Design Laboratory was much more than a trade school for commercial artists. Early publicity copy stressed the growing importance of professionalized industrial design and the perceived dearth of artists and designers trained according to a systematically modernist pedagogy; nonetheless, the Laboratory would never have been born without both the willingness of the Roosevelt Administration to dabble with the provisioning of a broad range of public goods and services, including the WPA cultural projects, as well as the determination of Popular Front activists to press the government to create a public sector base for its diverse cultural initiatives.[4] Once FAP director Holger Cahill had signed off on the proposal for a design school, immediate responsibility for recruiting a faculty rested with Frances Pollak, who supervised the various FAP educational activities in the New York metropolitan area. Despite the meager salaries, Pollak succeeded in attracting a diverse core of talented young artists and designers to teach at the Laboratory. A few, like interior designers Hilde Reiss and William Priestly, and graphic designer Lila Ulrich, had studied at the Bauhaus before the Nazis closed the school in 1933. Several others, like product design instructor Jacques Levy, held degrees from elite universities like Columbia and Yale. But the majority of the early instructors, including product design instructors William Friedman and Joseph J. Roberto, painters Irene Rice Pereira and Jack Kufeld, and sculptor Chaim Gross, had patched together their training from a combination of coursework in art, architecture or engineering at more plebian local institutions like City College, NYU, Cooper Union, Pratt Institute, and the Art Students' League. Most of them developed their pedagogy based on their own independent exposure to modernist aesthetics rather than their own educational experiences. With a few important exceptions like the teaching of avant-garde modernist painting styles in the cooperative school run by the Art Students' League, faculties in American schools of art and architecture largely resisted the rising worldwide influence of modernism through the 1930s. For the instructors at the Design Laboratory nearly as much as their pupils, the day-to-day operation of the fledgling school was itself a pragmatist exercise in "learning by doing."[5]

Inspired by prominent progressive intellectuals like Jane Addams, Charles and Mary Beard, John Dewey, Robert and Helen Lynd, and Lewis Mumford, and Thorstein Veblen, the Laboratory faculty believed that the purpose of properly conceived modern design must be to foster social democracy. To further their aesthetic and ideological objectives, they devised a highly innovative approach that combined artistic training in a wide range of media and techniques, inductive shop experimentation with various materials and forms, and coursework on society and culture (figure 3.1). Although the school's sponsorship as part of a temporary relief program made it difficult to implement a sequential curriculum for more systematic teaching, in the summer of 1936 the faculty nonetheless began a provisional three-year course of study. A year later, once the Laboratory was no longer funded by the FAP, the three-year program was expanded further into a four-year course of study comparable to the Bachelor of Fine Arts programs at established schools. Students responded enthusiastically to the curriculum, especially given the continuing lack of alternatives. Even schools that claimed to have courses in the emerging field of industrial design could not offer training remotely like that available at the Laboratory. Designer Don Wallance recalled that in 1934 he had enrolled in a class at Pratt taught by Donald Dohner, an early industrial designer who led in the in-house appliance styling

Figure 3.1 Students at the Design Laboratory School made these clocks in 1936 as part of their introductory coursework. Even though the pedagogy and curriculum were very much in flux at this early point in the school's development, the modernist sensibilities of the faculty and students are already evident in these clocks and in other student work from the first year. Photo courtesy of the Achieves of American Art, Smithsonian Institution, Washington DC

department for Westinghouse, but that he found it to be "mainly anecdotal and superficial." Following this disappointing experience, he "enrolled immediately" when he learned of the Design Laboratory in order to partake in its "comprehensive industrially oriented curriculum."[6]

In their efforts to formulate a visual idiom that they hoped would represent their progressive values, the Laboratory's faculty, students, and advocates battled on two fronts. First, the Laboratory's partisans challenged the ideology and style of the leading industrial design entrepreneurs who had influenced the emergence of the new profession as an integral element of marketing strategy. The initial commercial artists to call themselves industrial designers in the late 1920s and early 1930s had typically received a general, and sometimes quite informal, training. Some, like Raymond Loewy and Walter Dorwin Teague, had worked previously as advertising illustrators. Others, like Norman Bel Geddes and Henry Dreyfuss, had been theater set designers before redirecting their talents to the styling of products and packaging. The onset of the Depression at first threatened the nascent profession, but the severity of the slump in consumer demand induced corporate executives to embrace these designers' streamlined aesthetic as a way of bolstering sales through product differentiation and planned obsolescence. By the middle of the 1930s, a select group of successful entrepreneurs like Bel Geddes, Dreyfuss, and Loewy expanded from freelancing to heading their own agencies and employing numerous artists and designers to perform the rationalized and subdivided tasks involved in executing a continuous flow of commissions under the designers' brand name.[7]

The stars of the new profession cast themselves, and were likewise promoted by corporate publicists, as a new breed of master craftsmen supposedly able to transcend the division of labor at every step throughout the design, manufacturing, and distribution of goods for the mass consumer market. As evidence of their marketing celebrity, some of them even created "signed" goods like washing machines and radios. The industrial design entrepreneurs and the marketing and advertising executives with whom they collaborated sought to use streamlining as a way of representing their conviction in the eventuality of economic recovery and progress through privatized mass consumption under continuing corporate auspices. By giving the appliances, furniture, housewares, and retail outlets designed by their agencies a superficial appearance of organic unity, streamlining obscured the visual evidence of the various types of Fordist manual and mental labor involved in their creation. As objects and spaces that bore only minimal traces of the social relations of mass production, they proved well suited to convey the political values of corporate liberalism.

Although when the Laboratory first opened Pollak and Cahill enlisted Loewy and several other prominent designers to lend their names to its figurehead advisory board, the school's partisans quickly set forth an alternative vision of the nascent profession and its practitioners' role in the making of the material culture of mass consumerism. In sharp contrast to the streamlined representations of modernity offered by the industrial design entrepreneurs, the designers at the Laboratory developed a functionalist modernism with which they sought to focus attention on the labor involved in the imagination, rendering, fabrication, purchase, and everyday use of mass produced goods. In a declaration of principles from its 1937–1938 catalog, the Design Laboratory eschewed streamlining, instead imploring students to place "as little emphasis as possible on ornament," and to avoid "arbitrary" decorative features that lacked any "genetic connection to the functional and mechanical properties of an object whose surfaces they adorn superficially." Instead, the school maintained, "fabrication for function produces forms which have an inherent quality revealing both material and purpose." Antipathy toward the crass pretensions of the industrial design entrepreneurs even found humorous expression, as illustrated by student Milton Kalish's scathing cartoon in the school newspaper of Laboratory pupils roasting on a spit a designer who "was caught streamlining a coffee pot."[8]

The second front in the Design Laboratory's cultural war of position was against the creeping canonization of functionalist modernism as "high art" disassociated from political radicalism. Laboratory instructors acknowledged their debts to European interwar modernist projects, and the school was even described by some commentators as an "American Bauhaus." Yet the school's partisans insisted that functionalism must serve as a pragmatist means to a progressive political end, not just as a formalist signifier of elite status. A 1936 press release in which the Laboratory touted its role as the first school in the United States "to present in a coordinated and developed fashion the standards of taste and style already evolved elsewhere in the world in the so-called International Style," was also quick to note that its goal was not "to hand down dogmas about functionalism and modern design." Elaborating the distinction, school advocate Elizabeth McCausland wrote in August 1937, "the original Bauhaus, germinal as it was, suffered somewhat from the romantically individualistic self-expression of the men of genius who founded and conducted it." The Laboratory, by contrast, understood "that the most beautiful architecture, design, and art is not built by the individual, but by the coordination of talents and technics of individuals within the containing envelope of social relations." While fawning acolytes of Gropius or Breuer might merely appropriate "the outward form of the Bauhaus" and thereby recapitulate the "intellectual errors" of the Bauhaus luminaries, the designers at the Laboratory understood that the question of whether "the men who man the machines are dissatisfied by reason of too long hours and too low wages," McCausland concluded, was as important of a functional consideration for the aspiring modern designer as the selection of materials and fabrication methods.[9]

The identification of the majority of the faculty and students with the labor left was not merely rhetorical. The school seethed with the militancy and unrest that pervaded the WPA white-collar projects in New York City. Many students and faculty belonged to the Communist Party or to Communist-influenced Popular Front organizations like the Workers' Alliance and the League Against War and Fascism. Others belonged to Socialist or Trotskyist groups. Although they were a diverse band of radicals, they nonetheless participated in demonstrations and strikes directly related to the school, such as staffing and funding. Their involvement in a violent sit-down at the central WPA office in New York in December 1936 contributed in part to the waning support for the school by Cahill and others in the national FAP bureaucracy and the eventual elimination of funding for the Laboratory when the WPA appropriations were slashed in June 1937. Members of the Communist fraction within the school played a vital role in engineering the affiliation of the school with the left-led FAECT, without which the Laboratory would have been unable to continue. A council comprised of representatives from among the faculty, students, and the union's executive board assumed administration of the school, which was reorganized as a cooperative. Instructor William Friedman, who became chairman of the faculty upon the school's transition from public to labor sponsorship, recalled that "practically everyone who was on the original staff continued" because they believed the school was "important over and beyond its connection with WPA. It became a very important school educationally on the part of both students and staff."[10]

The FAECT hoped that its educational activities would furnish the cornerstone for an eventual "labor university." But putting Popular Front ideals into practice proved to be an arduous task. "We hear much about the progressive character of the Design Laboratory," an anonymous student wrote in the school newspaper in early 1938. Yet a "definite lack of understanding among students as to their role" persisted. "We must feel that we are not just isolated individuals attending classes and receiving instruction from teachers who have little in common with us, but that all of us are part of this cooperative scheme, with every phase of school activity the concern of each of us." Product design instructor Jacques Levy concurred in an open letter in which he made a renewed appeal to students and faculty alike to fulfill the ideological mission they had for the school. "Let us remember this: the school is no more important or valuable to society than the students or teachers make it," he admonished. "Great things must be in store for a school with such principles as ours has. We're in at the beginning, a responsibility is ours—let's not muff it."[11]

As difficult as it was to maintain the radical élan needed to sustain cooperative participation, an even more pressing challenge was the maintenance of an adequate stream of financial sponsorship. Retrenchment in the FAECT in the summer of 1938 compelled the ambitious white-collar union to end its limited support of the school, thus forcing the Laboratory to rely entirely upon tuition payments and a sporadic trickle of philanthropic contributions to continue its operations. The school's 1938–1939 catalog boasted that all instructors worked as designers in industry, giving them practical knowledge to pass along to their students, but in reality their paltry and irregular teaching salaries made this a necessity. Levy, for example, freelanced for General Electric's home appliance styling division, wrote interior design guidelines for the New York City Housing Authority, and even worked on the elaborate dioramas that comprised Bel Geddes' enormously popular Futurama exhibit for General Motors at the 1939–1940 New York World's Fair.[12]

Despite the ongoing financial uncertainty, in many respects this was the most successful phase of the Design Laboratory's tenuous existence. Teaching methods had been refined and improved, and the school made a number of new appointments in late 1938 and early 1939 that greatly enhanced the faculty. Some brought additional experience with artistic method and theory, like the muralist Burgoyne Diller, the Hungarian émigré painter Laszlo Matulay, and the sculptor Theodore Roszak. Other new instructors brought hands-on experience from design and advertising agencies and the mass media. Industrial designer Peter Schladermundt had worked for Dreyfuss and Bel Geddes, while Danish émigré architect and furniture designer Torben Müller worked in Loewy's office. Harrison Murphy, a former art director for the *Chicago Tribune*, and graphic design prodigy Paul Rand, who at twenty-three had become an art director for *Esquire*, brought their experience integrating the business of sales and marketing and the mechanics of print technology into the design process. Additionally, longtime Laboratory partisan Elizabeth McCausland finally joined the faculty to teach an ambitious new course sequence in cultural studies, while research chemist John Heasty drew upon his ongoing work in product testing at Consumers Union.[13]

From an ideological perspective, the left wing of the labor movement was the obvious patron of choice for the Laboratory. Events like the school's August 1937 exhibition at the American Contemporary Artists Gallery, run by leftist art dealer Herman Baron and Book and Magazine Guild (BMG) organizer Clara Grossman, had reinforced the links between the Laboratory's functionalist brand of modernism and the class-based cultural politics of the Popular Front. Yet, without any significant capacity to secure the production or distribution of functionalist design on a mass basis, labor sponsorship only had a limited effect on popular awareness of modernist styles or their possible connotations. Moreover, the efforts of the left-wing unions to lay claim to functionalist modernism were complicated by the preliminary efforts of cultural elites to appropriate functionalism. If the Laboratory's cultural war of position against the expressive streamlined modernism of the leading industrial design entrepreneurs was an uphill battle with long odds, at least it was relatively easy to discern where the front lines were. Not so when the school's partisans encountered those who sought to disassociate functionalist modernism from radical politics and instead deploy it as a signifier of elite status. The labor left and cultural elites continually contested the meanings of modernism until the final defeat of the Popular Front in the late 1940s, and their shared interest in promoting functionalism, albeit for very different reasons, made them frequent collaborators, as each side sought to use its partnership with the other to its own advantage.[14]

In December 1938, the Museum of Modern Art hosted a major retrospective exhibition on the Bauhaus, with former Bauhaus instructor and recent émigré Herbert Bayer as a guest curator to design the exhibit and supervise the installation. The token inclusion in the show of a small display of student work from the Design Laboratory augmented the struggling school's chances of tapping into private patronage while permitting it to skim off some of the Museum's prestige. But MoMA also benefited from the relationship. Although the Museum had wealthy patrons, in the late 1930s it was still struggling to make modern art and design into signifiers of refined taste and to establish its own elite status, and it gained in stature from using the Laboratory as a part of its own cultural front. In a caustic review of the show he wrote for *Architectural Record*, Levy reiterated many of the criticisms that McCausland had made earlier about the Bauhaus in an attempt once again to draw a clear distinction between the Laboratory's leftist functionalism and a de-radicalized formalist modernism that merely imitated the appearance of functionality. For Levy, Bayer's provocative installation did nothing to transcend the profound "discrepancy between theory and practice" that separated "Bauhaus ideas and principles" from "the work of the Bauhaus itself." He chided the Bauhaus masters for failing to appreciate that "the change from handicraft production to automatic and semi-automatic mass production" entailed "much more than the mere use of simplified forms and novel materials" for goods that were in fact not suitable for fabrication using mass-production technologies and could only be marketed to affluent consumers able to afford craft-made wares. Nonetheless, collaborations between the Popular Front left and liberal elites made it increasingly difficult to render such unambiguous political or aesthetic judgments. After all, how was an ordinary person supposed to know if a functionalist poster graphic, coffee pot, chair or building they encountered was intended to represent social democratic values or elite status?[15]

The blurring of the distinctions between the two competing claims on functionalism became even more apparent in the summer of 1939 with the publication of the *Design Students' Guide to the New York World's Fair*. Edited and designed by Rand, the guide was a joint production of the Laboratory and the New York Art Directors' Club. The top industrial design agencies of the 1930s created many of the most attended exhibits at the Fair, and their streamlined version of modernity dominated the look of the "World of Tomorrow." Dreyfuss' agency designed the "Democracity" exhibit inside the Fair's official Theme Center. Bel Geddes' Futurama exhibit, which offered fairgoers weary of the privations of the Depression a tantalizing glimpse of the abundance, convenience and technological mastery that supposedly awaited Americans a scant twenty years in the future, proved to be the Fair's most visited attraction. Yet, the *Design Students' Guide* largely ignored the central lures of the Fair, focusing instead on the examples of functionalist architecture and design to be found scattered in the midst of the streamlined pavilions and exhibits. In his foreword to the guide, MoMA curator and newly appointed Laboratory trustee John McAndrew praised the student contributors for scouring the Fair to find examples of "good modern design among the pseudo-modern fantasies." He admonished visitors to be wary of the "soft corners and fungoid bulges on the buildings by some of our most celebrated industrial designers" as they gleaned the Fair's saving remnants of "honest" modernism "shaped by the exigencies of function and materials" and "free of mannerisms." While the *Guide* upheld the school's aesthetic tenets, it did little to present the precious specimens of functionalist modernism as a coherent set of alternative symbols to convey Popular Front political ideals.[16]

Even as these collaborations compromised the ideological integrity of the Laboratory project, they were unsuccessful at generating enough conventional private patronage to sustain it. Dismal proceeds from a major fundraising drive in the second half of 1939 left the school insolvent and forced it to suspend its regular operations at the end of the year. Dozens of students continued to meet with their instructors in the hopes that the financial lifeline could be found for the Laboratory, but by the spring of 1940 it became painfully clear that a reprieve was not in store for the path-breaking school. In a final letter to the students, the school's governing committee assured them that their support had not been "entirely in vain," since "many of the basic ideas developed by the school during its four years of existence have already been incorporated in the teaching methods of other institutions and have certainly influenced the thinking of many individuals now working in the design field." Although conceding that the Laboratory was "technically dead," the committee contended that much "that was most important" about the school "stays alive."[17]

Another strategy for using modernism to convey leftist political meanings involved not the creation of an alternative institutional entity like the Laboratory that was under public or labor patronage, but rather the establishment of an adversarial subculture within the mass culture industries. The CIO's left-led unions of cultural workers constituted just such an internal oppositional network. During the 1930s and 1940s, these unions gained an impressive following in the fields of publishing, advertising, design, and commercial art. Especially in the greater New York metropolitan area, where many of the mass culture industries were concentrated, for a time unions like the BMG, the American Advertising Guild and the United American Artists (UAA) achieved sufficient prominence as to represent a credible alternative of professional and class solidarity to the ruthless competitiveness and insecurity that had characterized many aspects of culture production.[18]

As part of their organizing, union activists aggressively sought to re-appropriate modernism as a means of promoting class-consciousness among culture workers. The prolific use of various types of cubist, functionalist, and surrealist graphics and illustrations in flyers, pamphlets and union periodicals demonstrated the faith that white-collar union activists of the 1930s and 1940s shared with the founding generation of American modernists of the 1910s in the revolutionary potential of modernist aesthetics to provoke a pragmatist reconstruction of class identity (figure 3.2). In annual pageants like the mAD Arts Ball sponsored by the Ad Guild and the Surrealist Ball put on by the UAA, through which the struggling unions hoped to raise a little extra money and to cultivate a sense of radical community, commercial art and design workers flaunted their mastery of avant-garde styles and techniques in their promotional materials, their decorations, and their costuming. When the BMG had completed its wage survey among publishing workers in 1940, the union staged a Living Newspaper theatrical production of the findings for a mass meeting of the membership.[19]

The most important way in which these unions attempted to renew the association between modernist aesthetics and class-based politics was through the educational courses, workshops, and forums they offered where ordinary workers in the culture industries could gain exposure to innovations in design, graphic arts, typography, layout, copywriting, and editing. Open to members and non-members alike, these programs served to recruit new members to the unions who saw in modernist aesthetics the potential to represent their desire to become through collective action the agents rather than the mere instruments for making mass culture. But the extension programs also contributed to the growing acceptance of the unions as respectable entities within the parameters of normal professional practice. Given the limited opportunities available in the 1930s and early 1940s to obtain formal training in modernist styles and techniques, even individuals motivated by nothing other than crass opportunism might enroll in union classes to acquire marketable skills with which to better their own career prospects. As with so many of the collaborations of the Popular Front, these classes and forums brought together aspects of high culture, business culture, and labor culture in fluid and unpredictable ways.

The BMG launched its series of classes within months of its founding in 1935, and it sponsored an educational program on a continuous basis through the fall of 1947. In its earliest years, before it made the leap from a

Figure 3.2 The influence of Bauhaus graphic design is readily apparent in this illustration from the cover of pamphlet made in 1939 by the New York Joint Council of the United Office and Professional Workers of America to promote its new group health insurance for its members. The union consistently used modernist styles to represent the mental labor involved in the production of mass culture. Included in this design are figures for Local 18 (Book and Magazine Guild), Local 20 (American Advertising Guild) and Local 60 (United American Artists)

leftist professional advocacy group to a full-fledged trade union, classes were frequently held somewhat informally in apartments and cafeterias. Once the Guild had joined the CIO in 1937 through its affiliation with the United Office and Professional Workers of America (UOPWA), it moved its classes into its new offices at 69 Lexington Avenue. As part of the fall 1937 term, in addition to more mundane offerings on editing and proofreading, noted book designer and union president Robert Josephy repeated his popular course on typography, *Fortune* editor Louis Kronenberger taught a course on literary criticism, and *Harper's Bazaar* art director Alexey Brodovitch taught cutting-edge techniques in magazine layout and design. BMG class offerings for 1939 and 1940 still included Josephy's courses on typography and book design as perennial favorites along with *New Republic* editor George Soule's course on the role of progressive media in mass society and a course by Irving Simon, production manager for pulp powerhouse Macfadden Publications, on magazine layout and design to replace the one previously given by Brodovitch.[20]

Beginning in the fall of 1938, the classes run by the BMG were supplemented by additional educational initiatives sponsored by the Ad Guild and the UAA and coordinated by the UOPWA Greater New York Joint Council. As part of a series of standing-room-only forums for commercial artists held at the UAA hall in early 1939, Morris Rosenblum, art director for Bamberger's department store in Newark, presented a short movie, "A Day in the Life of an Ad," that documented the entire process involved in the production of a single print advertisement and highlighted the use of new styles and techniques. In the fall of 1939 and winter of 1940, the UAA again drew packed audiences to a series of forums, although in this case the emphasis was on the comparative evolution of contemporary aesthetics and the fine arts rather than on commercial applications. Speakers in this series, which was chaired by Elizabeth McCausland, included Stuart Davis, Philip Evergood, I. Rice Pereira, and Joseph Solman. Following the transfer of the Commercial Artists Section of the UAA to the Ad Guild in the fall of 1939, that local became the Joint Council's principal host for programs geared toward practical applications. The Ad Guild's classes on copywriting, graphics, illustration, advertisement layout, production, and sales attracted a growing following, with enrollment surpassing 200 students by November 1940. Significantly, 30% of the students in its courses were non-members, although for many who did join the Ad Guild the classes had been their first serious introduction into unionism. As Esther Handler of the Joint Council's education department pointed out, the classes brought into the union fold "many unorganized advertising workers who had to admit that here was an opportunity for expert professional training offered nowhere else at this price." Even its most expensive class, a course in advertising design that art director Paul Rand taught for the Ad Guild in the fall of 1941 that cost $15 for members and $25 for non-members, still was a bargain given the value of the experience.[21]

Of the various educational collaborations embarked upon by these unions, one of the most prestigious was between the Ad Guild and Herbert Bayer. Several months after the opening of the Bauhaus retrospective at MoMA, Bayer and Lila Ulrich, who had studied with him at the Bauhaus and subsequently taught at the Design Laboratory, chaired a wildly successful forum on modernist design jointly sponsored by the Ad Guild and the UAA. Following up on the positive response, Bayer and Ulrich agreed to teach a regular series of "laboratory" classes for the Ad Guild that continued from 1939 through the second half of 1941. The semester-long course, which stressed the practical application of constructivist and functionalist approaches to graphic design, was extremely popular, with sections continually oversubscribed by commercial artists in the advertising industry. In the spring of 1941, the New York Art Directors' Club hosted an exhibition of student work at its gallery and reproduced a selection of the compositions in its journal (figure 3.3). Bayer's position neatly demonstrates the complex and often competing loyalties and identities of Popular Front collaborators. He was at once an authentic Bauhaus veteran, a practicing designer with a record of commercial success that stretched back to his department store advertising in Weimar Germany and included his consulting for John Wanamaker department stores and the Container Corporation of America, a serial guest curator for MoMA, and a proponent of left-led, class-conscious unions of commercial artists and designers who made a real contribution of his talent to support their organizing efforts. Yet, trading on these multiple associations also implied a range of ambiguities and contradictions. Did Bayer's teaching for the Ad Guild somehow balance or counteract his involvement with the efforts of institutions like MoMA to promote avant-garde modernism as formalist high art rather than as a pragmatist tool to shock and to provoke new ways of thinking and seeing? Or did it merely compromise the union's aspirations to lay claim to modernism and deploy it as a means of furthering class-consciousness among white-collar workers and symbolizing the values of social-democratic consumerism?[22]

Politics, prestige, and patronage were inherently intertwined in the unions' educational and professional development programs. Union activists sought to deploy modernist aesthetics as a catalyst for radical political and social

Figure 3.3 A surrealist photomontage created in early 1941 by a student in Herbert Bayer's class for the American Advertising Guild in response to one of his assignments on developing technique. As with the Design Laboratory, union extension classes like Bayer's furnished a very important means for commercial artists and designers working in the culture industries to learn about modernist styles and techniques in the years before the academic institutionalization of modernism

change, but the attraction of rising elite institutions and liberal corporate executives as possible sponsors for cultural projects proved irresistible for the struggling unions. Even as MoMA's curators and patrons increasingly sought to define a formalist canon of high modernism cleansed of radical political connotations, the UAA, for instance, still hoped to appropriate a bit of the Museum's cachet to bolster its organizing activities when it held a conference there in late 1939 on the political and economic situation of artists in the United States. As with the Design Laboratory, collaborations directly involving the left-led culture worker unions with liberal individuals, organizations or institutions typically offered some benefit to all participants. Despite its future hegemonic position as the key arbiter of modernist taste in the postwar period, in the late 1930s and early 1940s MoMA could still reasonably expect to augment the legitimacy of its own mission through association with the unions as partners in the spread of functionalist "good design" and the battle against the alleged vulgarity of streamlining.[23]

Although they played a pivotal role in the development and dissemination of modernist techniques and styles, activists in the BMG, the UAA, and the Ad Guild were no more able to control the uses of modernism than their counterparts at the Design Laboratory. The unions' aggressive promotion of modernism did help to organize new members, but the broader cultural impact of these initiatives remained uncertain. As of the early 1940s, the contest for the meaning of modernism had been fought to a draw, as corporate liberals and cultural elites competed with Popular Front activists to define the significance of new aesthetic innovations. The unions undoubtedly abetted the appropriation of modernist aesthetics by American business, but as long as their supporters maintained a presence within the culture industries modernist art and design could not be deployed either to restore the legitimacy of corporate capitalism or to demarcate an updated hierarchy of taste without also evoking a heightened awareness of class.

The Design Laboratory and the left-led unions of culture workers had a lasting influence on the development of twentieth-century American material and visual culture. Instructors and students from the Laboratory as well as the extension classes of the BMG, the Ad Guild, and the UAA dispersed throughout the system of culture production, taking with them their particular understanding of modernist aesthetics. Although a handful of traditional schools of art and architecture in the United States did incorporate some elements of modernist pedagogy during the 1930s and early 1940s, only after World War II did this modernist approach to art and design education become the norm. Gropius' revamped School of Architecture at Harvard, Laszlo Moholy-Nagy's intermittently open School of Design in Chicago, and the retooled design programs at Pratt and Carnegie Tech borrowed elements of the Laboratory's pedagogy minus its radical politics, yet until the late 1940s they too remained the exception rather than the rule. At many schools, former participants in the modernist projects of the Popular Front made important contributions to the introduction and subsequent development of modernist curricula and teaching methods. I. Rice Pereira, for instance, brought her Design Synthesis course to Pratt, Friedman brought his expertise to the University of Iowa and the University of Minnesota, and Priestly rejoined his former mentors Bayer and Mies van der Rohe on the faculty of the School of Design in the late 1940s after it had affiliated with the Illinois Institute of Technology. Rand, arguably the biggest star associated with the Laboratory, joined the faculty at Yale in the late 1950s after establishing himself as one of America's most acclaimed graphic designers.[24]

As the hierarchy of modernist taste became more stratified following World War II, many of the artists, designers, and educators who had participated in the Popular Front contributed to the development of a type of modernism that corporations increasingly deployed as a refined visual idiom with which to represent themselves as institutions. The modernist principles embraced by the Laboratory and the left-led cultural workers' unions found expression after the war in corporate office buildings and interiors, in the sophisticated artwork and sculpture used to embellish these premises, and, most ubiquitously, in the new generation of logos created as part of corporate identity campaigns. Bayer, for instance, continued his work as a design consultant for Paepcke's Container Corporation of America as part of his long subsequent career. Rand designed corporate symbols, such as those for the ABC television network and for Westinghouse, that have remained in use for decades. Dozens of the lesser-known artists and designers who had received part of their training in modernist styles and techniques through the Laboratory or through the classes sponsored by the culture worker unions contributed to the dignified and elegant simplicity of this upscale corporate modernism. Their work stood in sharp contrast with the aesthetic treatment applied to the design and styling of mass consumer goods in the postwar period, as the streamlining of the 1930s evolved into the "Populuxe" look of the 1950s. Following a bifurcated aesthetic strategy, major manufacturers offered chrome and fins to lure buyers in the carnival of product merchandising while simultaneously presenting a respectable high modernist image when promoting the idea of the corporation as a responsible and enlightened entity in society.[25]

Yet, the kind of impact that the partisans of Popular Front modernism had hoped for remained elusive. Neither the public sector nor the labor movement proved to be reliable enough patrons to support the Design Laboratory adequately. Although the school's enthusiasts hoped for the development of alternative systems of either public or cooperative production and distribution through which its designs would find their way to consumers as bearers of social-democratic or radical meanings, such systems failed to flourish in mid-century America. Liberals and leftists alike continued to campaign for a restoration and expansion of government programs that provided public goods, including art and culture, rather than initiatives that only subsidized privatized consumption. After World War II, however, the prospect for such a public program seemed increasingly unlikely. Progressive unions were willing enough in principle to support the aims of the Laboratory, but in reality the labor movement remained sufficiently embattled that it was only able to implement a fraction of its cultural agenda. Even for large unions like the United Auto Workers (UAW), which aggressively pushed consumer cooperatives in the years after World War II, efforts to reshape the culture of American mass consumption into a tool for promoting class-conscious social democracy proved unsuccessful. The onset of the Cold War in the late 1940s permanently disorganized the Popular Front. The left-led unions of culture workers were suppressed, and the remnants of their cultural initiatives were expelled from the world of commercial art and design. Individual supporters of the Popular Front's political and cultural agenda either disassociated themselves from their radical pasts or risked finding themselves marginalized or even blacklisted.[26]

The ephemeral successes of these leftist activists in design, advertising, marketing, and publishing suggest the extent to which business cultures can accommodate alternative or oppositional subcultures. Over the last half-century, other subcultures within the corporate-dominated mainstream of design, advertising, and marketing have had a comparable aesthetic impact on American consumerism to that of the Popular Front, but without posing a substantive challenge to corporate hegemony. The purveyors of hip rebellion who appropriated countercultural styles in the 1960s and early 1970s helped to lead American business to shift from modernism to postmodernism as its predominant aesthetic strategy. Yet, while the anarcho-capitalist partisans of the 1960s as well as their dot-com descendants of the 1990s attacked the style and personal politics of mainstream advertising, design and marketing, they did not advocate the kind of fundamental challenge to the political economy of corporate capitalism that the Popular Front's backers had in their heyday. The Popular Front network of activists inside the mass culture industries remains the most strident adversarial subculture that the business mainstream has been capable of tolerating in the twentieth-century United States. Although its existence was largely expunged from the mainstream historical record, the institutions, organizations, and activities of the Depression-Era cultural left nonetheless played a vital role in turning modernist aesthetics into corporate aesthetics.[27]

Notes

1. For early examples of the "conventional" narratives of modernist design, see Henry-Russell Hitchcock, Jr., and Philip Johnson, *The International Style: Architecture Since 1922* (New York, NY: Norton, 1932), as well as the portrayal by the Museum of Modern Art (MoMA) of its own 1938 retrospective exhibition of Bauhaus design in *The Bulletin of the Museum of Modern Art* 6, no. 5 (December 1938). On the American modernist avant-garde of the 1910s and 1920s and its affinity for political radicalism, see Martin Green, *New York 1913: The Armory Show and the Paterson Strike Pageant* (New York, NY: Macmillan, 1989); William Leach, *Land of Desire: Merchants, Power, and the Rise of a New American Culture* (New York, NY: Vintage, 1993), 185–190; and Walter Kalaidjian, *American Culture Between the Wars: Revolutionary Modernism and Postmodern Critique* (New York, NY: Columbia University Press, 1993),

68 SHANNAN CLARK

19–187. On the role of MoMA in the 1930s as it tried to establish itself as an elite arbiter of modernist taste, see Terry Smith, *Making the Modern: Industry, Art and Design in America* (Chicago, IL: University of Chicago Press, 1993), 385–404; Barbara Staniszewski, *The Power of Display: A History of Exhibition Installation at the Museum of Modern Art* (Cambridge, MA: MIT Press, 1998), 143–190; William B. Scott and Peter M. Rutkoff, *New York Modern: The Arts and the City* (Baltimore, MD: Johns Hopkins University Press, 1999), 163–193; and A. Joan Saab, *For the Millions: American Art and Culture Between the Wars* (Philadelphia, PA: University of Pennsylvania Press, 2004), 84–128. On Paepcke's interest in patronizing modern art and design, see James Sloan Allen, *The Romance of Commerce and Culture: Capitalism, Modernism, and the Chicago-Aspen Crusade for Cultural Reform* (Chicago, IL: University of Chicago Press, 1983), 3–77; and Michele H. Bogart, *Artists, Advertising, and the Borders of Art* (Chicago, IL: University of Chicago Press, 1995), 259–269. On the emergence by the end of the 1930s of a cadre of modernist artists and intellectuals ideologically opposed to the Popular Front, see Serge Guilbault, *How New York Stole the Idea of Modern Art: Abstract Expressionism, Freedom, and the Cold War*, Arthur Goldhammer trans. (Chicago, IL: University of Chicago Press, 1983), 17–99; Erika Doss, "The Art of Cultural Politics: From Regionalism to Abstract Expressionism," in Lary May ed., *Recasting America: Culture and Politics in the Age of Cold War* (Chicago, IL: University of Chicago Press, 1989), 195–220; and Andrew Ross, *No Respect: Intellectuals and Popular Culture*, (New York, NY: Routledge, 1989), 1–64. For the prototypical formulation of the kitsch critique, see Clement Greenberg, "Avant-Garde and Kitsch," *Partisan Review* 6, no. 5 (Fall 1939): 34–49.

2. For an outstanding example of the strong ideological opposition that "populist" realist artists elicited among segments of the 1930s cultural left, see Stuart Davis, "*The New York American* Scene," *Art Front* no. 3 (Feb. 1935): 6. In this polemic, Davis, at the time one of the leaders of the Artists' Union, denounces the realism of Thomas Hart Benton and Grant Wood as the aestheticization of the conservative reaction associated with Hearst's *American* newspaper. Conversely, for a prime example of the preference within other segments of the Popular Front for realism over non-representational modernism as the supposedly most appropriate aesthetic strategy for the left, see O. Frank, "New Forces in American Art," *New Masses*, July 12, 1938, 23–24. For Macdonald's views, see Dwight Macdonald, "A Theory of Mass Culture," in Bernard Rosenberg and David Manning White eds., *Mass Culture: The Popular Arts in America* (Glencoe, IL: Free Press, 1957), 59–73; and Macdonald, *Masscult and Midcult* (New York, NY: Partisan Review/Random House, 1961). On the continued influence of pragmatism on many members of the postwar avant-garde, see Daniel Belgrad, *The Culture of Spontaneity: Improvisation and the Arts in Postwar America* (Chicago, IL: University of Chicago Press, 1998).

3. For the most thorough of the recent scholarly efforts to rehabilitate Popular Front culture and to promote a rethinking of its modernist affinities and sensibilities, see Michael Denning, *The Cultural Front: The Laboring of American Culture in the Twentieth Century* (New York, NY: Verso, 1996).

4. Design Laboratory brochure, Dec.1935, Records of the Federal Art Project of the Works Progress Administration, Archives of American Art, Smithsonian Institution, Washington DC (hereafter "FAP"), reel DC60, frames 563–565. The original documents in this collection are located in the Records of the

Works Progress Administration, Records Group 69, National Archives and Records Administration, College Park, MD. Also see "WPA Establishes Free Art School," *New York Times* (hereafter *NYT*), December 2, 1935, 19.

5. Holger Cahill to Frances Pollak, September 18, 1935, Francis O'Connor Collection, Archives of American Art, Smithsonian Institution, Washington DC (hereafter "FO"), reel 1084, frame 46; "American Bauhaus," *Architectural Forum* 64, no. 1 (January 1936): 17, 34; "Design Laboratory, New York" *American Magazine of Art* 29 (February 1936): 117; Federation Technical School Design Laboratory, *Catalog of Courses, 1937–1938*, Donald Wallance Collection, Cooper-Hewitt National Design Museum, New York, NY (hereafter DW), Biographical Material Series, Box 1, "Education—Design Laboratory, Circulars, 1936–1940" folder.

6. Frances Pollak to Holger Cahill, "Design Laboratory Bibliography," December 5, 1935, FO, reel 1084, frames 181–183; "Classes at Capacity in WPA Art School," *NYT*, April 17, 1936, 5; Jacqueline Keyes, "WPA Educators Blazing Trail with School in Industry Design," *NYT*, October 25, 1936, II, 5. On Wallance's account of his brief time as a student at Pratt and the contrast with the Laboratory, see Donald Wallance to Charles Hublitz, February 6, 1980, DW, Biographical Material Series, Box 1, "Biographical Statements, Questionnaires, and Related Materials" folder.

7. On the leading entrepreneurs of industrial design in the 1930s, see Jeffrey Meikle, *Twentieth Century Limited: Industrial Design in America, 1925–1939* (Philadelphia, PA: Temple University Press, 1979); Arthur Pulos, *American Design Ethic* (Cambridge, MA: MIT Press, 1983), 316–414; David Nye, *Electrifying America: Social Meanings of a New Technology* (Cambridge, MA: MIT Press, 1990), 339–380; Smith, *Making the Modern*, 353–383, 405–421; Roland Marchand, *Creating the Corporate Soul: The Rise of Public Relations and Corporate Imagery in Big Business* (Berkeley, CA: University of California Press, 1998), 265–311; and Shelley Nickles, "Object Lessons: Household Appliance Design and the American Middle Class, 1920–1960," Ph.D. diss., University of Virginia, 1999, 1–278. For an insightful contemporary survey of the early years of industrial design, see "Both Fish and Fowl," *Fortune* 9, no. 2 (February 1934): 40–43, 88, 90, 94, 97–98.

8. For the version of the Laboratory's statement of principles quoted here, see Federation Technical School Design Laboratory, *Catalog of Courses, 1937–1938*, 1–3, DW, Biographical Material Series, Box 1, "Education—Design Laboratory, Circulars, 1936–1940" folder. Kalish's cartoon appears in *Design Laboratory Perspective*, Jan. 1938, DW, Biographical Materials Series, Box 1, "Education—Design Laboratory, Student Activities, 1936–1940" folder.

9. "Design Laboratory" press release, August 22, 1936, Elizabeth McCausland Papers, Archives of American Art, Smithsonian Institution, Washington DC (hereafter "EM"), reel D374, frames 374–378; Elizabeth McCausland, "An 'American Bauhaus': Design Laboratory on Permanent Basis," *Springfield Union and Republican*, August 22, 1937, 6E.

10. On the radical sentiments of many students and faculty, see Lawrence Drake to Harry Hopkins, March 21, 1936, FO, reel 1086, frame 449; *American Student Designer*, May 19, 1936, DW Biographical Materials Series, Box 1, "Education—Design Laboratory, Student Activities, 1936–1940" folder; "WPA Art Executives Warned on Job Cuts," *NYT*, December 1, 1936, 6;

"WPA Artists Fight Police; 219 Ejected, Many Clubbed," *NYT*, December 2, 1936, 1, 16; Josiah Marvel to Hopkins, December 4, 1936, FAP, reel DC47, frame 73; Thomas Parker to Audrey McMahon, December 12, 1936, FAP. Reel DC47, frame 72; McMahon to Parker, December 15, 1936, FAP, reel DC47, frame 70; Marvel to McMahon, December 16, 1936, FAP, reel DC47, frame 71; McMahon to Cahill, December 21, 1936, FAP, reel DC47, frame 84; Theodore Draper, "Roosevelt and the WPA," *New Masses*, December 22, 1936, 14–16; "25 Strikes Called in WPA Here Today," *NYT*, March 31, 1937, 8; "WPA Ready to Drop 2,500 in Next Week," *NYT*, April 15, 1937, 14; "Sit-In at Art Project," *NYT*, May 15, 1937, 8; "10,000 Stop Work on WPA Projects," *NYT*, May 28, 1937, 1, 12; Milton Kalish to Suzanne Sekey, undated letter in my possession (although from the context it is clearly from late May or early June 1937); "WPA Art School Goes On," *NYT*, July 4, 1937, 2; "The Fine Arts," *New Masses*, July 6, 1937, 30–31; Liame Dunne, "Learning Design and Production: The Methods Used in the Design Laboratory of the F.A.E.C.T. School," *PM* 3, no. 12 (August 1937): 39–44; 'Design Laboratory at FAECT," *Architectural Record*, October 1937, 41; Interview with William Friedman by Mary McChesney, June 16, 1965, A New Deal for Artists Series, Archives of American Art, Smithsonian Institution, Washington DC, 6; Interview with Suzanne Sekey by Shannan Clark, May 30, 2003.

11. "Chapter School Grows in Influence," *Technical America* 4, no. 8 (September 1937): 10; "Student Responsibilities," *Design Laboratory Perspective*, January 1938, 1, DW, Biographical Materials Series, Box 1, "Education—Design Laboratory, Student Activities, 1936–1940" folder; Jacques Levy, "From a Faculty Member," *Design Laboratory Perspective*, January 1938, 2.

12. Design Laboratory 1938–1939 Catalog, DW, Biographical Materials Series, Box 1, "Education—Design Laboratory, Circulars, 1936–1940" folder; Jacques Levy, Curriculum Vitae, February 27, 1941, DW, Biographical Materials Series, Box 1, "Education—Design Laboratory, Correspondence, Announcements, Related Materials, 1934–1942" folder.

13. For technical reasons related to its accreditation and licensing by the state of New York, the school officially changed its name in the fall of 1938 from the Design Laboratory to the Laboratory School of Industrial Design (LSID). See "Laboratory School of Industrial Design Provisional Charter," EM, reel D384G, frames 970–977; LSID, "New Appointments to the Faculty for Spring 1939," DW, Biographical Materials Series, Box 1, "Education—Design Laboratory, Correspondence, Announcements, Related Materials, 1934–1942" folder; LSID, "1939 Bulletin," DW, Biographical Materials Series, Box 1, "Education—Design Laboratory, Circulars, 1936–1940" folder; LSID, "Spring 1939 Course Listings," EM, reel D375, frames 328–333; LSID, "Exhibit by Nine Instructors Recently Appointed to the Faculty of their Professional Work in Industrial Design and Graphic Arts," EM, reel D375, frames 317–318; Elizabeth Noble, "Industrial Design: Laboratory School Exhibits Achievements of New Faculty Members," *New Masses*, March 21, 1939, 31; LSID, "Instructors for Basic Courses, Fall 1939–1940," EM, reel D384G, frame 1250.

14. On the Design Laboratory show at ACA, see "Laboratory Design Project Show at the A.C.A.," *NYT*, August 15, 1937, X, 7; "Design Laboratory Exhibition, August 9th to 22nd, A.C.A. Gallery," EM, reel D375, frames 334–338; and McCausland, "An 'American Bauhaus'."

15. Levy, "Bauhaus and Design, 1919–1939," *Architectural Record*, January 1939, 71, 118. For examples of more sympathetic reviews of the MoMA exhibition from the left, see "Bauhaus," *Direction* 2, no. 1 (December 1938): 23; Elizabeth Noble, "The Bauhaus Exhibition," *New Masses*, December 20, 1938, 27; and *U.A.A. Commercial Artists Bulletin*, March 1939, 1, Rockwell Kent Papers, Archives of American Art, Smithsonian Institution, Washington DC (hereafter RK), reel 5242, frame 702.

16. *A Design Students' Guide to the New York World's Fair, Compiled for PM Magazine by the Laboratory School of Industrial Design* (New York, NY: Laboratory School of Industrial Design and the New York Art Directors' Club, 1939), DW, Biographical Materials Series, Box 1, "Education—Design Laboratory, Student's Guide to the New York World's Fair" folder. Also see "Designers Get Fair Guide," *NYT*, September 17, 1939, 48.

17. "LSID Report to the General Membership," August 22, 1939, DW, Biographical Materials Series, Box 1, "Education—Design Laboratory, Correspondence, Announcements, Related Materials, 1934–1942" folder; Minutes of Student Committee Meeting, October 18, 1939, DW, Biographical Materials Series, Box 1, "Education—Design Laboratory, Correspondence, Announcements, Related Materials, 1934–1942" folder; "Memorandum to All Students," November 14, 1939, DW, Biographical Materials Series, Box 1, "Education—Design Laboratory, Correspondence, Announcements, Related Materials, 1934–1942" folder; Minutes of Student Committee Meeting, December 27, 1939, DW, Biographical Materials Series, Box 1, "Education—Design Laboratory, Correspondence, Announcements, Related Materials, 1934–1942" folder; Student Committee of the Laboratory School of Industrial Design to All Students, June 6, 1940, DW, Biographical Materials Series, Box 1, "Education—Design Laboratory, Correspondence, Announcements, Related Materials, 1934–1942" folder.

18. The Book and Magazine Guild, the American Advertising Guild, and the United American Artists were all locals affiliated with the United Office and Professional Workers of America (UOPWA), which was the CIO's principal international union with jurisdiction over white-collar workers. In April 1946, the FAECT, which had had its own international charter from the CIO since 1937, was absorbed by the UOPWA. The UOPWA was one of the left-led international unions expelled from the CIO in 1949 and 1950 for alleged Communist influence.

19. Advertisement for mAD Arts Ball, *New Masses*, April 5, 1938, 29; "Arts Ball Rolls Around as Sober Citizens Batten Down Their Hatches," *Ledger* 4, no. 4 (April 1938): 8; "November Dances Planned by Artists and Book Guild," *UOPWA News* 5, no. 11 (November 1939): 7; "PM Shorts," *PM* 6, no. 3 (February 1940): 87; "Ad Guild to Stage 1940 in mAD Arts Jam," *Office and Professional News* (hereafter *OPN*) 6, no. 3 (March 1940): 5; "mAD Arts Ball Success," *OPN* 6, no. 4 (May 1940): 7; "Living Newspaper Plays to Standing Room," *Guild News* 12, no. 6 (June 1940): 3; "Local 60 Fun Helps Fund," *OPN* 6, no. 7 (October 1940): 6; "Artists' Frolic Packs 'Em In, But Surreally!" *OPN* 6, no. 8 (November 1940): 7; "mAD Arts Ball—Crazy," *OPN* 7, no. 3 (March 1941): 5.

20. "PM Shorts," *PM* 4, no. 3 (November 1937): 53; UOPWA Greater New York Joint Council, "Forums, Classes, Arts and Sports, 1939–1940," Trade Union File—United Office and Professional Workers, Tamiment

Institute, New York University; "Class Enrollment High," *Guild News* 12, no. 3 (March 1940): 5; "The Guild School," *Guild News* 12, no. 5 (May 1940): 12; "BMG School Begins Fall Term," *OPN* 6, no. 7 (October 1940): 7; "Guild School Opens Second Term," *Proof* 14, no. 3 (March 1942): 3; "Publishing Courses Swell School List," *Proof* 15, no. 5 (November 1942): 4; "Ad-Mag-Pub School Opens October 13," *Proof* (UOPWA Local 18 publication) 16, no. 10 (October 1943): 1, 4; "School Days Start at White Collar Center," *OPN* 12, no. 10 (October 1945): 10; BMG, "Book and Magazine Guild School—Fall Term 1946," American Business Consultants *Counterattack* Research Collection, Tamiment Institute, New York University, Box 21, Folder 13–31A.

21. "A Day in the Life of an Ad," *Commercial Artists Bulletin* (March 1939), RK, Reel 5242, Frame 702; "Three Locals Hold Forums," *UOPWA News* 5, no. 4 (April 1939): 5; UOPWA Greater New York Joint Council, "Forums, Classes, Arts and Sports, 1939–1940," Trade Union File—United Office and Professional Workers, Tamiment Institute, New York University; "Booklet Describes Cultural Program of New York Council," *UOPWA News* 5, no. 10 (October 1939): 7; UAA, 'United American Artists Lecture Series," 1939, Irene Rice Pereira Papers, Archives of American Art, Smithsonian Institution, Washington, DC (hereafter IRP), Reel 2395; "Artists Debate, But Surreally!" *OPN* 6, no. 2 (February 1940): 7; Esther Handler, "This Is Our School," *OPN* 6, no. 6 (September 1940): 9; "A-D Shorts," *A-D* 7, no. 1 (October 1940): 54; "Successful AAG Craft Classes Win Recruits," *OPN* 6, no. 8 (November 1940); 7; 'Guild Begins New Ad Craft Classes," *OPN* 7, no. 4 (April 1941): 9; "New York Dept. Set Up; Announces Fall Program," *OPN* 7, no. 10 (October 1941): 10.

22. UOPWA Greater New York Joint Council, "Special Series of Forums for those in the Art, Advertising, and Publishing Fields," RK, Reel 5242, Frame 717; "The Bauhaus Revived," *Commercial Artists Bulletin* (March 1939), RK, Reel 5242, Frame 702; "Famous Ad Man Teaches Guild," *OPN* 6, no. 3 (March 1940): 5; "Luncheons Build Ad Union," *OPN* 7, no. 1 (January 1941): 3; "A-D Shorts," *A-D* 7, no. 4 (April 1941): 57; "Herbert Bayer's Design Class," *A-D* 7, no. 5 (June 1941): 18–30; Percy Seitlin, "What Is Taught and Why," *A-D* 7, no. 5 (June 1941): 31–32.

23. On the UAA conference at MoMA, see "Artists to Hold Conference in N.Y.," *UOPWA News* 5, no. 12 (December 1939): 3; Richard Lewis to Officers and Members of All Art Locals and Divisions, 6 December 1939, RK, Reel 5243, Frames 664–665.

24. On Moholy-Nagy's School of Design in Chicago, see "Bauhaus Will Open in Chicago This Fall," *NYT*, August 22, 1937, II, 6; "Gropius Aide Here to Run Art School," *NYT*, September 2, 1937, 23; "Chicago's New Bauhaus," *NYT* September 12, 1937; "The New Bauhaus," *Architectural Forum* 67, no. 2 (October 1937): 22, 82; and Alain Findeli, "Moholy-Nagy's Design Pedagogy in Chicago (1937–1946)," *Design Issues* 7, no. 1 (Fall 1990): 4–19. On the introduction of systematically and rigorously modernist design pedagogy at Carnegie and Pratt, see Peter Müller-Munk, "Industrial Design," *Design* 40, no. 1 (January 1939): 12–15; and Alexander J. Kostellow, "Design and Structure Program of the Pratt Institute Art School," *Design* 42, no. 5 (May 1940): 6–9, 24; I. Rice Pereira, undated c.v., "Personal Documents and Biographical Information," IRP, Reel 1296.

25. On the aesthetics of the material culture of American mass consumerism in the 1950s, see Thomas Hine, *Populuxe* (New York, NY: Knopf, 1986); Arthur J. Pulos, *American Design Adventure, 1940–1975* (Cambridge, MA: MIT Press, 1988); Jeffrey Meikle, "From Celebrity to Anonymity: The Professionalization of American Industrial Design," in Angela Schönberger, ed., *Raymond Loewy: Pioneer of American Industrial Design* (Munich: Prestel Verlag, 1990), 51–62; John Heskett, "The American Way of Life: American Design in the Fifties," in Schönberger ed., *Raymond Loewy*, 115–122; David Gartman, *Auto Opium: A Social History of American Automotive Design*, (New York, NY: Routledge, 1994), 136–181; Shelley Nickles, "More is Better: Mass Consumption, Gender, and Class Identity in Postwar America," *American Quarterly* 54, no. 4 (December 2002): 581–622; and M. Jeffrey Hardwick, *Mall Maker: Victor Gruen, Architect of an American Dream*, (Philadelphia, PA: University of Pennsylvania Press, 2004), 118–161.

26. On the contested meanings of consumption and of the consumers' "interest" in mid-century America, see Charles McGovern, "Consumption and Citizenship in the United States, 1900–1940," in Susan Strasser, Charles McGovern, and Matthias Judt, eds., *Getting and Spending: European and American Consumer Societies in the Twentieth Century* (New York, NY: Cambridge University Press, 1998), 37–58; Lawrence Glickman, "The Strike in the Temple of Consumption: Consumer Activism and Twentieth-Century American Political Culture," *Journal of American History* 88 (2001): 99–125; Lizabeth Cohen, *A Consumers' Republic: The Politics of Mass Consumption in Postwar America* (New York, NY: Knopf, 2003), 8, 18–61; and Meg Jacobs, *Pocketbook Politics: Economic Citizenship in Twentieth-Century America* (Princeton, NJ: Princeton University Press, 2004), 95–261.

27. On the countercultural influences within the world of advertising in the 1960s, see Thomas Frank, *The Conquest of Cool: Business Culture, Counterculture, and the Rise of Hip Consumerism* (Chicago, IL: University of Chicago Press, 1997), 52–167. On the 1990s wave of hip rebellion in business, see Frank, *One Market Under God: Extreme Capitalism, Market Populism, and the End of Economic Democracy* (New York, NY: Anchor Books, 2000), 1–50, 220–306.

Chapter 4

Rationalizing Consumption: Lejaren à Hiller and the Origins of American Advertising Photography, 1913–1924[1]

Elspeth H. Brown

By the second decade of the twentieth century, the rationalization of the American economy threatened to founder, not on the shoals of production or distribution, where mechanization and national transportation systems had nearly vanquished challenges to middle-class material abundance, but on those of consumption. As numerous historians have argued, advertising matured as a profession in response to a new problem for American business: how to stimulate demand among white, middle-class consumers for the machined cornucopia of standardized products filling the shelves of American retail establishments. Whereas earlier advocates of American productive efficiency, such as the motion-study experts Frank and Lillian Gilbreth, had championed the use of photography in rationalizing the working body in production, by the 1920s the influence of applied psychology had reoriented managers toward an appreciation of the mind as the critical element of rationalized consumption.[2] Achieving greater sales in an increasingly competitive and national marketplace required convincing hesitant consumers that individual difference and personal meaning could be theirs, despite a regularized landscape of standardized goods. Corporations increasingly hired advertising agencies and their creative staffs, in Jackson Lears' phrase, to "surround mass-produced goods with an aura of uniqueness" designed to stimulate consumption through the promise of individuality.[3]

This article addresses the origins of American photographically-based advertising illustration in relation to modern consumer culture. The first section concerns the problematic status of photography as a medium for mass-market magazine illustration in the years before World War I, despite the medium's availability through halftone technology. As I will discuss, the lag between technological innovation and cultural practice reveals an unwritten history concerning photographic realism and advertising's middle-class audience. As the profile of the implied consumer shifted from that of "rational man" to "irrational woman" by 1915, photography's realist tendencies became a problem for a new school of advertisers seeking to harness the subjective for the benefit of corporate sales. In the second part of the essay, I will discuss how the problematic status of photography was resolved by an art-school trained illustrator, Lejaren à Hiller. Hiller successfully introduced fine art principles into his commercial photographs, creating for the first time a national market for photographically based advertising illustrations. His complex photographs, created for national brand manufacturers from the mid-1910s forward, severed photography from its slavish dependence on material reality, while at the same time retaining the evidentiary arguments implicit in the photographic medium.

Historians such as Roland Marchand, Stephen Fox, and Pamela Laird have provided us with thorough histories of the emergence of modern advertising, charting developments such as the birth of the advertising agency, the shift from newspaper as client to manufacturer as client, and the increasing reliance in advertising on what William Leach, in a slightly different context, has called "eye appeal."[4] My focus here is more on the advertisements (rather than on the advertisers) and, in particular, on the role of photographic illustration in engineering the shift to mass consumption. As Neil Harris and Estelle Jussim have discussed, the "ten-cent magazine revolution" of the 1890s ushered in a new technology, destined to redefine magazine illustration. The halftone screen process, gradually perfected between 1881 and 1893, enabled printers to reproduce photographic images with a full range of tonal gradients on the same sheet of paper receiving typeset copy.[5] By 1900, in Neil Harris's estimation, the halftone process was "firmly established as a major reproductive method for publishers of mass illustrated materials."[6] Despite the success of the ten-cent magazines and the financial incentive to shift to halftone, however, it was nearly twenty years before most national advertisers were willing to abandon their pen-and-brush artists in favor of commercial photography.

The historical problem I am posing is this: why, given the availability of halftone technology, as well as the reduced costs that it offered, was there *not* a wholesale shift to photographically based advertising illustration in the years between 1895 and 1920? Why was it that "class" magazines such as *Ladies' Home Journal* and *The Saturday Evening Post* continued to rely on pen-and-ink illustrators such as Charles Dana Gibson, when photography was readily available at a greatly reduced cost? The reason was simply that most commercial photography failed to meet advertisers' needs: it provided realism but not art, rationality but not emotion. Commercial photographers were aware of the new market, and throughout the years after 1890 photography invaded the small advertising cuts found in the back of popular magazines. Stilted advertisements for canned food, cameras, corsets, and carriages increasingly used photography as a method of showing the products' selling points in realistic detail. Products were displayed with the crisp insistence of edge-to-edge focus; advertisers assumed that photography's ability to reproduce the detail formerly lost with wood engravings or pen-and-ink drawings would persuade the customer of the product's fine workmanship. Eventually, static product still-lives were infused with "human interest"; babies and pretty female faces accessorized machine tools and breakfast foods; inventors' faces, in halftone, smiled warmly over industrious factories.[7]

Yet, despite the inclusion of an alluring young woman, the formal aspects of this type of advertising photography stayed safely within the confines of what generations of critics have understood as photography's privileged relationship to the real defined as the facticity of the material world. These portrait-based photographs, with their faithful recording of each and every tooth (both human and metallic), told, in the words of a contemporary critic, "everything about the facts of nature and left out the mystery!"[8] So long as advertising photography worked within a model of rational appeal, rather than emotion, this lack of mystery (referred to elsewhere as "art") was unproblematic; sharply focused, minimally composed photographic records were considered superior instruments of visual persuasion for many products. Early mass-circulation advertising photography corresponded with advertisers' belief that consumers made purchase decisions on a rational basis. The period before 1908 was the era of advertising as "salesmanship in print": the advertisement was a stand-in for the missing sales clerk, whose selling pitch had been based on the "reason why" the consumer should purchase a particular product over others—what became known in the business as "reason-why" copy. A good advertisement was a logical, persuasive argument concerning the product's superior merits; as one advertising executive argued, "True 'Reason-Why' Copy is Logic, plus persuasion, plus conviction, all woven into a certain simplicity of thought-pre-digested for the average mind."[9] Photography would seem to be the ideal medium for selling to an assumed "rational buyer." The faithful reproduction of detail offered by a halftone provided the visual analogue for "reason-why" copy. The early advertising photograph's indexical relationship to the product's material reality convincingly saturated the image with what Roland Barthes has called the denotative message, obscuring its connotative meanings.[10] The halftone became a transparent stand-in for the product itself, in all its superior workmanship.[11]

In an era of "reason-why" copy and efficiency mania, advertisers offered photography as providing an unmediated access to the real, with the "real" being defined as the product's material reality. Photographs denoted the superior product through the image's "having been there" quality, while photography, as a medium, implicitly connoted the efficiency of American business culture. Photography was the preferred medium in advertising copy directed to an implied rational consumer, usually (but not always) male. Especially in product advertising where the selling argument was based on efficiency, photography emerged as a favored medium, remaining popular long after advertisers had abandoned "reason-why" copy for most household products (figure 4.1).[12] Even in product advertising directed toward women, if the copy was based on logical argument (e.g., the portability of a Western Electric sewing machine), then the preferred illustration medium was often halftone. By the early 1910s, photography was widely understood (among advertisers, art directors, and consumers) to connote the logical rationality of

Figure 4.1 The photographic medium connoted the modern efficiency of American business culture and was used extensively in advertisements based on the rational appeals of "reason why" copy. Comptometer, *The Saturday Evening Post* (March 30, 1919), 96

reason-why copy. Thus, photographic illustration continued to dominate trade publications directed toward business and professional men, such as the magazine *System*, where the selling pitch was based on rational appeals of price, efficiency, or quality.

Although photography offered a sense of realism, for many years it failed to offer art. Art, however, was becoming increasingly indispensable to advertising, as advertisers shifted from an emphasis on the rational to the stimulation of the subjective. The value of photography as the preferred medium of efficient rationality became a distinct liability when, in the first decade of the twentieth century, advertisers and psychologists began to shift their model of the typical consumer from a rational to an emotional buyer. As the pioneering advertising psychologist Walter Dill Scott noted, "We have been taught by tradition that man is inherently logical, that he weighs evidence . . . and then reaches the conclusion on which he bases his action. The more modern conception of man is that he is a creature who rarely reasons at all."[13] By 1910, as Merle Curti has noted, the advertising trade press had replaced the dominant image of man as rational with a new conception of human nature, one based on nonrational impulses. The role of advertising shifted from educating consumers about a product's merits to creating desire through the stimulation of impulses, instincts, and emotions. Although advertising never abandoned "rational man" or reason-why copy completely, the shift to emotion sparked a new style in advertising.[14]

The new advertising featured a heavy emphasis on illustration as a means of connoting the high quality and class on which most advertising of these years depended. Pioneer advertising psychologists such as Scott emphasized the role of mental imagery in awakening the senses, and, as "the printed page cannot appeal directly to any of the senses except the eye" the role of visual imagery within the advertisement grew in importance.[15] Advertisers of breakfast cereals, soaps, and soft drinks reproduced original paintings, drawings, and sketches, often signed by the artist, as a way of building brand recognition and associating the product with the cultured aesthetic connoted by the featured illustration. The point of the illustrations was not to convince the consumer through logical argument, but, instead, to associate the product with the positive emotional responses triggered by what Roland Marchand has called the "visual cliches" of American advertising: the lovely bloom of American girlhood, the warm security of the family circle, or the small-town comforts of the settled village.[16]

Advertising, as a system of visual communication, is a symbolic language that traffics not so much in things as they are as it does in how (advertisers think) we would like things to be. Early-twentieth-century advertising professionals had begun to understand that consumers preferred an idealized reflection of the social world rather than an image of literal reality. Working in the genre of what Michael Schudson has called "capitalist realism" advertisers constructed a pictorial universe peopled by abstract types such as the loving wife or the elegant society lady, performing predictable, recognizable tasks such as picking up a child or enjoying the club—in abstract places easily recognized as Any town USA. Like the socialist realism of the 1930s, Schudson argued, American advertising simplifies and typifies. Individual idiosyncrasies of specific grandmothers (standing, yelling, non-white grandmothers, for example) are smoothed over into an abstracted "type" (seated, knitting, smiling, white grandmothers) that the targeted consumers recognize instantly, thereby expediting the sales message or product association.[17]

Pen-and-brush illustrations, with their signatures and distinctive marks and lines, clearly signaled the individual interpretation that provided one route for advertising's drive to what Schudson has called abstraction—not in the sense of a loss of figuration, but in the older sense of the word: "considered apart from concrete existence" or "without reference to a particular instance."[18] The advertising illustration signaled the concrete existence of the artist, but not the illustration's subject—which, except in testimonial advertisements, was always an abstract type. Consumers implicitly recognized the illustrations of James Montgomery Flagg or Harrison Fisher as ideal representations of American types, images that occupied the powerful emotional borderlands between the mundane specificity of the known and the alluring abstraction of fantasy. Illustrations acted as psychological handmaidens to consumer desire: they announced their status as idealized abstractions while simultaneously licensing subjective flights of consumer longing.

So where did this evolution leave photography? It seemed hamstrung as a medium: its faithful reporting of material fact, and its overwhelming enthusiasm for endless, superfluous detail, seemed to suggest its unsuitability for idealist representation. Stilted halftones for "Brown's Jackets" had difficulty competing with the visual sophistication of "Holeproof Hosiery;" and color, though important, was not the only distinguishing difference. As one author stated in 1918, the "almost unavoidable realism of photographic illustrations as usually made killed the effective impression demanded of the picture used to illustrate a story . . . An illustration must get away from this very definite thing and give to all classes of readers an idealistic vision of the hero or heroine of the book or story."[19]

By 1913 it was clear what advertisers wanted of illustrations, and photographers seemed unable to meet the demand. The shift to impressionistic copy required the merchandising, not so much of the product itself, but of the benefit the product offered. Advertisers sought dynamic images marked by both formal and conceptual clarity. They needed to tell a "striking or interesting story" through dramatic lighting, harmonious composition, balanced use of lines and visual contrast, and other formal elements that had been considered more the province of the artist than of the photographer. However, unlike art-school trained illustrators such as Howard Pyle or N. C. Wyeth, few photographers could boast any formal art training; they lacked, as a rule, the knowledge of composition, line, and chiaroscuro learned through academic study in the fine arts.

The problem of how to introduce a more sophisticated photographic practice into advertising illustration was addressed by a Milwaukee resident who moved to New York in 1907. Lejaren à Hiller, a young photographer with three years of formal art training at the School of the Art Institute of Chicago, saw himself as an artist, illustrator, and photographer—in that order. Through his innovative use of the camera in both fiction and advertising, Hiller essentially invented modern photographic illustration.

Hiller began his career in 1905 as a commercial illustrator in Chicago, where he worked for J. T. Mitchell, a future partner in the well-known advertising firm Lennen and Mitchell. Arriving in New York in 1907, Hiller soon joined the Society of Illustrators and made his living as a freelance commercial illustrator, producing both pen-and-ink drawings and cover art for *Good Housekeeping*, *Cosmopolitan*, *Harper's Bazaar*, and other magazines between 1908 and 1913, when he turned to photography. After a period of time competing with the greats of magazine illustration, Hiller began photographing his models rather than drawing them. He developed a portfolio of photographically based illustrations and made the rounds of the New York publishers. After numerous rejections, Hiller succeeded in convincing W. G. Gibson, the editor of *Cosmopolitan* and a prior client, to give him a story to illustrate.[20]

Anna Katherine Green's short story "The Grotto Specter" appeared in the June 1913 issue of *Cosmopolitan*.[21] The story, about a mysterious murder in a cave-like grotto, was illustrated by six signed photographic illustrations by Lejaren à Hiller. Hiller photographed a street excavation pit as a cave background for his fictionalized tableau. The photograph's documentary tendencies were softened through dramatic chiaroscuro: dark tones frame the figures, who emerge, hazily, from dense backgrounds and whose contours, though photographically rendered, remain nonetheless suggestive. The resulting images made a dramatic impact: *McClure's* magazine editors spotted the story and offered Hiller an exclusive contract, but *Cosmopolitan* counteroffered, and Hiller signed a one-year contract with Hearst Publications for $7,500.[22]

The aesthetic foundation for Hiller's commercial illustration was pictorial, or artistic, photography. Pictorialism, a popular movement in American photography from the mid-1890s through the 1920s, was built upon nineteenth-century English models that argued for the camera's creative possibilities. The goal of the pictorialists was to elevate photography to the status of fine art by moving the camera away from the tyranny of fact.[23] Deeply influenced by the simplicity of natural beauty, European painting, and Japanese aesthetics, early-twentieth-century pictorialist photographers sought to infuse their work with an emotional and spiritual intensity. The preference for classical tableaux, as well as the allegorical dimensions of the natural landscape, pushed the camera image beyond the mechanical recording of social fact to express intimacy, ecstasy, ambiguity, and revelation—all of which prior generations had considered beyond the capability of photographic representation.

Hiller was an accomplished pictorialist photographer, and his status as an "artist" helped legitimize his use of photography in commercial illustration. Although maintaining his reputation as an artist separate from his commercial work, Hiller also sought to merge the two worlds, and his illustrations for "The Grotto Specter" represented his first halting effort to yoke pictorialist aesthetics to commercial ends. The illustrations launched Hiller on a prominent and lucrative career illustrating fiction, not only for *Cosmopolitan*, but also for *The Saturday Evening Post* and other middle-class magazines. This experience in illustrating fiction, as well as a series of articles about psychic reality and the nonmaterial world, perfectly positioned Hiller for the advertising contracts that came his way after 1913. As he alone among commercial photographers seemed to recognize, selling no longer depended on the verisimilitude of material reality; sales required the motivation of subjective realms of emotion and psychology. Advertisers had begun to recognize the point made by a *Printer's Ink* columnist after World War I: "the same people who thrill and suffer and cry and grow hot-tempered over the tempests and joys of fiction, further ahead in the same magazines, are touched and influenced by that heart which is put into advertising."[24]

The visual strategies used to motivate the reader's engagement with works of fiction soon became indistinguishable from the visual strategies used to spark the consumer's desire to purchase. A 1917 advertisement for the Aeolian Company suggests how Hiller's work in illustrating the subjective held direct relevance for advertising work (figure 4.2). In this photographic tableau, an old man wears a "rapt expression, sad but very tender" as the phonograph, memory's handmaiden, returned the vision of his lost love, hovering in ghostly lavender outside the open doorway. The advertisement's appeal to memory and the subjective, illustrated by Hiller's montaged and heavily retouched photograph as well as by the copy's fictionalized narrative, demonstrates how the lines between fiction and advertising, between the material and the nonmaterial worlds, were growing profitably indistinct. Aesthetic innovations made in pursuit of the irrational became yoked, through advertising, to the rationalization of consumption. As Hiller pointed out in 1920,

> modern advertising, as it is exemplified in the higher class of periodicals, must often possess qualities that appeal to the reader with infinitely more subtlety than a mere statement of such material facts as widths, lengths, weights, colors, and prices . . . there are luxuries of the mind which must be hammered out no less than those for the body.[25]

Hiller's visual strategies relied on illustrating the mind's fictions through the short story or through the emotional benefit promised by the consumption of mass-produced goods.

Drawing on his pictorialist background, Hiller introduced a number of aesthetic innovations into advertising photography, successfully pushing the medium past the obsessive imperative to record. The soft-focus lens, long familiar to pictorialist photographers, but a new tool for commercial illustrators, enabled Hiller to soften contours. In the darkroom, combination printing allowed him to duplicate the images of a few models at various scales, which he then pieced together and rephotographed. He heavily retouched his images, painting on them to exaggerate shadows, remove unnecessary details, or disguise seams. For grand-scale environments, such as the Egyptian pyramids or a schooner at sea, Hiller constructed toy models, photographed the objects at a comparatively large scale, and then inserted smaller figures made

Figure 4.2 Hiller's experience in illustrating the subjective became relevant for his later work in advertising. Ad for the Aeolian Company, Lejaren à Hiller, photographer. *The Saturday Evening Post* (November 24, 1917), 46

from posing models in the studio. For smaller settings, such as an evening by the piano or a group of bathing beauties, Hiller had the set constructed on site. As his business expanded after the war, his staged tableaux became more complex. By 1918 he had a full-time talent scout, who scoured the streets of New York searching for the perfect social type; contemporary accounts claimed that Hiller had a physiognomic archive of over two thousand models, amateur and professional.

In an advertisement for the Aeolian Company, a sophisticated composition with a full set, Hiller used lighting to discipline the eye (figure 4.3). Light cradles the enraptured features of "John Smith, merchant, by day" but "artist, dreamer, poet" while he plays the pianola. The edges of the picture are thrown into darkness, while the image's pyramidal composition and selective illumination send the viewer's eye in two diagonal lines of illuminated points: one commencing at the left sofa arm (where a woman lounges) and ending at the spot of light on the rear windowpane; the other beginning with Hiller's own signature and continuing through Smith's hand (where another triangle is formed with the face, hands, and sheet music) to his face, and then back to the windowpane. The eye moves restlessly between the dramatically lit faces. The compositional tension is held by the absent center: the distance between the two figures is a little too great, the angle of couch and piano a bit too severe. In search of resolution, the eye moves downward to the text, which both anchors the pyramid visually and works to resolve, through narrative, the image's subtle tensions.

In these complex images, lighting, composition, and other formal strategies work together, leading the eye through the image to the product or narrative suggested by the gathered figures. Lighting directs the viewer's attention through the photograph, disciplining the eye's movements on behalf of the product's selling point. As *Printer's Ink* columnist W. Livingston Larned argued in 1925, "Light is perhaps the most potent of all directing and guiding visual influences. It can signpost anything. It compels attention."[26] Lighting, composition, cropping, background, accessories, use of white space—all were formal strategies used to focus viewers' attention on the product or its benefits, while keeping "the eye from wandering from the edges of the picture."[27]

Hiller's work is remarkable not only for his use of pictorialist strategies to overcome photography's realist tendencies but also for how early he came upon these solutions. The few historians who have charted the beginnings of modern advertising photography have focused on the well-known photographers Edward Steichen and Clarence White, and they date the introduction of photography for commercial illustration to a later period, usually the early or mid-1920s. Their interpretations follow the groundbreaking work of Patricia Johnston, whose research on Edward Steichen has helped to complicate historians' understandings of the relationship between art and commerce during the 1920s.[28] Michele Bogart in her work on commercial illustrators, as well as Bonnie Yochelson in her work on Clarence White's students, follow Johnston's lead in marking the 1920s as the origin of photographically based advertising illustration.[29] But the recent historiographic focus on Steichen and White, though a much-needed corrective to generations of scholarship on Alfred Steiglitz and his battle for the aesthetics of photography, understates the degree to which pictorialist aesthetics had become part of advertising photography well before Steichen and White's students transformed the field in the 1920s. By the time Steichen returned to the

Figure 4.3   As Hiller's advertising work progressed, he relied increasingly on set design and lighting rather than on combination printing to achieve his effects. Ad for the Aeolian Company, Lejaren à Hiller, photographer. *The Saturday Evening Post* (September 22, 1917), 78

United States from Europe in 1923, Hiller had been creating photographically based advertisements for ten years.

By 1920 Hiller's advertising work was attracting the *most* sophisticated of clients and continued to garner national recognition. In 1919, for example, Hiller worked with the illustrator and future industrial designer Walter Dorwin Teague on a lush, multipage catalogue for the upscale men's clothier Adler-Rochester.[30] Hiller illustrations were featured in national advertising campaigns for IBM, Armstrong Linoleum, Corning Glass, Senreco toothpaste, General Electric, S.D. Warren paper, 1847 Rogers Bros. flatware, Victrola, Fatima cigarettes, and Pond's cold cream, among other companies and products—all before 1923. Nearly every issue of the "quality" magazines such as *The Saturday Evening Post* and *Ladies' Home Journal* featured his distinctive photographic tableaux, usually signed by the artist. By the later period, Hiller's lighting, set design, and dramatic narratives owed less to pictorialism than to cinema, an interest that he pursued in his own film productions of the early 1920s. Hiller's work was selected for each of the Art Directors' Club's annual exhibitions of advertising art during the early 1920s.[31] After years of skepticism about the role of photography in advertising illustration, the editor of the 1924 *Annual of Advertising Art* confidently asserted, "The place of the photograph in advertising is unquestioned. It can accomplish things which no drawing or painting can possibly do."[32]

Hiller's compositions relied on the aesthetics of pictorialist photography and painting to spark an emotional longing on the part of the viewer, a yearning of the spirit that the product promised to satisfy. As Hiller remarked,

> If the maker of a great piano desires to demonstrate the wonders of that instrument to the cultured ones for whom it is specially designed, he does not exhibit a mere photograph of the piano, with a detail of its structure and a statement of its price; he obtains a picture that cannot fail to arouse deep and truly aesthetic emotions in the soul of any clod who may chance to see it.

While this aesthetic approach was not especially difficult for the charcoal or pen-and-ink artist, the photographer needed to manipulate his tools to achieve the same effect on the viewer's subjective life. In the shift to emotional copy and advertisers' appeal to the subjective, pictorialism provided Hiller with the tools necessary to move photography away from its "almost unavoidable realism" to the abstracted idealism necessary to modern advertising.[33] With this shift, which moved commercial photography from the tyranny of fact to the triumph of longing, Lejaren à Hiller launched the photographic revolution of modern advertising illustration.

Notes

1. This essay is reprinted from *Enterprise & Society* 1 (December 2000): 715–738. My thanks to the Business History Conference for permission to reprint the essay here.
2. See my chapter on the Gilbreths in Elspeth H. Brown, *The Corporate Eye: Photography and the Rationalization of American Commercial Culture* (Baltimore, MD: Johns Hopkins University Press, 2005).
3. T. J. Jackson Lears, *Fables of Abundance: A Cultural History of Advertising in America* (New York: Basic Books, 1994), 270. For the role of trademark legislation and brand identity in developing markets, see Susan Strasser, *Satisfaction Guaranteed: The Making of the American Mass Market* (Washington D.C..: Smithsonian, 1989), 29–57; and Richard Tedlow, *New and Improved: The Story of Mass Marketing in America* (New York: Basic Books, 1990).
4. Roland Marchand, *Advertising the American Dream: Making Way for Modernity, 1920–1940* (Berkeley, CA: University of California Press, 1985); Stephen Fox, *The Mirror Makers: A History of American Advertising and its Creators* (New York: Morrow, 1984); Pamela Walker Laird, *Advertising Progress: American Business and the Rise of Consumer Marketing* (Baltimore, MD: Johns Hopkins University Press, 1998); see also William Leach, *Land of Desire: Merchants, Power, and the Rise of a New American Culture* (New York: Pantheon, 1993).
5. David Phillips, "Art for Industry's Sake: Halftone Technology, Mass Photography, and the Social Transformation of American Print Culture, 1880–1920" (Ph.D. Diss., Yale University, 1996), 54–62. For further discussion of the technologies and inventions relating to halftone, see Estelle Jussim, *Visual Communication and the Graphic Arts: Photographic Technologies in the Nineteenth Century* (New York: R.R. Bowker, 1974).
6. Neil Harris, "Iconography and Intellectual History: The Half-Tone Effect" in *New Directions in American Intellectual History*, ed. John Higham and Paul K. Conkin (Baltimore, Md.: Johns Hopkins, 1979), quotation at p. 197.

7. For a discussion of the advertising approach in personalizing the "soulless" corporation, see Roland Marchand, *Creating the Corporate Soul: The Rise of Public Relations and Corporate Imagery in American Big Business* (Berkeley, Calif.: University of California Press, 1998), 31.
8. Henry Peach Robinson, *The Elements of a Pictorial Photograph* (Bradford, England, 1896), 70. The definition of realism, especially in relationship to photography, has never been static; the term has been a site of contestation used to define photography's capacities and goals throughout the nineteenth century and into the twentieth. For a review of some of the nineteenth-century debates, see Mary Warner Marien, *Photography and Its Critics: A Cultural History, 1839–1900* (Cambridge, England: Cambridge University Press, 1997). For a discussion of realism in relationship to American culture more generally, see Miles Orvell, *The Real Thing: Imitation and Authenticity in American Culture, 1880–1940* (Chapel Hill, N.C., UNC Press 1989); and David Shi, *Facing Facts: Realism in American Thought and Culture, 1850–1920* (New York: Oxford University Press, 1995).
9. Quoted in Fox, *The Mirror Makers*, 50. Later, with the shift to emotion and atmospheric advertising, the notion of salesmanship in print was retooled to reflect the "human touch," "When you put salesmanship into print you are trying to make it take the place of a living salesman" argued Herbert N. Casson. "People do not care to read about facts . . . this is especially true of women, and most of our sales literature—fully eighty percent of it—is intended to influence women. Most goods are bought by women." See Herbert N. Casson, "The Human Touch in Printed Salesmanship," *Printed Salesmanship* (Sept. 1926), 27; see also Karl Thayer Soule, "Silent Salesmen," ibid., 32–33.
10. Roland Barthes, "The Photographic Message" in *Image/Music/Text*, trans. Stephen Heath (New York: Hill and Wang, 1977), 18.
11. As David Nye has discussed, this factual style of presentation was especially attractive in industrial photography. See David E. Nye, *Image Worlds: Corporate Identities at General Electric, 1890–1930* (Cambridge, MA: MITS Press, 1985), 31–58. See also Jennifer GreenLewis, *Framing the Victorians: Photography and the Culture of Realism* (Ithaca N.Y.: Cornell University Press, 1996), 26–27.
12. For the connection among photography, efficiency, and reason-why copy after World War I, see "Pictorial Demonstration Instead of the Superlative," *Printer's Ink Monthly* (Jan. 1923), 65–66; and K. B. White, "Old Man Specific Gets Direct Sales with Institutional Advertising," ibid. (Jan. 1922), 31–32.
13. Walter Dill Scott, *Influencing Men in Business: The Psychology of Argument and Suggestion* (1911; New York: The Ronald Press Company, 1914), 35. Scott's work on advertising psychology began appearing after 1901, when Thomas L. Banner, western advertising manager for *The Delineator* and other Butterick magazines, asked Scott to give a talk on the psychology of advertising to a group of advertising professionals. Scott's numerous articles and books helped move advertisers away from reason-why copy to methodologies that are more suggestive. For more on Scott, see Leonard W. Ferguson, *Walter Dill Scott: First Industrial Psychologist* (n.p., 1962); Edmund C. Lynch, "Walter Dill Scott: Pioneer Industrial Psychologist," *Business History Review* 42, no. 2 (Summer 1968): 149–157.
14. Fox, *Mirror Makers*, 70; see also Martha 1. Olney, *Buy Now, Pay Later: Advertising, Credit, and Consumer Durables in the 1920s* (Chapel Hill, N.C.,

UNC Press, 1991), 135. This period also marked the growing recognition among advertisers and consumer advocates that women made the majority of household purchases. See Christine Frederick, "Teach Women What Advertising Does," *Printer's Ink* (June 20, 1920), 177–183.

15. Walter Dill Scott, "The Psychology of Advertising," *Atlantic Monthly* (Jan. 1904), 34; see also Mary Fenton Roberts, "What the Photograph Means to the Magazine," *Photo-Era Magazine* (Sept. 1925), 121–126.

16. Marchand, *Advertising the American Dream*, 153, 235–284. On this point, see also Ronald Berman, "Origins of the Art of Advertising," *Journal of Aesthetic Education* 17, no. 3 (Fall 1983): 62. For a contemporary critique of advertisers' overreliance on visual cliches, see W. Livingston Larned, "Finding the Theme for the Illustration," *Printer's Ink* (October 29, 1920), 105–109; W. Livingston Larned, "Peopling the Advertisements with Characters That Really Live," ibid. (February 12, 1920), 59–64; and W. Livingston Larned, "When Is an Illustration Unconventional," ibid. (October 7, 1920), 165–169.

17. Michael Schudson, *Advertising: The Uneasy Persuasion* (New York: Basic Books, 1986), 209–223. Roland Marchand has described advertising as a Zerrspiegel, or fun-house mirror, which reflects back a distorted image, not wholly fictive, but exaggerated in places. Marchand, *Advertising the American Dream*, xvii.

18. *American Heritage College Dictionary*, s. v.

19. "Our Cover Portrait and Hall of Fame," *Portrait* 9, no. 2 (June 1919): 11–13.

20. Hiller's only illustration (so far as I have been able to find) for *Cosmopolitan* before his photographic work commenced in 1913 appeared in the October 1909 issue, pp. 658–659: a pen-and-ink drawing for Ella Wheeler Wilcox's poem "Lord Speaks Again." Brief narratives concerning this period of Hiller's career can be found in Joseph Katz, "Perfect Host," *Advertising and Selling* (May 23, 1935), 54. Lejaren à Hiller, autobiographical typescript, February 2, 1950, Hiller Archive, Visual Studies Workshop, Rochester, N.Y. (hereafter cited as Hiller Archive, VSW). Hiller claimed that he made his first photographically based illustration for a St. Louis newspaper while working at the Fair in 1904; the images illustrated a story of a farm family visiting the Fair, and he was paid $1.50 each. Lejaren à Hiller, autobiographical typescript, September 25, 1945, p. 2.

21. Publishing entrepreneur William Randolph Hearst had bought one of the nation's leading illustrated magazines, *Cosmopolitan*, in 1905 as his first venture into the general magazine market. In 1914, the magazine had a circulation of one million, with each issue averaging 144 pages. In 1912, the magazine dropped its muckraking emphasis and turned to a major reliance on fiction, with an increasing emphasis on sexual or romantic subjects. See Frank Luther Mott, *A History of American Magazines, 1885–1905* (Cambridge, Mass., 1957), 480–505.

22. Lejaren à Hiller, "Illustrating Magazine Articles and Advertising by the Use of the Camera," *Commercial Photographer* 3, no. 1 (Oct. 1927): 17; "They Chose Photography" clipping about Hiller, Bourke-White, and Platt Lynes, 194, publication not noted, Hiller Archive, VSW, p. 38; see also Joseph Katz, "Perfect Host" *Advertising and Selling* (May 23, 1935), 54.

23. Pictorialism has an extensive historiography; as an introduction, see Robert Doty, *Photo-Secession: Steiglitz and the Fine-Art Movement in Photography*

(New York: Dover, 1978); William Innes Homer, *Alfred Stieglitz and the Photo-Secession* (Boston: Little, Brown, 1983); Christian A. Peterson, "American Arts and Crafts: The Photograph Beautiful 1895–1915," *History of Photography* (Autumn 1992), 189–232.

24. W. H. Heath, "Heart Throbs as the Pictorial Theme," *Printer's Ink* (November 11, 1920), 157–158.

25. Lejaren à Hiller, "Combining Brush and Camera," Printer's Ink Monthly (June 1920), copy in Hiller Archive, VSW.

26. W. Livingston Larned, "A Little Light on Dark Pictorial Subjects," *Printer's Ink* (April 16, 1925), 77–81; see also W. Livingston Larned, "Catching the Eye of the Lazy Reader," ibid. (November 18, 1920), 150–152.

27. Wilbur Perry, "How Much Should the Advertising Photograph Show?" *Printer's Ink Monthly* 5, no. 7 (Dec. 1922): 35–36. For a discussion of backgrounds and accessories in product still-life advertising photography, see "Hats-And Photographs That Sell Them," *Commercial Photographer* 1, no. 2 (Nov. 1925): 43–47; and D. P. Foster, "Accessories That Make the Half-Tone Interesting," *Printer's Ink* (April 15, 1920), 133–136.

28. See Patricia Johnston, "Edward Steichen's Commercial Photography," *Exposure* 26, no. 4 (1989): 4–22; and ibid., *Real Fantasies: Edward Steichen's Advertising Photography* (Berkeley, Calif.: University of California Press, 1997).

29. Michele Bogart, *Artists, Advertising, and the Borders of Art, 1890–1960* (Chicago: University of Chicago Press, 1995); Bonnie Yochelson, "Clarence White, Peaceful Warrior," in *Pictorialism into Modernism: The Clarence H. White School of Photography*, ed. Marianne Fulton (New York: Rizzoli, 1996).

30. For Teague's advertising work before 1925, see Clarence P. Hornung, *The Advertising Designs of Walter Darwin Teague* (New York, 1991); Clarence P. Hornung and Fridolf Johnson, *200 Years of American Graphic Art* (New York: G. Braziller, 1976), 164–165; and Charles Dalton Olson, "Sign of the Star: Walter Dorwin Teague and the Texas Company, 1934–1937" (MA Thesis, Cornell University, 1987), 1–39. Teague worked for Phoenix Hosier, as did Hiller; the borders on the White and Wycoff's calendars seem to be Teague's work as well. Teague worked for the high-quality illustration advocate Ernest Elmo Calkins, in his advertising agency Calkins and Holden, between 1908 and 1912, when he went out on his own as a freelance advertising artist specializing in decorative design and typography. For further information about Teague, see Jeffrey Meikle, *Twentieth Century Limited: Industrial Design in America, 1925–1939* (Philadelphia, PA: Temple University Press, 1979), 87.

31. These important early commercial photographers need additional research. Hiller's 1921 photographs were loaned by J. A. Migel and exhibited by Street & Finney. The 1922 Royal Typewriter ad was exhibited by H. K. McCann Company, while the Fatima photograph was loaned by Liggett & Meyers and exhibited by the Newell-Emmett advertising agency. See *Annual of Advertising Art in the U.S.*, 1921, pp. 5 and 21; *Annual of Advertising Art in the U.S.*, 1922, pp. 104 and 109. For further information about these important exhibitions, see "Advertising Art Promoted by New York Art Center," *Printer's Ink* (November 10, 1921), 50–52; "Art Directors' Club Holds First Annual Exhibition," ibid. (March 10, 1921), 80–84; "Awards at Art Directors' Club Exhibition," ibid. (April 30, 1925), 61–62; as well as Bogart, *Artists, Advertising, and the Borders of Art*, 128–132.

32. *Third Annual of Advertising Art*, 1924 (there was no exhibition in 1923), p. 122. W. Livingston Larned, noting the advances in photographic illustration, declared as early as 1920 that "the artist can howl the winds down and the fact still remains that there are more photographic illustrations than ever—and they are superlatively better" than painted illustrations. W. Livingston Larned, "The Hidden Beauties of the Photographic Illustration," *Printer's Ink* (March 25, 1920), 57.

33. "Our Cover Portrait and Hall of Fame," *Portrait* (June 1919), 11–15. This article, which appeared in an Ansco company house organ, appeared next to an article by Sadakichi Hartman detailing the compositional structures of master painters such as Botticelli, Raphael, and Boucher.

Chapter 5

Art and Commerce: The Challenge of Modernist Advertising Photography

Patricia Johnston

In his 1939 essay "Avant-Garde and Kitsch," now a landmark in the history of American modernism, Clement Greenberg lamented the paradox in which artists who produced high culture struggled to remain apart from bourgeois society, yet were tied to "an elite among the ruling class" by "an umbilical cord of gold." Unhappy as he was that the primary support for high culture came from this tiny, wealthy faction, Greenberg was even more troubled that support for the arts among this class was fast disappearing, with no other champion in sight. "The masses have always remained more or less indifferent to culture," Greenberg bemoaned. They were satisfied with kitsch—"popular, commercial art and literature"—that he characterized as "the debased and academicized simulacra of genuine culture."[1] In this enormously influential essay, Greenberg articulated binaries often used to define modernism, binaries that powerfully shaped critical understanding of the fine arts for the next several decades. Avant-garde and kitsch still echo in formulations such as high and low, fine and applied, elite and popular, art and commerce.

Greenberg's essay can be seen as the culmination of a period of intellectual contest and consolidation between the wars. The expressive modes and political resonances of modernist visual culture had long been in play, with numerous national variants. Greenberg himself dated the emergence of modernism to the mid-nineteenth century, developing simultaneously, and not accidentally, along with the "first bold development of scientific revolutionary thought in Europe," that is, Marxism. Because much modernist art after World War II became resolutely apolitical, the politics of the young Greenberg's prescriptions for maintaining a healthy, authentic culture are often overlooked. Greenberg's ideas must be seen in his historical context: he lived in an unstable era on the brink of world war. He was horrified by the rise of fascism in Germany. And he was disillusioned with the Stalinist branch of the Left. He condemned kitsch as one of "the inexpensive ways in which totalitarian regimes seek to ingratiate themselves with their subjects . . . they will flatter the masses by bringing all culture down to their level." But Greenberg saw no redemption in capitalism. Rather, he correlated the origins of the modernist avant-garde with the breakdown of capitalist society and its continuing crisis—in essence, avant-garde culture offered a critique of capitalism. There was only one solution: a socialist culture that will preserve "whatever living culture we have now" and extend a new complex, sophisticated culture to everyone.[2]

Greenberg's essay came after two decades during which advertising integrated the medium of photography and the visual language of modernist art. His writing conveys a flavor of the period, when the roles and overlaps of the artistic and commercial spheres were debated in literary magazines and the popular press.[3] Though clean divisions into art and commerce (or avant-garde and kitsch) may be useful for analysis and debate, in practice, firm borders are rare. In retrospect, two ironies emerge from Greenberg's position. The first is that despite his clear political bearings in the late 1930s, by the mid-1940s Greenberg became a force advocating formal analysis as a method of art criticism, which contributed to the erasure of overt politics from modernist art in the postwar period.[4] (There is great similarity between this critical approach and the literary New Criticism of the 1950s.) The second irony, which is further explored in this essay, is that commerce widely adopted modernist visual culture in the interwar period, despite the fundamental view, as Greenberg outlined, that the fine arts were removed from commercial interests and early modernism was driven by its critique of capitalism.

The challenge to histories of this period is to illuminate the interrelationships between art and commerce, in the face of sometimes adamant arguments that the two were (and are) separate spheres. In histories of photography, the shadows of avant-garde and kitsch remain, and obscure the understanding of both practices as variant expressions of modernity that derive much from each other, even as they often define themselves in opposition to one another. This essay will explore how this tension has shaped the critical reception of advertising photographs by Paul Outerbridge (1896–1958), Charles Sheeler (1883–1965), and Edward Steichen (1879–1973).

Greenberg's concept of high culture derived from ideas solidly embedded in western thought. Art academies from the Renaissance on had defined and policed the concept of high art; they emphasized hierarchies of subject matter, with paintings of history, religion, and classical mythology at the top. The key moment for theorizing the construction and functions of high art came in the late eighteenth century. Philosopher Larry Shiner described the "great fracture in the older system . . . finally severing fine art from craft, artist from artisan, the aesthetic from the instrumental and establishing such institutions as the art museum, the secular concert, and copyright."[5] Immanuel Kant's renowned *Critique of Aesthetic Judgment* articulates this shift. Kant conceptualized artistic form as aesthetic and universal, emphasized the distinction between art and craft, and contended that beauty in a work of art cannot be utilitarian—it is not instructive, commercial, or otherwise instrumental. Kant called this aesthetic state "disinterestedness," a quality essential for experiencing beauty. Kant's influence on modernist thought can be seen in two major ways: the philosopher's emphasis on disinterestedness implies a suspicion of commercial art, and Kant shifted the criteria for evaluating art from its subject to its form, foreshadowing the formalist critical method Greenberg came to promote.[6]

Modernist concepts of high art as uplifting also derived from the ideas of Victorian poet and critic Matthew Arnold, who in his enormously influential 1869 book *Culture and Anarchy*, defined culture as "the best that has been thought and said in the world." Arnold continued: culture is "a study of perfection," which society needed "to minister to the diseased spirit of our time." Though Greenberg mirrored Arnold's definition of high culture, they could not be more different in interpreting the political implications. Where the young Greenberg believed socialism would deliver a true and elevating culture to everyone, Arnold, who was concerned by the decline of the aristocracy and working-class demands for democracy, suggested that culture could be used to retain the status quo. "Culture," he said decisively, "is the most resolute enemy of anarchy."[7] The connection from Arnold to Greenberg was not direct. The intervening years saw the development of the "art-for-art's sake" movement and the "significant form" criticism of Roger Fry and Clive Bell.[8]

Modernist theory thus employed firmly established philosophical ideas to conceptualize art and commerce as separate enterprises that were implicitly ranked—high over low, elite over popular. However, the use of modernist photography by advertising agencies in the interwar period disrupted such neat categories, allowing us to see complexities in the cultural landscape beyond the binaries established by critics such as Arnold and Greenberg. While modernist theory tried to draw clear lines between fine and applied arts (and culture and commerce), advertising practice blurred and overlapped the boundaries. Corporations engaged creative staff at the agencies to design advertisements, and art directors and photographers suggested effective, aesthetic solutions to advertising needs. The balance between selling and aesthetics was always in motion. Modernist advertising was a prevalent and influential visual form in the interwar years, and there was much overlap between fine art and commercial photography. Rather than standing apart from capitalism, modernism was employed to advance it.

The history of photography, as it has been written so far, echoes the binary structure articulated by Greenberg. The historical narratives defining art photography are well known—from the British Victorian debates of H. P. Robinson and P. H. Emerson (which coincided with Arnold's theories of high culture), to the Arts and Crafts movement that promoted photography through its emphasis on technology and printing, to the founding of the Photo-Secession by Alfred Stieglitz and his promotion of art photographers through his gallery *291* and journal *Camera Work*. Around 1900 art photography was synonymous with Pictorialism, a painterly style featuring soft-focus images created by manipulating the photographic process. By World War I modernist artistic photography developed, characterized by higher contrast, sharper focus, and a direct representation of the subject with an emphasis on the underlying abstract geometric structure. Emphasis on the metaphorical content of abstraction increased. Stieglitz, with his nineteenth-century training, came to this through Symbolist art. His younger colleague, Paul Strand, used formal elements along with some social analysis to translate metaphysics or moral components into visual terms.[9] Members of the Stieglitz circle rigorously monitored the perceived borders of photographic fine art, leading to legendary antagonistic personal relationships and acrimonious public quarrels.

The Stieglitz circle represented a small, if very visible, segment of New York photographers. Other photographers in the interwar years saw less rigid lines between art and commerce. The photographic historian Bonnie Yochelson has demonstrated that photographic modernism had at least two fathers. Stieglitz's campaign for photography's recognition as a fine art is the more commonly recognized lineage. The other lineage stems from the many modernist commercial photographers who were trained at the Clarence H. White School of Photography; through White's efforts many photographers learned a modernist vocabulary, which they brought to a wide public through the mass media. White had been a successful Pictorialist photographer associated with Stieglitz's Photo-Secession, until their falling out around 1910. He began to teach photography in 1907 and opened his own school in 1914, with a curriculum that emphasized design principles and encouraged work in the applied arts. White based the philosophy of his school—the "fusion of beauty and utility"—on the philosophy of his colleague at Columbia Teachers College, Arthur Wesley Dow, who advocated a democratic ideal of art appreciation and urged the application of fine art principles to industrial and commercial design. Some of White's students, including Anton Bruehl, Margaret Bourke-White, Paul Outerbridge, Ralph Steiner, and Margaret Watkins became New York's top commercial photographers. They practiced a modernist style based on close-up views, spare geometric compositions, oblique vantage points, tonal contrast, and sharpened focus that dominated advertising photography for the next two decades.[10] This second lineage of modernism refused to acknowledge a split between art photography and commercial work; the photographers believed they were engaged in both enterprises.

Many photographic historians of the past two decades (particularly in the fields of American studies, and visual communication, sociology, and anthropology) have worked to incorporate advertising photographs, as well as images generated by journalism, medicine, anthropology, and countless other fields into an historical overview.[11] However, when photographers worked in both artistic and commercial modes (or a mixture of them), art historical literature has had difficulty addressing the situation. Usually the fine art aspect of photography is privileged over other concerns as the basis for evaluating cultural significance. For instance, the Metropolitan Museum of Art's catalogue for *The New Vision: Photography Between the World Wars* distinguished between the "strict modernism" of Stieglitz and Strand, and "a rearguard or derivative modernism which might be termed modernistic [that] found application in commercial portraiture and fashion and advertising photography." Separating "modernistic" from "modernism" constructs cultural hierarchies. The terminology implies that "modernistic" is a derivative (and by implication, corrupted) form of fine art—when many artists made both art and commercial photography at the same time, and both practices informed each other. The term modernistic did not have such a precise meaning between the wars, though it was often used for Cubist-inspired compositions and in association with Art Deco and other industrial design styles. Rather than separating "modernistic" from "strict modernism," a more useful interpretive strategy is to see these different photographic practices as representations of different aspects of modernity that overlap and help construct each other.[12]

Despite a growing branch of research in photographic history that demonstrates how extensively modernist imagery was incorporated into American commercial culture, the art historical discourses that have shaped the language and understanding of modernist photography remain deeply entrenched. We might call these older narratives *modernist discourses*, in that they reflect the ideas, which Greenberg articulated, that art and commerce are two completely separate enterprises.[13] I am, of course, arguing that *modernist imagery* crossed these rhetorical boundaries.

Paul Outerbridge

In some art historical accounts, the commercial production of photographers is absent from narratives of their careers—even though almost all photographers, including those known strictly as art photographers such as Strand and Ansel Adams, did some advertising work. In other cases, modernist histories attempted to separate art from commerce, with the consequence that the origins of images are omitted and the formal qualities emphasized, in effect decontextualizing the image and turning commerce into art.

Paul Outerbridge is a photographer whose commercial production has been ignored in an attempt to recategorize his advertising images as art. His *Ide Collar* has only rarely been reproduced in its original context as an advertisement in the November 1922 *Vanity Fair*—with a Victorian "spinach" border and text that illustrates that the art director with whom he worked had little understanding of Outerbridge's modern approach with the camera (figure 5.1). It is most often reproduced as an isolated modernist art photograph, with attendant discussion typically focused on its advanced geometric formal construction and its relationship to Cubism.

Outerbridge studied at the Clarence H. White School of Photography, and the young photographer obtained the Ide Collar commission through White, who was an active proponent of New York's Art Center, where graphic designers, illustrators, and art directors often met. In 1921 and 1922 White's friend Heyworth Campbell, an art director for Condé Nast Publications, ran a series of features on modern photography in *Vanity Fair*

Figure 5.1   Advertisement for Ide Collars, *Vanity Fair*, November 1922, p. 5. Paul Outerbridge, Jr., photographer

that included work by White School students Ira Martin, Margaret Watkins, and Outerbridge, as well as better known photographers such as Man Ray and Charles Sheeler. Outerbridge did a good deal of work in the advertising industry before he left for Europe in 1925. After he returned in 1929, he became an expert in the carbro-color process, which he used for advertising and magazine features, as well as personal work.[14]

The three monographs published on Outerbridge pass swiftly over his advertising career to emphasize the photographer's later surrealistic nude studies, and thus ignore the integral cross-influences between the fine art and the commercial worlds.[15] Such studies perpetuate a view of modernism in which commercial photography is thought to be either artistically conservative imagery or corrupted modernist art and thus a drag on the artist's qreputation. More significantly, such a perspective reveals how deeply ingrained is the conception of art as separate from everyday life.

In the Outerbridge literature one can barely find a mention of his position in the advertising industry; works for clients like *Jello* from 1923 and *Chesterfield cigarettes* from 1931 are given titles like *Pattern No. 342* and reproduced without context or comment, as if it is obvious that they were modernist art experiments. Paradoxically, it is Outerbridge's advertising photographs that are more highly regarded than his later personal work, if one is to judge by the number of reproductions in books and the commentary in exhibition reviews. His early commercial works are frequently reproduced (out of context) as pinnacles of American modernism.[16] In one monograph, the authors felt compelled to argue that Outerbridge "kept his photographs uncompromised by the commercial illustrative and advertising market to which most of his work was sold."[17] In fact, if the market that eagerly sought Outerbridge's work had been disturbed by its modernism, he would not have been in such demand. Rather, modernism was recognized as an effective selling tool by advertising agencies, clients, and magazine editors. But in modernist art historical accounts, the industry's influence on photographic style is minimized and the vision of the individual artist is celebrated.

Charles Sheeler

Charles Sheeler's 1927 images of the Ford Motor Company's River Rouge plant illuminate the inseparability of some aspects of art and commerce in the interwar period, particularly the treatment of industrial imagery (figure 5.2). The N. W. Ayer agency offered Sheeler a commission to photograph Ford's new, state-of-the-art factory. At the enormous plant, Ford controlled all aspects of its business: receiving raw materials, processing them into parts, assembling and distributing the final product. The Rouge plant employed about 75,000 people on over 1100 acres, with 93 miles of railroad track and 23 main buildings.[18] The work Sheeler produced for Ford brought him wide public attention and secured his reputation as a preeminent photographer of modern life. Yet within the critical literature on the River Rouge commission, there are still debates about how to assess his achievement.

Sheeler had trained in both the fine and applied arts. He followed three years at Philadelphia's School of Industrial Art (1900–1903) with three years of painting at the Pennsylvania Academy of the Fine Arts (1903–1906). In the first decade of the twentieth century he made three trips to Europe to study its old masters and absorb its emerging abstraction, and on his return worked as both a painter and photographer. In 1913, he exhibited six paintings in the monumental Armory Show, which introduced European and American

Figure 5.2   Charles Sheeler. Ford Plant, River Rouge, Criss-Crossed Conveyors, 1927. The Lane Collection, Museum of Fine Arts, Boston

modernism to a large audience for the first time. His paintings of the mid-teens reflected the compositional structure of Cubism and the sparkling colors of the Fauves. And Sheeler was familiar with the witty, original creations of artists and collectors loosely connected under the umbrella of New York Dada. His closest friend, Morton Schamberg, created paintings of mechanical abstractions; he knew Francis Picabia's mechanomorphic portraits and Marcel Duchamp's sensational Cubist paintings; and Sheeler was warmly invited into the Arensberg family circle, perhaps the most influential collectors of American Dada.

By 1912, photography was his main source of support, and Sheeler employed it concurrently as an alternate artistic medium. The 2002 exhibition at the Museum of Fine Arts, Boston, renewed attention to this early period of Sheeler's career. The documentary aspect of Sheeler's earliest commissions, architectural photographs for Philadelphia-area architects (1912–1914), was acknowledged as contributing to his eye for sharp, geometric compositions, and, understandably, treated as but a passing moment in his long career.[19] The exhibition held some surprises, such as pushing back the date of Sheeler's *Bucks County Barn*, one of the key icons of photographic modernism from 1917 to 1915, thus situating him as perhaps the earliest proponent of a radical new vision in America.[20] The exhibition reinforced Sheeler's early visibility as a photographic artist, winning prizes, along with Schamberg and Strand, in a 1918 photography exhibition judged by Stieglitz. Stieglitz, reportedly, was thinking of devoting an issue of his journal *Camera Work* to Sheeler, but it never came to fruition.

Unlike others, such as Stieglitz, Strand, and Steichen who refuted their soft-focus Pictorialist past for a sharper-focused, more abstract modernism, Sheeler began his photographic career meeting commercial photography's demands for crisp reportage. Yet the museum's treatment of this practice was contradictory; much of the exhibition and its accompanying catalogue elided the commercial and the artistic aspects of Sheeler's work in order to emphasize the artistic and obscure the instrumental. Photographs of African sculpture (1916–1917) for Marius de Zayas's Modern Gallery and similar work for the collector John Quinn (1918–1919) were treated as the essence of modern art, presented in a ten-page portfolio. While acknowledging their documentary origins, curator Theodore E. Stebbins argued Sheeler "did almost the impossible, taking (or expropriating) objects that had their own roles and powers in the masquerades of Dan society and creating from them new objects that exude an equivalent spirituality in modern Western culture."[21] But whether or not they were considered art works from the beginning is open to some question. When the photographs of African art were shown at the Modern Gallery, the New York *Evening World* reviewed them as art: "Mr. Sheeler has specialized in photographs of the original African carvings . . . and on modernistic motifs" (April 7, 1917). But the *Christian Science Monitor* saw them as documentary, the pages "of a limited edition album de luxe . . . which should take its place in art libraries" for the study of African art (February 4, 1918).[22] The compelling images of African art illustrate the dilemma posed by Sheeler's work: in modernist narratives, when does the creativity of the photographer trump the fact that he was paid to make the image? As the MFA catalogue demonstrates, whether or not something is considered art it is clearly a subjective call.

Sheeler was interested in city subjects from his earliest years in New York. In 1920, he made the short film *Manhatta* in collaboration with Strand, and in subsequent paintings and photographs Sheeler explored the city's crowds, skyscrapers, and transportation. Throughout the 1920s, he had a high profile as a commercial photographer. In addition to doing work for numerous advertising clients, in 1926 Sheeler joined the staff of Condé Nast Publications, taking fashion shoots for *Vogue* and celebrity portraits for *Vanity Fair*.

Given Sheeler's early involvement with artistic photography and his close association with Strand and Stieglitz until their break in 1923, it is not surprising that he developed strong views about the medium.[23] Echoing the philosophy of straight photography, he told Constance Rourke, his first biographer, "I have come to value photography more and more for those things which it alone can accomplish." His goal was "the best statement of immediate facts," though he was quick to add that photography was an art with its own characteristics.[24] These words might have been spoken by Strand, Edward Weston, or other modernist photographers, but Sheeler's openness to commercial applications of photography simultaneously aligned him with others such as the White School photographers and his friend Edward Steichen, who made artistic commercial photographs. Sheeler told Rourke "the term artist should have a wider application than is implied by reference to the fine arts."[25] In his 1937 unpublished *Autobiography* he wrote that because industry "concerns the greatest number, finding an expression for it concerns the artist."[26] And he took great pleasure in industrial design. He loved his car, a 1929 Ford, which he was then photographing for the company's advertising: "to sit at the wheel is a revelation . . . My pleasure in it is akin to my pleasure in Bach or Greco and for the same reason—the parts work together so beautifully."[27]

When the N. W. Ayer agency approached Sheeler to spend six weeks in Detroit to photograph the new Ford plant, he must have known it would be a good fit. The reality of the job exceeded his expectations: he wrote to Arensberg, "The subject matter is incomparably the most thrilling I have had to work with."[28]

A prevalent theme in 1920s America, even among intellectuals, was an appreciation for business, and Henry Ford was often mentioned as its symbol. In the October 1923 issue of the literary magazine *Broom*, for example, editor Matthew Josephson presented a satirical yet celebratory view: "Mr. Ford, Ladies and Gentlemen, is not a human creature. He is a principle, or better, a relentless process . . . Let Ford be President. Let him assemble us all into a machine."[29] Coincidentally, this same issue featured some of Sheeler's work, and it may have influenced Sheeler's ideas about industry in general, and Ford's approach to mass production in particular. Sheeler's admiration for Ford increased upon experiencing the River Rouge plant. He wrote to Walter Arensberg, "Even having seen it, one doesn't believe it possible that one man could be capable of realizing such a conception."[30] Sheeler echoed this appreciation in a number of published statements. When *Fortune* magazine reproduced *American Landscape*, one of his paintings based on his Ford experience, the editors wrote a caption that connected Sheeler's modernist aesthetics with industrial production: "From the huge machine that cuts steel plates at a pressure of a thousand pounds to the square inch to the gauges which measure thousandths of inches, efficiency of function and its accompanying beauty is evident. Here is to be seen the machine working with an infallibility which precludes human competition. . . . It becomes evident one is witnessing the workings of an absolute monarchy. It confirms a preference for that type of government with the proviso that the monarch be of the calibre of Henry Ford."[31] While clearly this is hyperbole that one might expect in a business magazine, art historian Terry Smith noted that over a number of years Sheeler repeated similar paeans to industry "often and without irony."[32]

Ford engaged Sheeler to use his sophisticated artistic interpretation to represent the company's mechanized automobile production (as symbolized by the River Rouge plant) in order to convey a modern image for the company. As Smith observed, Sheeler's "work was valued because he photographed spark plugs, cars, and society ladies as if they were works of art." He employed stylish "modernist techniques of isolating, cropping, bold lighting, contrasting sharply different with even surfaces."[33]

If we look at the publication history of the best-known image from River Rouge series, *Criss-Crossed Conveyors*, we see dual canonization processes (figure 5.2). This image and others from the Rouge series have become emblems of both modernist art and advertising photography—but considering them in two separate discourses has been problematic. Though photographic histories discuss the Rouge photographs as an example of how modernism has had an impact on advertising photography and vice versa, the N. W. Ayer and Son archives do not have any records of even a single instance in which they were used as advertising photographs in mass-market consumer magazines. In essence, they functioned more as general publicity than as advertising. They were used in annual reports for Ford, and house magazines such as *Ford News*. And they established visual conventions that were replicated for many years in the company literature by Ford house photographers.

Sheeler's Rouge photographs were presented to the public through another route. Ayer's art director Vaughn Flannery distributed portfolios of selected prints to upscale magazines to generate publicity for Ford. *Criss-Crossed Conveyors* appeared in literary magazines like *Transition* and trendy high-style consumer magazines like *Vanity Fair. Vanity Fair*'s caption played on the almost religious significance of the factory in American capitalist culture: "It is natural that the largest factory, turning out the most cars in the least time, should come to have the quality of America's Mecca, toward which the pious journey for prayer."[34] Critic Samuel M. Kootz praised the Rouge photographs in *Creative Art*, arguing that Sheeler's "freshness of vision" achieved through his artistic skills "elevates photography to a new beauty." The artist, Kootz believed, "has articulated the very soul of steel, in a series of the truest portraits of our times."[35] As Smith observed, the fact that the River Rouge series was used in general public relations rather than in specific advertisements has led to the "polite fiction" that they are not commercial photographs—that Sheeler was creating independent, artistic photographs.

In Sheeler's case, the photographic literature, by its refusal to situate the image in context, has made commerce into art and art into commerce.

Museum interpretations of Sheeler's River Rouge photographs have followed the long shadow cast by late-nineteenth-century battles to define photography as a fine art. Sheeler's retrospective exhibitions in both 1987 and 2002 emphasized his identity as an artistic photographer and discounted his achievements as a commercial artist. At the 1987 exhibition, two warmly toned photographs *Kodascope Model C* and *L. C. Smith Typewriter* were framed and hung on the wall as art photographs, with no hint in the labels that the works had been advertising commissions. The accompanying catalogue essay simply glided over the issue, not mentioning that an art director and other members of N. W. Ayer's advertising staff had been involved in their collaborative production.[36] To do so would have detracted from the implicit assertion of Sheeler's photographic originality; this omission was necessary to incorporate the works into modernist narratives of art photography.

In the catalogue for the 2002 exhibition, Theodore Stebbins saw Sheeler's great success in the "warmth and even spirituality" he imparted to his best prints: "many of the Bucks County images, some of the African prints, and much of the Chartres series, and he did it even here at the Rouge." In effect, Stebbins uses this subjective criterion—one that even Stebbins himself admits is "almost impossible for the art historian to describe"—to categorize photographs into art or commerce. Because of the frequent critical discourse defining Sheeler's photographs as machine-age artifacts, Stebbins argues, "it is easy to overlook the transcendental nature of many of his most successful photographs." In some of the interior factory images, Sheeler "emphasizes the sensuous, animalistic shape of each object, suggesting the mysterious and elemental rather than the mechanical and the literal." According to Stebbins, this quality of spirituality is manifested further in the Rouge photographs, with "the fiery furnaces and looming, altarlike machinery at the Rouge suggesting an irrational, unknowable side even to the most rationally organized factory on earth."[37] Stebbins continued a long tradition of decontextualizing the Rouge images to turn them into art.

Much scholarly work has debated Sheeler's views on twentieth-century technology and industry. Miles Orvell perceives an ambiguous view of industry in the River Rouge photographs. The images appear to be "celebrations of Ford and, by implication, of American capitalism," but Orvell argues that by "aestheticizing industry" Sheeler is "maintaining the purity of the artwork as a defense against the severities of industrial life."[38] Karen Lucic sees his film, *Manhatta*, as his "most positive treatment of a machine-age subject," reminiscent of "Whitmanesque optimism," though it had occasional undertones criticizing the anonymity of urban life and no doubt incorporated ideas from his co-producer Strand.[39] In Sheeler's 1920s city scenes and skyscrapers, such as the painting *Park Row Building* or the lithograph *Delmonico Building*, Lucic detects a subtle ambivalence to the urban experience, expressed through city architecture that seems fragmented, dark, and impersonal, a portrait of the "fundamental hollowness" of the city's businesses. In such images he employed an "exaggeratedly impersonal" approach that paradoxically became his signature style.[40] Ultimately, Lucic concludes, Sheeler was haunted by "a divided and unresolved attitude toward the subject."[41] Lucic's characterization of Sheeler's industrial imagery as measured and even ambivalent toward modernity effectively allows Sheeler to stand on both sides of the issue—to be "thrilled" by his individual subject, even as he critiques them.

Sharon Corwin proposes to find Sheeler's ideas about industrial America in the formal qualities of his images. Like Lucic, she finds ambivalence: "To say that the formal project of Precisionism engages the rhetoric of the rationalized factory is not necessarily . . . a visual endorsement." Rather, she perceives a "conflicted stance toward the status of labor," expressed in paintings through the glassy surfaces that deny the brushwork that made them, and other characteristics that suggest the "effacement of artistic labor." Works of art thus achieve a "visual rhetoric of efficiency" by "*over*looking the visible traces of labor."[42]

Where some have seen ambivalence, others have seen a celebration of corporate capitalism.[43] In my view Sheeler's treatment of figures provides the key. As has been frequently observed, in the River Rouge series Sheeler constructed elegant abstractions from the geometry of the plant, and rather purposefully ignored the laborers on Ford's famous assembly line. When he pictured people, the workers functioned as measurement tools by which the vast scale of the whole enterprise may be gauged. Avoiding the workers allowed Sheeler to more easily transform the lines and shapes of the factory into abstract art. The comparison with Diego Rivera's murals of the Ford plant at the Detroit Institute of Arts is striking—in Rivera's paintings powerful, muscular workers force machines to do their jobs. Given the context of the emerging labor movement between the world wars, it seems impossible to ignore that the two artists posit very different political outlooks. Rivera was out front—activist, even strident, in advancing his Marxist politics. Sheeler, with his more withdrawn personality and restrained artistic style, may allow more variety in reading his work, but his joy in representing the mechanical engines of industry cannot be dismissed.

In Terry Smith's view, the River Rouge photographs represent the "meeting of different modernities—Ford Company, industrial design, upper-class fashion, and avant-garde modernism."[44] As Smith noted, "in the design of advertisements, the reach toward the visual culture of the [upper] class is also imperative, given the advertiser's imperative to sell to these people. Modern artists had a double role here: not only to modernize the subculture of the rich through updating its tokens of taste (paintings, sculpture, architecture) but also to modernize the advertising directed at them."[45]

Sheeler's Rouge photographs also demonstrate the fluidity of stylistic features between art and commerce—and the wider audience for modernist style. Following modernist theory, articulated in one version by Greenberg, observers may expect to find a critique of capitalism in Sheeler's modernist imagery. When it is lacking, they find ambivalence rather than admiration for industry. In practice, modernism is a style not tied to any politics, as the Italian Futurists demonstrated with their support of Mussolini. Style and politics must be read together in historical context.

In the telling of Sheeler's career, his advertising work has been consistently minimized. There are persistent legends of how he gave up photography in 1931 at the behest of his art dealer, Edith Halpert of the Downtown Gallery, in order to focus on painting. However, in a 1934 interview with *Commercial Photographer*, Sheeler acknowledged that while he was preparing for a painting exhibition that coming fall, "my photography is practically all advertising."[46] This suggests that although Sheeler still had to earn a living, his dealer believed that promoting the myth of a non-commercial artist would ultimately be more lucrative.

Sheeler has been particularly vulnerable to decontextualization, and, as in the case of Outerbridge, the consequence of such distortion is a reinforcement of the modernist idea of the fine artist as a unique and original thinker. Much of the cultural resonance of the imagery in its time period is lost. In the 1930s, Sheeler emphasized the content of his imagery when he told Rourke "our factories are our substitute for religious expression."[47] By the 1950s, the formalism Greenberg articulated in the 1940s was triumphant—perhaps having more to do with changes in the social and political climate of the United States than art criticism. Social commentary in art became linked to the social realist style of the 1930s and the many leftist artists who practiced it, an uncomfortable connection in the age of McCarthyism. Modernist abstraction was a safe and rewarded course, politically and aesthetically. In the postwar period, Sheeler absorbed modernist narratives and lost interest in contextualizing his work, preferring formalist interpretation. "I don't believe I could ever indulge in social comment," the photographer told an interviewer in 1954.[48]

Edward Steichen

Advertising agencies certainly acknowledged the importance of modernist fine art as a category of cultural production. By the 1920s, art directors had become professionalized. Most had art school training, and quite a few continued to paint and exhibit their work on the side. The art directors, as well as the commercial photographers, saw art as an essential part of commerce.

The 1936 Cannon Mills towel campaign for *Vogue* magazine is an example of an advertising campaign in which the photographer and the art director consciously worked to cross borders between art and commerce. In this campaign, N. W. Ayer's art director Charles Coiner commissioned a series of twelve graceful nude studies to evoke the idea of a figure emerging from her bath (figure 5.3). Steichen's images used the vocabulary of high art to try to make themselves noticed. To be noticed was, and is, among the primary goals of advertising photography. The references to the ideal figure, used intermittently through the history of art to signal beauty and perfection, staked a claim for a status closer to art, if not within art.

Figure 5.3 Advertisement for Cannon towels, *Vogue*, June 15, 1936, inside cover. Edward Steichen, photography. Charles T. Coiner and Paul Darrow, art directors, for N. W. Ayer and Son agency

Coiner recalled that he wanted a particularly artistic look for the advertisements for the 1936 Cannon Towel campaign and he selected Steichen because of the photographer's solid reputation as an artist. Steichen had established this reputation through Pictorialist exhibitions in the first decade of the century. By the time Coiner hired him thirty years later, it is impossible that the high profile designer did not know of Steichen's advertising work, as examples of it were published almost annually in the Art Directors' Club yearbooks. Perhaps Coiner claimed Steichen was "the best non-commercial photographer in the United States at the time" because he considered the photographer's work for *Vogue* and *Vanity Fair* "editorial" rather than "commercial."[49] For his part, Steichen must have welcomed the Cannon account, because, like the portraits he did for *Vanity Fair*, they occupied a critical space situated between his fine art photographs and his more obviously applied art imagery.

The polished fine art appeal of Steichen's Cannon work echoed images more likely found in art museums and Steichen's own early Pictorialist photographs than images found on the pages of mass magazines. And, unlike the audience the advertising agency sought for inexpensive beauty products, the placement of the Steichen's Cannon advertisements in high fashion magazines—*Vogue* and *Harper's Bazaar*—rather than in the "home" magazines—*Good Housekeeping* and *Ladies' Home Journal*—superficially indicates the manufacturer was targeting a more affluent, more refined audience, an audience they thought would be flattered by the pictorial references to the long tradition of reclining Venuses dating back to the Renaissance. They also thought this audience was sophisticated enough to accept the display of women's bodies as a technique for merchandising towels in a more daring manner than any previously used in mass media advertising. Steichen's images were printed in sepia tones, not the new color processes. This gives them a more "artistic" look that also tacitly reinforced the fine art status of Steichen's photographs, quelling any residual doubts from the nineteenth-century debate "can photography be art?" Or, in this case, "can commercial photography be art?"

It is difficult to ascertain how the targeted upper-class female viewers read and reacted to Steichen's figures in the 1930s, draped, as it were, with the status of high art. No doubt the cultural strength of the status of the fine arts led many women to view the images as Coiner proposed they do: as the latest in the display of women's bodies in the western tradition, as examples of ideal beauty, as great appreciations for the female form, as evidence of the audience's sophistication as spectators. The women *are* art. Because of the heavy weight of gendered ideologies, many women may have viewed the female form as Coiner did, with a male gaze, or shifting among possible viewer positions, bringing both male and female values and judgments to the female form. Thus, upper-class women were positioned as authoritative viewers (art admirers), even though such authority was otherwise inconsistent with women's relation to looking at the high art nude, where women traditionally take the place of passive object and men typically take the role of active viewer.

One of the great mysteries and paradoxes of Steichen's career is how he was able to keep his identity as a fine art photographer as the primary defining element of his career while most actively pursuing his commercial work. Part of the story is the more open-ended ideas of modernism prevalent before World War II. In the interwar years, Steichen considered himself both an art and commercial photographer simultaneously. Throughout the 1920s and 1930s in his public statements, Steichen continually praised commercial art for its ability to bring good art and design to a mass audience and he celebrated its purpose of showcasing the best products of American capitalism. He delighted that "now I have an exhibition every month that reaches hundreds of thousands of people through editorial and advertising pages."[50] Despite his early exploration of socialism, Steichen strongly internalized the business culture of the 1920s; he believed that his high fees proved both his popular appeal and his artistry.

Another part of the story is Steichen's strong belief in the artistic merit of his commercial production. Steichen frequently sent advertising photographs to art exhibitions during the 1920s and 1930s. He sent *Vanity Fair* portraits and *Vogue* fashion photographs to the 1929 *Film und Foto* exhibition in Stuttgart and the 1936 International Contemporary Photography Exposition in Paris. His 1938 retrospective at the Baltimore Museum of Art featured his advertisements for Jergens' Lotion, Steinway Pianos, Douglass Lighters, Coty Lipstick, Kodak Film, and Hexylresorcinol as well as his early landscapes, abstract experiments, and portraits.[51] Much later, when he was director of the Department of Photography at the Museum of Modern Art, he donated to MoMA's permanent collection images commissioned by the Douglass Lighter Company and other advertising clients. In these ways, Steichen insisted on collapsing the distinctions between the fine and popular arts, insisting that both should be seen as aspects of modernism.

Like Sheeler, Steichen's view of the art and commercial worlds was sometimes contradictory. Despite his visibility as a spokesperson for commercial photography, Steichen occasionally harbored reservations about the nature and value of advertising photography. His biographer, Carl Sandburg, noted in 1929 that Steichen believed, "The only choice for an artist is collaboration or revolution."[52] With his advertising photography, Steichen consciously chose collaboration. In this he seems to accept the position of the Stieglitz circle (with whom he was affiliated early in his career, until he parted with Stieglitz over commerce and World War I), which articulated a strict separation between commercial art and fine art. But in his actions, Steichen challenged the terms of polarity—between "collaboration" and "revolution,"—publicly and frequently identifying himself as a commercial artist (in the company, he argued, of Michelangelo, Leonardo, and others, who worked for private patrons). Along with his art directors, Steichen restructured Stieglitz's argument, placing work created for commercial patrons on a continuum with fine art rather than in opposition to private expression. Thus, Steichen reframed the discussion to accentuate the social and cultural nature of imagery, enlarged the scope of art, and situated commercial art within the whole.

The art historical literature is beginning to recognize the interplay between fine and commercial art in Steichen's work. Steichen's early romantic landscapes have long been at home in museums, even when his commercial work was excluded.[53] My own book, *Real Fantasies: Edward Steichen's*

Advertising Photography, described the extent of his commercial practice between the wars and the interplay of his art and advertising photography. His retrospective at the Whitney Museum of American Art in 2000 included Steichen's advertising photographs, fabric designs, and tear sheets of fashion features from *Vogue*.[54] This inclusion attests to a trend in current photographic criticism to recapture and better reflect the vitality and inclusiveness that characterized modernist practice in the early twentieth century.

Modernist criticism has typically had a difficult time accounting for commercial art as a cultural expression, particularly in the postwar period. The cultural critics of the 1930s, however, engaged in lively debates. Some, like Greenberg, saw the fine and popular arts as polar opposites: individual vs. corporate, free expression vs. commercial culture, engaged spectator vs. passive observer. Others, such as Steichen, saw quality commercial art as valuable for improving the public's aesthetic taste.

A number of observers engaged in discussion of visual culture believed a quality popular art might reach and edify the public. Lewis Mumford, sometimes an unsparing critic of modern life and consumerism, described the paucity of high culture as the "problem of trying to live well in a régime that is devoted to the production of T-beams and toothbrushes and TNT." Preceding Greenberg's description of kitsch, Mumford complained "the urban worker escapes the mechanical routine of his daily job only to find an equally mechanical substitute for life and growth and experience in his amusements."[55] Mumford argued that the public would accept fine art, if only they had the chance. He took aim at the same issue that troubled Greenberg—the correlation between money and access to high culture. Without public access, art was consigned "to the sphere of mere connoisseurship and wealthy patronage." Though he acknowledged a difference between fine and popular arts, he did so without condescension toward audiences. He believed a municipal gallery and art center run by artists would "help make art part of the daily routine of the mass of people, and so bring painting and sculpture as close to them as the moving pictures and comic strips are now."[56]

The noted art historian Meyer Schapiro in 1936, in a passionate defense of the New Deal Works Progress Administration employment for artists, recognized the cultural importance of engaging audiences of mass distributed imagery. "A public art already exists," he said. "The public enjoys . . . the movies with a directness and whole-heartedness which can hardly be called forth by the artistic painting and sculpture." Like Greenberg's kitsch, Schapiro considered much popular culture "low-grade and infantile public art . . . [that] reduces art to a commercial device for exploiting the feelings and anxieties of the masses." But Schapiro believed that the public could be mobilized to demand access to the fine arts. Artists, he argued, must work for the "support of the organized working class" by providing "a program for a public art which will reach the masses of people." If artists "produce simply pictures to decorate the offices of municipal and state officials . . . then their work has little interest to the workers." Schapiro also advocated increasing quality in the industrial arts, and worried that so few people could afford good design.[57]

The cultural critics expressed sentiments that Outerbridge, Sheeler, and Steichen certainly shared: although much commercial imagery was of low quality, ambitious imagery need not be confined to high art; the public would accept and understand thought-provoking ideas and styles presented in popular media. Modernist photographers in the early decades of the twentieth century did not strictly segregate different types of photographic practices into immutable categories such as art photography, advertising photography, journalistic photography, and so on. These boundaries hardened and became more hierarchical in the postwar years. It was the great contribution of postmodern critics to challenge the hierarchies of late modernism and to change the terms of the debates. Interest in analyzing culture has replaced interest in describing style and ranking genres. And historical context is being restored. Although some resistance remains, visual historians are now free to study the full spectrum of visual production to understand society. And art historians have begun to reconstruct the careers of photographers whose narratives have been shaped by mid-century modernist ideas.

Notes

My thanks to Joanne Lukitsh and Patricia Hills for inspiration and constructive criticism, and to Elspeth Brown for her support of this work.

1. Clement Greenberg, "Avant-Garde and Kirsch," (1939) rpt. in Greenberg, *Art and Culture: Critical Essays* (Boston: Beacon Press, 1965). Quotations from pp. 8, 10.
2. Greenberg, "Avant-Garde and Kirsch," pp. 4, 19, 21. Greenberg argued that avant-garde culture furnished "an historical criticism" that revealed "our present bourgeois social order was shown to be, not an eternal 'natural' condition of life, but simply the latest term in a succession of social orders" (p. 4). For a critique of Greenberg's politics see T. J. Clark, "Clement Greenberg's Theory of Art" (1982), rpt. in *Postmodern Perspectives: Issues in Contemporary Art*, Howard Risatti ed. (Englewood Cliffs NJ: Prentice Hall, 1990).
3. There is an extensive literature critiquing the idea of fine art as a special realm removed from political and commercial interests going back to the 1970s. One might even argue that demystifying fine art was one of the central focuses of certain aspects of postmodern thought, though there has been no consensus on its application and adoption. Thomas Crow's work, for example, investigated how "the artistic avant-garde has discovered, renewed, or re-invented itself by identifying with marginal, 'non-artistic' form of expressivity and display–forms improvised by other social groups out of the degraded materials of capitalist manufacture." "Modernism and Mass Culture in the Visual Arts," in *Modern Art in the Common Culture* (New Haven: Yale University Press, 1996), pp. 3–37. Quotation on p. 3.
4. Clement Greenberg, "Abstract Art," *The Nation* 158 (April 15, 1944): 450–451, rpt. in *Modern Art in the USA: Issues and Controversies of the 20th Century*, Patricia Hills, ed. (Upper Saddle River NJ: Prentice-Hall, 2001), pp. 146–150. Five years after "Avant Garde and Kitsch" Greenberg's ideas about the avant-garde artist's responsibility to critique society reversed course

in several respects. On formalism he writes: "Let painting confine itself to the disposition pure and simple of color and line, and not intrigue us by associations with things we can experience more authentically elsewhere." He also accepted a distancing of art from society, so unlike the earlier connections he made between avant-garde art and a critique of capitalism. He concluded: "Art is under no categorical imperative to correspond point by point to the underlying tendencies of its age . . . the most ambitious and effective pictorial art of these times is abstract or goes in that direction" (p. 150).

5. Larry Shiner, *The Invention of Art: A Cultural History* (Chicago: University of Chicago Press, 2001), p. 9. For an extended discussion of the history of the concepts of high and low art, see my "Critical Overview of Visual Culture Studies," in *Seeing High and Low: Representing Social Conflict in American Visual Culture*, Patricia Johnston, ed. (Berkeley: University of California Press, 2006).

6. On Kant, see Shiner, *The Invention of Art*, pp. 146–151, and for commentary on his influence on twentieth-century art history see Keith Moxey, *Peasants, Warriors, and Wives: Popular Imagery in the Reformation* (1989; rpt: Chicago: University of Chicago Press, 2004), pp. 1–2.

7. Matthew Arnold, *Anarchy and Culture*, Samuel Lipman ed. (1869 rpt: New Haven: Yale University Press, 1994). Quotations on pp. 5, 31, 51, 136. On Arnold's importance, see John Storey, *An Introductory Guide to Cultural Theory and Popular Culture* (Athens: University of Georgia Press, 1993), pp. 21–25.

8. For example, see Roger Fry, *Vision and Design* (New York: Bretano's, 1921) and Clive Bell, *Art* (1913, rpt: New York: Oxford University Press, 1987).

9. Paul Strand, "Photography," *Seven Arts* 2 (August 1917): 524–525, rpt. in *Photography: Essays and Images*, ed. Beaumont Newhall (New York and Boston: MoMA and New York Graphic Society, 1980). The emphasis on metaphysical content grew stronger as the literature on straight photography developed. For an overview see Bonnie Yochelson, "Clarence H. White Reconsidered: An Alternative to the Modernist Aesthetic of Straight Photography," *Studies in Visual Communication* 9 (Fall 1983): 24–44.

10. Bonnie Yochelson, "Clarence H. White, Peaceful Warrior," in *Pictorialism into Modernism: The Clarence H. White School of Photography* (New York: Rizzoli and Rochester: George Eastman House, 1996), pp. 10–119; and Yochelson, "Clarence H. White Reconsidered."

11. This perspective is now incorporated into the standard textbooks for history of photography courses; however, it has been slow to penetrate museum exhibition catalogues. The two most frequently used current texts see art photography as one of many photographic practices, along with photojournalism, scientific imaging, vernacular portraiture, and numerous other photographies. Naomi Rosenblum, *A World History of Photography*, 3rd ed. (New York: Abbeville Press, 1997); and Mary Warner Marien, *Photography: A Cultural History* (Upper Saddle River NJ: Prentice Hall, 2002).

12. For a model of this type of study, see Terry Smith, *Making the Modern: Industry, Art, and Design in America* (Chicago: University of Chicago Press, 1993). He advocated examining "a new way of seeing . . . across a variety of visualizing domains . . . located precisely within the psychosocial economies which were, in turn, constructing them" (pp. 6–7).

13. These ideas are the legacy of modernist photographic historians such as Beaumont Newhall, John Szarkowski, and Weston Naef, whose careers

collectively span from the 1930s to the 1990s. Many of their ideas resonate with those developed by photographers Strand and others associated with the later years of the Stieglitz circle.

14. Yochelson, "Clarence H. White, Peaceful Warrior," pp. 84, 90.
15. Another example: Outerbridge's image of bracelets for a Macy's ad is titled *Musical Semi-Abstraction*. Graham Howe and G. Ray Hawkins, *Paul Outerbridge, Jr.: Photographs*, text by Graham Howe and Jacqueline Markham (New York: Rizzoli, 1980), p. 34. [It is identified in Margaret Watkins, "Advertising and Photography," *Pictorial Photography in America* 4 (1926), n.p.] See also Bernard Barryte, Graham Howe, and Elaine Dines, *Paul Outerbridge, A Singular Aesthetic: Photographs and Drawings, 1921–1941, A Catalogue Raisonné* (Laguna Beach: Museum of Art, 198CA: Museum of Art, 1981); and Manfred Heitung, ed., text by Elaine Dines-Cox, *Paul Outerbridge* (New York: Taschen, 1999).
16. For example, see John Szarkowski, *Looking at Photographs: 100 Pictures from the Collection of the Museum of Modern Art* (New York: MoMA, 1973), p. 80.
17. Howe and Hawkins, *Paul Outerbridge, Jr.: Photographs*, p. 7.
18. Theodore E. Stebbins, Jr. and Norman Keyes, *Charles Sheeler: The Photographs* (Boston: Little Brown and Company, 1987), p. 25. This book also served as the exhibition catalogue for Sheeler's 1987 retrospective at the Museum of Fine Arts, Boston.
19. Gilles Mora, "Charles Sheeler: A Radical Modernism," in *The Photography of Charles Sheeler, American Modernist* (Boston: Bulfinch Press, 2002), p. 82.
20. Theodore E. Stebbins, Jr., "Sheeler and Photography," in *The Photography of Charles Sheeler, American Modernist* (Boston: Bulfinch Press, 2002), pp. 9–25. Stebbins explains that since the 1987 exhibition at the Museum of Fine Arts, which he also curated, he has examined "a half-dozen vintage prints of this image, all of which are inscribed on the reverse in Sheeler's hand, 'Bucks County Barn / 1915.' " The curators previously assigned the date of 1917 because the image had won a photographic prize in 1918 (p. 23, n. 8).
21. Stebbins, "Sheeler and Photography," p. 14. The images for De Zayas seem to have been intended as both documentation and as the centerpiece of a co-authored book *African Negro Wood Sculpture*. The book included Sheeler's original photographs, and it seems less than 10 out of a planned edition of 22 were produced. For another discussion of the issues raised by these images, see Helen Shannon, *From "African Savages" to "Ancestral Legacy": Race and Cultural Nationalism in the American Modernist Reception of African Art*, Ph.D. diss., Columbia University, 1999.
22. Marius de Zayas, *How, When, and Why Modern Art Came to New York*, ed. Francis M. Naumann (Cambridge MA: M.I.T. Press, 1996), pp. 70, 114.
23. Sheeler was very close to Strand and Stieglitz until they took offense to a supportive review that Sheeler wrote in *The Arts* about Stieglitz's exhibition at the Anderson Galleries. Sheeler drew similarities to old master paintings and commented on the preciousness of platinum paper. Charles Sheeler, "Recent Photographs by Alfred Stieglitz," *The Arts* 3 (May 1923): 345. This review and the fallout are discussed in Stebbins and Keyes, *Charles Sheeler: The Photographs*, p. 22.
24. Constance Rourke, *Charles Sheeler: Artist in the American Tradition* (New York: Harcourt, Brace, and Co, 1938), p. 120.
25. Rourke, *Charles Sheeler: Artist in the American Tradition*, p. 131.

26. Quoted in Susan Fillin Yeh, "Charles Sheeler: Industry, Fashion, and the Vanguard," *Arts Magazine* 54 (February 1980): 154–158, quote on p. 158.

27. Charles Sheeler to Walter Arensberg, February 6, 1929, Arensberg Archives, quoted in Stebbins, "Sheeler and Photography," p. 16.

28. Charles Sheeler to Walter Arensberg, October 25, 1927, Arensberg Archives, quoted in Lucic, *Charles Sheeler and the Cult of the Machine*, p. 92.

29. Matthew Josephson, "Henry Ford," *Broom* 5 (October 1923): 142.

30. Charles Sheeler to Walter Conrad Arensberg, October 25, 1927, Arensberg Archives, Philadelphia Museum of Art, in Fillin Yeh, "Charles Sheeler: Industry, Fashion, and the Vanguard," quoted on p.156.

31. *Fortune* (March 1931): 57, quoted in Smith, *Making the Modern*, p. 127.

32. Smith, *Making the Modern*, p. 111.

33. Smith, *Making the Modern*, p. 112.

34. "By Their Works Ye Shall Know Them," *Vanity Fair* 29 (February 1929): 62.

35. Samuel M. Kootz, "Ford Plant Photos of Charles Sheeler," *Creative Art* 8 (April 1931): 264–267.

36. Stebbins and Keyes, *Charles Sheeler: The Photographs*, p. 23.

37. Stebbins, "Sheeler and Photography," p. 19.

38. Miles Orvell, "The Artist Looks at the Machine: Whitman, Sheeler, and American Modernism," in *After the Machine: Visual Arts and the Erasing of Cultural Boundaries* (Jackson: University Press of Mississippi, 1995), pp. 3–27. Quotes on pp. 15, 17, 18.

39. Karen Lucic, *Charles Sheeler and the Cult of the Machine* (Cambridge: Harvard University Press, 1991), p. 53.

40. Lucic, *Charles Sheeler and the Cult of the Machine*, pp. 53–74.

41. Lucic, *Charles Sheeler and the Cult of the Machine*, p. 108.

42. Sharon Corwin, "Picturing Efficiency: Precisionism, Scientific Management, and the Effacement of Labor," *Representations* 84 (2004): 139–165. Quotes on pp. 150, 160. For examination of these issues in a somewhat earlier time period, see Elspeth H. Brown, *The Corporate Eye: Photography and the Rationalization of American Commercial Culture, 1884–1929* (Baltimore: Johns Hopkins University Press, 2005).

43. For example, Matthew Baigell called Sheeler "the true artist of corporate capitalism," in "American Art and National Identity: The 1920s," *Arts Magazine* 61 (February 1987): 51.

44. Smith, *Making the Modern*, p. 127.

45. Smith, *Making the Modern*, p. 186. On Rivera's murals see Mary Jane Jacob and Linda Downs, *The Rouge: The Image of Industry in the Art of Charles Sheeler and Diego Rivera* (Detroit: Detroit Institute of Arts, 1978) and Laurance P. Hurlburt, *The Mexican Muralists in the United States* (Albuquerque: University of New Mexico Press, 1989).

46. Lillian Sabine, "Charles Sheeler, New York City" 9 (June 1934): 253–258. Quote on p. 255. For a discussion of the relationship between Sheeler's photography and painting, see Karen E. Haas, " 'Opening the Other Eye': Charles Sheeler and the Uses of Photography," in *The Photography of Charles Sheeler, American Modernist* (Boston: Bulfinch Press, 2002), pp. 119–139.

47. Rourke, *Charles Sheeler: Artist in the American Tradition*, p. 130.

48. Frederick S. Wight, et al., *Charles Sheeler: A Retrospective Exhibition* (Los Angeles: UCLA, 1954), p. 28, quoted in Lucic, *Charles Sheeler and the Cult of the Machine*, p. 108.

49. Charles T. Coiner, "Recollections of Ayer," Oral history interview by Howard L. Davis and F. Bradley Lynce (March 16, 1982), p. 15, N. W. Ayer & Son, Inc. Archives, New York. The Cannon campaign is discussed more extensively in my book, Patricia Johnston, *Real Fantasies: Edward Steichen's Advertising Photographs* (Berkeley: University of California Press, 1997), pp. 204–214.

50. Presentation of Edward Steichen, "Minutes of the Representatives Meetings," January 31, 1928, pp. 2–3, J. Walter Thompson Archives (now at Duke University). Steichen's comments on commercial art are discussed in my book, Johnston, *Real Fantasies: Edward Steichen's Advertising Photographs*, pp. 25–41.

51. Johnston, *Real Fantasies*, p. 36.

52. Carl Sandburg, *Steichen the Photographer* (New York: Harcourt, Brace, 1929), p. 53.

53. This museum practice is paralleled in the vast literature on Steichen. Most of the books on the Stieglitz circle pay homage to Steichen's Pictorialist prints, as do museum catalogues such as Denis Longwell, *Steichen: The Master Prints, 1895–1914* (New York and Boston: MoMA and New York Graphic Society, 1978), and more recently, Joel Smith, *Steichen: The Early Years* (Princeton University Press in association with the Metropolitan Museum of Art, 1999). The overview by his widow also devotes little attention to his commercial work, Joanna Steichen, *Steichen's Legacy: Photographs, 1895–1973*, as does the book by the talented biographer Penelope Niven, *Steichen: A Biography* (New York: Clarkson Potter, 1997).

54. Barbara Haskell, *Edward Steichen* (New York: Whitney Museum of American Art, 2000).

55. Lewis Mumford, "The City," (1922) quoted in Lucic, *Charles Sheeler and the Cult of the Machine*, p. 45.

56. Lewis Mumford, "Letters from Our Friends," *Art Front* 1 (November 1934), n.p.

57. Meyer Schapiro, "Public Use of Art," *Art Front* 2 (November 1936), pp. 4–6.

Part II

Business and the Politics of Difference, 1900–1930

Chapter 6

"New York is Not America": Immigrants and Tourists in Post–World War I New York

Angela M. Blake

In contrast to the prevailing public image of New York before World War I, when the burgeoning skyscraper "landscape" seemed its greatest new attraction, by the 1920s observers of New York had lowered their gaze to the streets, as it were, and seemed more interested in assessing New York's status by means of its population rather than its buildings. "It is not so much the place . . . as the people," mused renowned British writer and frequent visitor to New York, Ford Madox Ford, in his 1927 book *New York Is Not America*, when considering New York's appeal. He dismissed the urban landscape as the city's defining characteristic in favor of its diverse urban population.[1]

Ford's book suggested the inextricable links between geography and identity in the 1920s. To Ford, and to many Americans living west of the Hudson River, heterogeneous, cosmopolitan New York was not America, was not representative of the nation. However, the city's seemingly precarious relation to national culture cut both ways. To social conservatives, New York represented disruptive postwar cultural changes, and the threat to "old stock" Americans posed by immigrants. On the other hand, for the growing number of Americans spending their vacations as tourists in their own country, much of New York's appeal lay in its exotic, somewhat un-American reputation. For these consumers New York was best marketed as *both* American and un-American. For the tourist industry this contradictory mix required deft reinterpretations of widely circulated pejorative images and rhetoric about the city's immigrants and their neighborhoods.

In the postwar period, New York continued—as it had since the late nineteenth century—to struggle against persistent national doubts about where it fit in the national imaginary. During a period of intense anti-immigration campaigning and legislation, New York's reputation as a city of immigrants potentially worked against the efforts of city boosters and tourist industry advocates to sell the city as a suitable middle-class tourist destination. Tourism promoters in New York, using the image of the city's famously diverse population and apparently distinct ethnic neighborhoods, successfully built on old and new fashions for "slumming" in the city's "foreign" quarters, helping to construct the ethnic identities of various areas of the city in opposition to the supposed "whiteness" of "native" New York. Boosters and tourism promoters used the very aspect of the city that threatened to undermine their business—its cosmopolitan heterogeneity—to attract average American tourists.

Locating America, Identifying Americans

National press and political attention to immigration intensified before and after American involvement in World War I. Between 1880 and 1919, over twenty-three million immigrants arrived in the United States, seventeen million of whom entered through New York. The numbers of immigrants arriving from Eastern and Southern Europe increased exponentially, reaching almost a million as early as 1907. By 1920, almost forty per cent of New York City's population was foreign born, with 480,000 Russian Jews forming the largest ethnic group of that population.[2] In 1917, Congress passed a new immigration act that imposed literacy tests on immigrants, in an attempt to keep out the Eastern and Southern Europeans. The war in Europe put an effective stop to the rising trend of immigration due to the practical and political difficulties of population movement during wartime. As the war ended, however, concern rose again in the United States that immigration, static for a few years, would surge once more following the Armistice.

At stake in the attacks on New York's American-ness, in the intense campaigns to restrict immigration, as well as in the postwar "red scare," was a larger crisis of identity and geography: Where was "America" in the postwar world? Was America represented by, and located in, the small town or in the big city? What landscape represented America? Earlier in the century, what had seemed most American, because least European, was the rocky landscape of the Far West. However, after World War I, with Europe both fragmented and no longer the dominant political and financial region of the world, what was American had to be defined by means of domestic, not international, comparisons. The anxiety over foreignness was not only about Jews or immigrants; it also represented a deeper anxiety about new attitudes, new social mores, deemed "foreign" to a real or imagined America.

Much of the discourse about New York's un-American qualities relied for its credibility on larger national, rather than local, concerns about locating American identity in the postwar period. As numerous scholars have argued, America's postwar prosperity undergirded a renewed conservatism, and a refocus on domestic issues in the 1920s.[3] Such self-examination raised questions about who was American and what an American looked like. New York, port of entry for most immigrants, and home to the largest urban foreign-born population, became the focus of national attention to matters of identity, ethnicity, and race. As the center of the growing advertising and public relations industries, New York was also the national center for image-making. More than any other place at the time, New York City was the location in which the image of America and of Americans was daily created and recreated. From the Gibson girl to the flapper, from the "other half" to the "demi monde," New York types became national types; the gap between local and national almost imperceptible. It was this imbrication of New York and the nation to which the rest of America increasingly objected. How could New York be the nation's metropolis when a large proportion of its residents looked not "American" but "foreign"? New York's apparent disregard for Prohibition, its reputedly risqué cabaret and theater productions, and its tendency to attract "bohemians" and other political and social eccentrics added to the outsider's impression that New York could not, and should not, represent America.

The objections to New York's status as the nation's metropolis emanated in particular from cities and states outside the Eastern seaboard whose editorial writers and journalists refused to see their cities and local cultures labeled by New Yorkers as parochial and simpleminded, representative of a mass-produced, suburban Babbittry.[4] National culture was now truly national in origin and geography, they argued. New York, populated by the lost and the liminal of the world, should not look down its nose at the stable values and populations of the Midwest. George Ade, a nationally known journalist, author and playwright, living happily in small-town Indiana, argued against what he called the "Great Myth" perpetuated throughout the nation that "[e]verything on the wrong side of the Hudson River is Siberia," and that "the sun shines over Fifth Avenue all the time that rain is descending on Omaha." New York, according to Ade, was not only snobbish, its reputation based on myth rather than fact, but also un-American. He described New York's wealth, with thinly veiled anti-Semitism, as "more Oriental than Yankee," with "flash, vulgarity, self-advertising . . . more in evidence than rugged New England traits."[5] In an era of tension around immigration and its possible effects on "American stock," the assumed Northern European heritages of New England cultures and "bloodlines" carried greater than usual racial and cultural capital.

New York's large Jewish population made the city a particularly appealing target for out-of-town critics of the city's national reputation and image. Anti-Semitism had built steadily throughout the twenty-year period of rapidly increasing immigration from Eastern and Southern Europe. The most commonly expressed fear was that Jewish immigrants from the last twenty years had displaced both the more familiar Irish and German immigrants who had arrived in the mid-nineteenth century, as well as the old stock "native" Anglo-American population. A lengthy illustrated article in the popular monthly magazine *World's Work* in 1916 described the achievements of the city's inhabitants in recent years, boasting of New York's size, wealth, and cultural progress. The last seven pages of the sixteen-page article dwelled on New York's Jewish population, suggesting that Jews were both too numerous and too successful. They had arrived as "ragged immigrants" twenty years before and were now "many of them . . . millionaires." Jews, the author suggested, were taking over the city: "They are rapidly becoming New York's largest landowners; . . . They are displacing the Irish from the municipal civil service; nearly all the new appointments now made are Jews." The article included various photographs of New York. Three photographs on one page worked to back up the author's argument about the city's apparent Jewish "problem." One image, entitled "The Ghetto," showed a crowded Lower East Side street, with a caption remarking on the great number of Jews living in the city. Another image, entitled "Lower Fifth Avenue," ran with the caption "The one-time aristocratic residential section of the city, now almost entirely occupied by Jewish dry-goods firms. Every fourth person in the Borough of Manhattan is a Jew."[6] Such rhetoric brought ancient anti-Semitic stereotypes and prejudices into New York's contemporary debates about race, immigration, and the American identity of places and people.

According to this article, not only were the Jews taking over many areas of business and employment, they were also taking over increasing amounts of city space, beyond the confines of the so-called "Ghetto" on the city's Lower East Side. Of course, Jews had lived in many different areas of the city since the founding of New York in the seventeenth century but, for the purposes of this article, it was more convenient to suggest that New York's Jewish community had spread out from one single "Ghetto" area on the East Side. As Deborah Dash Moore has shown, in the 1910s and 1920s, New York's Jews did gradually move out of the overcrowded tenement neighborhoods on the east side to establish communities in other areas of Manhattan, Brooklyn, and the Bronx. However, of more concern to the author of this article was the impression that Jews had begun to encroach on areas of Manhattan regarded as the preserve of the city's Anglo gentry. This apparent incursion, whereby immigrant Jews had "demolished the homes of the Knickerbocker aristocracy on Fifth Avenue . . . and replaced them with clothing factories," showed the power struggle behind anti-Semitism and anti-immigration rhetoric in postwar New York.[7] From the mid-1910s, racial and commercial geographies came under increasing scrutiny and reorganization. The 1916 zoning ordinance, new building codes, and the regional plan of the early 1920s, were all attempts to re-order the city, and to more clearly designate what—and who—belonged in which spaces. Opponents of further Jewish immigration defined the city's Jewish population, particularly working-class Jews, no matter how long their residence in the city, as foreign interlopers into "American" space and culture.[8]

Mapping Race and Politics

In the summer of 1919, State Senator Clayton Lusk headed a committee set up by the New York State Legislature to investigate sedition. Senator Lusk soon went beyond the original rubric for the committee and conducted raids, targeting immigrants as dangerous political radicals, against various institutions in New York City such as the controversial Rand School of Social Science, similar to the infamous raids conducted that same year elsewhere in the nation by U.S. Attorney General Palmer.[9] The Lusk Committee produced a map of New York City based on their investigations, the commercial version of which was entitled "Map of the Borough of Manhattan . . . Showing the Location and Extent of Racial Colonies," issued in 1920 by the A. R. Ohman Company of New York. The large patches of red on the map indicated the neighborhoods inhabited by "Russian, Polish and Other Jews." The map also showed smaller patches of green, yellow, brown, pink, maroon, and black, indicating the presence of other "racial colonies," such as Irish, Chinese, and Italian.[10]

The Racial Colonies map, with its carefully demarcated areas of foreign occupation, suggested the encroachment on all fronts feared by local and national nativists. The non-colored area of Manhattan apparently represented the population that had no race: the "white" Anglo population regarded as native to the city. From north and south, from east and west, the colored areas seemed to close in on the spine of whiteness down the center of Manhattan. The map defined ethnic and national groups as racial groups, in keeping with contemporary notions of racial identity. Popular books on racial identity written at the time by anti-immigrationists and eugenicists, such as Madison Grant's *The Passing of the Great Race* and Lothrop Stoddard's *The Rising Tide of Color*, familiarized a broad American readership with these ideologies. As historian Matthew Jacobson has suggested, American society only gradually recognized Jews and other "probationary whites" as fully "white" or "Caucasian" in the years between the Johnson immigration act of 1924 and the end of World War II. This 1920 map was designed to represent the presence of foreign racial groups, their tendency to live in proximity to one another, and above all to suggest the diminishing space of whiteness.

The map, based on data from 1919, does not suggest the "colored" threat as coming from the city's African American population. By 1920, Harlem in upper Manhattan was beginning its rapid rise as the nation's Black metropolis, due in part to the Post–World War I migration of African Americans from the South to Northern cities such as New York, Detroit, and Chicago. In 1919–1920, with Harlem's sons returning home as war heroes, and their generation's push for civil rights not yet a threat to the white establishment, the city's nativists and conservatives could focus their anxieties on the "racial" and political threat posed by European immigrants. The color red on the map, chosen to represent "Russian, Polish and Other Jews," catches the eye most immediately and carries with it that color's traditional suggestion of danger as well as the more current 1920 association with the political and cultural threat posed by "Reds"—socialists and communists.[11]

In the early and mid-1920s, New York's—and the nation's—pre-eminent African American neighborhood did not have to mount the same arguments about the "American-ness" of its inhabitants as did the Lower East Side. In fact, leading figures in the Harlem Renaissance in the mid-1920s drew attention to the fact that Harlem and its Black population was American, not "foreign." "[T]he language of Harlem is not alien; it is not Italian or Yiddish; it is English. Harlem talks American, reads American, thinks American," wrote James Weldon Johnson in 1925 as he and others of the Talented Tenth pushed Harlem's writers and artists to the attention of the white cultural establishment.[12] Some Black Americans may well have wished to assert their American identity in the face of fierce competition from European immigrants for jobs and for affordable living space. Johnson's comments do carry an anti-immigrant tone, more than a hint of agreement with the Anglo nativists who had so successfully by 1925 campaigned to end continued mass immigration from Southern and Eastern Europe. Whatever tensions may have existed between African-Americans and European immigrants over their claims to "American" identity, to the resurgent Ku Klux Klan, as well as its less violent political allies, both "races" ranked high on their list of undesirables and degenerates in the postwar era.

New York's densely populated immigrant neighborhoods provided an easy target for political scaremongers. The presence in the nation's most important city of such large groups of new immigrants, especially Russian Jews tarred by association with the recent Bolshevik revolution, caused alarm among immigration opponents which they attempted to convey to the larger public via magazine and newspaper articles. In an inflammatory article in the *Forum* magazine in the spring of 1919, journalist John Bruce Mitchell described the city's Lower East Side as "the breeding place of revolt in the New World." According to Mitchell, few realized the extent or pattern of the geography of Bolshevism in New York: "Have you ever been to Forward Hall on East Broadway, the Manhattan Labour Lyceum at 66 East 4th Street, or the Rand School at 133 East 15th Street?" Mitchell, like Senator Lusk and other "red scare" proponents, represented the Jewish neighborhoods of the city's east side as the location of increasing danger, areas fomenting revolt, attacking American political, religious, and cultural values.[13]

Culture, Nostalgia, and "Race"

The voices raised in challenge to New York's American-ness came not only from the pages of national magazines and the Babbitts of the heartland but also from within the city itself. These voices bore the haughty vowels of the Union and Century Clubs, of Gramercy Park and Washington Square. The Knickerbocker and Astor crowds had particular reasons for allying themselves with the cowtown critics. Members of these social elites, many of them "native" New Yorkers and "old stock" Americans, had experienced since the late nineteenth century growing challenges to their economic, social, and cultural power in the city of their birth. By World War I, the population and the power structure of Manhattan seemed increasingly alien to this class of New Yorkers. As sociologist Frederic Cople Jaher has argued: "Most of the Old Guard . . . attributed its demise to demagogues who hoodwinked the bovine masses and to robber barons who seized commercial supremacy from a class too noble to adopt their malevolence. Beleagured patricians saw in democracy, immigration, racial degeneracy, and industrialism the essence of the modern era and the enemies of the fallen elite."[14] Some members of the old elites joined forces in business and marriage with the newer, industrial and financial elites but such alliances did not remove the sense of alienation. Many *nouveau-riche* Anglo railroad entrepreneurs, bankers, and corporate leaders felt no more comfortable in the postwar world than did members of the older blueblood or mercantile elites. The old elites responded to this cultural crisis with efforts to preserve their heritage. Their preservation efforts took various forms—architectural, spatial, and demographic—not the least of which comprised a concerted effort to retain the power of their class and ethnic group by restricting the numbers of immigrants entering the city and the country.[15]

Old stock New Yorkers, those with the least investment in the city's growing consumer economy, felt the most alienated from the cultural changes taking place in the city they had once called their own. This class group, descendants of the old colonial mercantile elite and of the second wave elite of Mrs. Astor's famous "Four Hundred," had a strong attachment to the city, but were devotees of an older version of metropolitan life: a nineteenth-century New York, largely homogenous in terms of race and religion, with social position clearly demarcated, and political power accompanying cultural power. To a generation raised in the 1870s and 1880s, the rapidly changing and increasingly heterogeneous power structure of 1920s New York City, in which political and cultural power spread across a range of elites and constituencies, was bewildering and threatening.

Old "WASP" New Yorkers, facing increasing anxiety about racial superiority in the face of mass immigration into their city, turned to biology, culture, and theories of evolution to bolster their claims to power in the postwar world. In September 1921, New York's American Museum of Natural History (AMNH) hosted the Second International Congress of Eugenics, with an accompanying month-long exhibition. Mrs. Edward H. Harriman, wife of the railroad magnate and Museum Trustee, and herself founder of the Eugenics Record Office at Cold Spring Harbor, in Long Island, contributed $2500 toward the staging of the exhibit. Other patrons included Honorary President of the Congress, Alexander Graham Bell, and Herbert Hoover.[16] The 1921 Congress and exhibit provided a public forum for Old Guard New Yorkers, and their allies around the country, to re-assert their political power in the national and international spotlight, under the cover of a scientific event at one of the city's most prestigious and well-loved institutions.[17] Henry Fairfield Osborn, driving force behind the 1921 Congress and exhibition at AMNH, was a biologist and paleontologist, and became President of the American Museum of Natural History in 1908, having been a curator at the Museum since 1891. Under Osborn's leadership, the AMNH became one of the nation's most important sites for the promotion of eugenics and racial classification, and played a major role in national political debates about immigration.[18]

One of Osborn's chief associates in the popularization of racial and eugenic theories in relation to immigration was fellow-New Yorker and class peer, Madison Grant (1865–1937). Grant, gentleman scholar of natural history, paleontology, and human evolution, knew Osborn both from New York social circles and from their service together on the Museum and the Bronx Zoo's boards of trustees. Like Osborn, Grant came from a well-established and wealthy New York family, with both paternal and maternal roots in the city dating back to colonial times. Madison Grant is best known as the author of the four-times reprinted and revised treatise on the rise and vaunted decline of the "Nordic" race, *The Passing of the Great Race*, first published in 1916. Henry Fairfield Osborn wrote two enthusiastic introductions to later editions of the book.[19] In Grant's view, the new immigration of the 1890s and early years of the twentieth century represented the lowest racial stocks of Europe, the "sweepings of . . . jails and asylums," which European governments were glad to let go. The "whole tone of American life" had been "lowered and vulgarized" by "this human flotsam."[20]

For both Grant and Osborn, present-day immigration from Southern and Eastern Europe into New York, which they observed around them every day, provided evidence for their racial theories. They believed that immigration by the eugenically inferior "Alpine" and "Mediterranean" races was causing the birthrate of "Nordic" Americans to drop "because the poorer classes of Colonial stock, where they still exist, will not bring children into the world to compete in the labor market with the Slovak, the Italian, the Syrian and the Jew." The passivity of the "man of the old stock" meant that "he is to-day being literally driven off the streets of New York City by the swarms of Polish Jews."[21] To Grant, New York represented the epitome of the dire direction in which the "race" was heading. "Large cities from the days of Rome, Alexandria, and Byzantium have always been gathering points of diverse races, but New York is becoming a *cloaca gentium* [human sewer] which will produce many amazing racial hybrids and some ethnic horrors that will be beyond the powers of future anthropologists to unravel." He argued that the conditions of life in large cities such as New York threatened the Nordics and Anglo-Saxon old stock Americans: "The 'survival of the fittest' means the survival of the type best adapted to . . . the tenement and factory, . . . From the point of view of race it were better described as the 'survival of the unfit.' "[22]

The New York daily press covered the papers and discussions at the 1921 eugenics Congress but showed less interest in the exhibit, which suggests that this anti-immigration elite possessed relatively little power to garner mass publicity.[23] Given the muted criticisms contained in some editorial comments on the Congress, it is possible that the editors of the New York dailies deemed the Congress's aims wrong-headed or pernicious. It is also possible that, even if individual newspaper owners or editors agreed with some of the aims of the Congress, they simply wished to avoid alienating their readership and advertisers, many of whom were from immigrant backgrounds. More in keeping with the largely pro-immigrant, anti-racist politics of the city, *The Sun* and *The World* instead ran frontpage stories throughout the month of September 1921 about the resurgence of America's most controversial racist and anti-Semitic organization, the Ku Klux Klan.[24]

Henry Fairfield Osborn and Madison Grant's mourning for the decline of Nordic civilization fit with the larger sense of loss or embattlement felt by others of their class and generation in New York. The image of Old Guard New Yorkers Osborn and Grant, ensconced in their Museum on the Upper West Side, carefully preserving the remains of sundry dinosaurs while railing against the purported near extinction of their own species, is telling. Nostalgia for an apparently lost New York, a New York that existed before the new immigration, preoccupied many of the city's upper classes. Largely recalling and extolling the virtues of the 1870s and 1880s, their publications and activities represented another attempt to lay claim to the city and its identity. However, unlike Henry Fairfield Osborn or Madison Grant, the majority of these writers were not committed to a political program to undo the demographic and cultural changes wrought in the city since the turn of the century. They seemed more resigned to the end of their era and content to describe it nostalgically for their own satisfaction.[25]

Since the Hudson–Fulton celebration in 1909, efforts to preserve New York's Anglo-Dutch past had become more popular. Bastions of the city's Old Guard such as the City History Club, the New-York Historical Society, and branches of patriotic genealogical organizations such as the Colonial Dames of America, sponsored local history and preservation activities. Such activities gained greater momentum in the late teens and after World War I, with major efforts such as the rebuilding of Theodore Roosevelt's birthplace at 28 East 20th Street following his death in 1919, and the building and opening of the American Wing at the Metropolitan Museum of Art in November 1924.[26] Elaborate events marking an anniversary or other commemoration had become increasingly popular in the early twentieth century. Referencing older traditions of parades and fairs, the historical pageants staged by patriotic organizations in large cities such as New York represented the re-assertion of an older order, and laid claim to a past frequently not shared by more recent inhabitants.

A New Itinerary and A New Geography

The vast array of images of immigrants in newspapers and popular national magazines, while helping to generate support for immigration restriction, also peaked readers' curiosity about such foreign racial types and their cultures. Certainly by the early 1920s, art, fashion, literature, and the tourist industry all catered to a new interest in ideas of the "primitive," and in the "picturesque" qualities of peoples and cultures regarded as having retained "old world" ways of life, culture, dress, and language. It was a romantic, consumerist reinterpretation of the racial typing and classifying promoted by anti-immigration advocates.[27]

The 1920s witnessed the maturation of the American consumer economy as a result of higher wages, mass production, national distribution of material goods, and a highly effective advertising industry. A crucial component of the decade's aura of mass material progress was the automobile. The number of automobiles in the United States increased twenty times between 1913 and 1931; by the end of the 1920s, over twenty percent of Americans owned cars.[28] This increased mobility, along with increasing leisure time and even paid vacations for some workers, drew more Americans out onto the nation's roadways or railways as tourists. By the early 1920s, guidebooks claimed New York received about 200,000 visitors per day. While this number probably included a range of regular daily visitors—from suburban shoppers to traveling salesmen—it does indicate both the popularity of New York as a sightseeing destination and the economic value of such visitors to many of the city's businesses.[29]

Representations of New York's immigrant populations and neighborhoods as enhancements to the city's entertainment facilities became increasingly common in the descriptive literature about the city in the mid- and late-1920s. While older guides to the city's attractions had included the immigrant neighborhoods on their itineraries, they did so in terms of "slumming" trips, as slightly risky excursions marginal to the main itinerary, revealing populations largely marginal to the city's life and identity. As new laws gradually reduced the numbers of new immigrants to a relative trickle, authors and publishers of tourist literature more confidently recommended the city's ethnic neighborhoods to sightseers.

The city presented in New York guidebooks since the urban tourism trade had started its boom in the 1890s was a site of commercial consumption, edited and described most often by a corporate, not an individual, author. The old New York of George Foster's or James McCabe's sensationalist guides from the 1850s to the 1880s had given way to an image of New York sponsored by a downtown hotel, or seen via a souvenir album of views supplied courtesy of a soap company, or published by the local newspaper company and sent with the compliments of the local church.[30] For example, *How to Know New York*, published in 1887 in Boston by the Rand Avery Company, an early example of this trend, was compiled under the sponsorship of the Grand Union Hotel, though this is not stated explicitly. The guidebook's title page mentions the hotel as the starting point of their itinerary, the second page of the guide is an advertisement for the hotel, the introduction mentions the hotel, and two pages of advice to the reader depict a visitor getting useful information from a hotel clerk at the Grand Union Hotel, at which establishment the reader was recommended to stay while in the city. As business products, largely funded by selling advertising space, the style and content of the guides changed considerably from those of the mid-nineteenth century. The city presented to visitors in these publications was a city of hotels, of manufacturing and retail establishments, of commercial institutions featured in the guide itself or pictured in its advertising spaces. The personal tone of an individual author, warning of thrilling urban dangers or extolling the virtues of the city's leading politicians, was replaced in the early twentieth century by a corporate anonymity and by the blandness of boosterism.

During the 1920s, the tone and range of travel writing and guidebooks changed somewhat, allowing for a more personal tone to re-emerge. Individually authored magazine articles about travel excursions and travel memoirs increasingly appealed to the more well-to-do traveler. The authors of such materials were, or presented themselves as being, from the well-educated background assumed of their intended readers, though the authors' ethnic backgrounds were left unstated. Thus, an upper-middle-class Anglo reader might comfortably, though not necessarily correctly, assume she shared a cultural perspective with the author. Certainly, the manner in which such writers presented New York's "ethnic" neighborhoods suggested they found them as "foreign" as might their readers.

By the mid-1920s, these travel writers encouraged their readers to understand that Little Italy, Chinatown, and the "Ghetto," had become part of the mainstream tourist itinerary and were as accessible and as safe to explore as any other area of the city. This growing genre of travel literature, aimed at the burgeoning American tourist classes, served to counteract contemporary Anglo-Saxonism and nativism by re-describing New York's immigrant neighborhoods as picturesque and available for consumption. In this manner, the images and rhetoric of tourist guidebooks and travel literature worked to argue for a new, multicultural version of American identity, in keeping with the contemporary arguments of Randolph Bourne and Horace Kallen.

This commercial, tourist industry spin on erstwhile undesirable populations and neighborhoods took specific issue, in the immediate postwar period, with the images of immigrants produced by eugenicists and nativists calling for immigration restriction. Popular national monthly magazines such as the *Saturday Evening Post*, *Literary Digest*, *Good Housekeeping*, and *Collier's* ran scores of articles in the 1910s and early 1920s touting eugenicist arguments for immigration restriction.[31] Not only did these articles run in major popular magazines, but they were also authored by well-known Americans whose opinions carried great weight: President-elect Calvin Coolidge wrote an article entitled "Whose Country Is This?" for *Good Housekeeping* in 1921; George Creel, who had led the U.S. government's wartime propaganda unit, the Committee on Public Information, wrote an article for *Collier's* magazine that same year entitled "Melting Pot or Dumping Ground?" These articles argued that immigrants from Eastern and Southern Europe were physically and mentally defective, diseased, criminal, and racially unassimilable. Often accompanied by photographs of Ellis Island, or of New York's Lower East Side, these articles posed a threat to the tourist industry boosters' positive "spin" on the city (figure 6.1).

To counteract such widespread negative propaganda about New York's immigrants, guidebook publishers and travel writers promoting the city to middle-class American tourists knew that, despite the obvious contradiction, they needed to market New York as both American and un-American, as offering both the reassurance of familiarity as well as the excitement of difference. Therefore, while promoting the more conventional attractions of the theater district's Great White Way, they also sold Little Italy, Chinatown, and the Ghetto as New York attractions, contradicting the interpretations offered by Coolidge, Creel, and others.[32]

Throughout the early 1920s, producers of tourist guides and other travel literature and ephemera worked to re-position New York's immigrant

Figure 6.1 This image, accompanying an article by well-known government propagandist George Creel, entitled "Meeting Pot or Dumping?" appeared in *Collier's* magazine, September 3, 1921. The accompanying photographic images of disheveled and infirm-looking immigrants serves as an example of how anti-immigration and eugenicest forces used photography to support their effort. New York tourism promoters could not then easily re-deploy similar photographic images of immigrants in guidebooks or other tourist ephemera encouraging tourists to visit the city's immigrant neighborhoods. Travel and guidebook writers instead turned to non-photographic illustrations to convey the supposed charms of the Lower East Side's ethnic neighborhoods

neighborhoods within the American tourist itinerary by marketing to tourists those immigrant cultures and neighborhoods with the best potential to offer positive consumer experiences, and the least vulnerability to American post-war politics of race and national identity. This "re-spinning" of New York's foreign peoples and places as part of an American's tour of his/her own country served to Americanize the always-suspect identity of New York while maintaining enough sense of difference to make the tour worthwhile. The tourist and travel industry achieved this seeming sleight of hand by editing their itineraries, moving away from photographic representations, and by continually working with the lexicon of contemporary racism if only to undermine its anti-immigration intent.

Itineraries recommended in guides and travel literature published in the early and mid-1920s worked to draw a broad middle class of tourists into a variety of New York neighborhoods, including selected immigrant areas. *Rider's New York City*, one of a series of Rider's guides to American cities that began publication shortly before World War I, aimed to attract a broad middle-class readership. The editor, author, and compiler Fremont Rider modeled the guides on the well-established Baedeker guidebook series in Europe. Baedekers were part of every American tourist's equipment for seeing Europe in the 1910s and 1920s. As T.S. Eliot suggested in his 1920 poem "Burbank With a Baedeker: Bleistein With a Cigar," the carrying of a Baedeker connoted "American tourist" in pre- and Post–World War I Europe. Rider's *Guides* imitated the Baedekers, both in the presentation of itineraries tailored to a particular length of stay, and in the use of asterisks to denote especially significant sites or highly recommended restaurants and hotels. For middle- and upper-middle-class Americans developing the habit of tourism in their own country, Rider's overt referencing of the Baedeker guides suggested the suitability of the destinations described.[33]

In his 1923 guide to New York, Rider offered both a fourteen-day and a five-day itinerary for visitors with limited amounts of time. His fourteen-day itinerary included a visit to the "foreign quarters" during the afternoon of the sixth day. He listed the Italian quarter, Chinatown, and the "Yiddish and Russian" quarters, giving the street locations of each, but warning readers of the "long walk through narrow, sordid streets, teeming with an overcrowded population . . . ." Only those visitors most determined to go in search of the urban picturesque were likely to follow up on such a backhanded recommendation. In the brief five-day itinerary, Rider left out the "Yiddish and Russian" quarters, sending his readers only to the Italian quarter and to Chinatown.[34] The foreign cultures of Italy and China, consumed in the form of immigrant communities in America, Rider apparently regarded as more palatable to American tourists. Although both carried somewhat unsavory reputations for violence and gang-oriented skulduggery, nonetheless guidebook writers more easily promoted these two "colorful" cultures as picturesque and quaint. Especially in the context of the postwar redscare, with anti-Semitic and anti-immigration rhetoric running high, authors such as Rider more readily excised from their itineraries the predominantly Jewish neighborhoods of New York that offered the wrong sort of "otherness." Chinatown and Little Italy had longer established traditions of satisfying the visiting "slummer" with curio shops, restaurants, music, and festivals, whereas Jewish neighborhoods offered comparatively few opportunities for ethnic consumption.[35]

Beginning in the mid-1920s, guidebook and travel writers more frequently encouraged tourists to explore ethnic neighborhoods on their own, taking self-guided walking tours with the aid of a guidebook. Freed from fears of exploring these neighborhoods, and from the tyranny of the sightseeing bus with its set itinerary and its pat megaphone narratives, tourists could create for themselves a more personal experience of the city, a tailored search for ethnic authenticity. After the 1924 immigration act, ethnic neighborhoods may have seemed less "foreign" than before the war. By the late 1920s, large numbers of the neighborhoods' inhabitants had grown up in New York, or been born in the city. They formed a more assimilated, more "modern" generation of ethnic New Yorkers. It is also worth considering that this dynamic may have been complicated by second- or third-generation "ethnics," in search of the "old neighborhood" or other connections to their past, themselves forming part of the late-1920s clientele for these visits to "ethnic" New York. Regardless of the visitor's background, ethnic neighborhoods in the late 1920s offered a mix of safety, accessibility, and reassuring impressions of assimilation and Americanization while also still offering the thrill of an authentically foreign experience.[36]

In the fall of 1925, *Outlook* magazine published an article by well-known New York Italian-American writer Edward Corsi which suggests the tensions at play between consumers, the business of tourism, and racial politics over the perception or promotion of places and people as either "foreign" or "American." Entitled "My Neighborhood," the headline under the article title read: "Edward Corsi finds in the polyglot boarding-house of New York the makings of the America of to-morrow. It is an article to make Americans of the old stock pause and think." Corsi's article captured the contradictory argument made by writers encouraging people to visit immigrant neighborhoods that the area was both American *and* foreign: American enough that "Americans of the old stock" should not denigrate its inhabitants, but foreign enough that tourists might patronize the neighborhood, making the most of a vanishing "old world" culture.[37]

Corsi suggested that it was New York's multiracial, multicultural population, not that of its perceived Midwestern or New England "heartland," which represented America's future and formed the nation's emerging identity. Corsi quoted an immigrant intellectual friend from the neighborhood who claimed that when the "Great American Novel" eventually appeared "its background will not be Main Street, but the East Side of New York. Its central figure, furthermore, will not be a Babbitt or a New England farmer or a Kentucky colonel, but an immigrant's son, a child of the melting-pot." His friend insisted that "the East Side, with its peoples from many lands, speaking many tongues, and gradually building a civilization which, in the end, will be ours and not Europe's, is America." Corsi explained his friend's unconventional viewpoint to his implied Anglo, middle-class readership by describing how the limited geography of the city's immigrants affected their concept of "America": "to the Italian mother on Mulberry Street, imprisoned in her four-room flat, or to the overworked Jewish tailor on East Broadway . . . 'America' is a hodge-podge of toiling millions, tenements, crowded subways, busy sweatshops, and fenced-in playgrounds—in other words the East Side."[38] By implication, his immigrant friend's perspective on America was similarly shaped by his immersion in an immigrant neighborhood.

Both crusaders for immigration restriction and promoters of tourism within New York's "racial" neighborhoods discussed the city's immigrants as physical as well as cultural types. Being able to identify visually a Russian Jew, a Syrian, an Italian, or a Greek comprised an important aspect of the tourist's encounter with the authentically foreign. Building on the physical, racial typing familiar to middle-class readers from periodical articles and from contemporary notions of race, tourism promoters and torchbearers for the immigrant neighborhoods echoed the images and language of scientific racism.

Tourists came in search of what guidebooks and travel articles referred to as the "real" Jew or the "real" Italian. Hutchins Hapgood, a well-known chronicler of the Jewish Lower East Side, described the "real Jew" as one who "remains steadfastly faithful to the spirit of the old culture . . . whether he be push-cart peddler, scholar, or worshiper in the synagogue." The location of the "real" Jews, the New York Ghetto, Hapgood argued, "when interpreted by the sympathetic artist" was "deeply picturesque."[39] Edward Corsi encouraged readers to see the foreign-ness of his immigrant neighborhood, visible not only in "the flags of many colors, [and] the foreign papers on every news-stand, but [also] in the types one meets on the streets—tall blond Nordics, olive-skinned, dark-haired Mediterraneans, long-bearded Semites and Slavs, massive Africans, East Indians, gypsies, Japs, and Chinese." The terms Corsi used, such as "Nordic" and "Mediterranean," borrowed directly from the racial typologies that were first delineated at the turn of the century by social scientists such as W. Z. Ripley, and further popularized and legitimized by Madison Grant and others. But Corsi warned his readers that the quaint, picturesque Old World as represented in his neighborhood would soon disappear: "America's doors are fast closing, and the tide of a new civilization, . . . which is not Anglo-Saxon or Latin or Slav, but 'American,' is setting in."[40] Corsi suggested that the assimilation deemed impossible and even undesirable by immigration restrictionists was indeed occurring. While Corsi seemed to welcome such assimilation in terms of the greater security and respect it brought to immigrants, he also seemed to regret its coming as it would break down the distinct foreign racial types and cultures so appealing to tourists and, apparently, to him.

Unlike the articles and books calling for immigration restriction, tourist literature encouraging ethnic tourism depicted the supposedly available ethnic types, the "real" Jews and Italians and their neighborhoods, using images that avoided photographic realism. Instead, guidebooks and travel literature used pencil, charcoal or ink-wash sketches, often by well known artists, photography's reform connotations. Artists and illustrators, well known to many readers from their books of sketches or their illustrations in magazines, hired to work on tourist literature included E. H. Suydam, Vernon Howe Bailey, Joseph Pennell, and Loren Stout. The extensive use of pen and ink illustration, at a time when neither cost nor technology inhibited the reproduction of photographic images, came about because, by the postwar period, most middle-class Americans could not view photographic images of immigrants and their neighborhoods without their conjuring negative connotations. From Jacob Riis's 1890s photographs of New York's tenement neighborhoods, to Lewis Hine's images of Ellis Island immigrants, to eugenicist images of "undesirable aliens," photography had for too long served the aims of reform movements to allow its successful use by businesses invested in the promotion of the city's immigrant neighborhoods as tourist attractions.[41]

In an early example of this trend in illustration, Caroline Singer, an accomplished travel writer, focused her attention in 1921 on an Italian neighborhood in New York's Lower East Side. Singer made specific reference at the start of her article to the contrast between old and new representations of New York's immigrant neighborhoods. The conventional but, she suggested, outdated image of this neighborhood was of "framed silhouettes of family groups sitting with hunched shoulders about allotments of piece-work," a reference recalling old photographs of the Lower East Side taken by Jacob Riis and other social reformers, still familiar to most of her readers. The new view she and her illustrator, Cyrus LeRoy Baldridge, provided was from the consumer's perspective, taking pleasure in "the pageants of the market-place, the plumed marionettes of Mulberry Bend, and the softly flaring tapers of the holy feast." Baldridge's images of the neighborhood's streets and people emphasized the picturesque details of craggy-visaged old men, cluttered vegetable markets, and dark-eyed, dark-haired young Italian women. The images were captioned either with quotations from Singer's text, adding to the veracity of her account, or with titles such as "A twentieth-century Mona Lisa," "The blind flute-player," and "A Madonna of the balcony," providing another layer of ethnic romance. The use of quality illustrations, with their romantic and picturesque connotations, evoked (as with Rider's guides) the elite pleasures of the European tour, equating New York neighborhoods and their middle-class tourists with well-established but more exclusive travel experiences.[42]

This new tourist literature, whether article, guidebook or collection of travel essays, made direct appeal to a female audience. Writers and publishers knew that American women comprised a large proportion of the touring classes, and participated in decisions about where to travel and what to do on vacation. Increasingly, starting in the 1920s and growing in numbers in the 1930s, women also wrote guidebooks and travel features, placing more emphasis on assurances of comfort and safety; guidebooks included many more details about shops and shopping, including what one could buy in the small shops and pushcart markets of the Lower East Side. The illustrations accompanying these articles or guidebook chapters featured women and children, not as the victims of poverty but as characters in vibrant neighborhood scenes. The two female authors of *New York in Seven Days*, published in 1925, constructed their tourist narrative through the eyes of a fictional male protagonist guiding a female acquaintance around the city. This knowledgeable male guide reassures his female companion as she hesitates on the borders of Chinatown that he knows "many women" who come to the area "alone or in pairs to shop." The two browse the shops of "Brasstown," a commercial district in the Jewish quarter, and he suggests she return alone on Sunday to see the local Orthodox population of bearded men and bewigged women.[43]

However, the still-thorny issue of urban geography tempered guidebook and travel writers' perceptions of the immigrants as "picturesque." Most regarded such populations as picturesque only when they remained within their ethnically defined neighborhoods. One writer encouraged his readers to experience New York's foreign neighborhoods, to see the "magic and mystery of the Orient" in Chinatown, or the "veritable Naples" of Little

Italy. But he also described those same immigrants as a potential threat. Referring to the sight of striking workers marching on Fifth Avenue, he wrote: "There was not an American face in the entire twenty-five thousand . . . It was an object lesson as to whose are the hands into which we are throwing control of our country."[44]

If visitors stayed within the geography of immigrant neighborhoods, as promoted by the tourist trade, they need have no fears, but could instead relish the opportunity for a form of world travel, moving from one "country" to the next, as they strolled around the city. Journalist and author Konrad Bercovici described New York in the mid-1920s as "not a city but a world." Like the anti-immigration campaigners and red-scare proponents, guidebook and travel writers mapped the location and borders of New York's immigrant neighborhoods. Bercovici's *Around the World in New York*, for example, took the reader through "Africa," "Greece," "China," and various other "countries."[45] Despite his book's echoes of more conservative versions of the city's foreign geographies, as seen in the "Racial Colonies" map of 1920, Bercovici's imagined map of New York suggested orderly consumer pleasures, not political, racial threats. Norman Borchardt's illustrations offered pleasing interpretations of Bercovici's text, featuring foreign-looking streets and people whose appearance exuded charm not menace.

This type of literature seeking to boost the city, to promote the immigrant neighborhoods as attractions, and locate the urban picturesque had its counterpart in the tourist brochure maps of the late 1920s and the 1930s. Brightly colored and frequently covered in cartoon images or caricatures of ethnic or urban "types" meant to represent a particular neighborhood, these maps depicted the whole of Manhattan as a site of easy entertainment. Earlier maps designed for tourists had mostly comprised fold-out appendices to guidebooks and usually showed only practical information such as major railroad, elevated, and subway lines, and perhaps a handful of well-known sites such as the Metropolitan Museum, Trinity Church, and the American Museum of Natural History. Beginning in the late 1920s, map and guidebook publishers, banks, hotels, sightseeing companies, and independent mapmakers issued brochure maps of New York, available in bookstores, hotel lobbies, newsstands, railroad offices, and other commercial venues frequented by visitors. Building on the work done by the guidebooks and travel literature of the mid-1920s, these maps displayed the changes brought by new zoning laws that had banned garment lofts and their Jewish immigrant workers from Fifth Avenue. The racial "others" now stayed in their own neighborhoods—more convenient for tourists and more acceptable to white, Anglo New Yorkers. These maps presented a city open for exploration by the visitor, designating all parts of the city as equally part of the tourist itinerary.[46]

The open, city-wide territories of the tourist maps represented the successful commodification of the city's space by the 1930s. The dominance of New York by a mass consumer economy, underway in the city since the turn of the century, shifted the center of political and economic power away from the old Anglo-Saxon elites toward new immigrant entrepreneurs deeply embedded in the new economy as retailers, bankers, property developers, mass entertainment moguls, and advertisers. The promulgation of the immigrant neighborhoods as tourist attractions on a par with the Metropolitan Museum and Broadway resulted from the successful re-casting of New York's image in the mid- and late-1920s by the rising business elites of the city. Working with their class and ethnic peers in the city government, this new breed of boosters re-organized and re-packaged New York City, creating a new, less stratified geography.

Throughout the 1920s and on into the 1930s, racial categories remained critically important in the United States, but the uses to which they were put shifted. As historians of world's fairs and other "public amusements" have shown, experiencing the "other" as entertainment had a long history by the 1920s, and continues to be an important aspect of contemporary tourism. Although nativist forces seemed to win the day in 1924, in fact their power to influence the image of New York was already waning. By the mid-1920s, organized commercial forces, led by New York's businessmen's associations, had already amassed far more capital—financial and cultural—than the "old stock" nativists. Conscious of their diverse constituencies, both the city government and the trade associations became adept in the 1920s at marketing both the immigrant neighborhoods and Times Square as native to New York, part of the city's identity as both American and un-American. An important part of that project, running parallel with the re-spinning of the city's "foreign quarters," was the invention of Midtown as New York's brand image, its avowedly American heart.

Notes

1. Ford Madox Ford, *New York Is Not America* (New York: Albert and Charles Boni, 1927), 107. See especially chapters four and five. Ford Madox Hueffer (1873–1939), changed his last name to Ford after World War I. Ford, perhaps best known for his novel *The Good Soldier* (1915) was a novelist, essayist, and literary review editor whose circle of acquaintances included Gertrude Stein and others of the American ex-patriate circle in Paris in the war period and the 1920s, as well as most of the leading younger writers in London both before and after the war. See Alan Judd, *Ford Madox Ford* (Cambridge, MA: Harvard University Press, 1991), and Bernard J. Poli, *Ford Madox Ford and the Transatlantic Review* (Syracuse: Syracuse University Press, 1967).

2. John Higham, *Strangers in the Land: Patterns of American Nativism, 1865–1925* (New Brunswick: Rutgers University Press, 1955). On early twentieth-century immigration, see also Alan M. Kraut, *Silent Travelers: Germs, Genes, and the "Immigrant Menace"* (Baltimore: Johns Hopkins University Press, 1994).

3. For studies of Post–World War I American culture and politics see Michael E. Parrish, *Anxious Decades: America in Prosperity and Depression, 1920–1941* (New York: W.W. Norton, 1992); Lynn Dumenil *The Modern Temper: American Culture and Society in the 1920s* (New York: Hill and Wang, 1995); Frederick Lewis Allen, *Only Yesterday: An Informal History of the 1920s* (New York: Harper and Brothers, 1931); Arthur M. Schlesinger, Jr., *The Crisis of the Old Order, 1919–1933* (Boston: Houghton Mifflin, 1957); William E.

Leuchtenburg, *The Perils of Prosperity, 1914–1932* (Chicago: University of Chicago Press, 1958); Lawrence Levine, "Progress and Nostalgia," in *The Unpredictable Past: Explorations in American Cultural History* (New York: Oxford University Press, 1993); T.J. Jackson Lears, *No Place of Grace: Antimodernism and the Transformation of American Culture, 1880–1920* (New York: Pantheon, 1981).

4. Sinclair Lewis's novel *Babbitt* (New York: Harcourt, Brace and Company, 1922), satirized life in the fictional town of Zenith, located in the Midwest, and became both a bestseller and cultural shorthand for contemporary suburban consumerism, and small town social conformity. Sherwood Anderson wrote harsher condemnations of small town American life and values. See Anderson's *Winesburg, Ohio: A Group of Tales of Ohio Small Town Life* (New York: B.W. Huebsch, 1919).

5. George Ade, "Oh, Yes! We Will Visit New York—But We'll Pin a Return Ticket Inside Our Vest," *The American Magazine* 91 (March 1921): 14–15. Other examples of this debate about New York are Mark Sullivan, "Why the West Dislikes New York: The Eternal Conflict Between City and Country," *World's Work* 51 (February 1926): 406–411; "Why A Cartoonist Would Rather Live in Des Moines Than in New York," *Literary Digest* 62 (July 12, 1919): 86–90; Editorial, "New York City as the World's Prize 'Borough of Bunk'," *Literary Digest* 70 (August 27, 1921): 37–38. Part of this debate about New York focused on especially contentious neighborhoods, such as Greenwich Village. See, for example, "The Lure of Greenwich Village," *Literary Digest* 65 (May 8, 1920): 46–47, and "Greenwich Village Virus," *Saturday Evening Post* 194 (October 15, 1921): 14–15.

6. James Middleton, "New York the Stupendous," *World's Work* 31 (March 1916): 538–554. See also Editorial, "One million six hundred and forty-three thousand Jews in New York City," *World's Work* 47 (November 1923): 20–22. For more on the geography of New York's Jews, see Deborah Dash Moore, *At Home in America: Second Generation New York Jews* (New York: Columbia University Press, 1981) and her article, "On the Fringes of the City: Jewish Neighborhoods in Three Boroughs," in David Ward and Olivier Zunz, *Landscape of Modernity: New York City, 1900–1940* (New York: Russo II Suge Foundaton, 1992).

7. Middleton, 554.

8. M. Christine Boyer, *Dreaming the Rational City: The Myth of American City Planning* (Cambridge, MA: MIT Press, 1983), 91–95, 155–159, 178–185. See also Keith Revell, "Regulating the Landscape: Real Estate Values, City Planning, and the 1916 Zoning Ordinance," in Ward and Zunz, *Landscape of Modernity*, 19–45; Robert Fishman, "The Regional Plan and the Transformation of the Industrial Metropolis," ibid., 106–125.

9. The Rand School was an adult education facility sponsored by the Socialist Party, founded in 1905. Although many of its faculty and students were socialists, the faculty also included such non-socialist luminaries as Charles Beard and John Dewey. For more on the Rand School, see Mari Jo Buhle, Paul Buhle, and Dan Georgakas, eds., *Encyclopedia of the American Left* (New York: Garland, 1990). The Rand School and other New York institutions and publications were named as sources of high school students' knowledge of Bolshevism, according to an article in the *Literary Digest* in July 1919. According to the article, a questionnaire given to high school students in the city that summer revealed publications such as *The New Republic*, *The Nation*, the New York *Call*, and *The Liberator*, as well as the Rand School, as sources of Bolshevik

information. See "Bolshevism in New York and Russian Schools," *Literary Digest* 62 (July 5, 1919): 40–41.

10. The original version of the map, as used by the Lusk Committee, is housed in the New York State Archives at Albany. A photograph of the map can be found in Paul E. Cohen and Robert T. Augustyn, eds., *Manhattan in Maps, 1527–1995* (New York: Rizzoli, 1997).

11. Madison Grant, *The Passing of the Great Race*, 4th ed., (New York: Scribner's, 1921); Lothrop Stoddard, *The Rising Tide of Color Against White World-Supremacy* (New York: Charles Scribner's Sons, 1920); Matthew Frye Jacobson, *Whiteness of a Different Color: European Immigrants and the Alchemy of Race* (Cambridge, MA: Harvard University Press, 1998), 75–90, 92–102, 176. See also David Roediger, *The Wages of Whiteness: Race and the Making of the American Working Class* (London: Verso, 1991).

12. James Weldon Johnson, "Harlem: The Cultural Capital," in *The New Negro*, ed. Alain Locke, quoted in David Levering Lewis, *When Harlem Was In Vogue* (New York: Oxford University Press, 1989), 113.

13. John Bruce Mitchell, " 'Reds' in New York Slums: How Insidious Doctrines are Propagated in New York's 'East Side,' " *The Forum* 61 (April 1919): 442–455. See also Nicholas M. Butler, "Our Bolshevik Menace," *The Forum* 63 (January 1920): 49–56; Franklin M. Giddings, "Bolsheviki Must Go," *Independent* 97 (January 18, 1919): 88; Editorial, "Is Bolshevism in America Becoming a Real Peril?" *Current Opinion* 67 (July 1919): 4–6; Editorial, "How the Russian Bolshevik Agent Does Business in New York City," *Literary Digest* 61 (May 17, 1919): 60–63; Clayton R. Lusk, "Hatching Revolution in America," *Current Opinion* 71 (September 1921): 290–294 and "Radicalism Under Inquiry," *Review of Reviews* 61 (February 1920): 167–171.

14. Frederic Cople Jaher, *The Urban Establishment: Upper Strata in Boston, New York, Charleston, Chicago, and Los Angeles* (Urbana: University of Illinois Press, 1982), 276.

15. The Immigration Restriction League, though founded in 1894 by a group of Boston Brahmin Harvard classmates, attracted members from other North East elites, especially old New Yorkers. On membership in the League, see Higham, *Strangers in the Land*, 102. See also Jaher, *Urban Establishment*.

16. Fundraising form letter, from Henry Fairfield Osborn. Henry Fairfield Osborn Papers; Correspondence: Organizations; Eugenics: Second International Congress, 1921. Archives, Department of Library Services—Special Collections, American Museum of Natural History.

17. Robert W. Rydell, *World of Fairs: The Century-of-Progress Expositions* (Chicago: University of Chicago Press, 1993), 47–48.

18. Details of Henry Fairfield Osborn's family background and career are from Ronald Rainger, *An Agenda for Antiquity: Henry Fairfield Osborn and Vertebrate Paleontology at the American Museum of Natural History, 1890–1935* (Tuscaloosa: University of Alabama, 1991). See Osborn's own works relevant to this chapter, such as Henry Fairfield Osborn, *Men of the Old Stone Age: Their Environment, Life and Art* (New York: Scribners, 1915); "Our Ancestors Arrive in Scandinavia," *Natural History* 22 (1922): 116–134; "The Approach to the Immigration Problem Through Science," *Proceedings of the National Immigration Conference*, No. 26 (1924): 44–53. On Osborn's involvement in the evolution debates of the 1920s, see his *Evolution and Religion* (New York: Scribners, 1923). Some of the most significant criticism

of Osborn's views came from Franz Boas, a colleague at the American Museum of Natural History, who was already one of America's most respected anthropologists by the second decade of the twentieth century. See, for example, Franz Boas, *The Mind of Primitive Man* (New York: The Macmillan Company, 1911). For Boas's views of Osborn and others' eugenical beliefs and "scientific racism," see Boas, "Question of Racial Purity," *American Mercury* 3 (October 1924): 163–169, "This Nordic Nonsense," *Forum* 74 (October 1925): 502–511, and "Fallacies of Racial Inferiority," *Current History* 25 (February 1927): 676–682. See also the very popular works of his pupils, Margaret Mead, *Coming of Age in Samoa* (New York: William Morrow, 1928) and Zora Neale Hurston, *Mules and Men* (Philadelphia, London: J.B. Lippincott Company, 1935).

19. Grant, *Great Race*. Grant later went on to write other books on the issue of race and immigration in the United States, such as *The Conquest of a Continent, or, the Expansion of Races in America* (New York: Scribners, 1933) and, with Charles Stewart Davison, *The Alien in Our Midst; or, "Selling our birthright for a mess of pottage"* (New York: The Galton Publishing Company, Inc., 1930).

20. Grant, *Great Race*, 89–90.

21. Ibid., 91.

22. Ibid., 92.

23. "Melting Pot Has Proved Failure in America as Vices of Mingled Races Are Perpetuated," New York *World*, September 23, 1921, p. 3; "Nature Leader of Man in Mechanics," ibid., September 24, 1921, p. 9; "Warns of Race Decline," ibid., September 25, 1921, p. 9; "Eugenist Denies Bars To Marriage Can Improve Race," ibid., September 27, 1921, p. 7. In the New York *Sun*, see "Noted Scientists Here For Eugenics Conference," September 22, 1921, p. 2; "Questions Darwinian Theory," September 24, 1921, p. 2; "Decries Beauty in Picking Mate," September 27, 1921, p. 9; "Race War Seen In Class Clash," September 28, 1921, p. 8. in the *New York Times*, see "Tracing Parentage By Eugenic Tests," September 23, 1921, p. 8; "Want More Babies in Best Families," September 25, 1921, p. 16; "Eugenists Uphold Control of Birth/Scientists Come Out for Limitation of Families Where Poverty and Disease Are Perils," September 27, 1921, p. 20; "Sees American Man as Superior of Woman," September 28, 1921, p. 11. See also editorial in New York *World*, September 26, 1921, p. 10; see also "America and the Man," New York *Sun*, September 27, 1921, p. 16, and "Who Are The 'Fittest'?" same paper, September 28, 1921, p. 14.

24. See, for example "Ku Klux Klan Used Army and Navy Club Address to Peddle Memberships in Campaign By Mail; The World Reproduces 'Grand Goblin' Documents," New York *World*, September 8, 1921, front page. The KKK remained on *The World*'s front page for the rest of the month.

25. Books of nostalgic reminiscences published by this generation included James H. Callender, *Yesterdays in Little Old New York* (New York: Dorland Press, 1929) and Charles Townsend Harris, *Memories of Manhattan in the Sixties and Seventies* (New York: The Derrydale Press, 1928). See also Editorial, "The old Bowery wouldn't know itself now," *Literary Digest* 65 (May 8, 1920): 70–75; Robert and Elizabeth Shackleton, "Vanishing New York," *The Century Magazine* 100 (June 1920): 150–164; Theodore Dreiser, *The Color of a Great City.* (New York: Boni and Liverwright, 1923); Mrs. J. B. Harriman,

"Hither and Yon," two-part series of articles on old New York, *The Century Magazine* 106 (September 1923): 651–663 and (October 1923): 873–886; Herbert Asbury's articles in *The American Mercury*, late 1920s, such as "Days of Wickedness," vol. 12 (November 1927): 359–369.

26. For more on both preservation activities in New York, and the history of the preservation movement throughout the United States, see Charles B. Hosmer, Jr., *Presence of the Past: A History of the Preservation Movement in the United States Before Williamsburg* (New York: G.P. Putnam's Sons, 1965); Susan Porter Benson, et al., *Presenting the Past: Essays on History and the Public* (Philadelphia: Temple University Press, 1986).

27. On "primitivism" in American art and culture in the early twentieth century, see Warren Susman's essay on concepts of "civilization" in the 1920s in his *Culture As History* (New York: Pantheon, 1984); for New York specifically, see Ann Douglas, *Terrible Honesty: Mongrel Manhattan in the 1920s* (New York: Farrar, Straus, Giroux, 1995) and W. Jackson Rushing, *Native American Art and the New York Avant-Garde: A History of Cultural Primitivism* (Austin: University of Texas Press, 1995). For a broader study, see Marianna Torgovnik, *Gone Primitive: Savage Intellects, Modern Lives* (Chicago: University of Chicago Press, 1990). For the theoretical background of primitivism and early anthropology, see James Clifford, *The Predicament of Culture* (Cambridge, MA.: Harvard University Press, 1988).

28. Lynn Dumenil, *The Modern Temper: American Culture and Society in the 1920s* (New York: Hill and Wang, 1995), 77. See also Boyer, *Dreaming*, 139–140, 183–184.

29. Magazine articles on the joys and perils of automobile touring rapidly increased in numbers in the 1920s. See, for example, George W. Sutton, "Rolling Vacations," *Colliers* 68 (August 6, 1921): 13; Alexander Johnston, "America: Touring Ground of the World," *Country Life* 37 (January 1920): 25–34; V. Gurney, "Auto-burro honeymoon," *Sunset* 43 (July 1919): 40–42; Elon H. Jessup, "Flight of the tin can tourists," *Outlook* 128 (May 25, 1921): 166–169; Myron J. Whitney, "Fording the Atlantic Coast," *Outing* 75 (January-February 1921): 231–234, 282–285; Helen M. Mann, "May Day Motorists," *Overland* 75 (May 1920): 419–424. See also Warren Belasco, *Americans on the Road: From Autocamp to Motel, 1910–1945* (Cambridge, MA: MIT Press, 1979); John A. Jakle, *The Tourist: Travel in Twentieth-Century North America* (Lincoln, Neb.: University of Nebraska Press, 1985); Marguerite Shaffer, *See America First* (Washington, DC: Smith Sonian Institution Press, 2001).

30. Other examples are *New-York* Compliments of Joseph Biechele Soap Company, Canton, Ohio (n.d.; c.1884); *The Gate to the Sea* (Brooklyn, New York: Eagle Press, c.1897). The *Eagle*, the daily newspaper of Brooklyn, also ranked among the important and widely read papers of the New York area. The title page of this guide is stamped "Compliments of the Third Universalist Church, North Henry Street and Nassau Avenue. Look for the Pink Sheets." The pink sheets referred to were stapled in the center of the guide and contained information about the church and its services, and advertisements by Brooklyn businesses and manufacturers.

31. See Edwin G. Conklin, "Some Biological Aspects of Immigration," *Scribner's Magazine* 69 (March 1921): 352–359; Henry H. Curran, U.S. Commissioner of Immigration at the Port of New York, "Fewer and Better, Or None," *Saturday Evening Post* 196 (April 26, 1924): 8–9, 189; Lothrop Stoddard,

"Is America American?" *World's Work* 41 (December 1920): 201–203; Kenneth L. Roberts, "East is East," *Saturday Evening Post* 196 (February 23, 1924): 6–7, 138, 143, 145–146; Editorial, "An Alien Antidumping Bill," *Literary Digest* 69 (May 7, 1921): 12–13; Calvin Coolidge, "Whose Country Is This?" *Good Housekeeping* 72 (February 1921): 13–14; George Creel, "Melting Pot or Dumping Ground?" *Collier's* 68 (September 3, 1921): 9–10; Editorial, "Ellis Island Sob Stuff," *Saturday Evening Post* 194 (November 26, 1921): 20; Owen Wister, "Shall We Let the Cuckoos Crowd Us Out of Our Nest?" *American Magazine* 91 (March 3, 1921): 47; Willet M. Hays, "Immigration and Eugenics," *Review of Reviews* 69 (April 1924): 405–406.

32. See Louis Dodge, "The Sidewalks of New York," *Scribner's Magazine* 70 (July–December 1921): 584–592. On the relationship between American identities and New York's metropolitan status, see Editorial, "New York's Big Foreign Population," *Literary Digest* 73 (April 29, 1922): 13; Editorial, "Is New York American?" *Saturday Review of Literature* 2 (January 2, 1926): 457; Mary Agnes Hamilton, "Red-Haired City," *Atlantic Monthly* 139 (April 1927): 491–497; Editorial, "Why Hate New York?" *The Outlook* 142, (March 17, 1926): 404; Jacques LeClercq, "Why I Live in America," *The American Mercury* 6 (September 1925): 25–31; Chester T. Crowell, " 'Welcome, Stranger!' Said Little Old New York," *The Independent* 102, (April 24, 1920):121–122.

33. Fremont Rider, *Rider's Guide to New York City* (New York: Henry Holt and Company, 1923). For more on the use of Baedeker guides by American tourists in Europe, see Harvey Levenstein, *Seductive Journey: American Tourists in France From Jefferson to the Jazz Age* (Chicago: University of Chicago Press, 1998), especially p. 33 and 158–159.

34. Rider, *Rider's Guide*, 122, 124.

35. In the first edition of his New York guide, Rider made only passing references to the immigrant neighborhoods of the Lower East Side. See Fremont Rider, *Rider's New York City* (New York: Henry Holt and Company, 1916), 149–150.

36. On the ethnic and racial "mainstreaming" of white ethnics after the 1924 Act, see Jacobson, *Whiteness*, 91–135. See also Higham, *Strangers*.

37. Edward Corsi, "My Neighborhood," *Outlook* 141 (September 16, 1925): 90–92. See also the series of articles by Rollin Lynde Hartt that appeared in the summer of 1921, giving portraits of racially or ethnically distinct New York neighborhoods. Hartt's articles offer an excellent example of the type of popular discourse opposing negative views of immigrant, or "foreign," neighborhoods in the early 1920s. See Rollin Lynde Hartt, "New York and the Real Jew," *Independent* 105 (June 25, 1921): 658–660; "Made in Italy," *Independent* 106 (July 23, 1921): 19–20; "More Irish Than Ireland," *Independent* 106 (August 20, 1921): 68–69. Hartt also wrote an article about Harlem, unusual not only because magazine articles about Black Harlem were very rare, but also because of his laudatory tone: "I'd Like to Show You Harlem!" *Independent* 105 (April 2, 1921): 334–335.

38. Ibid., 90.

39. On the history of "seeing" Jewishness in the face or body of a Jew, see Jacobson, *Whiteness*, 171–202.

40. Hutchins Hapgood, "Picturesque Ghetto," *Century Magazine* 94 (July 1917): 469–473; Corsi, "My Neighborhood." By 1917, Hapgood was well

known as the author of *The Spirit of the Ghetto: Studies in the Jewish Quarter of New York*, published in 1902. Hapgood hired a then-unknown artist, Jacob Epstein, to illustrate the book with sketches of the Lower East Side's Jewish population. Epstein used the proceeds from this work to pay his way to France, where he trained as a sculptor. Epstein later moved to England, where he achieved great success and became one of twentieth century's most acclaimed sculptors. See Hutchins Hapgood, *The Spirit of the Ghetto* (New York: Funk and Wagnalls, 1902). For more on Epstein, see Jacob Epstein, *Let There Be Sculpture* (New York: G.P. Putnam's Sons, 1940). On racial typologies, see earlier discussion of Osborn and Grant. See also W. Z. Ripley *The Races of Europe; A Sociological Study* (New York: D. Appleton and Company, 1899).

41. Some examples of the work of these and other illustrators include Will Irwin, *Highlights of Manhattan*, illus. E. H. Suydam (New York: The Century Company, 1927); Vernon Howe Bailey, *Magical City: Intimate Sketches of New York* (New York: Scribners, 1935) and *Skyscrapers of New York* (New York: W.E. Rudge, 1928); Helen Josephy and Mary Margaret McBride, *New York is Everybody's Town*, illus. Margaret Freeman (New York: G.P. Putnam's Sons, 1931); Scudder Middleton, *Dining, Wining, and Dancing in New York*, illus. Loren Stout (New York: Dodge Publishing Company, 1938); J. George Frederick, *Adventuring in New York. With Ten Etchings* (New York: N.L. Brown, 1923); Joseph Pennell, *The Glory of New York* (New York: W.E. Rudge, 1926); Rian James, *All About New York: An Intimate Guide*, illus. "Jay" (New York: The John Day Company, 1931); Charles G. Shaw, *Nightlife*, illus. Raymond Bret-Koch (New York: The John Day Company, 1931).

42. Caroline Singer, "An Italian Saturday," *Century* 101 (March 1921): 590–600. Caroline Singer and illustrator Cyrus LeRoy Baldridge frequently worked together. Subsequent publications, for both adults and children, on which they collaborated include *Turn to the East* (New York: Minton, Balch and Company, 1926); *White Africans and Black* (New York: W. E. Rudge, 1929); *Boomba Lives in Africa* (New York: Holiday House, 1935); *Ali Lives in Iran* (New York: Holiday House, 1937); *Half the World Is Isfahan* (New York: Oxford University Press, 1936); *Race? What the Scientists Say* (Camden, N.J.: The Haddon Craftsmen, 1939); and *Santa Claus Comes to America* (New York: A.A. Knopf, 1942).

43. Helena Smith Dayton and Louise Bascom Barratt, *New York in Seven Days* (New York: Robert M. McBride and Company, 1925). See also Sarah M. Lockwood, *New York: Not So Little And Not So Old* (Garden City, N.Y.: Doubleday, Page and Company, 1926). Journalist and illustrator Helen Worden wrote several guides to New York, some of which she illustrated herself: *The Real New York; A Guide for the Adventurous Shopper, The Exploratory Eater and the Know-It-All Sightseer Who Ain't Seen Nothin' Yet* (Indianapolis: The Bobbs-Merrill Company, 1932); *Round Manhattan's Rim* (Indianapolis: The Bobbs-Merrill Company, 1934), *Discover New York With Helen Worden* (New York: American Women's Voluntary Services, 1943), and *Here Is New York* (New York: Doubleday, Doran and Company, 1939). More guides by women include: Rosalie Slocum and Ann Todd, *A Key to New York* (New York: Modern Age Books, 1939); Marjorie Hillis Roulston, *New York, Fair or No Fair; A Guide for the Woman Vacationist* (Indianapolis: The Bobbs-Merrill Company, 1939); Gretta Palmer, *A Shopping Guide to*

New York (New York: R.M. McBride and Company, 1930); Eva McAdoo, *How Do You Like New York? An Informal Guide* (New York: The Macmillan Company, 1936); Clara Laughlin, *So You're Visiting New York City!* (Boston: Houghton Mifflin, 1939); Elizabeth Hubbard Lansing, *Seeing New York* (New York: Thomas Y. Crowell Company, 1938).

44. Robert Shackleton, *The Book of New York* (Philadelphia: The Penn Publishing Company, 1920), 178. See also Elizabeth Frazer, "Our Foreign Cities: New York," *Saturday Evening Post* 195 (June 16, 1923): 6–7.

45. Konrad Bercovici, *Around the World in New York* (New York: The Century Company, 1924). Information on Bercovici's background is from his obituary, *New York Times*, December 28, 1961, 27:1.

46. The Map Division of the New York Public Library has an extensive collection of pictorial maps of New York. Some examples from the 1920s and 1930s in this collection include "The Heart of New York as Served by New York Central Railroad" (New York: Rand McNally, 1930); "A Pictorial Map of New York, Necessarily Incomplete, On Which are Displayed the Cultural Centers of the City," *New York Times Magazine*, July 31, 1927; "East Side, West Side, All Around the Town" (New York: Empire State Sightseeing Corporation, 1932); and "A Pictorial Map of that Portion of New York City Known as Manhattan" (Winchester, MA: Ernest Dudley Chase, 1939).

Chapter 7

"The First Thing Every Negro Girl Does": Black Beauty Culture, Racial Politics, and the Construction of Modern Black Womanhood, 1905–1925

Tiffany M. Gill

Adina Stewart, mother of international labor leader Maida Springer Kemp, known best for her work with the International Ladies Garment Worker's Union (ILGWU), realized shortly after immigrating to the United States that there were limited opportunities for black women in the labor force. Born in Panama, Adina Stewart was among the estimated 300,000 Caribbean people who immigrated to the United States between 1900 and 1930.[1] Arriving at Ellis Island in 1917 along with her husband and seven-year-old daughter, the family settled in Harlem. Not long after, Stewart and her husband separated and she was faced with the challenge of raising her daughter on her own. Wanting her daughter to get an education and learn a trade that would eventually allow her to earn a living, Stewart enrolled her in the Bordentown Manual Training and Industrial School for Colored Youth in New Jersey in 1923 where Maida received a standard industrial education. For girls, this consisted of training in domestic science.

Domestic labor, Adina Stewart soon found out, was also her only option for work. Kemp later recalled that her mother's first job in the United States was as a day-worker making $2.10 a day. However, Stewart did not last long at that job due to a confrontational incident with her white employer. While Stewart never returned to day work, she subsequently worked as a laundress and then as a cook at a country club in Connecticut. Frustration with her limited labor prospects led Stewart, like many of her Caribbean counterparts, to pursue a career in the beauty culture industry. While never becoming wealthy, she eventually opened up her own beauty salon and never worked again as a domestic laborer.[2]

Adina Stewart's story was not uncommon. She, like so many other black female migrants from the Caribbean and the Southern United States, entered the beauty trade as an alternative to domestic labor. Fueled by a desire for personal independence and financial autonomy, these women arrived in northern and mid-western cities at a crucial moment in the early twentieth century. With the United States' population overall becoming increasingly urban, black women migrants tapped into the discourse of the "New Negro" and the "New Woman" to assert a new sense of themselves and demonstrate their ability to function and thrive in these new urban environments.[3] Among the many new aspects of modernity these women embraced when they arrived in these urban spaces was a flourishing black beauty industry with salons ready to help them achieve a modern and urban look as well as schools equipped to train them to become professionals and entrepreneurs. The black beauty industry played a crucial role in providing black migrant women with the personal dignity and financial stability they desired and was instrumental in ushering these women into the modern experience by empowering them as consumers and laborers.[4]

This essay attempts to show the complexities of modern black womanhood by focusing not only on the economic and social culture that the black beauty industry fostered in northern and mid-western cities, but also by emphasizing how the women within this industry cultivated a climate of political activism. Adina Stewart not only found financial stability in the beauty industry, but also used the financial autonomy afforded by her profession to support her extensive political work as a supporter of Marcus Garvey's Universal Negro Improvement Association (UNIA). The role that black female beauticians and beauty entrepreneurs played in the black female club movement, the labor movement, and in Marcus Garvey's UNIA—movements that on the surface seem ideologically opposed to one another and to a business based on hair straightening and styling—illuminate how black women navigated through the complex terrain of black modernity in the early twentieth century. The networks created among women in the beauty industry fostered a larger movement culture within black communities that supported various struggles against racial injustice. These movements, though varied in their ideologies and approaches, relied heavily upon the connections among beauticians as well as their access to their black female clientele. These networks were particularly important in the early twentieth century, as blacks faced a time of great transition, not the least of which was the mass exodus of African Americans out of the south to northern and mid-western cities between the two World Wars in the period known as the Great Migration.[5]

Migrant Women as a Social Problem

Most of the black female migrants that arrived in northern cities during the Great Migration were single women, usually between 13 and 30 years of age, who came in search of independence, financial and otherwise.[6] In these cities, migrant women numerically outnumbered men. This combined with the ways migrant women boldly embraced the new forms of leisure and amusements available to them caused white and black social reformers to band together to address what was considered the "negro migrant girl problem." Fearing that these women would fall into crime and partake in what they considered immoral activities during their leisure time, social reformers created institutions to limit the migrants' interactions with their new urban environments.

Middle-class reformers' perception that migrating women represented a 'problem' was heightened due in part to the perceived inability of black women to be gainfully employed. As early as 1905, white progressive reformer Frances Kellor, founder of the National League for the Protection of Colored Women, explained: "the problem of the unemployed negro woman in New York City is probably more serious than that of any other class of worker."[7] This seemingly hyperbolic observation was underscored by the limited employment opportunities for black women who, constrained by the totalizing effects of racial and gender discrimination, found it difficult to maintain stable employment. Kellor further lamented that African American women, often recruited to work as domestic servants in cities, were often forced into prostitution when domestic labor did not fulfill their economic needs. One of the recommendations that Kellor made to remedy the migrant girl situation was the creation of training schools that would help "the green helpless negro woman brought up here from the South—on promises of easy work, lots of money and good times" adjust to the efficiency required of them in the urban workforce and protect them from the vice of the city.[8] Kellor and many of her contemporaries did not address the employment problems that black women encountered as a result of the compounded affect of racial and gender discrimination in the labor market, but instead blamed the women themselves for their inability to secure viable and respectable employment. In other words, little attention was given to challenging the economic system; instead the focus of Kellor and even black reformers like Jane Edna Hunter and Nannie Helen Burroughs was on the perceived lack of efficiency and poor morals of black women.[9]

Beauty entrepreneurs and the networks of beauty schools they established in northern cities sought to address many of the same issues as progressive reformers, but instead of fearing the perils of modern urban life, they sought to help black women navigate and even capitalize on the trappings of modern urban life. In 1924, a reporter from the Saturday *Evening Post* commented that, "the first thing every negro girl does when she comes from the South is . . . have her hair straightened."[10] Beauty entrepreneurs understood that this phenomenon spoke of black women's desire to embrace some of the trappings of modern life as well as provide an opportunity for black women to gain an economic benefit in the process. They did not try to restrict black women's engagement with modern urban life, particularly consumer culture. Instead beauty entrepreneurs celebrated and encouraged black women's engagement with commerce through beauty culture. Settlement houses and domestic training schools were designed to protect women from entering into crime and prostitution; beauty colleges, on the other hand, offered a viable financial alternative by providing black women with the marketable skills they needed to keep them from turning to the sex trade or low paying domestic servant work.

As early as 1907, in the nascent stages of the Great Migration, the beauty culture industry was widely recognized as providing economic opportunities for black women who wished to escape domestic labor. In a *Voice of the Negro* article, Katherine Tillman, an essayist and playwright, explained that hairdressing was indeed a worthwhile profession for black women. She explained, "some colored hairdressers earn a good living by giving scalp treatments to colored women's heads and a nice growth of soft healthy hair replaces the short, harsh hair of former days."[11] Madam C.J. Walker, founder of the Walker Manufacturing Company and arguably the most successful beauty entrepreneur of the early twentieth century, declared in a series of lectures given in Washington, DC in August of 1913 that the time had come for "women of the race to rise above the laundry and the kitchen."[12] Later that summer at the annual meeting of the National Negro Business League, Walker asserted that she was helping black women rise above domestic labor by "employing hundreds of Negro girls and women all over the country" as Walker product sales agents and beauty operators.[13] Maggie Wilson, a Walker Company sales agent from Pittsburgh lauded Walker for opening economic doors for women like her who were migrants to northern and mid-western cities. In language that echoed the concerns of progressive reformers, Wilson explained, "you have opened up a trade for hundreds of our colored women to make an honest and profitable living." Wilson continued that African American women appreciated the fact that they could "make as much in one week as a month's salary would bring from any other position a colored woman can secure."[14] With over 80 percent of African American women in Northern cities engaged in domestic labor, it is likely that Wilson was comparing the opportunities of the beauty industry with the lack of financial opportunities in domestic work, the vocation so embraced by progressive reformers. National statistics bear witness to the increasing appeal of beauty work to black women in the twentieth century. In 1890, the census reported 514 black women worked as beauticians; by 1900, the number grew to 984; by 1910, 3,093. By 1920, the number quadrupled to 12,666.[15]

Walker, herself a former laundress, explicitly compared not only the economic prospects her company provided vis-à-vis domestic labor, but also the easier workload: "I feel I have done something for the race by making it possible for so many colored women and girls to make money without working hard."[16] While settlement houses and training schools emphasized hard work as a sign of moral character, beauty schools demonstrated that they better understood the desires of black women migrants who wanted more free time to engage in the leisure activities of the city. Beauty culture was appealing to black women not only because of its financial dimension, but also because it allowed these women to have more control of their free time. While progressive reformers described their agenda as modern, they minimized the role of commercial leisure activities and commercial beauty culture in helping black women achieve this goal. The intersection of commercial pursuits with the politics of appearance that encouraged black women to groom and straighten their hair became an important way by which African American women began to define their modern selves.[17]

The Modern Woman

In 1916, Mamie Garvin Fields recalled going to a lecture by Mary Church Terrell, the president of the preeminent black female reform organization, the National Association of Colored Women, on "The Modern Woman" in Charleston, South Carolina. For Fields, who though living in Charleston had previously migrated to Massachusetts and New York City, it was Terrell's appearance, including her "beautifully done hair," perhaps more than her words, that embodied the title of her speech.[18] Fields recalled that Terrell told the black women at the Mt. Zion African Methodist Episcopal (A.M.E.) Church that they had their own lives to lead and that as black women they should learn to care for themselves. Terrell encouraged the women in attendance "to go into [their] communities and improve them . . . to go out into the nation and change it. Above all, [to] organize [themselves] as Negro women and work together."[19]

While watching Terrell had a great impact on Fields and the racial uplift work she would later engage in, it is perhaps even more significant that by the time Terrell came to Charleston another "modern woman," Madam C.J. Walker, had already come through town on more than one occasion. Walker proclaimed a similar agenda, but added another dimension—financial opportunity. And while Madam Walker, dark-skinned and of humble birth, at first glance bore little resemblance to the lighter hued, refined Terrell, Fields' descriptions of the two women and their messages were strikingly similar. Referring to Walker, Fields noted:

> that lady really could inspire you with her lectures . . . she had a beautiful face, beautiful hair, dressed elegantly. When she stood up to talk, a *go-ahead, up-to-date* black woman was talking, and the women listened to what she had to say.[20]

In particular, Fields' reference to Walker as a "go-ahead, up-to-date black woman" was reminiscent of the way she described Terrell as the embodiment of the modern woman. However, Walker brought something more than the rhetoric of racial uplift and personal betterment. She also brought a tangible way for black women to obtain economic stability, which enabled black women to change and improve their communities just as Terrell admonished. Mamie Garvin Fields' life demonstrates the possibilities for an African American woman who embraced the messages of both these modern women.

Born Mamie Garvin, in Charleston, South Carolina, in 1888, Fields was first educated in a one-room schoolhouse and eventually attended Claflin University where she learned, among other skills, dressmaking, millinery, and pedagogy. Upon graduating from college, she taught in rural schools in South Carolina, but after a few tough years, she migrated to Massachusetts to work as a live-in domestic servant. Disappointed by the lack of free time and low pay, she recalled, "we felt that if we did go out to work, then we ought to make as much money as possible. The money was the point. If we were not doing the best financially, it was time to move."[21] Fields then took a job in a sewing factory where she made more money than she ever had before. After getting married, shortly before the United States entered World War I, Mamie Garvin (now Fields) moved to Charlotte, North Carolina and New York City before resettling permanently in Charleston.

While Fields' career as a teacher and a clubwoman has been chronicled by historians, her work as a beautician for the Poro Company (the Walker Company's main rival, established by Annie Malone) has not garnered much attention.[22] Fields started the Modern Priscilla Club and served as two-term president of the Federation of Women's Clubs, an organization that eventually became affiliated with the National Association of Colored Women (NACW). As a teacher, she worked as the head instructor of the Society Corner School on James Island, South Carolina for almost 20 years. However, her traditional progressive reform work and her beauty work emerged in the same context and was born out of the same sense of duty to the race and desire to be a modern woman. The beauty work, however, also emerged out of financial necessity.

Despite her teaching credentials and experience, Fields found that when she returned to Charleston "there were more Negro teachers than jobs, even though many children had nobody to teach them." It was at this time that Fields formed a close friendship with another Mamie—Mamie Rodolph, an Avery College graduate. Fields explained:

> As young brides and neighbors, we were the kind of pals who would experiment together: read a cookbook one afternoon and then make something we never heard of before, or plan how to copy a design out of a woman's magazine. But the big experiment we did together had nothing to do with cooking or serving. We experimented with "the Poro System."[23]

According to Fields, the Poro System came to Charleston via the wife of the Reverend Jesse Beard, a local A.M.E. minister, who heard Malone speak at a denominational meeting "up north somewhere." Mrs. Beard enrolled in Malone's beauty course, which consisted simply of a short demonstration with potential students "working on each other's heads" using "sage rinses, the egg rinses, the pressing oil, the hair-growing pomade, and the special finger movements to make thin hair grow."[24] At the end of this cursory training, the women would receive a certificate of completion and a set of products to get started on heads in their own communities. Once Mrs. Beard went back home to Charleston, she found an eager group of women anxious to learn the skills she had acquired. Interestingly enough, most of the women who were interested in learning about beauty culture came from within Beard's social circle—well-educated upwardly mobile race-conscious women like Fields and Rodolph. In other words, beauty culture was not just a meaningful economic opportunity for poorer black women who were trapped in domestic labor, but was also a viable alternative for educated black women who found that their opportunities in the more traditional middle-class professions were still limited despite their credentials.

Historical treatments of Fields' life that overlook her hair work while highlighting her club work are ironic, since the two were inextricably interwoven. As married black women were not allowed to teach in Charleston, when Fields decided to return to teaching in 1926, she was sent to a rural school on James Island. While Fields happily taught the three Rs, she was most excited about the other things she was able to bring to her students and their communities. Fields explained that the "black teachers in the country schools served as extension agents, community workers, and a lot else besides: one day I took hairdressing over to my school." And while many of her students were excited to have their hair dressed, some of the mothers of the rural girls were angered and even insulted at Fields' attempt to introduce them to beauty culture. Fields, in her attempt to spread modernity to the young women of South Carolina encountered resistance from those who saw hairdressing as compromising the values of rural life as well as resentment among the rural poor to those in the burgeoning middle class.

Beauty Work as Race Work

Other women had better luck than Fields in merging racework and beauty culture. Ezella Mathis Carter was both the consummate clubwoman and the successful entrepreneur. Her life provides insight into how these seemingly incongruous worlds of business and social reform intersected. Her 1935 biography, written by Kathryn Johnson, sheds light on this historically obscure yet accomplished woman.[25] Carter was born in Girard, Alabama, and her family moved to Atlanta when she was one month old. Later in life, she earned money by teaching and eventually attended Spelman Seminary where she specialized in "Teachers' Professional and Missionary Training Courses."[26] She graduated from Spelman in 1907 and subsequently went on to teach at Kowaliga Academic Institute, a school several miles from Booker T. Washington's Tuskegee Institute.

Carter's marriage in September 1909 (Johnson does not give any information concerning her husband) "naturally changed her career." Shortly thereafter, she migrated to Chicago and studied to become a beauty culturist at the Enterprise Institute. Upon graduating, Carter received a certificate and opened up her own beauty shop where she taught the "art of hairdressing." Like Madam C.J. Walker and Annie Malone, Carter "experimented with various oils for the hair, and was finally successful in compounding her own hair preparations," which were still in demand at the time Johnson's biography was published in 1935. Madam Carter did more than sell beauty products. Carter took advantage of the intimacy of selling beauty products in women's homes to further her involvement in the black club movement. Using a door-to-door sales approach, Carter entered black women's homes, and taught them how to care for their hair. Biographer Johnson explains:

> She would go into the cabins, which probably had no more than two or three rooms; there she would heat water on the open fireplace, and with what conveniences she could find, shampoo the hair; then with infinite patience, apply the pressing oil; the straightening comb and the presser, and at the end of an hour and half or perhaps, two hours, she would be talking to the woman, giving her a lesson on how to improve her condition and her neighborhood.[27]

Madam Carter seized the opportunity offered by entering black women's homes under the non-threatening guise of selling beauty products to do racework.

Madam Carter clearly understood that the home was a site in which she could not only advance herself entrepreneurially, but a place where she could act as a social reformer and establish herself as a true race woman. The NACW took notice of her abilities and named her the chair of the organization's Business Section.[28] In addition, she also sponsored clubs at the local level. After training other women in the beauty trade and in their role as racial uplifters, Madam Carter gathered her sales agents into "Life Boat clubs," appropriately named since the clubs "were designed to save the people in the sections where [the agent] traveled."[29] These clubs were educational, industrial, and benevolent in nature. They collected dues, distributed money to those who were ill, and in the event of death, provided funeral expenses. These Life Boat clubs were eventually incorporated under the laws of the State of Illinois, and even became affiliated as an associate member of the National Council of Negro Women (NCNW). In 1927, the club expanded its mission and established a center for rural girls.

The strategy used by Madam Carter, namely meeting the needs of and administering to the poor within their homes, was a staple strategy of clubwomen in the early decades of the twentieth century. As a part of what they termed the "good" homes project, clubwomen targeted poor black women in their dwellings. Mary Church Terrell, the first president of the NACW, explained in a 1902 essay that it was only through the home "that a people can become really good and great. More homes, better homes, purer homes is the text upon which sermons have and will be preached."[30] Other clubwomen echoed the importance of the black household. "The Negro home," Josephine Bruce said, "is rapidly assuming the position designated for it. It is distinctly becoming the center of social and intellectual life; it is building up strength and righteousness in its sons and daughters, and equipping them for the inevitable battles of life which grow out of the struggle for existence."[31] Madam Carter clearly understood that the home was a site in which she could not only advance herself entrepreneurially, but a place where she could act as a social reformer and establish herself as a true race woman.

Although Fields and to a greater extent, Carter synergized beauty work and race work, traditional clubwomen, at the forefront of discussions about black womanhood in the early twentieth century, debated the role of the beauty industry in black women's lives. In the very early years of the century, they often led the charge against the burgeoning commercialization of beauty. Cornelia Bowen, one of Tuskegee Institute's first graduates, gave a report to the NACW in 1904 lauding Mt. Meig's Anti Hair Wrapping Clubs, where members pledged "not to wrap their hair in an effort to straighten it." Bowen explained, "It is foolish to try [to] make hair straight, when God saw fit to make it kinky."[32] And while the black beauty industry in this period minimized the connection of the products they sold to the practice of hair straightening, for most in the black community, these products were associated with the practice.[33] In that same year, Nannie Helen Burroughs, a leader of the Women's Auxiliary of the National Baptist Convention, and founder and president of the National Training School for Women and Girls, told women that the true way to improve their lives was not through cosmetics and hair treatments, but through moral purity, education, and cultural refinement. She argued that improving one's appearance undermined the more important work that a black woman should engage in, namely improving her "real self." Burroughs continued, "a true woman wouldn't give a cent for a changed appearance of this sort- a superficial nothing. What every woman who bleaches and straightens needs, is not her appearance changed, but her mind. . . . Why doesn't she wish [instead] to improve her real self?" For Burroughs, the rise of beauty culture contradicted ideas of authenticity, and not just racial authenticity, but a gendered one as well. Beauty culture, ironically, seemed to disrupt a sense of true womanhood based on the cultivation of moral character.[34]

Still, beauty culturists were able to exploit part of the rhetoric employed by clubwomen to promote their products. The very things Burroughs emphasized, namely respectability and self-improvement, left room to include physical deportment and good grooming. Indeed, for all of her public lament about the emphasis black women placed on their physical appearance, the young women who participated in Burroughs' National Training School had their hair, body, odor, and clothing checked daily to see if it measured up to Burroughs' high standards.[35] Beauty culturists, in these early years, also connected their services with good grooming and modernity, arguing that they were not trying to change the appearance of black women. They even went so far as to say that there was nothing wrong with black women's natural attributes; they simply sought to enhance the beauty and good characteristics that were lying dormant. A school textbook, *A Complete Course in Hair Straightening and Beauty Culture*, written by Mrs. B.S. Lynk in 1919, went even further. She described the quest for beauty not as a luxury, but as a "duty."[36] The purpose of the textbook book was stated in its preface: "If this volume shall be the means of some girl or woman taking hope and gaining information that will lead to success, happiness, and prosperity, these lines would not have been in vain."[37] The rhetoric of uplifting black womanhood, a cause clubwomen saw as their primary goal, was adopted by beauty entrepreneurs who openly connected good grooming practices to moral character and economic advancement.

Financing the Race: Beauty Culturists and Philanthropy

Madam Walker first encountered the ladies of the National Association of Colored Women, the preeminent African American female reform organization of the early twentieth century, at their fourth biennial convention in 1903 while she was living in St. Louis, working as a washerwoman, dabbling in the beauty business and known as Sarah Breedlove. The church Walker attended, St. Paul's African Methodist Episcopal, hosted the 200 NACW delegates representing the "better" women of the race. However, Walker, an unknown washerwoman with high aspirations, was not embraced by the organization's mainly middle-class members.[38] By 1910, once Walker began to experience a modicum of success, she realized that she needed to get out word about her products on the African American convention circuit, especially at meetings where large numbers of black women gathered. She attended the NACW's seventh biennial in Louisville, Kentucky in the summer of 1910, where she was a part of the official delegation from Indiana; yet her presence was not noted in any substantial way.

In 1912, when Walker was formally introduced to the crowd of NACW women who barely knew her just two years earlier, she did not speak of her Wonderful Hair Grower. Instead, she pledged to pay for the travel costs of Mary Church Terrell and two other women to travel to Richmond, Virginia and appeal to the governor on behalf of Virginia Christian, a seventeen-year-old washerwoman who was set to be executed for killing her white employer. The women of the NACW applauded Walker and praised her for her demonstrated "interest in race progress" by publicly commending her not just on this donation, but also on her well-known contribution to the YMCA fund in Indianapolis.[39] Walker's popularity with the NACW only grew over the following years: in 1914, Victoria Clay Haley presented a motion endorsing Walker's work for the race and in 1916 Walker captivated the elite clubwomen by showing pictures of her business establishment and her lavish home.

By the time the NACW met in Denver in 1918, Madam Walker was one of its most well-known delegates, even leading a panel discussion on women in business where she questioned the elitism of clubwomen and expressed what she felt was a sense of duty to African Americans migrating from the South. She implored clubwomen, "Shall we who call ourselves Christians sit still and allow them to be swallowed up and lost in the slums of these great cities." Walker went a step further, not just lamenting the state of the new migrants, but also wishing to see them join the ranks of the better classes: "Bring them into your clubs and other organizations where they can feel the spirit and catch the inspiration of higher and better living."[40] Walker, in many ways, earned a platform to make this exhortation because she was known as one of the largest financial contributors to the organization and its causes. After Madam Walker's death in 1919, the NACW memorialized her in their official record stating that Walker stood out "not so [much] because of her great contribution to improve the personal appearance of her race, as the fact that she realized and provided for honorable employment for developing the manhood and womanhood of the race. The influence of this great woman will never die. Not only in life did she generously aid individuals and institutions, but in death by the provisions of her will, does her generosity still influence almost every phase of our race's life and institutions."[41]

Walker's giving, as the NACW noted, was not limited to the NACW's causes. In 1914, in response to a request from Ella Croker of Indianapolis for a detailed "statement of gifts, donations, and charitable undertakings of Madam C.J. Walker," Walker's lawyer and business manager F.B. Ransom recounted a three page list of her philanthropy, which included everything from giving holiday turkeys to the needy, to purchasing a wheelchair for a paralytic man, donating to orphans' homes, maintaining an industrial mission school in South Africa, and donating legal assistance to a "poor boy" serving a life sentence for killing a white man.[42] Not to be outdone, Annie Malone, Walker's primary business competitor and also a member of the NACW, offered financial support to many racial causes, especially the St. Louis Colored Orphan's Home (that was renamed in her honor in 1946), though much of her philanthropy was devoted to religious institutions, especially the St. James A.M.E. church.[43]

Philanthropy was at the center of the way beauty culturists voiced their strength and dignity to the black community. Wanting the financial power of beauticians to be felt beyond their personal philanthropic work, Walker and Malone also established incentives for their employees to engage in financially supporting the race. For example, Poro employees were organized into welfare associations that raised money for benevolent causes. In 1916, Madam C.J. Walker began making plans for the organization that would eventually become the Walker Hair Culturists' Union. Walker explained to F.B. Ransom that she wanted to "call a meeting of all the agents and form a National which would be similar to the Women's Federated Clubs."[44] While the Union was organized to deal directly with issues relating to the beauty industry, like learning new hair care techniques and introducing agents to new products, the organization was also established to demonstrate the financial and political clout of Walker agents. In a letter to F.B. Ransom, Walker instructed Ransom to "form a letter to be sent to all the agents" appealing to them to donate one dollar each to the Booker T. Washington Memorial Fund. Walker explained, "It will show the world that the Walker Agents are doing something other than making money for themselves . . . I don't want my agents to fall behind any body of women in this ralley [sic]."[45] Prizes were given to the local clubs of Walker Agents that did the most charity work. As journalist George Schuyler reported in the *Messenger*, "through these clubs, Madam Walker [has] perpetuated her great spirit of benevolence in every section of the world."[46] This tradition of giving to race causes would continue as a strong part of what beauty culturists were taught in college curricula until the 1970s.

The philanthropy of Madam C.J. Walker, while born out of her generosity and sense of duty to her race, was also strategic. Recognizing her power among clubwomen, Walker was quick to make sure her desires were expressed through her philanthropy. She explained in a letter to Ransom:

> My lectures in Pittsburgh were a success and the club women are planning to have me stop over on my way South as they want to give a big affair for the Old Folks Home and want me as an attraction and I said that I would, provided they divide the spoils with me for the Old Folks Home of Indianapolis and if it is a success whatever I get I will send it to them.[47]

The very woman who was made to feel like an outcast among the ladies of the NACW less than ten years earlier was now powerful enough to demand the terms of her contributions. Indeed, Walker's philanthropy was so renown that she was inundated with seemingly unending requests from organizations and individuals to provide financial assistance. For example, she instructed Ransom to tell the YWCA to stop pestering her to contribute more money, explaining, "I think I do enough for all of those organizations without them bothering me. I just gave them fifty dollars when I was there in May."[48] Still, despite her frustrations, Walker took full advantage of her position as a philanthropist to gain status for herself and for beauty culturists as a whole. To that end, she encouraged those who worked for her company to be at the forefront of giving in their communities.

While the average beauty culturist was not able to make contributions on par with Malone and Walker, their collective philanthropic achievements made an impact. The authority they gained in their communities through their giving led beauty culturists to see themselves not merely as laborers but as professionals. Even Nannie Helen Burroughs who voiced such a vociferous denouncement of the black beauty industry in 1904, by the 1930s recognized the industry's ability to provide black women with the skills needed to be gainfully employed—the very thing that her own domestic training schools advocated. In 1936, Burroughs addressed graduates of the Apex beauty system at their commencement. In direct contradiction to the words she penned in her previous *Voice of the Negro* article, Burroughs proudly proclaimed, "The beauty industry is ours, and we should keep it as ours." Instead of telling women that they should cultivate their inner beauty and not waste their time on their appearance, Burroughs asserted that, "we must look our best and less than our years at all times in order to hold our husbands if we have one, or our jobs if we haven't."[49] Indeed, the racial uplift ideology Burroughs' advocated in her National Training School, namely racial pride, respectability, and a strong work ethic, combined with Burroughs' appeal to black women of all classes closely aligned her ideology with what was taught at beauty colleges like Apex.[50] Beauticians had, by the time Burroughs addressed the Apex graduates, become respected citizens and professional women within their communities. One of the reasons they had become so well respected was their economic power and their ability to support financially the causes that clubwomen advocated.

The Professional Woman

Much of the historical literature on black women in the professions has emphasized teaching and nursing as the most promising avenues to becoming a professional woman.[51] However, many women who initially wanted to become nurses or teachers, eventually entered the beauty trade after realizing the financial and time commitments necessary to achieve traditional professional status. A beautician from Charlotte, North Carolina, for example, recounted that she planned to enter nursing school after completing high school, but that once she married, her husband talked her out of it and "pushed her toward marriage and motherhood." After the birth of her first child, she enrolled in a course in beauty culture saying that "it seemed more convenient and easier to do at the time" since it did not take as long as nursing school to complete.[52]

Beauty college was cheaper than teacher's colleges and nursing schools and more significantly was marketed to black women who may have otherwise seen a professional career beyond their reach. Walker Company promotional literature explained that, "age, family tree, cultural background, professional connection, etc . . . have no bearing on your chance to succeed in Beauty Culture. It is a new day profession, open to all whose ambition leads them to study, prepare themselves properly, and make the sacrifice necessary to succeed."[53] Beauty school was also less expensive than teacher's college or nursing school. During her travels to Washington, Georgia, in 1916, Madam Walker wrote to her business manager that she "found so many poor people who cannot raise twenty five dollars" that she decided to reduce the price to earn a beauty certificate to ten dollars. Walker added, "I just put them on their honor to pay whenever they can and as soon as they pay it all, we'll give them their contract."[54] For black women desiring a steady income and professional status who did not have the luxury of time and money necessary for extensive professional education, beauty school was a welcome alternative.

Indeed the beauty schools Walker and others created, the majority of which were in northern and mid-western cities, served as key social, political, and economic institutions for black women getting acclimated to urban life. For the women who chose to learn the beauty trade, they were not only introduced to a vocation, but also to a profession. Beauty college curricula instilled in their students the strategic importance of using their position to influence their communities.[55] Graduations were grand events where beauticians showcased their professionalism and proclaimed their importance to their families, friends, and neighbors. Programs from beauty school graduations in places like Harlem, Detroit, and Indianapolis show pictures of hundreds of perfectly coiffed women dressed in white, "their hair and complexion beaming with evidences of care to themselves even as they are prepared to give unto others."[56] These gala events were held in the neighborhood's most coveted sites like the Dunbar Ballroom, or in prestigious churches like Harlem's Mother A.M.E. Zion. Valedictorians and salutatorians addressed their classmates and diplomas were conferred by the school's president. The graduations were always covered in the black press.[57]

Beauty culturists understood that one way to help professionalize their career was by creating a national organization and therefore formally legitimize themselves as clubwomen.[58] Following the lead of organizations like the National Association of the Colored Graduate Nurses (NACGN), organized in 1909, a group of beauty culturists and hair-care manufacturers convened in October 1919 in Philadelphia. There, Mr. R.V. Randolph, organized what was then called The National System Hair Culture League. After merging with many smaller beauty clubs, the name was changed to the National Beauty Culturists' League. The organization was incorporated in March 1920 and held its first convention in Philadelphia that same year, electing Madam J.E. Pennick its first president. The first officers, all women except Mr. Randolph who is credited with being the National Organizer, adopted as their national slogan, "Link Up With Us."[59]

The schools and professional organizations founded by beauty entrepreneurs offered more than a moral defense of black womanhood, professional identity, and even more than training in grooming hair. They were able to offer black women the chance to become self-employed entrepreneurs, and in many instances, social, economic, and political leaders. In 1918, Madam Walker, in a speech to the NACW, speculated that "I shall expect to find my agents taking the lead in every locality not only in operating a successful business, but in every movement in the interest of our colored citizenship."[60] Secure in their economic status and professional status, beauty culturists now turned their attention to using their authority and leverage within the African American community to make a political impact.

Beauticians and the New Urban Politics

One of the first graduates of Madam C.J. Walker's Leila College in New York City was a woman named Lucille Campbell Green. Described as a light-skinned woman of medium height and build with a head of short cropped hair, Green was born Lucille Campbell in Christianburg, Virginia in 1883.[61] She attended Howard University where she studied to become a schoolteacher and met and married Joseph Green, who died shortly after the couple moved to New York City. Lucille Green gave up school teaching upon the death of her husband and enrolled in Leila Beauty College. After graduating, Green "not only started her own salon on 135th Street, but also became a close friend of Madam Walker and a member of the 'society' that grew up around her in Harlem."[62] It was during her trips back and forth to her hair salon on 135th Street and Lenox Avenue (which just happened to be down the corridor from Ernest Welcome, who in 1914 was the head of the Brotherhood of Labor) that Ms. Green caught the attention of twenty-five-year-old Asa Philip Randolph. Randolph's biographer Jervis Anderson describes their subsequent courtship as "brief and unspectacular," stating that Philip took Lucille to stage shows, movies, and, of course, political lectures.

Mr. Randolph was not very fond of parties or dances; and when Lucille invited him to Madam Walker's soirees, he declined and said that he did not have time to waste on "fly-by-night people."[63]

Even if A. Philip Randolph was not impressed with Madam Walker's parties and her cohort of "successful speculators of recent vintage, community club-women, new urban professionals, and other parvenu varieties," he certainly learned to respect the lucrativeness of the haircare industry.[64] In fact, it was the marriage of the "socialist and the socialite" on April 15, 1913 that in many ways made A. Philip Randolph's career and political activism possible. The new Mrs. Randolph joined the Socialist Party shortly after the marriage; and as a couple, they committed themselves to political activism, campaigning to elect Socialist candidates to local offices.

"I had a good wife. She carried us," A. Philip Randolph noted of Lucille, whose financial backing was crucial to his socialist newspaper, *The Messenger*. Lucille Randolph distributed the paper from her exclusive salon and periodically used her earnings to pay its debts. In 1919, the Justice Department described *The Messenger* as "by long odds the most dangerous of all the Negro publications." When eulogizing Mrs. Randolph, a columnist for the *New York Post* later wrote:

> Lucille Greene [sic] Randolph seems entitled to the honor of being called the one time second most dangerous Negro in America. The title would certainly have once been official if the agents of the U.S. Justice Department had had the initiative and wit to intercept her postal money orders which helped support A. Philip Randolph's subversive activities.[65]

When A. Philip Randolph was asked to organize the Brotherhood of Sleeping Car Porters (BSCP) in 1925, he discussed the job with Lucille, who enthusiastically supported his decision to assist the then-fledgling union. Her financial support became even more crucial while her husband held this post since Philip did not receive a regular salary from the organization until 1936.[66] She also persuaded her friend and colleague, A'Lelia Walker, daughter of Madam Walker and heir to her beauty empire, to donate money to the BSCP, and organized other Walker salon operators to contribute money and prizes for the beauty contests that the Brotherhood held.

Mrs. Randolph's support of her husband was not only financial, but social as well. Through her contacts, he met wealthy African Americans and prominent left-wing whites who added prestige to his political pursuits. She was the one to introduce Philip to Chandler Owen, the person with whom he partnered at the Brotherhood.[67] Clearly Lucille's relationship to her husband is significant, but her accomplishments as a hairdresser and salon owner in Harlem should be explored in their own right. Jervis Anderson explains:

> Lucille became one of the more accomplished and sought after of the Walker students. Her customers ranged from the black elite in Harlem to well-to-do crinkly haired whites from "downtown." And one day a week she traveled out

to the fashionable Marlborough Blenheim Hotel in Atlantic City, to serve a
similar white clientele. Her prices seem to have been high, and brought her a
considerable income.[68]

Anderson argues that as Philip's reputation as a "wild-eyed radical" spread,
Lucille's patrons began to shy away, forcing her to abandon her salon in
1927. Yet, Gwendolyn Keita Robinson argues that "nationalism, radicalism,
and high classed life styles were often fused in those days. . . . Lucille, though
a socialite, ran for the New York City Board of Alderman on the Socialist
Party ticket in the 1930s, while at the same time, maintaining her beauty
salon, without suffering any apparent pangs of contradiction."[69] The reality
is perhaps somewhere in the middle of these two analyses. In the late 1920s,
Lucille seemed to want to devote more of her time to formal politics, and the
demands from the beauty industry may have begun to interfere. In addition,
her clients may not have been as comfortable with the radical politics advocated by Randolph and others in this period.[70]

Lucille Green Randolph was not the only person involved in the labor
movement who started her career in the beauty industry. International labor
leader Maida Springer Kemp, known best for her work with the International
Ladies Garment Worker's Union (ILGWU), found early on that that there
were limited opportunities for black women in the labor force and turned to
the beauty culture industry. Kemp's brief foray in the industry came as a
result of her mother Adina Stewart, the Panamanian immigrant whose
history opened this essay.

Adina Stewart wished for her daughter to follow in her footsteps as a beautician, and Maida did eventually earn a certificate from Poro Beauty College
in Harlem. Maida worked as a receptionist at Poro College in 1927, but
turned down a request from Annie Malone to work as a field representative
for the company, in part because of Malone's strict religious beliefs and personal standards. After marrying, Maida (now Springer) left the workforce
temporarily, as her husband was able to support their family, which soon
included a son Eric, born in 1929. However the Depression changed the
financial situation of the Springer family and in 1932 Maida returned to the
workforce, not in the beauty industry, but as a garment worker.[71]

While both Lucille Green Randolph and Maida Springer Kemp are best
known for the work they engaged in after their careers in beauty culture, their
exposure to that industry certainly influenced their later political and
economic choices. In many ways, the economic activism they eventually
dedicated their lives to should be seen as an outgrowth of what was instilled
in them in their beauty school training. Furthermore, exposure to the
lucrativeness and economic independence of women in the industry provided
living examples of the importance of economics to the racial struggle.

Although Maida Springer Kemp's mother could not instill her own
enthusiasm for beauty culture in her daughter, she did expose her daughter
to political activism. Adina Stewart was an avid supporter of Marcus
Garvey's UNIA and introduced her daughter to this world of racial pride,

pan-Africanism, and economic nationalism. Started during World War I, UNIA became the largest African American secular organization in history with chapters and membership in the United States, Africa, and the Caribbean. The Jamaican-born Garvey arrived in New York City in 1916 with a distinctly modern political agenda that was economically and racially nationalist.[72]

In all likelihood, Stewart was introduced to Garveyism through her work in beauty culture. According to Barbara Bair, many women who were actively involved in the UNIA earned a living in the beauty culture industry. However, quantifying the number of beauty culturists who were involved in the Garvey movement is difficult, due in part to the fact that a person's employment was usually subsumed under their title and position within the UNIA.[73] Still, the organization's emphasis on economic independence and institution building would have made it appealing to women practicing beauty culture. Furthermore, the relationship between Garveyism and beauty culture was cultivated through the *Negro World*, the official publication of the UNIA, which heavily marketed the beauty industry to its readers through its advertisements.

Business and economic development were central to the UNIA's philosophy. In 1919, Garvey and the UNIA founded the Black Star Steamship Line, an international shipping company that was designed to establish "an independent economy, business, industry, and commerce, and to transport our people . . . on business and pleasure."[74] Although selling stocks for the Black Star Line through the mail led to Garvey's imprisonment, his plan for the economic development of blacks around the world had a more far-reaching impact. Greatly informed by the economic policies of Booker T. Washington, Garvey believed in the primacy of economic power in racial struggle.[75] In 1919, the same year as the Black Star Line was launched, Garvey established the Negro Factories Corporation, which manufactured black dolls as well as uniforms for UNIA members and employees. The UNIA also started and encouraged small businesses by creating restaurants, grocery stores, and steam laundries, primarily in Harlem, the organization's headquarters. The organization also attracted many blacks who were already involved in business enterprises. Emory Tolbert's analysis of the Los Angeles local UNIA chapter demonstrates that much of the leadership and many of the rank-and-file were businessmen and women, who were no doubt attracted to the organization's strong entrepreneurial leanings.[76]

Garvey's belief in a strong independent economic base went beyond sustaining black businesses; it also informed his rejection of white philanthropy for his organization. Unlike Booker T. Washington and even W.E.B. DuBois, who also advocated the establishment of an indigenous economy under the control of blacks, Garvey refused any financial input from whites, even though it was "white financial institutions [that] held mortgages on UNIA properties."[77] Still, the UNIA attempted to create and encourage an independent black economy that depended upon the black masses and attempted to instill a sense of racial pride based on their financial autonomy.[78]

Ironically, when viewed from the perspective of the many black female beauticians who embraced Garveyism, much of the racial pride upheld in the Garvey movement celebrated and prescribed a narrow view of masculinity.[79] The organization's discourse of firm patriarchal leadership, while always an aspiration, was a contested space among male and female Garveyites. Beauty entrepreneurs, who as guardians of successful African American enterprise emblematized the UNIA's philosophies of economic nationalism, simultaneously undermined UNIA theories of racial pride and patriarchal order. In many ways, examining Garveyism through the lens of black beauty culture provides insight into the ways that urban African Americans in the early twentieth century navigated through their increasingly complicated political, economic, and social terrain.

When it came to black women as entrepreneurs, women within the Garvey movement were not discouraged from joining the business community because they were thought to be inept, but because their involvement in commerce might reflect poorly on the abilities of black men as providers. A *Negro World* article proclaimed this sentiment: "Let us go back to the days of true manhood when women truly revered us . . . let us again place our women upon the pedestal from whence they have been forced into the vortex of the seething world of business."[80] Indeed, the very fact that women participated in the workforce was seen as an embarrassment and an indication of black men's inability to provide for and protect their families. However, the organization had to confront the reality of black women in the workforce. For example, a 1924 *Negro World* article described how black women were leaving domestic work to become "barbers, hairdressers, manicurists, and stewardesses," occupations that the article was glad to report, "do not have the objectionable features of personal domestic employment."[81]

Despite the limitations imposed on the proper role of black ladies, women in the Garvey movement, under the leadership of Amy Jacques Garvey, defied the prescribed norms and used the rhetoric of the movement to their advantage. Nowhere was this contestation over meaning more evident than in the woman's page of the *Negro World*, entitled "Our Women and What They Think." Jacques Garvey wanted the woman's page to reflect more than fashion and domestic concerns; in an editorial on one of her women's pages, Jacques Garvey paid homage to the "woman of today [who] has a place in nearly all phases of man's life," including business and commerce.[82] In fact, one area of commerce that the *Negro World* was dependent upon was, ironically, the predominately female beauty culture industry.

In many ways, beauty culture fit into the UNIA's conception of black womanhood. Whereas business defined black manhood in Garveyism, beauty, in many ways was a cornerstone of black female identity. For example, the UNIA and *Negro World* sponsored beauty contests and fashion shows that celebrated the beauty of black womanhood. Marcus Garvey was even inspired to celebrate the beauty of black woman in poetic verse.[83] However, the UNIA's notion of black beauty did not depend on cosmetic artifice, but on a supposed natural inner beauty. An article in the January 17, 1925 edition of *Negro World* explained that "real beauty cannot be put on with cosmetics." Another article, printed a year earlier asserted that "true beauty" was not seen in the face, but in the heart and soul of a woman, "a woman's worth is to be estimated by the real goodness of her heart, the greatness of her soul and the purity and sweetness of her character."[84]

Paradoxically, these discussions of natural black female beauty often shared the page with large advertisements for Madam Mamie Hightower's Golden Brown Beauty Preparations, Madam Rhoda's Twelve Minute Hair Straightener, Pluko's Hair Dressing Treatment, and, of course, the then world famous Madam C.J. Walker's Wonderful Hair Grower. Chandler Owen publicly criticized Garveyites for what he saw as a dissonance between rhetoric and practice concerning beauty preparations. In a *Messenger* article published in 1924, Owen explained: "Garveyites and other dark people constantly inveigh against the white man and the Negroes imitating the white man—yet to take this very crowd away from the world would bankrupt Madame Walker, the Poro, Overton, Dr. Palmer's, the Apex, and all other skin whitening and hair straightening systems, in a few weeks."[85] In many ways, the pages of the *Negro World* embodied the tensions of Great Migration era blacks anxious to embrace the beauty of all things "black," yet who also wished to assert a modern consumer identity, which for black women in the early twentieth century was often expressed through beauty preparations. In addition, the *Negro World* and the organizations and ideologies it sought to reflect, had to hold their convictions about the meaning of blackness against the very real acknowledgement that it was the advertising of hair treatments and cosmetic preparations that financially supported the very words they wrote.[86]

An August 1925 article on the woman's page of the *Negro World* asked its readers a pointed question in the essay's title, "Are We Proud of Our Black Skins and Curly Hair?" The author answers this question with a resounding no and elucidates the lack of pride blacks, particularly women, have in their God-given appearance. "Surely, the Almighty did not make a mistake when he created millions of black men and women. No, instead of being proud of their black skins and curly hair, they despise them rather than build up a great nation with a proper economic basis. . . ."[87] Ironically, in another editorial on the woman's page, economics was cited as the reason why blacks straightened their hair and bleached their skin. When asked why blacks would go to such lengths, the writer responded, "To the end that they may be admitted to better jobs, moneyed circles, and in short, share the blessings of the prosperous white race."[88] Blacks were also openly chastised for using modern technology not to advance the race in any significant way, but to beautify it. "Negroes use the laboratories, not to discover serums to prevent disease and experiment in chemicals to protect themselves in case of war, but to place on the market grease that stiffens curly hair, irons that press the hair to look like a horse's mane, and face cream that bleaches the skin overnight."[89]

Marcus Garvey and the UNIA's relationship to the beauty industry is best characterized as reciprocal and not antagonistic. Garveyite women worked in the industry, and Marcus Garvey himself actively forged relationships with beauticians and beauty product manufacturing companies. One of Garvey's most loyal supporters was a beautician named Ethel Collins. Collins, like Garvey, was born in Jamaica and immigrated to New York in 1919. A year later, she joined the UNIA and became a stockholder in the Black Star Line. By the late 1920s, she was a featured speaker at UNIA meetings and eventually became the Lady President of the New York Garvey Club. Collins never married and lived with her siblings while working as a secretary at the UNIA headquarters. Perhaps out of financial necessity or out of sheer desire to do hair, Collins worked as a beautician simultaneously. This was not uncommon.[90] Described as a "Garvey loyalist," Collins worked with the UNIA for over twenty years, working as a key player mainly behind the scenes.[91]

Collins also wrote for the *Negro World*. For Garvey's thirty-ninth birthday, for example, she penned a poignant article chronicling Garvey's contributions to the race. "Thirty nine years ago a babe was born. Little did that mother know that she was contributing the greatest gift to civilization and to her race in that he is the greatest channel which God has used to remove the scales from the eyes of his fellow men." In that same article, Collins expressed enthusiasm for Garvey's economic policies. "If we remain in a consumers' position all the days of our lives," Collins asserted, "then we will be trampled upon."[92] In 1929, Collins became Acting Secretary General of the UNIA; after Garvey's death in 1940, Collins continued her close working relationship with Amy Jacques Garvey and was instrumental in the relocation of UNIA headquarters to Cleveland.

Based both on the close relationship that Madam Walker had with Marcus Garvey and the large numbers of women from the Caribbean who attended Lelia College in Harlem, it is not surprising that Collins advertised her services as a Walker-trained beautician operating a salon located at 56 W. 135th Street in Harlem.[93] Walker was given credit for contributing "the funds with which he started the *Negro World* and acquired what was later to be known as Liberty Hall."[94] Walker and Garvey also shared a notion of black business as a way to connect what is now commonly referred to as the African Diaspora.

Even after Walker's death, Garvey's organization had a close bond with her company. In 1929, the National Supervisor of the Madam C.J. Walker Manufacturing Co., Marjorie Stewart Joyner, was sent as an official delegate from the Walker Company to the UNIA convention in Jamaica, the same convention where Collins was named Acting Secretary General. The theatrically trained Joyner also performed a dramatic recitation at Garvey's birthday celebration at Edleweiss Park. The *Negro World* proudly proclaimed that during her visit, Joyner would "conduct lectures on Beauty Culture at several of the leading department stores in the island that handle the complete line of Mme. Walker preparations."[95] Even the politically cautious F.B. Ransom, who took over the day to day operations of the Walker company after Madam Walker's death, showed his support for Garveyism at a New York meeting of the UNIA where the purchase of Liberty Hall was announced by delivering an address on the viability of black owned and black-supported enterprises.[96]

The *Negro World* seemed to enjoy giving the Walker Manufacturing Co. in particular positive publicity. A 1926 article lauded the company for providing all of its employees with a $500 life insurance policy for Christmas, while another article proclaimed that the "extension of Mme. Walker's Business Helps the Race." Walker College graduations were also covered in the newspaper, and Madam C.J. Walker's birthday was posthumously celebrated in its pages.[97] The Walker Company sponsored a Trip Around the World contest in 1925, where people who bought Walker products were encouraged to send proof of their purchases into the Walker Company in support of a race leader to win the contest. The UNIA took out full-page ads in the *Negro World* asking for votes for P.L. Burrows, the Assistant Secretary-General of the UNIA. The advertisement explained that "Mr. Burrows' participation in the contest has the sanction of the Hon. Marcus Garvey." As the only way to vote was through buying products, Garvey was essentially encouraging the purchase of Walker products.[98]

Conclusion

Navigating the complex social, economic, political terrain of the early twentieth century, black beauticians with their nuanced understanding of black women's desires to embrace modern consumer culture, established a profession for black women that was, for the most part, under the complete control of black women. They served as the manufacturers, sales agents, and beauty operators of this very successful business enterprise. Striving to be among the best women of the race, they secured a professional and financial autonomy through institution building and philanthropy, and became highly regarded members of their respective communities.

Moreover, beauticians had a high degree of independence relative to other blacks—especially black women—whose occupations were usually under the watchful eye of whites. Throughout the early years of the twentieth century, black women worked primarily as domestics, doing work that was often isolating and constantly supervised, clearly not offering a site to organize collective resistance. Even black professional women like schoolteachers within segregated school systems faced constraints due to their dependence upon white-run school boards and city councils. Beauticians worked within black female owned establishments, supplied by black manufacturers, patronized by black female clients, within segregated communities. Black beauty culturists, with the foundation laid for a secure financial endeavor, only increased the political risks they took on behalf of African Americans in the remaining years of the twentieth century. They used their position not only to fix black women's hair, but also to try to fix their lives.

Notes

1. For more information on Caribbean migration to the United States in the early twentieth century, please see, Irma Watkins-Owens, *Blood Relations: Caribbean Immigrants and the Harlem Community, 1900–1930* (Bloomington, IN: University of Indiana Press, 1996).

2. Information on the life of Adina Stewart can be found in Yvette Richards, *Maida Springer Kemp: Pan-Africanist and International Labor Leader* (Pittsburgh: University of Pittsburgh Press, 2000), pp. 13–35 and Elizabeth Balanoff, "Maida Springer Kemp Interview," in Ruth Edmonds Hill, ed. *The Black Women Oral History Project: The Arthur and Elizabeth Schlesinger Library on the History of Women in America* (Westport, CN.: Meckler Press, 1991).

3. For more on the discourses on the "New Woman" see: Judith M. McArthur, *Creating the New Woman: The Rise of Southern Women's Progressive Culture in Texas, 1893–1918* (Urbana: University of Illinois Press, 1998); Joanne J. Meyerowitz, *Women Adrift: Independent Wage Earners in Chicago, 1880–1930* (Chicago: University of Chicago Press, 1988); Kathy Peiss, *Hope in a Jar: The Making of America's Beauty Culture* (New York: Metropolitan Books, 1998); *Cheap Amusements: Working Women and Leisure in Turn-of the-Century New York* (Philadelphia: Temple University Press, 1986); Stephanie J. Shaw, *What a Woman Ought to Be and to Do: Black Professional Women Workers during the Jim Crow Era* (Chicago: University of Chicago Press, 1996). For a discussion of the "New Negro" see Alain Locke, ed. *The New Negro* [1925] (New York: Touchstone Books, 1991); David Levering Lewis, *When Harlem Was in Vogue* (New York: Oxford University Press, 1979); and Jervis Anderson, *This Was Harlem: A Cultural Portrait* (New York: Ferrar, Strauss, and Giroux, 1981).

4. This argument is at the center of the work on beauty culture by Kathy Peiss, *Hope in a Jar*. See also A'Lelia Bundles, *On Her Own Ground: The Life and Times of Madam C.J. Walker* (New York: Scribner Books, 2001); Noliwe Rooks, *Hair Raising: Beauty Culture and African American Women* (New Brunswick, NJ.: Rutgers University Press, 1996); and Susannah Walker, "For Appearances Sake: African American Women's Commercial Beauty Culture from 1920 to 1970," Ph.D. Diss., Carnegie Mellon University, 2001.

5. For a more detailed discussion of the period known as the Great Migration, see Joe William Trotter, ed. *The Great Migration in Historical Perspective: New Dimensions of Race, Class, and Gender* (Bloomington, IN: Indiana University Press, 1991); Carole Marks, *Farewell, We're Good and Gone: the Great Black Migration* (Bloomington, IN: Indiana University Press, 1989); Beverly Bunch-Lyons, *Contested Terrain: African American Women Migrate from the South to Cincinnati, Ohio, 1900–1950* (New York: Routledge Press, 2002); Milton Sernett, *Bound for the Promised Land: African American Religion and the Great Migration* (Durham, NC: Duke University Press, 1997); and Victoria Wolcott, *Remaking Respectability: African American Women in Interwar Detroit* (Chapel Hill, NC: University of North Carolina Press, 2001).

6. For more information on the demographics of the women who journeyed to northern cities see, Sharon Harley, "For the Good of Family and Race: Gender, Work, and Domestic Roles in the Black Community," *Signs* 15 (Winter 1990). For a discussion of the reasons black women migrated north, see Darlene Clark Hine, "Black Migration to the Urban Midwest: The Gender Dimension, 1915–1930," in Joe William Trotter, ed. *The Great Migration*, 127–146; Victoria Wolcott, *Remaking Respectability*, and Beverly Bunch-Lyons, *Contested Terrain*.

7. Frances Kellor, "Southern Colored Girls in the North: The Problem of Their Protection," *Charities*, 18 March 1905. For more information on Kellor's life see, John J. Miller, "Miss Americanizer: Frances Kellor," *Policy Review: the Journal of American Citizenship* 83 (May–June 1997): 64–65.

8. Frances Kellor, "Southern Colored Girls in the North," *Charities*, March 18, 1905.
9. Hazel Carby, "Policing the Black Woman's Body in an Urban Context," *Critical Inquiry* 18 (Summer 1992): 741.
10. Quoted in Kathy Peiss, *Hope in a Jar*, p. 231.
11. Katherine Tillman, "Paying Professions for Colored Girls," *Voice of the Negro* (January and February 1907): 55.
12. "The Negro Woman In Business," *Indianapolis Freeman*, September 20, 1913.
13. Minutes of the Fourteenth Annual Convention of the National Negro Business League, p. 211.
14. Maggie Wilson to Madam CJ Walker, Oct. 1, 1913, in "Walker's Hair Parlor and Lelia College Brochure" quoted in A'Lelia Bundles, *On Her Own Ground*, p. 179.
15. Statistics compiled in Bundles, *On Her Own Ground*, p. 353. It must be remembered that these statistics do not indicate the number of women doing hair work in their homes or in informal settings. While I am focusing on beauty culture in Northern cities, it is important to note that by the 1930s, beauty culture had become an important part of life even in the rural south. See Hortense Powdermaker, *After Freedom: A Cultural Study in the Deep South* (New York: Russell&Russell, [1939] 1966), p. 180.
16. *New York Age*, undated Hampton Institute Archives, quoted in Bundles, *On Her Own Ground*, p. 180.
17. Use of the word "straighten" to describe the styles and grooming practices advocated by Madam Walker and her agents is problematic, as it was a word that Walker did not use herself in any advertisement. Still, this is perhaps the best word to describe the grooming practices of the day. For more on this, see Noliwe Rooks, *Hair-Raising: Beauty, Culture, and African American Women* (New Brunswick, N.J.: Rutgers University Press, 1996).
18. For a description of Fields' impressions of Mary Church Terrell, see the opening pages of Deborah Gray White, *Too Heavy a Load: Black Women in Defense of Themselves* (New York: WW Norton, 1999), pp. 21–23.
19. Mamie Garvin Fields with Karen Fields, *Lemon Swamp and Other Places: A Carolina Memoir* (New York: The Free Press, 1983), pp. 189–190.
20. Fields, *Lemon Swamp*, p. 187–188.
21. Fields, *Lemon Swamp*, p. 151.
22. For example, in two biographical summaries of her life, one by Karen Fields in "Mamie Elizabeth Garvin Fields," in Darlene Clark Hine et al. eds, *Black Women in America: An Historical Encyclopedia* (Bloomington: Indiana University Press, 1993), 426–428 and the other by Stephanie Shaw, *What a Woman Ought to Be and To Do*, there is no mention of Fields' profession as a Poro Beauty Culturist.
23. Fields, *Lemon Swamp*, p. 187.
24. Fields, *Lemon Swamp*, p. 188.
25. Information on Ezella Mathis Carter is reprinted from, Tiffany M. Gill, "I Had My Own Business So I Didn't Have to Worry: Beauty Salons, Beauty Culturists, and the Politics of African American Female Entrepreneurship," in Philip Scranton, ed. *Beauty and Business: Commerce, Gender, and Culture in Modern America* (New York: Routledge Press, 2001). See also Kathryn Johnson, *What A Spelman Graduate Accomplished: Ezella Mathis Carter—A Biography and An*

Appeal (Chicago, 1935). Johnson actually accompanied Carter on her southern journeys.

26. Johnson, *What A Spelman Graduate Accomplished*, p. 12.
27. Ibid. 14.
28. Ibid. 23.
29. Ibid. 32.
30. Terrell is quoted in Paula Giddings, *When and Where I Enter: The Impact of Black Women on Race and Sex in America* (New York, 1984), 99. Originally from Mary Church Terrell, "What Role Is the Educated Negro Woman to Play in the Uplifting of Her Race?" *Twentieth Century Negro Literature*, D.W. Culp, ed. (Naperville, Ill., 1902), p. 175.
31. Bruce is quoted in Giddings, *When and Where I Enter*, 100. Originally from Josephine Bruce, "What Has Education Done for Colored Women," *The Voice of the Negro* (July 1905), 296.
32. Quoted in A'Lelia Bundles, *On Her Own Ground: The Life and Times of Madam CJ Walker* (New York: Scribner Books, 2001), p. 77.
33. For a more detailed discussion of the connection between beauty products and hair straightening, see Noliwe Rooks, *Hair Raising* and Susannah Walker, "For Appearances Sake."
34. Nannie Helen Burroughs, "Not Color But Character," *The Voice of the Negro*, July 1904. See also, Peiss' discussion of the distinctions between make-up and cosmetics; Peiss, *Hope in a Jar*.
35.. See Noliwe Rooks, *Hair Raising* and Evelyn Brooks Higginbotham, *Righteous Discontent: The Women's Movement in the Black Baptist Church, 1880–1920* (Cambridge: Harvard University Press, 1993).
36. See, Mrs. B.S. Lynk, *A Complete Course in Hair Straightening and Beauty Culture* (Memphis: 20th Century Art Co., 1919), p. 7.
37. Lynk, A Complete Course, p. 6.
38. A'Lelia Bundles, *On Her Own Ground*, p. 75.
39. For a recounting of Walker's appearance at the NACW's eighth biennial see Bundles, *On Her Own Ground*, p. 129.
40. This speech to the NACW convention in Denver 1918 is recounted in Bundles, *On Her Own Ground*, pp. 227–228.
41. Davis, *Lifting as they Climb*, p. 263.
42. F.B. Ransom to Ella Crocker, November 19, 1914, Box 9 Folder 1, Madam CJ Walker Papers, Indiana Historical Society (hereafter MCJW, IHS).
43. For more information on Annie Malone's philanthropy see, Gwendolyn Keita Robinson, "Class, Race, and Gender: A Transcultural Theoretical and Sociohistorical Analysis of Cosmetic Institutions and Practices to 1920," Ph.D, Dissertation, University of Chicago, 1984.
44. Madam C.J. Walker to F.B. Ransom, April 17, 1917, Box 1 Folder 4, MCJW, IHS.
45. Madam Walker to F.B. Ransom, April 17, 1917, Box 1 Folder 4, MCJW, IHS.
46. George Schuyler, "Madam C.J. Walker: Pioneer Big Business Woman of America," *Messenger*, August 1924, p. 264.
47. MCJW to FB Ransom, February 22, 1916, Box 1, Folder 3, MCJW, IHS.
48. MCJW to FB Ransom, September 18, 1916, Box 1 Folder 5, MCJW, IHS.
49. "Nannie Burrough's Address at Apex Commencement," *Apex News*. (January/February/ March 1938).

50. For a detailed discussion of the racial uplift ideology of Nannie Helen Burroughs and the National Training School see, Victoria Wolcott, " 'Bible, Bath, and Broom': Nannie Helen Burroughs's National Training School and African-American Racial Uplift," *Journal of Women's History* 9 (Spring 1997): 88–110 and Darlene Clark Hine, " 'We Specialize in the Wholly Impossible': The Philanthropic Work of Black Women," in *Lady Bountiful Revisited: Women Philanthropy, and Power* ed. Kathleen D. McCarthy (New Brunswick: Rutgers University Press, 1990), pp. 70–93.

51. See Darlene Clark Hine, *Black Women in White: Racial Conflict and Cooperation in the Nursing Profession*, 1890–1950 (Bloomington: Indiana University Press, 1989), xv.

52. Almetto Alexander, Interview by Karen Ferguson, June 11, 1993. Behind the Veil Collection, John Hope Franklin Research Center for African and African American Documentation, Duke University.

53. Walker Beauty Colleges, MCJW, IHS.

54. Madam Walker to F.B. Ransom, September 26, 1916, Box 1, Folder 5, MCJW, IHS.

55. See Julia Kirk Blackwelder, *Stylin' Jim Crow: African American Beauty Training During Segregation* (College Station: Texas A & M Press, 2003). Although she deals primarily with the Franklin Beauty School in Texas, many of the same tropes existed nationwide.

56. "C.J. Walker College Graduates Large Class," *The Negro World*, February 21, 1925.

57. See Myrtle Evangeline Pollard, "Harlem As It Is: Sociological Notes on Harlem's Social Life" Volume I (MBA Thesis: College of the City of New York, 1935).

58. Hine argues that black professionals as early as the 1890s "embraced the ideology of self-determination" and began "the arduous task of creating a separate network of professional associations." Darlene Clark Hine, "The Intersection of Race, Class, and Gender in the Nursing Profession," in *Speak Truth to Power: Black Professional Class in United States History* (Brooklyn: Carlson Publishing, 1996), p. 171.

59. Vernice Mark, *The National Beauty Culturists' League, Inc.*, 2nd edn, (Detroit: Harlo Press, 1994), p. 18.

60. This speech to the NACW convention in Denver 1918 is recounted in Bundles, *On Her Own Ground*, pp. 227–228.

61. Information on Lucille Campbell Greene Randolph is reprinted from, Tiffany Gill, "I Had My Own Business So I Didn't Have to Worry."

62. Jervis Anderson, A. *Philip Randolph: A Biographical Portrait* (New York: Ferrar, Straus, Giroux, 1972), p. 70.

63. Anderson, A. *Philip Randolph*, p. 72.

64. Anderson, A. *Philip Randolph*, p. 72.

65. William Dufty quoted in Melinda Chateauvert, *Marching Together: Women of the Brotherhood of Sleeping Car Porters* (Urbana: University of Illinois Press, 1998), p. 8.

66. Chateauvert, *Marching Together*, p. 8.

67. Anderson, A. *Philip Randolph*, p. 73.

68. Anderson, A. *Philip Randolph*, p. 70.

69. Robinson, "Class, Race, and Gender," p. 395.

70. Beth Tompkins Bates argues that 1925 witnessed the burgeoning of a new moment in radical black politics, which she describes as "new-crowd protest politics." In particular, Bates highlights the role of the Brotherhood of Sleeping Car Porters and A. Phillip Randolph in advocating a politics that linked economic and political citizenship and rights. This shift, as Bates notes, was initially met by opposition by many blacks in positions of leadership. While this is an agenda that black beauty culturists would come to embrace in the 1940s, perhaps this transition period was difficult for Lucille Randolph's clients and colleagues to support, thereby causing a decline in her business. For more discussion of the shift in black politics that occurs around 1925, see Beth Tompkins Bates, *Pullman Porters and the Rise of Protest Politics in Black America*, 1925–1945 (Chapel Hill: University of North Carolina Press, 2001).

71. Richards, *Maida Springer Kemp*, pp. 34–35.

72. Judith Stein, "Marcus Garvey," in Eric Foner and John Garraty, eds. *The Reader's Companion to American History* (New York: Houghton Mifflin, 1991), pp. 440–441.

73. According to Barbara Bair: "It is very difficult to track employment of Garveyites, even through mention of them in the *Negro World*, because the focus there was on UNIA activism and opinion, versus what a person "was" or "did" for a job or profession outside the movement (they "were" the movement/ activists/ auxiliary members, and not elevator operators, nurses, beauticians, lawyers, etc., when they participated in the UNIA dialogue and activities)." Barbara Bair, email to the author, September 15, 2002.

74. From Amy Jacques Garvey, *Garvey and Garveyism* (New York: Collier Books, 1970), p. 86, quoted in Juliet E.K. Walker, *History of Black Business in America Capitalism, Race, Entrepreneurship* (New York: Macmillan Reference Library, 1998), p. 219.

75. Tony Martin, *Race First: The Ideological and Organizational Struggles of Marcus Garvey and the* UNIA (Boston: The Majority Press, 1976), p. 33.

76. Emory Tolbert, *UNIA and Black Los Angeles: Ideology and Community in the American Garvey* Movement (Los Angeles: UCLA Press, 1980).

77. Walker, The History of Black Business in America, p. 222.

78. For more analysis of the economic dimensions and ideologies of Marcus Garvey and the UNIA, see Milfred Fierce, "Economic Aspects of the Marcus Garvey Movement," *Black Scholar* 3 (March–April 1972): 50–61; "Garvey and Negro Business," *Negro World*, April 7, 1923; Mrs. Johnie Terry, "Talk Alone Cannot Liberate a Race," *Negro World*, July 10, 1926.

79. For a larger discussion of the gendered nature of Garvey's racial pride, see, Martin Summers, *Manliness and Its Discontents: The Black Middle Class and the Transformation of Masculinity, 1900–1930* (Chapel Hill: University of North Carolina Press, 2004); Michele Mitchell, *Righteous Propagation: African Americans and the Politics of Racial Destiny after Reconstruction* (Chapel Hill, NC: University of North Carolina Press, 2004); Barbara Bair, "True Women, Real Men: Gender Ideology, and Social Roles in the Garvey Movement," in *Gendered Domains: Rethinking Public and Private in Women's History*, Dorothy O. Helly and Susan Reverby, eds. Ithaca: Cornell University Press; 1992 and "Renegotiating Liberty: Garveyism, Women, and Grassroots Organizing in Virginia," Beryl Satter; "Marcus Garvey, Father Divine, and the Gender Politics of Race Difference and Race Neutrality," *American Quarterly* 48 (March 1996): 43–76; Ula Taylor, *The Veiled Garvey: The Life and Times*

of Amy Jacques Garvey (Chapel Hill: University of North Carolina Press, 2002); also see Deborah Gray White's discussion in *Too Heavy a Load*, Chapter 4.

80. Quoted in White, *Too Heavy a Load*, p. 121.

81. "Negro Women Leaving Domestic Service Alone," *Negro World*, December 6, 1924.

82. Ula Taylor, "Negro Women are Great Thinkers as well as Doers," p. 112.

83. The full text of Marcus Garvey's poem, "The Black Woman," is quoted in Rupert Lewis and Patrick Bryan, eds. *Garvey: His Work and Impact* (Trenton: 1991), p. 75.

84. "For the Searcher of Beauty," *Negro World*, January 17, 1925; "True Beauty Not of Face but of Heart and Soul," *Negro World*, November 8, 1924.

85. Chandler Owen, "Good Looks Supremacy: A Perspicacious Perusal of the Potencies of Pulchritude by a Noted Authority," *The Messenger*, March 1924.

86. The *Negro World* was certainly not the only black newspaper that relied heavily on advertising dollars from the black beauty industry. One need only to examine the pages of the *Messenger, Crisis, Pittsburgh Courier*, and *Chicago Defender* to see that the black beauty industry almost single handedly supported the black press. For further analysis, see Owen, "Good Looks Supremacy."

87. "Are We Proud of our Black Skins and Curly Hair?" *Negro World*, August 1, 1925.

88. "I Am a Negro-And Beautiful," *Negro World*, July 10, 1926.

89. *Negro World*, August 1, 1925.

90. Bair, "True Women, Real Men," p. 165.

91. Bair, "True Women, Real Men," p. 165.

92. "Marcus Garvey's Contribution to His Race," *Negro World*, August 28, 1926.

93. See Advertisement on Woman's Page, *Negro World*, November 20, 1926.

94. *New York Amsterdam News*, July 6, 1940.

95. *Negro World*, August 24, and September 7, 1929.

96. *Negro World*, July 24, 1926.

97. *Negro World*, February 21, 1925.

98. See *Negro World*, August 8, 1925, and January 24, 1925. It is important to point out that Burrows did not garner enough votes to win.

Chapter 8

The Sentimental Work of Play: Manhood and the American Toy Industry, 1900–1930[1]

Woody Register

In 1919, a writer in the trade journal *Playthings* recalled the lengths to which the "American toy man" once had to go to "disguise or hide the fact" that he made or sold toys for a living: the toy manufacturer would call his operation a "wood-working plant" to make it sound more dignified when he applied for a loan; wholesalers would mention the toys they kept in stock only if they were asked about them; and during the brief Christmas season when toys *were* featured, retailers would stick them in the basement. In all aspects, the writer suggested, toymaking and toyselling in the United States had once been questionable occupations, "Unworthy the Respect of Sound Business Men," as the subtitle to the article put it. But today, he concluded, "there is a change—a wonderful change—all along the line. There is a pride everywhere." Or, as another toy man boasted in 1913, "The domestic toy manufacturers comprise today a sturdy industrial body. Barely a decade ago this could not be said."[2]

These claims of the "wonderful change" of the American toy man from a shrinking, dissembling object of ridicule to a proud and "sturdy" embodiment of respectability composed the toy man's narrative of lost-and-found manhood. This narrative was a familiar and persistent feature of the toy trade press between 1910 and 1930. During this period new mass manufacturing techniques, soaring consumer demand, and the virtual elimination of German competitors turned the United States into the world's largest producer of and market for toys. As toy men conventionally told their success story, the transformation of the industry also entailed a transformation of the man himself. Men who made or sold toys invariably started out as weaklings on a path that was scorned and belittled: "In years past," as one veteran of the trade confessed, toyselling was "neglected, even despised . . . kicked into the worst corner of the store and throttled completely on Christmas Day." But the beatings they took prepared them for greater days to come: "The wonderful possibilities of toys . . . have [lately] become apparent to far-seeing men . . . ," the editors of *Playthings* observed in 1910. The "trade is surely coming into its own . . . [as] one of the most important of any in modern merchandising"[3] (figure 8.1).

PRESIDENT OF DRY GOODS COMPANY: "Not until to day, Jones, have I realized what this business has missed without a toy department. We want the FAMILY trade—we want to break in customers when they're YOUNG—we want to humanize our business—and we want to do it THE WHOLE YEAR ROUND. What's more we're going to START RIGHT NOW. Now you are the man to put the deal across—are you game for the fight"?

JONES THE NEW TOY BUYER: "I'm with you from the start—and let me say that you have made the one big decision that can make this house the best known business in the state—and the one decision that will electrify every department you operate with the life blood of business—new and permanent customers.

Figure 8.1 Far-seeing businessmen, this illustration from a 1917 issue of *Playthings* contends, were finally appreciating toys as serious business and looking for managers who were man enough to lead it out of the "Christmas tree class" of seasonal sale

Source: Illustration reproduced from the Collection of the Library of Congress.

Given the growth of the American toy industry in the last century, this statement was prescient editorializing. Yet considering how often toy men asserted these claims to each other between 1910 and 1930, one is left wondering if they did not, perhaps, protest too much. Collectively, their self-congratulatory proclamations read less as statements of undeniable fact than as therapeutic pleas for assurance. Although manning the helm of one of the fastest growing areas of twentieth-century business, toy men still found themselves on the defensive as "men." One reason for their gender anxiety was what they sold—playthings, or "mere gewgaws," to quote the phrase that stung toy men the most. But the problem also reflected the paradoxical demands of the work they had to perform. As toy men told each other time and time again, the only way to penetrate markets and to secure the territory of Toyland was for themselves to become the child-man inhabitants of Fairyland, the playful, goodhearted friends of their little customers. The sentimental work of play—or what *Playthings* called "dealing with childhood"—combined executive management, profit considerations, and boyish dreams.[4] The difficulties of juggling these elements of their job assignments in part reflected the peculiar needs of their manufacturing and retailing tribe. But in a more important sense, the cultural transformations indicated by their example suggest broader dilemmas faced by the growing population of urban middle-class men whose wealth and well-being were invested in the proliferating consumer industries of the twentieth century.

"Toy man" was a broad ontological category, although it did not encompass the retail clerks selling playthings or the laboring women or men who worked in factories making them. Rather, the American toy man was a member of the managerial middle-class: the owner of a factory, the manager or drummer at a wholesale house dealing in toys, the buyer for a department store, a designer of playthings, or a writer for the trade press. To be sure, there were female "toy men" who distinguished themselves in all of these occupations. Such exceptions to the rule, however, did not call into question the universality of the term, which was cast in the image of the managerial man—a figure who was presumed to represent all sexes and classes.[5]

If the sex or class of the "toy man" rarely was ambiguous, gender was another matter. The toy man's narrative of lost-and-found virility was part of the more general remaking of middle-class gender codes after 1890. Through most of the nineteenth century, manliness had been regarded as a matter more of having character—acting with self-restraint, independence, and contempt for "effeminate" leisure and luxury—than of possessing a male body. By the late nineteenth century, this model of ideal manhood was weakening under broad social and economic changes: women were defying the prescribed boundaries of the domestic sphere and encroaching on the prerogatives of their husbands and fathers; immigrant Jews and eastern and southern Europeans were successfully bidding against native-born men for power in America's growing cities and dominating the new economies of commercial entertainment; a corporate consumer culture was subverting the ethos of self-restraint even as it promised freedom and fulfillment through consumption; and, looming over all, opportunities for self-employment and self-determination were diminishing in an overly-determined urban, consumption-driven, bureaucratic, corporate, ethnically diverse world. Much of the scholarship on masculinity in this period has underscored how these changes caused a "crisis of masculinity" or "gender malaise." These changes, observes Gail Bederman, "not only affected men's sense of identity and authority, they even affected men's view of the male body." Middle-class white men, feeling that they had become too civilized, turned against much of what they had once valued as the essence of the "manly achiever" ideal: self-control, emotional restraint, and the existential commitment to the idea that "the full liberty of manhood" was achieved through productive work or business ownership. Instead, they appropriated qualities as well as social roles that they traditionally had regarded as subversive of manliness *and* social order, especially the rough physical competition and energy of working-class and immigrant life, and the unbridled playfulness of boys. Whether men were participating in or just watching (or reading about) the action, the hypermasculine compensations of the new "passionate manhood"—vigorous sports, bodybuilding, cowboy art and fiction, wilderness and imperialistic adventures, or the challenges of mortal combat—treated the male body itself, rather than the character inside it, as the most promising field for renewal of personal strength and self-mastery.[6]

Where did "toy men" fit into this boisterous lot of would-be strongmen? As the vanguard of the new consumption economy, toy men occupied a precarious cultural terrain on which to chart a new frontier for manly endeavor—the commercial world of play and children's toys. Beefing themselves up, whether physically to demonstrate their fearlessness and invincibility, or figuratively through aggressively conquering markets and winning sales, could work against them.[7] Success in their field, they believed, was not like that in other areas of commerce; the sentimental work of play required a different approach. As *Playthings*, the industry's leading publication, explained, toy men had to realize and accept that they were not making or selling merchandise; they were dealing in "the stuff that dreams are made of." Whether "from choice or circumstance," they were the chosen representatives "of Peter Pan the Playfellow."[8]

As dealers in dreams and illusions, toy men were engaged in a business that was at the conceptual center of the twentieth-century consumer culture of "desire," the new institutions, social roles and practices that aimed "to merchandise virtually every moment in the human life cycle."[9] To that end businessmen and many women developed a visual vocabulary not only of pleasure, delight, and astonishment, but also of luxury, artifice, impermanence, theatricality, fantasy, illusion, and magic. All of these qualities were traditionally identified as dangers to middle-class order. But by the end of the century, concerns about the "arts of deception" championed by such master showmen as P. T. Barnum were fading from the middle-class landscape as tricks and deceptions became "an intrinsic component of the commercial entertainment industry."[10] By this time, too, artists of deception were thriving in the new institutions of consumption that proliferated in urban America after 1890: department stores, theaters, advertising agencies, restaurants, dance halls, amusement parks, to name only a few. Such figures, from window dressers to stage managers to toy men, filled the ranks of these businesses in the first third of the twentieth century. They developed and deployed a commercial aesthetic that aimed, obviously, to sell goods, but more importantly to sell goods by reinventing the city as a theatrical landscape of pleasurable commodities. In the process, they struggled to domesticate the more subversive aspects of their illusions and became a troubling, if largely accepted part of the consumer marketplace and twentieth-century life as a whole.[11]

Fred Thompson, the designer of Coney Island's Luna Park amusement park, stated the emerging consensus on consumer desire in 1910: men and women, he said, were not rational-choice-making adults, but "grown-up children [who] want new toys all the time . . . Each year the grown children become more insatiable. They are thrill-hungry. They ask a new thought; they demand a new laugh; they clamor for a new sensation."[12] Toy men had a stake in the notion that adults are actually insatiably desiring children at heart. That idea, combined with the earlier reference to *The Boy Who Would Not Grow Up* (the subtitle of J. M. Barrie's drama *Peter Pan*), linked the new occupations, marketing strategies, and commodities of the toy industry to another key aspect of consumer capitalism: the commercial culture of Peter Pan. This phrase describes the array of businesses and businessmen who embraced the figure of the eternal boy to explain who they were and why they believed that, to prosper in the new century, a man must never stop playing or being a boy. This model of manly behavior overlapped with the "passionate" ideal at a number of points, but with important differences. For one, Peter Pan was no epitome of tree-swinging muscularity like Edgar Rice Burroughs's Tarzan. For the last century, he has, with rare exception, been portrayed on stage and in film by lithe, petite female actors, from Maude Adams in the original 1905 American staging to, recently, the Olympic gymnast Cathy Rigby. Such casting inevitably suggests that refusing to grow up carries its share of liabilities, leaving a man in a vague intersection of the masculine, feminine, and childlike. And yet the eternal boy who shuns the duties and concerns of adulthood for a life of freedom and adventure in Never Land has endured as an enticing, if persistently troubling, masculine ideal. Where hypermasculine fiction, such as Burroughs's Tarzan series or *The Moon Men*, fantasizes about the restoration of a master-class of native-born men, Peter Pan's continuous appeal has been its alternative vision of male authority and power—the lure of dodging the disabling responsibilities of growing up by escaping to Never Land. As an early-century spectator explained, the eternal boy stands for "the time when the universe was but our playground."[13]

The aspirations and anxieties of Peter Pan's chosen representatives, or toy men, signal that too much attention to hypermasculine forms of compensation may lead us to underestimate the enthusiasm with which many men sought, not to escape the malaise of modernity, but to adjust their expectations as men to accommodate the new commodities and social roles of early twentieth-century consumer capitalism. Toy men did not just represent or perform gender; they used it to construct and defend a new masculine identity that incorporated the commodity world of toys and "play." In the most obvious sense, they labored to overcome the stinging suspicion that men who dealt in playthings for a living did not measure up as men. At the same time, they endeavored to absorb the peculiar qualities of toys as they were merchandised in the consumer marketplace, to become themselves boys who had never grown up or stopped playing. For men born after 1870, as most toy men were, these were rival, even contradictory imperatives. With the prospect of unprecedented chances to exploit new consumer markets, yet concerned that their work and product were unworthy of a man, toy men invented alternative middle-class ideals of manhood more in tune with the priorities and opportunities of the consumer marketplace. They followed two interrelated strategies: on one hand, they used toys and play to reinvent gender, providing new ways of describing and enacting male power in and for a culture of consumption. On the other hand, they used gender to masculinize toys and play as "constructive," especially of sturdy, powerful manhood, thereby lending legitimacy to a commodity and industry that were not only new, but also, because of their associations with childhood and play, of questionable character. Their mixed success acutely points out the enduring unease of American men as they have tried to carve out an identity for themselves as men in the shifting and uncertain ground of consumer capitalism.

A Commercial Business with Sentimental Work to Perform

In 1908, F. A. O. Schwarz, the German immigrant who had been selling toys in New York for more than half a century, recalled that when he began, the American industry amounted to "practically nothing, and the product was a crude article, often meaningless."[14] Before 1890, toys were a rare and expensive commodity in American stores and homes, even among the "well-to-do," who regarded them as a "luxury," not a necessity.[15] The major supplier of playthings sold in the United States and the rest of the world was Germany, where craft traditions organized by toy merchants and brokers dominated especially the lines of dolls and mechanical playthings. R. H. Macy opened the first toy department among large-scale American retailers in New York in the 1870s, and as early as 1882 the pioneering Philadelphia merchant John Wanamaker sent a buyer to Europe to purchase playthings independently of import wholesalers for his store. But Macy and Wanamaker were ahead of other mass retailers in the emphasis they gave toyselling.[16] The great change began between 1900 and 1910, when large urban department stores across the country greatly expanded Christmas toy merchandising; then again after 1910, as the "year-round," permanent toy department became the standard in large-scale retailing. From that point, the great urban stores, although they accounted for a minority share of toy sales, nevertheless dominated the industry, developing the principal merchandising strategies and techniques, in effect, inventing both the child consumer and the toy department, an "oasis" of play and delight for selling toys to adults and children.[17]

Although initially lagging behind domestic retailers, American toy manufacturing began its "revolution" around 1905. The extraordinary growth of the domestic industry resulted from the combined forces of new mass manufacturing techniques, the "visible hand" of marketing and tariff protection, and the assistance of unanticipated historical developments. Fortuitous for American manufacturers, between 1914 and 1920 the soaring demand for toys intersected with, first, the European war, which eventually cut off German toy suppliers, and, second, the economic boom of the war years. Circumstances thus conspired to provide American toymakers a protected environment at a time when many middle-class Americans had money to spend and, with inflation running high, ample incentive to spend it. What followed, in the words of one toy man, was "a great revolution of the *toy* industry." The output of 55 leading manufacturers nearly tripled from 1913 to 1919, from $5.5 million to nearly $16 million. The fourteen domestic doll factories that labored in the shadow of their German superiors in 1913 grew to ten times that number by 1919.[18] Retail growth was equally spectacular during this period. "We have never experienced anything like it," said R.C. Gibson, the buyer for Chicago's Marshall Field, where 100 clerks worked year-round in the toy section. While the American toy industry grew to be the world's largest, retailers, no longer confined to Christmas, sought to commandeer other holidays—Easter, St. Valentine's Day, Lincoln's and Washington's birthdays—to make toy-buying a year-round, never-ending affair. In all, the industry grew 1300 percent in the two decades after 1905, producing more than $58 million worth of toys in 1925. *Playthings*, which had begun in 1903 with twenty pages, published its largest issue ever (514 pages) that year.[19]

Although the growth of the American toy industry constituted a story of steady and impressive commercial success, the white-collar men who actually worked in or supervised the businesses still felt they had to prove themselves as men. As they conventionally told the story, in the "boyhood" of the business (before 1910) the domestic industry and toys in general constituted an incidental, even despised part of American life. In the days of German-made toys, *Playthings* explained in 1919, toys "boasted of no mercantile prestige . . . The public bought them because children had to have playthings of one kind or other." Descriptions of these early days emphasized the petty stature, the physical weakness and dependency of the business. Compared with other commercial ventures, the toy industry seemed either "young" (which toy men regarded as a slight to their pride) or "trivial." Manufacturers and leading urban stores viewed toymaking and selling "as a side show" limited to the Christmas season.[20] Many of the century's earliest domestic producers began making toys as a seasonal sideline, often as a production consideration to use up scrap materials or to keep a factory busy during times when the principal line of business was not in production.[21] In addition, the men who were put in charge of the scorned retail department were ill fit to resist their marginalization. They tended to be marked by a condition of dependence and powerlessness: "the boss's little brother," or the "unfortunate" man "whose good nature prevented refusal," or, finally, the "uninformed buyer from another department" who knew nothing about toys and simply bought and sold what he was told. In all respects, the body of the early toy business and of the toy man himself resembled that of toyless children as the industry defined them in the salubrious post-war years: "Poor, pale little devils, flat chested, spindle legged and hollow cheeked with sunken and lack lustre eyes . . ."[22]

Toy men sought to build themselves up in a number of ways. Some tried to hire men instead of women for the department. However, even if they believed "every toy department should have at least one man on the permanent selling force," they were unable to keep the "sterner sex" in the department. Men would clerk anywhere—suits, furniture, even millinery—before toys. The male clerk, an exasperated buyer complained, "seems to feel that such departments offer a man 'man's' work." The trade publication *Toys and Novelties* advised this buyer to try to bribe "a good man, or a likely boy" with a higher salary.[23]

If they could not hire men, retailers could assert their seriousness by building an expanded, year-round market for toys and play. Playthings had to be "taken out of the Christmas tree class and put into every day life."[24] For toy men, "making" a market was a kind of frontiersmanship in a post-frontier society, an expression of masculine aggression and independence as opposed to the passive and weakly dependent position of the "boss's little brother." It meant actually acquiring or conquering territory in the store, a kind of property ownership, expanding the temporary Christmas toy section to the permanent toy floor for every day life.[25] As *Playthings* editorialized, toys were "not an industry which was creating a field for itself." During the war years, when German supplies dried up, toy demand grew so rapidly that even smaller stores established permanent toy displays, following the example set by some of the largest stores a decade before. Yet toy men preferred to see themselves not as the beneficiaries of fortunate circumstances, but as aggressive, self-made men who were masters of their destinies. "It is by this method of creating a market rather than following blindly along established lines," explained *Playthings*, "that the great strides have been made by American toy manufacturers." No longer content to let children decide what they wanted, toy men were, as an ad for the Erector line of construction toys claimed, going "Over the Top in 1918," conquering new markets, acquiring new territory in the store, and telling children what they desired. In early 1920, a toy man requested "just another year or two"; by then, "the toy industry will have imbedded itself in the world of commerce so deeply, substantially and permanently that nothing under the sun will ever move it or distract it from its rightful position." Other toy men already felt the changes. As one had proclaimed a year earlier, "we are finding all our latent talents coming to the surface. We are giving expression to the best in us and thus becoming creators, not imitators. We are relying more on our own resources."[26] These toy men were becoming toy *men*.

Yet, in conquering their territory and moving stock by selling to children, toy men had to answer to a paradoxical imperative. As one toy writer insisted, "each toy department and each toy store must consider itself as a commercial business, with a sentimental work to perform."[27] This prescription would have made no sense in the nineteenth century, when "sentimental" was a synonym for "unmanly."[28] To mix business with such emotions was not just to confuse the separate moral spheres and natures of men and women, but to invite disaster.[29] But the marketplaces of Peter Pan culture required a new kind of man, one more in tune with the emerging suburban ideal of "masculine domesticity." In the early twentieth century, magazines and other sources of expert advice were urging middle-class fathers to claim a greater presence in their children's lives. Rather than acting like stern Olympian patriarchs, they should pal around with the kids, act like a caring older companion, especially with their sons.[30] Merchants commercialized this ethos, adjusting themselves both to the new child-centeredness of the suburban ideal and to the demands of the marketplace. As the buyer for New York's Fourteenth Street Store asserted in 1909, the "girls and men" of the toy department "must enter into the spirit of hearty childhood themselves; they must be children to their friends, calling them by name, if possible. . . . If a little girl gets her little toe stepped upon, she is kissed and comforted. If a small boy bumps into a swing that refuses to get out of his way, his wounds are rubbed and he is coaxed into a new game." Another suggested the best way to get the "customer's viewpoint of playthings" was to have his clerks "dress in the well loved costumes of Mother Goose and the Fairy Tales"[31] (figure 8.2).

Costuming salesclerks as Bo-Peep and Jack Horner and other prescriptions for commercializing the "spirit of hearty childhood" indicated how toy selling was at the center of significant changes in American retailing. Christmas toy sales had been an increasingly important aspect of urban retailing since around 1905, and special decorative features, particularly in window displays, had frequently accented the Christmas seasons.[32] Beginning in 1912, leading American department stores substantially increased the use and elaborateness of holiday decorations and entertainment features. "It is not sufficient to get the customers into the stores," *Playthings* observed that year; "they must be entertained there, and this is the real secret of merchandising at this season." That year, for example, the Wanamaker store in New York abandoned the "distinctly businesslike atmosphere" that had marked its toy department in the past and installed a "Fairyland," decorating the sales floor with "impressive green dragons" and "plaster heads of comic figures." Wanamaker's idea, *Playthings* reported in 1915, "was to delight and dazzle beyond description . . ." Prior to 1915, the magazine noted, the New York Gimbel's toy department had been weighted down with "a sort of majestic dignity that . . . had some of the purely educative atmosphere of the museum." No longer; that year, Gimbel's installed a "Santa Claus Land" and some of its decorations and features resembled "a three-ring circus gone

The Real Way to Sell Dolls

First Pick Out Maidens of Rare and
Radiant Beauty. Second, Dress Them
to Represent the Dolls they are to
Sell. Third, Give Them a Chance at
the Susceptible Public. Hegeman of
R. H. Macy & Co., did this Very
Effectively this Year with these Three
Dainty Little Misses Dressed as
Madame Hendren Dolls

Figure 8.2 A commonly used strategy for disguising the transparent commercialism of toy-selling with the "hearty spirit of childhood" was to integrate sales clerks into the commodities they sold. These clerks at Macy's are costumed to look like popular dolls

Source: Illustration reproduced from the Collection of the Library of Congress.

mad."[33] Retailers were scorning seriousness and sternness to sell toys in the spirit of the child at play.[34]

Dazzling adult and child customers with decorative features was part of a larger scheme to banish—or, rather, disguise—the commercialism and pressure sales tactics that permeated the "adult" areas of the store. "If possible," advised one toy man, "get away from the fixed and stiff business-like appearance of the adults' end of the store because nothing so grates on the soul of the child as a matter-of-fact stiffness." W. G. Hegeman, the toy buyer for Macy's and an influential figure in the industry, instructed fellow buyers in 1913 to appeal to the "happy, care-free nature of the child" and to expel from their departments "the ordinary more or less sordid merchandising appeal" that was used to sell apparel, furniture, and appliances.[35] "Let the spirit of play" rule the toy department, urged Kitty Walker, the buyer for the Grand Leader store in St. Louis. "Without it the child feels restrained and stricken with awe." In 1919, Bloomingdale's in New York advertised its "Happyland" as "just the sort of [place] that every child will love—not one of those cold, *stand-off, hands-off* shows with 'Don't Touch' signs bobbing up everywhere, but an Affair of *toys* and *joys* . . ." Yet toy men knew that the people who read ads and bought toys usually were adults. The elaboration of the "fairyland spirit of toys" actually was aimed at grown-ups. "By all means," implored a writer in *Playthings*, "let us realize that the dear public is just begging for merchants to forget the strictly commercial, particularly in respect to toys, and to give them the glimpse of Fairyland that toys by their nature promise all of us." Ads told women and men to come to Toyland to "forget about your troubles—forget that you are grownups—go back to your childhood days."[36]

In part, this sales strategy reflected the dominant retail service ideal that the great urban merchants, Marshall Field and John Wanamaker, pioneered in the late nineteenth century. To banish the transparently commercial was not unusual advice; most merchants sought to "disarm the customer by replicating the [anti-commercial] ambience of a bourgeois home."[37] Yet the "toy department spirit," as it was often described and proposed, aimed completely to transform merchandising, disarming adult and child customers by creating an anti-patriarchal atmosphere of parentless freedom, intergenerational equality, and wish fulfillment. Managers of toy departments were urging a version of "masculine domesticity" on each other. To make sales, they had to become a new kind of man, by suppressing the male passions of selfishness and determination to acquire wealth and by assuming what was usually a woman's role as selfless nurturer and companion of children. The "toy man's proposition," as one writer defined it, was "to put sharp commercial considerations aside." A veteran of the doll firm Fleishaker & Baum urged the buyer to "put all of himself and all of his love for the littles[t] ones into his work and while he may not get as big a money return for his labor as some other departments may, the reward in the happiness brought to the children will pay better than gold." Another cautioned that "the makers and sellers of play[th]ings must know children and must have a high regard for children"; obvious advice perhaps, but also necessary because middle-class men had, for most of the nineteenth century, spent little time with their children, male or female.[38] In fact, few of the preconditions for success as a "toy man" conformed to nineteenth-century prescriptions of respectable manhood. What kind of Victorian man could fulfill what *Toys & Novelties* cited as the foremost quality for successful toy selling, "*Can be a child once again yourself*"?[39]

As all of these quotations suggest, the illusion of free play and spontaneous desire, of "childhood days" in "Happyland," was more important than actually letting adults or children do as they wanted or get what they wished. Appearances and assurances notwithstanding, liberty in the toy department was largely structured by and subordinate to the merchandising needs of the store. The idea of making the child feel as if she or he were the "proprietor" of the store was founded on the faith that loyalty won during childhood insured "a good customer in after life." The meanings and symbols of the toy department were designed not to free children or adults but, as a veteran clerk explained in 1929, "to create the desire for ownership whenever the children come into the store. Place the toy doll or game in their hands, place him astride the velocipede. In every case make the kid believe he or she owns that toy." Yet as toy men talked to each other and encouraged these schemes and practices, they insisted that it was both good business and actually the case that the toy department was, as it should be, not "cold or so lonely," but an "oasis" of innocence in the pecuniary "world commercial."[40] Toyland offered an icily instrumental market solution to the antimodernist yearning for a refuge of warmth and community in the heartless, impersonal, pervasively commercial modern world.[41]

In truth, hiding the pecuniary reality of the toy department only meant masking the exercise of power. For toy men to become children again did not amount to infantilization. On the contrary, by cultivating the boy inside, toy men did not surrender power so much as devise new ways of enacting it by disguising it as influence.[42] W. A. Finnerty, the toy man at New York's Wanamaker Store, was a case in point. "Friendliness," advised Finnerty, must be "the prevailing spirit" of the department, but they were to be decidedly lopsided friendships. Like most toy men, he maintained that the "pressure of high-powered salesmanship" did not work in the toy department, which should have the atmosphere of freedom and ease. According to the Finnerty plan, when a mother brings her children to Wanamaker's, a salesclerk does not pounce on them but waits for an opportunity to play with the children, to become their friend. "No one urges [the mother] to buy, but as she strolls through the department with her children, friendly eyes keep track of them." If interest is shown, the clerk is "ready to serve, but otherwise, she plays the part of a friend of the child." Here selling was not only "playing" but also playacting. Retail toy men like Finnerty practiced the art of "handling people," of winning them as friends in order to influence them as customers by playing with them. The issue at stake in these prescriptions was power, how to have it and how to use it invisibly, inoffensively but effectively in an era of salesmanship and administration.[43]

By the end of the 1920s, these apparently contradictory imperatives—to be the sturdy man and the winsome boy, the playful friend and the playacting salesman, the conquering proprietor and the yielding servant, the dealer in fancy and the generator of profits—were uneasily contained in the model of manhood embodied by toy men, such as Bob Davis, whom a 1926 Christmas ad for Hanke's Department Store in Cincinnati described as the "Richest Man" in town. As toybuyer, Davis had "the next happiest job to being Santa Claus himself." But he was not handed the job on a plate; no, "he made this job!" His success was attributed to a number of factors: a youthful eye that could see "into several million [child] hearts so understandingly"; a determination to drive hard bargains, dealing directly with overseas producers, making "huge contracts with toy factories," to bring the savings home to "nearly all the children of Greater Cincinnati"; and, finally, skillfully "directing the many duties of more than one hundred able assistants." And yet, for all this hard work, "there isn't a younger person in Hanke's than 'Bob' Davis. If you could see him today, . . . you would never believe that he has been a full grown man for more than forty years." The ad concludes, "See Toyland tomorrow—lose your worldly worries in a fairyland of children's joys . . ."[44] Bob Davis had more fun and was a better man *and* manager for staying a boy at heart, which constituted a new kind of manhood that was enacted in and made necessary by a culture of consumption.

Play is the Business of the Child

"Bob" Davis (or at least the advertised version of him) may have figured out how to combine managerial science and industrial ideas with the fairyland spirit of toys, but the very way in which the claim was voiced suggests the ad copy was not describing reality so much as pleading a case for it. Toy men felt that the battle for the status of their wares and of themselves was far from over. Even with a decade of mounting sales behind them, the editor of *Playthings* scolded the annual gathering of the industry in 1927: "We [toy men] must, ourselves, remember and we must make the world understand that toys of today are tools of youth . . . [and] no longer mere gewgaws to distract the juvenile mind . . ."[45] Such an argument, with its juxtaposition of constructive tools and fancy gewgaws, was partly a reminder never to be satisfied with existing sales; but it also indicated that toy men did not separate market expansion from their continuing struggle to show that they, like the wares they dealt in, were not a shameful sideshow. During and after the war years, efforts within the industry to build sales by defining the meaning and importance of toys often engaged the suspicion that toys corrupted children. The debate revolved around the concerns that continued to worry the sales force of Peter Pan culture: were toys "mere playthings" that effeminized or weakened the child, or "constructive tools for learning" that prepared the manly bearing of the child?

Selling toys, then, almost inevitably meant selling middle-class Americans—and toy men themselves were included in this category—on the authentic virility of toys and the men who dealt in them. For example, in 1910, a writer in *Playthings* explained why girls' and boys' toys were fundamentally different: "The first lives in a land of unreality, the latter in one of stern roughness and practicality." There was little unusual for the time in categorizing tender idealism as feminine and muscular, factual realism as masculine. The mere act of drawing the distinction here, though, betrayed the toymakers' jumpiness. Defining a hierarchy that favored the manly child who combined knowing with doing or preferred toys that "fill the youthful brain with burning facts about the great world in which it is to live . . ." may have been more effective at explaining away the trouble than actually alleviating the discomfort of being a toy man.[46]

In 1919, Marshall Field's toy-buying handbook expressed the central metaphor for the masculinization of play as "the business of a child," a version in miniature of the peculiarly adult male behavior of middle-class work. By 1920, the New York *Journal* was demanding "more toys . . . [for] the boy half working, half playing, intensely interested and willing, to develop his mind along the line of his future work."[47] This instrumentalist ethos became an essential component of the sales pitch for the many new "educational toys" and the vast array of American-made playthings that duplicated the material life of adults in miniature, all of which rolled out of American factories in record numbers after 1910. Toy men quoted and often worked closely with the new child experts, who confirmed that "toys are the means by which children live in miniature the daily life of their elders."[48] Notwithstanding the use of gender-neutral references, the universal model of playing child implicit in this view of play almost invariably was the little masculine doer, the toy man himself in miniature. A 1920 editorial in *Playthings* identified the "purchasing power" of playing boys as the backbone of the new American industry. The universal child at play (they named him "Johnny") was "a thinking, reasoning personality with the ideas of manhood and of business surging in his brain. He wants to do things, he wants to create things . . ." For Johnny no less than for the toy man, play was serious business. Marshall Field's "Inspiration" advertisement for its toy department, which identified commodity play as the foundation of man-made civilization, was celebrated in the trade in the early 1920s: "As kings dream of dynasties, warriors of conquest, and explorers of continents—so children dream through the inspiration of toys." In America, children had no time for "mere amusement" (figure 8.3). As the editor of *Playthings* asserted in 1924, American toys "are made for useful play rather than for playful use."[49]

After 1914 and continuing into the 1920s, however, some American toy men used the words, which conventionally had distinguished boys' from girls' toys, to construct a new hierarchy that was more attuned to the circumstances of the war and postwar era. They sought to masculinize play as an activity that, with the right *American-made* commodities, led to the acquisition of the sturdy body of manhood. Beginning in the war years, toymakers initiated a

INSPIRATION

AS kings dream of dynasties, warriors of conquest, and explorers of continents—so children dream through the inspiration of toys.

What philosophy, science and art are to civilization, business to man, the fireside to woman, toys are to youth. Toys are the child's WORLD!

Our Toy Section is a fountain of impulse for child nature and nurture. Boys and girls find here their priceless treasure—their friends; their comrades; their ambitions.

In this Universe of Playdom are the milestones marking the road to maturity. Here are toys constructive and instructive—for occupation, recreation, and education. Here is Science at its source; Art in its adolescence; Power at its portal! *FOURTH FLOOR*

MARSHALL FIELD & COMPANY

Figure 8.3 Toy men praised Marshall Field's "Inspiration" ad, with its civilization-building boy at play and doll-playing girl at his knee, for its success in expressing the vital necessity of toys as tools for hardy growth, instead of gewgaws for mere amusement

Source: Illustration reproduced from the Collections of the Center for Research Libraries.

national campaign advertising American toys as an essential element of "The Trinity that Builds Patriotism / The Home—The School—The Playhour," the last of which was designated the "greatest" of the three, "the toy hour."[50] During but especially after the war, toy men also endeavored to establish the masculine character and manly effects of all domestically produced toys—not just those made for boys—as the distinguishing mark of their specifically American quality. Toy men defended their newly won market monopoly by setting their commodities against the marked femininity and effeminizing effects of the German-made variety. This chauvinization of play and toys was a profitable mix of sentiment and business, gender hierarchies, "100% Americanism," and the particular market interests of domestic producers. According to the new convention, American-made toys were sturdier, "more stable and last longer," educational, "health-building," scientific, "well built substantial," made for a definite purpose, realistic, original, priced for value, and tailored to children's "needs" not whims or desires.[51] In comparison, German-made toys were the gendered "other": "hanky-panky, flimsy," "frail," "made only for amusement," cheap, imitative, "baubles to last for a day."[52]

However sturdy American toys seemed in comparison to the German competition, there were problems with envisioning play as the manly business of the child. For instance, what constituted the difference between a child and an adult, or more precisely, between a boy and a man? The marketing of toys obviously destabilized the time-honored moral boundary between manhood and boyhood, an effect that appealed to an increasing number of middle-class men who envied the energy and fun-loving zest of boys. Also, however committed retailers were to pitching toys as educational tools, almost everyone in the business understood that selling toys required using sentiment, theatricality, and fantasy—putting on shows, dealing in illusion, and promising fun. Many sought to banish practical concerns from the toy department and to make it a place of "sheer joy" where "the ghosts of dead fireflies go."[53] What, then, was Toyland: a laboratory of "burning facts" or a garden of fanciful fireflies? It seems that Toyland, like toy men, was not so much either as both, a syncretic combination of these contrasting and gendered qualities. When the maker of the popular construction toy, Structo, introduced in 1917 the advertising slogan, "Makes Men of Boys—Makes Boys of Men," it effectively summarized the uncertain returns of the sentimental work of play.[54]

A Boy Wants Fun

The toy man who most effectively exploited the formula of Structo's slogan was actually its formidable competitor, A. C. Gilbert. In 1913, Gilbert introduced Erector, a construction toy consisting of a box of miniature metal girders and axles with which a child (presumably a boy) could build miniature suspension bridges, skyscrapers, or cranes. His aim, Gilbert explained, was to stimulate "the constructive side of a boy's nature" and "the ambition to become somebody, to be something big." He also made Erector one of the industry's most popular and recognized brand-name commodities.[55] But Gilbert's success and notoriety were only partly attributable to the particular ingenuities and talents reflected in his toy. Tapping into the sudden proliferation of new market outlets and consumer demand for commodities of childhood, he also capitalized on the profit potential of making boys into men and men into boys. Publicizing his work as "play" and his identity as a boy who never grew up, he demonstrated that his manhood was not compromised, but enhanced by his investment in arrested development. Gilbert made himself the most visible representation of the sturdy body of the domestic toy industry during its extraordinary growth period from 1915 to 1925. In 1915, he was instrumental in founding the Toy Manufacturers of the U.S.A. The trade association united domestic manufacturers independently of wholesale houses, which had dominated the American market through their control of imported playthings. Elected the first president of the organization, Gilbert led it through the critical years during and after the Great War and commanded the association's campaign to define the meaning and vital national importance, not of playthings in general, but of American-made toys. His goal, as he put it, was to build an Erector-like domestic toy industry that "exert[s] the sort of influences that go to form right ideals and solid American character."[56]

Gilbert's biography, however, suggests the troubles that toy men faced in finding a solid footing in a consumer industry that mixed hard facts with the ghosts of fireflies. Born in 1884 in Salem, Oregon, where his father was a businessman and insurance broker, Gilbert was an intensely competitive and athletically gifted youth who displayed little interest in or patience for his father's modest pursuits. On the athletic field, he became a champion pole vaulter, making it to the 1908 Olympics.[57] Even closer to his heart, though, was performing magic tricks.[58] A crack amateur magician from a young age, Gilbert eventually abandoned a medical degree from Yale to devote himself to Mysto Manufacturing, a company that he and a partner started in 1908 to produce boxes of magic tricks for would-be boy performers like himself. Their success encouraged them to expand to a full line of magic supplies for professionals and to open a retail outlet on Times Square, while Gilbert himself dramatized his talents in clubs and in store windows, where he demonstrated Mysto's wares.

A contemporary performer once called magic "a sort of pleasant fraud . . . upon a good-natured public," but Gilbert claimed to be a new kind of magician. He may have relished tricking people, but he avoided the dark trappings of the typical vaudeville Mephisto. Instead he portrayed a clean-shaven, virile sorcerer for the modern age. Moreover, he wanted "to place magic on a footing where it has never been before . . . . to build up a reputation . . . for honesty and reliability." Magic, stated the Mysto catalogue, "is legitimate merchandise if manufactured by honest and reliable firms." For Gilbert, trickery did not undermine character, or magic and illusion conflict with sincerity and reliability. "Be a man and a magician," the catalogue exhorted its boy customers.[59]

Gilbert's determination to combine magic, performance, and character took an important turn in late 1911, when he began thinking "how fascinated boys might be in building things out of girders," the idea behind the Erector set. The magic business was "fun," he explained, but "not enough to satisfy me."[60] Perhaps, but he may have sensed the limitations to the magic market and worried as well that a man who dealt in deception for a living would never achieve a reputation for honesty and reliability. Erector, although a toy, seemed to present fewer such problems. With aggressive marketing and advertising, sales were approaching $2 million by 1920.[61]

Yet tricks remained Gilbert's stock in trade. The ads for Erector and his later autobiography integrated his athletic virility, energy, love of magic, eternal boyishness, and desire to win public affection through performance in a coherent narrative for achieving boy-manhood by way of constructive play with his particular commodity. Much like the friendly-eyed toy retailers, Gilbert played the part of playful buddy to his young customers. In the hearty salutation that appeared in Erector ads—"Hello, Boys! Make Lots of Toys!"—he addressed his potential customers as he himself claimed to be, a fellow boy, a pal and playmate. He wrote ads to read "as if they were personal messages from me to the boys." He invited boys to write back to him, and the "best letters" were published in *Toy Tips*, an advertising publication disguised as a newspaper and circulated freely "to any boy who wrote in for it." The company boasted a distribution of 75,000 in 1921. As *Printers' Ink Monthly* put it, the boy "is made to feel that he is writing direct to A. C. Gilbert, and the letter he gets in reply is signed by A. C. Gilbert." The letters were, like the ads, a pleasant fraud. As *Playthings* reported in 1920, "about 1,500 letters a day come into the Gilbert office, and all are answered, most of them necessarily, by form letters . . ."[62]

Gilbert's finest bit of sentimental work occurred in 1918 during a much-publicized debate over whether, as a wartime necessity, Christmas gift giving should be temporarily suspended. So recommended the federal Council of National Defense, which included a number of cabinet-level officials. Even though retailers predicted the council's action would have little effect on Christmas spending, the toy trade association weighed in as if the nation's heart were at stake. To "rob American *children* of their joy on Christmas—,"Gilbert's company protested in an ad, "to cheat children of childhood play—that must not be." Gilbert, as the toy association's president, led a mission to Washington to defend the interests of American children. He won a retraction and a bonanza of publicity. Gilbert insisted American toys were neither luxuries nor gimcracks. "The greatest influences in the life of a boy are his toys . . . A boy wants fun, not education." Then he opened cases of sample toys, and the decorum of the meeting broke apart. Cabinet members, one newspaper reported, began to play with the toys as though they "were boys again." A council member explained: "Toys appeal to the heart of every one of us, no matter how old we are." Gilbert was widely praised for saving the holiday *and* for boosting the prestige of domestic toys. The toymaker regarded the event as "one of the happiest and most successful undertakings" of his career and attributed his achievement to a simple, if redundant, approach: "I was earnest, I was honest, and I was sincere."[63] Few lobbyists have ever claimed otherwise. But for Gilbert, his stratagems did not constitute undue influence because they were deployed in the spirit of play. After all, he had made serious men break down and have some fun—and saved Christmas in the bargain. This formula worked for him. As he explained in 1923, "To many men business is a burden: something to be taken solemnly and groaned over. Not to me! I am having the time of my life."[64]

Gilbert believed that the example of his life and his toys were essentially conservative in function, solidifying manliness, instructing boys and their fathers in the stern duties that their sex had always honored, "the ambition to become somebody, to be something big." But his designs for dealing with childhood also showed man-boys and boy-men how to perform as men in the commodity marketplace. In doing so, he was like other American men who sought a practical resolution to the dilemmas of working in a culture of consumption. In the historical context of social change, the feminization of consumption and the workplace in general, and the growing recognition that the consumer marketplace would provide commodities for use and enjoyment, toy men struggled to reformulate the contours of manliness to incorporate play and eternal childishness as both commodities and opportunities. Yet such figures do not easily conform to the gender-crisis model of early twentieth-century men seeking to escape from the "frustrations, the routine, and the sheer dullness of an urban-industrial culture."[65] Rather, they were aggressively reinventing manhood in a way that both accommodated and rejected older gender codes for new ways of thinking about, enacting, and embodying manhood.[66] By the end of the 1920s, the idea that a man should simultaneously be a child and adult or that his work could be play still stirred anxieties, but they were no longer inconceivable in plotting the route to manly achievement, pleasure, and wealth in a consumer age. The designers of the twentieth century's consumer economy were not forsaking work or divorcing their sense of entitlement and self-realization from commanding the factory or store. Instead, the sentimental work of play contributed to the invention of an alternative ideal of manhood, one that accommodated facts as well as fireflies and enabled men to be magicians. For Gilbert and others like him, embracing consumption and having fun were becoming preconditions of a sturdy body, for their industries no less than for themselves.

Notes

1. Portions of this article originally appeared as chapter six in Woody Register, *The Kid of Coney Island: Fred Thompson and the Rise of American Amusements* (New York: Oxford University Press, 2001). I am especially grateful to John L. Thomas, whose intellectual friendship inspired this work, and to John Grammer, whose support is immeasurable.
2. "The Transition of Toys," *Playthings* 17 (January 1919): 132; "To the Front—American Toy Industry," *Toys and Novelties* 9 (July 1913): 23. For other similar "narratives," see "The Toy Trade," editorial, *Playthings* 9 (July 1911): 51; and "Toys in America," editorial, *Playthings* 8 (June 1910): 79; "Buyers Boost American Toys," *Toys and Novelties* 12 (June 1915): 34.
3. "Toys in America," 79.
4. "Salesgirls in Costume," *Playthings* 25 (October 1927): 69.

5. On female dollmakers, see Miriam Formanek-Brunell, *Made to Play House: Dolls and the Commercialization of American Girlhood, 1830–1930* (New Haven: Yale University Press, 1993). For other female toy men see, for example, "Katherine Gifford, Cleveland Toy Buyer," *Playthings* 19 (June 1921): 74; "Boston Buyer Talks of Toys," *Playthings* 20 (February 1922): 162. Perhaps the most impressive and important "toy man" of the twentieth century was Ruth Handler, mastermind of Mattel's Barbie doll. Although two generations younger than the figures discussed here, she had to face down her husband and others in Mattel to get them to add Barbie to their line of boy-oriented guns and other toys. See Ruth Handler with Jacqueline Shannon, *Dream Doll: The Ruth Handler Story* (Stamford, Conn.: Longmeadow, 1994).

6. Gail Bederman, *Manliness and Civilization: A Cultural History of Gender and Race in the United States, 1880–1917* (Chicago: University of Chicago Press, 1995), 37. On these gender transformations in general, see also John F. Kasson, *Houdini, Tarzan, and the Perfect Man: The White Male Body and the Challenge of Modernity in America* (New York: Hill & Wang, 2001); Kristin L. Hoganson, *Fighting for American Manhood: How Gender Politics Provoked the Spanish-American and Philippine-American Wars* (New Haven: Yale University Press, 1998); Peter G. Filene, *Him/Her/Self: Sex Roles in Modern America* (1974; Baltimore: Johns Hopkins University Press, 1986), 69–93, 71–80; Carroll Smith-Rosenberg, "The New Woman as Androgyne: Social Disorder and Gender Crisis, 1870–1936," in Smith-Rosenberg, *Disorderly Conduct: Visions of Gender in Victorian America* (New York: Knopf, 1985), 245–296; William R. Leach, "Transformations in a Culture of Consumption: Women and Department Stores, 1890–1925," *Journal of American History* 71 (September 1984): 319–342; Susan Porter Benson, *Counter Cultures; Saleswomen, Managers, and Customers in American Department Stores, 1890–1940* (Urbana: University of Illinois Press, 1986), 75–226; William Leach, *Land of Desire; Merchants, Power, and the Rise of a New American Culture* (New York: Basic Books, 1993); E. Anthony Rotundo, *American Manhood; Transformations in Masculinity from the Revolution to the Modern Era* (New York: Basic Books, 1993), 167–246; John D'Emilio and Estelle B. Freedman, *Intimate Matters: A History of Sexuality in America* (2nd edition, Chicago: University of Chicago Press, 1997), 222–235; Gail Bederman, " 'The Women Have Had Charge of the Church Work Long Enough': The Men and Religion Forward Movement of 1911–1912 and the Masculinization of Middle-Class Protestantism," *American Quarterly* 14 (September 1989): 432–465; Elliott J. Gorn, *The Manly Art: Bare-knuckle Prize Fighting in America* (Ithaca, N.Y.: Cornell University Press, 1986).

7. For examples of hypermasculine men who made spectacles of their personal metamorphoses from milquetoast youth to masterful manhood, see Kasson, *Houdini, Tarzan, and the Perfect Man.*

8. "Salesgirls in Costume," 69.

9. Leach, *Land of Desire,* 90. On the significance of the toy industry to this development, see the extended discussion in Leach, "Child World in the Promised Land," in *The Mythmaking Frame of Mind; Social Imagination and American Culture,* ed. James Gilbert et al. (Belmont, Calif.: Wadsworth, 1993), 209–238.

10. James W. Cook, *The Arts of Deception: Playing with Fraud in the Age of Barnum* (Cambridge, Mass.: Harvard University Press, 2001), 29.

11. Cook, *Arts of Deception*, quotation appears on 29. On "tricksters" in nineteenth and early twentieth-century America, also see Neil Harris, *Humbug: The Art of P. T. Barnum* (1973; Chicago: University of Chicago Press, 1981); Karen Halttunen, *Confidence Men and Painted Women; a Study of Middle-class Culture in America, 1830–1870* (New Haven, Conn.: Yale University Press, 1982), especially 198–210; William Leach, "A Trickster's Tale: L. Frank Baum's *The Wonderful Wizard of Oz*," in L. Frank Baum, *The Wonderful Wizard of Oz*, ed. Leach (Belmont, Calif.: Wadsworth, 1991), 174–175; Jackson Lears, *Fables of Abundance: a Cultural History of Advertising in America* (New York: Pantheon, 1994), especially 17–133.

12. Frederic Thompson, "Amusing People," *Metropolitan* 32 (August 1910): 604–605, 610.

13. "Childhood Young and Old: What Some Grown-Ups Learned at a Performance of 'Peter Pan,' " *New York Times*, December 17, 1905: part 4, 4. I discuss Peter Pan culture and gender at length in *The Kid of Coney Island*, especially 12–15, 179–184. A different, but related set of considerations are examined in Marjorie Garber, *Vested Interests: Cross Dressing and Cultural Anxiety* (New York: HarperPerennial, 1993), 165–185.

14. "Pioneers in the Toy Trade: Frederick A. O. Schwarz," *Playthings* 7 (June 1909): 60, 64.

15. "Toyland on State Street," *Toys and Novelties* 12 (April 1915): 31; Leach, "Child World," 211–212; Bill Brown, "American Childhood and Stephen Crane's Toys," *American Literary History* 7 (Fall 1995): 443–444. The best history of the American toy industry is Gary Cross, *Kids' Stuff: Toys and the Changing World of American Childhood* (Cambridge, Mass.: Harvard University Press, 1997).

16. Formanek-Brunell, *Made to Play House*, 15–16; "Pioneers in the Toy Trade: John T. Doll," *Playthings* 5 (May 1907): 32.

17. Leach, "Child-World," 210–211.

18. "The Great American Toy Industry," *Toys and Novelties* 15 (February 1918): 123; Leach, "Child World," 212–213; James T. Patterson, *America in the Twentieth Century: A History*, 3rd ed. (Ft. Worth: Harcourt Brace Jovanovich, 1989), 119–122; "Made-In-America," *Toys and Novelties* 14 (February 1917): 69. In 1914, the United States imported $7.7 million in German toys; in the five months prior to declaring war in 1917, $19,045. See "Allies Compete for World's Toy Market," *Toys and Novelties* 15 (March 1918): 99; Franklin Butler, "United States Supreme Toy Market," *Toys and Novelties* 15 (February 1918): 169; "Toy Manufacturers Association of the U.S.A. File Brief with Ways and Means Committee," *Toys and Novelties* 18 (June 1921): 72. The TMAUSA represented only a fraction of the industry. The value of domestic toys compared to imports also suggests the rapidly mounting dominance of American makers. In 1914, the United States imported $9 million and produced $13.7 million; in 1917 imports dropped to $3 million while domestic production soared to $26 million, which represented 90% of the domestic market. See Butler, "United States Supreme Toy Market," 169.

19. "Toyland on State Street," 31; "Chicago Christmas Season Smashes All Records," *Playthings* 18 (January 1920): 260–262; Harry Edwin Booth, "Buyers Preparing for Record Business in 1920," *Toys and Novelties* 17 (January 1920): 235; "How 'Go to It Gibson' Made Good," *Playthings* 18 (January 1920): 270–271; "American Appetite for Toys Insatiable," *Toys and*

Novelties 20 (December 1923): 162; Leach, "Child World," 213; "New and Old Merchandising Problems in the Toy Industry," *Toys and Novelties* 24 (December 1927): 177; "Keep and Use This Book," *Playthings* 23 (January 1925): 361.

20. "How American Toys Made Good," *Playthings* 17 (April 1919): 87; "We Are Proud of Our Veteran Toy Men," *Toys and Novelties* 14 (April 1917): 49; "Buyers Boost American Toys," *Toys and Novelties* 12 (July 1915): 34; "The Toy Trade," 51.

21. Richard O'Brien, *The Story of American Toys, From the Puritans to the Present* (New York: Abbeville, 1990), 72–76; "Playthings Pioneers," *Playthings* 15 (January 1918): 66–77; August Belden, "When the Side-line Becomes the Big Profit Maker," *Printers' Ink* 125 (December 6, 1923): 73–76.

22. "The Toy Trade," 51; "Toys in America," editorial, *Playthings* 8 (June 1910): 79; Robert H. McCready, "The Toy Department," *Playthings* 15 (December 1917): 10; Thomas K. Black, "Feature Blood Building Toys!" *Playthings* 18 (May 1920): 99.

23. "The Question Box; That Man in the Department," *Toys and Novelties* 9 (September 1913): 36. The debate over the relative merits of men and women in toy sales followed larger discussions over the gender of selling, to which women seemed—in the eyes of most retailers—naturally suited. On the natural kinship of "womanhood" and retail selling, see Susan Porter Benson, *Counter Cultures: Saleswomen, Managers, and Customers in American Department Stores, 1890–1940* (Urbana: University of Illinois Press, 1986), 31–74, 124–176. Men who fit the retail ethos of eagerness to please and service at any cost often were regarded as "sissies" or womanly; men who served often seemed servile. See Rotundo, *American Manhood*, 273; on the problems of service in a "republican" culture, see Gordon S. Wood, *The Creation of the American Republic, 1776–1787* (New York: W. W. Norton, 1972), 71, and Halttunen, *Confidence Men*, 33–55.

24. "Toys Bring Children's Trade; Why the Youngsters Are the Best Spenders," *Toys and Novelties* 9 (June 1913): 70; "Going After Toy Business," *Toys and Novelties* 12 (July 1915): 44–45; "What Has the Future in Store?" *Playthings* 9 (January 1911): 51–52; "Toys Bring Children's Trade; Why the Youngsters Are the Best Spenders," 70; Robert H. McCready, "The American Toy Industry," *Playthings* 22 (January 1924): 308.

25. My American Studies colleague John Grammer suggested this phrasing and insight to me.

26. "Editorial Comment," *Playthings* 17 (January 1920): 227–228; advertisement for Erector set, *Toys and Novelties* 15 (January 1918): 19; "Toy Fair Wonderful Success," *Toys and Novelties* 17 (February 1920): 200; "At the Threshold of a New Era," *Toys and Novelties* 16 (January 1919): 129.

27. "The 'Oasis' of the Mercantile World," *Playthings* 7 (February 1909): 66.

28. Bederman, *Manliness and Civilization*, 37.

29. "Sentimental business" would have seemed unnatural in a culture that honored the independence of "masculine achievers." See the discussion of Stephen Girard in Bruce Dorsey, *Reforming Men and Women: Gender in the Antebellum City* (Ithaca: Cornell University Press, 2002), 105.

30. Margaret Marsh, "Suburban Men and Masculine Domesticity, 1870–1915," in *Meanings for Manhood: Constructions of Masculinity in Victorian America,*

ed. Mark C. Carnes and Clyde Griffen (Chicago: University of Chicago Press, 1990), 111–127.

31. L. Shoneman, "The Fourteenth Street Store (N.Y.) Toy Department," *Playthings* 7 (December 1909): 35; "Salesgirls in Costume," *Playthings* 25 (October 1927): 69.

32. Leonard S. Marcus, *The American Store Window* (New York: Whitney Library of Design, 1978), 12–13; "To Suit Every Fancy," *New York Times*, November 27, 1888: 8.

33. Warfield Webb, "Christmas in Chicago," *Playthings* 10 (December 1912): 45; "Christmas Displays in New York," *Playthings* 10 (December 1912): 41–42; Sidney J. Rockwell, "The Christmas Displays of New York," *Playthings* 13 (December 1915): 52–58, quotations on 52, 55, 54.

34. The Marshall Field store in Chicago was remarkable for its refusal to join in on the dramatization of toys and Christmas. Its toy merchandising perennially emphasized "a splendid, dignified simplicity which is the height of good taste . . ." See "Marshall Field Merchandising," *Playthings* 10 (May 1912): 46–49, quotation on 46. On toy spectacles outside major cities, see " 'Santa Claus Arrival' in Boonville, Mo.," *Playthings* 11 (January 1913): 117–118.

35. "Essentials in the Toy Department Interior," *Toys and Novelties* 9 (June 1913): 44; "Pointers from the Macy Toy Section," *Toys and Novelties* 9 (September 1913): 30. The word "sordid" was used frequently to describe merchandising outside the toy department. See "Little Schemes Which Draw the Children," *Toys and Novelties* 9 (July 1913): 26.

36. "From a Success Note Book," *Toys and Novelties* 9 (June 1913): 63; Bloomingdale's ad, *Toys and Novelties* 16 (January 1919): 128; "Capitalize Toy Atmosphere," *Playthings* 15 (March 1917): 78; "A 'Real Estate' Development," *Playthings* 14 (January 1916): 87–88.

37. Benson, *Counter Cultures*, 83.

38. "The 'Oasis' of the Mercantile World," 66; F.W. Trumpore, "Confessions of a Reformed Toy Buyer," *Toys and Novelties* 15 (February 1918): 157; "The 'Art' in Toy Selling," *Playthings* 25 (July 1927): 73; Formanek-Brunell, *Made to Play House*, 57–58; Rotundo, *American Manhood*, 36–37.

39. W. Barrett Hankins, "Toy Talks," *Toys and Novelties* 15 (August 1918): 42.

40. Warfield Webb, "Christmas in Chicago," *Playthings* 9 (December 1911) 56; "Flapper Filosofy by Sunshine Sue (The Girl Behind The Toy Counter)," *Toys and Novelties* 26 (October 1929): 58; Marie H. Anderson, "You Must Put Heart Interest Into Your Toy Advertising," *Playthings* 19 (August 1921): 86–87; " 'Oasis' of the Mercantile World," 66.

41. Richard Wightman Fox, "The Discipline of Amusement," in *Inventing Times Square: Commerce and Culture at the Crossroads of the World*, ed. William R. Taylor (1991; Baltimore: Johns Hopkins University Press, 1996), 97.

42. On "influence," see Dorsey, *Reforming Men and Women*, 1–2, 106–107.

43. "The Fine Art of Helping Children Buy Toys," *Toys and Novelties* 24 (December 1927): 211. On lop-sided friendships, see T. H. Breen and Stephen Innes, *"Myne Owne Ground": Race and Freedom on Virginia's Eastern Shore, 1640–1676* (New York: Oxford University Press, 1980), 32–35. I have been influenced by Donald Meyer's examination of Dale Carnegie and the era of salesmanship and administration in *The Positive Thinkers: Popular Religious Psychology from Mary Baker Eddy to Norman Vincent Peale and Ronald Reagan* (1965; reprint, Middletown, Conn.: Wesleyan University

Press, 1988), esp. 177–194, and Warren Susman, "The Culture of the Thirties," in *Culture as History; the Transformation of American Society in the Twentieth Century* (New York: Pantheon, 1984), 150–183. See also Dale Carnegie, *How to Win Friends and Influence People* (1936; New York: Pocket Books, 1981), esp. 3–50.

44. "Cincinnati Store Pays Fine Tribute to Its Toy Buyer," *Toys and Novelties* 24 (November 1927): 66–67.

45. Robert H. McCready, "Children's Day a New Era in Toy Selling," *Playthings* 25 (July 1927): 146.

46. "The Little Girl's Doll," *Playthings* 8 (January 1910): 75; "A Little Knowledge is a Dangerous Thing," *Playthings* 7 (January 1909): 63.

47. "Every Toy Salesman Should Know," *Playthings* 17 (November 1919): 94; "Toy Problems Get 'Lead-Editorial' Attention in Metropolitan Newspaper," *Playthings* 19 (January 1921): 352.

48. William Leach, "Child World," 226–234; Cross, *Kids' Stuff*, 121–145.

49. "Editorial Comment," *Playthings* 18 (January 1920): 227–228; ad reprinted in *Toys and Novelties* 17 (December 1920): 130; on "useful play," see McCready, "American Toy Industry," 308. On the "manliness" of civilization, see Bederman, *Manliness and Civilization*.

50. These ads are reprinted in *Toys and Novelties* 16 (October 1919): 70–73.

51. "At the Threshold of a New Era," *Toys and Novelties* 16 (January 1919): 129; "Lord and Taylor Plans To Do Business Twelve Months a Year," *Toys and Novelties* 16 (April 1919): 59; H. E. Rodenbaugh, "New York Stores Have Greatest Toy Season," *Toys and Novelties* 16 (January 1919): 127; "Uninterrupted Toy Season Assured," *Toys and Novelties* 15 (September 1918): 29; "How American Toys Made Good," 87.

52. "Uninterrupted Toy Season Assured," 29; Rodenbaugh, "New York Stores Have Greatest Toy Season," 127; "Lord and Taylor Plans To Do Business 12 Months a Year," 59; "How American Toys Made Good," 87; Ernest W. J. Hughes, "The American Child of Today Demands Better Toys," *Toys and Novelties* 17 (January 1920): 298.

53. "Salesgirls in Costume," 69; Anderson, "You Must Put Heart Interest Into Your Toy Advertising," 86–87. As one "Successful Middle Western Toy Buyer" claimed, it was a mistake to try to sell adults on the "constructive" qualities of toys, how they "would help the children grow up to be sturdy men and women . . . The vast majority of toys, I feel sure, are purchased by the grown folks because the purchasers feel that the toys will please and amuse the youngsters." See "What I've Learned by My Mistakes," *Toys and Novelties* 20 (March 1923): 107.

54. Advertisement for Structo, *Toys and Novelties* 14 (April 1917): 32–33.

55. Advertisement for Gilbert Toys, *New York Times*, December 19, 1920, part 7, 5. Erector, like its competitor Structo, reflected and encouraged the imperial ambitions of American culture during this era. An ad for Structo in 1915 hailed playing boys as "Empire Builders." See *Toys and Novelties* 12 (November 1915): 45.

56. A. C. Gilbert with Marshall McClintock, *The Man Who Lives In Paradise: The Autobiography of A. C. Gilbert* (New York: Rinehart, 1954), 150–156, quotation on 156.

57. Gilbert, *Man Who Lives In Paradise*, 18, 16.

58. Gilbert, *Man Who Lives In Paradise*, 19, 21.

59. Gilbert, *Man Who Lives In Paradise*, 19, Mysto ad on 106. See the following catalogues collected as "Conjuring: A Collection of Pamphlets," Billy Rose Theatre Collection, New York Public Library at Lincoln Center, Astor, Lenox, and Tilden Foundations: The Mysto Manufacturing Company, *Mysto Magic* (New Haven, Conn.: Mysto Manufacturing, 1911), cover, 2–3; Donald Holmes Alsdorf, *Tricks and Conjuring apparatus for parlor and stage* (Kansas City, Mo.: Donald Holmes Alsdorf, 1916), 2, and Hornmann Magic Company, *The 20th century wonders, illustrated and descriptive; the latest European novelties, magical effects, etc., the latest books, music & stage instructions* (New York: Hornmann Magic Company, 1916). Other images of "modern" magicians summoning demonic figures appear in Cook, *The Arts of Deception*, 168, 207.

60. Gilbert, *Man Who Lives In Paradise*, 115, quotations on 119, 123. A slightly different account attributing the inspiration to "an overhead signal stand of structural iron" appears in "Fine Tribute to A. C. Gilbert by American Magazine," *Toys and Novelties* 20 (December 1923): 165.

61. Gilbert, *Man Who Lives In Paradise*, 135–139; Roland Cole, "Gilbert, Maker of Scientific Toys," *Printers' Ink Monthly* 2 (January 1921): 96.

62. See Erector ad reprinted in *Playthings* 14 (October 1916): 82; Gilbert, *Man Who Lives in Paradise*, 130, 131; Cole, "Gilbert, Maker of Scientific Toys," 96; "Gilbert Talks On Scientific Toys," *Playthings* 18 (April 1920): 89. Gilbert's secret, so he claimed, was that he was a boy at heart; when he announced innovations to Erector in 1924, he explained that "for these last two years I have been a boy again, building models which far surpass any models ever built with any construction toy." See ad in *Playthings* 22 (January 1924): 35.

63. "Toys are 'Essential' So Long as There Are Children in the World," *Toys and Novelties* 15 (July 1918): 26; ad for Gilbert Toys, *Toys and Novelties* 15 (August 1918): 21; "This Is The Revised Order of the Council of National Defense," *Toys and Novelties* 15 (September 1918): 29; Gilbert, *Man Who Lives In Paradise*, 145–157. Gilbert used essentially the same strategy in 1921 in testifying for tariff protection for the American toy industry against German competition. "It is our purpose to couple fun and education," he told the Senate Committee on Finance. Robert McCready, editor of *Playthings*, similarly argued that American toys "lay the foundation for lives of usefulness" and deserve protection from cheap German manufacturing. See United States Senate, *Hearings on the Proposed Tariff Act of 1921*, 67th Congress, 2d Session, 1921–1922, Senate Documents, vol. 5, part 5 (Washington: Government Printing Office, 1922), 4088, 4095.

64. "Fine Tribute to A. C. Gilbert by American Magazine," 166.

65. John Higham, "The Reorientation of American Culture in the 1890s," in *Writing American History*, ed. Higham (Bloomington, Ind.: Indiana University Press, 1970), 79.

66. Gail Bederman makes this point especially well in *Manliness and Civilization*, 5–15.

Part III

Commerce and the Built Environment, 1900–1940

Chapter 9

The Metropolitan Life Tower: Architecture and Ideology in the Life Insurance Enterprise

Roberta Moudry

Financial institutions, among them life insurance companies, are prominent builders and owners of skyscrapers. These institutions are known for their corporate headquarters, symbolic markers on the cityscape—one thinks of the TransAmerica Building in San Francisco, the John Hancock Building in Chicago, or New York Life's recent television campaign featuring their 1920s Madison Avenue home office.[1] The imprint of these powerhouses of capital on the urban landscape is more extensive than the singular architectural event, as mortgages, bonds, and philanthropic activities direct the financial sector's funds and visions into the built and human structures of the city. However, the skyscraper headquarters is the corporation's public face, occupying space in the city and providing a visual object to which a range of corporate values and products are linked and marketed to the public.

This study brings focus to the corporate headquarters of one such institution, the Metropolitan Life Insurance Company. In 1890, Met Life, an emerging insurance powerhouse, made a surprising break from the financial district of downtown Manhattan and built an eleven-story home office uptown at the southeastern edge of Madison Square, then a fashionable social center. In 1909, it completed its full-block expansion with a 700-foot tower, then the tallest inhabited building in the world (figure 9.1). Through all stages of an expansion that continued into the 1950s, the home office, with the tower as centerpiece, served as both a highly efficient nerve center for a paper-intensive industry and a powerful public relations device, a representation of a corporate ideology that bound together the dispersed, imagined community of the "Metropolitan family."[2]

Met Life's building enterprise, particularly the raising of the skyscraper tower onto the city's skyline, captured the attention of turn-of-the-century architects, engineers and artists, millions of policyholders, and an attentive public. Nearly a century later, the home office and tower has attracted scholarly attention across the disciplines. Business and cultural historians have studied

Figure 9.1 Metropolitan Life Insurance Company Home Office, ca. 1909. Looking across Madison Square Park, the 700-foot campanile appeared as a freestanding building situated next to the full block home office building. To the left of the tower is Stanford White's Madison Square Presbyterian Church, which replaced the congregation's gothic sanctuary that once stood at the site of the tower. Library of Congress. Prints and Photographs Division. Detroit Publishing Company Collection [LC-D4-39238]

the home office, particularly its interior spaces and practices, in relationship to corporate structure and gender theory.[3] Other scholars have considered the tower's use as an advertising tool, its role in the development of a modern urban photographic sensibility, its meaning to factory workers and communist organizers, and its frequent appearance in popular romance/disaster novels.[4]

Architectural historians construct building histories as a means of examining why structures or landscapes, typically those noted for aesthetic qualities or political/social significance, were designed in a particular way. While these works have traditionally focused on aesthetics and technology, and the persons of the architect and client, a growing number of studies in recent decades have considered their architectural subjects through the lenses of political and social history, anthropology, economics, and even biological science.[5] At the same time, a group of urban historians and geographers— Thomas Bender, Richard Sennett, and David Harvey are the most prolific and well known of this group—have seized upon the physical city as a means of furthering their investigations about culture, community, human relations, and social/economic systems.[6]

Like these ambitious investigations that highlight the connection between built environment and culture, this study endeavors, in David Harvey's vernacular, to spatialize a corporate history through the study of architecture. It defines architecture broadly, as structures and their physical contexts, as well as their uses and meanings, both assigned and acquired. Integrating materials and methods from architectural, business, and urban history, this building history traces the three-dimensional impact of a corporation and its culture on the spaces of the city. It places Met Life's home office within the context of the life insurance enterprise and the company's ideological constructs, and considers its relationship with the city's physical and cultural landscapes. By posing cultural questions about architecture and its two-dimensional representation, we may specify the home office's critical role in transmitting corporate values of thrift, health, and civic responsibility to a dispersed "family" of employees and policyholders, and the broader urban population.

The Life Insurance Enterprise

Achieving popular acceptance only in the mid-nineteenth century, life insurance was both modern and urban. It offered industrial workers and capitalists financial security upon the death of the breadwinner, replacing a matter once managed by church or extended family with an impersonal business contract, based on mortality statistics and administered with scientific efficiency. Because life insurance broached the sensitive topic of mortality, and commodified life and death, it evoked suspicion from religious leaders and the general public. Thus it was essential that companies appear responsible, responsive, and supremely trustworthy, and these institutions turned to architecture to convey authority, strength, and a spectrum of conservative virtues.[7]

The post–Civil War decades saw major expansion of the insurance industry, and the rise of a series of home office buildings in New York City, clustered along lower Broadway, in the vicinity of City Hall Park. Encompassing the maintenance of long-term contracts as well as financial services, life insurance was a paper-intensive business requiring large spaces for clerical workers and records management. All insurance companies, and especially the few—Prudential, John Hancock and Met Life—that specialized in the labor-intensive industrial, or working-class, insurance, employed large clerical staffs, new technologies, and systematized procedures to handle the volume of correspondence and recordkeeping.[8] And because state regulations limited the industry's commercial real estate investments to their own office structures, companies typically overbuilt to include a large rental component in their building program.[9] Driven by these requirements, and competition within the industry, major companies produced monumental structures distinguished by elegant detailing and technological innovation.

Because life insurance, unlike the Ford Company or the railroads, lacked a visible practice or product that bespoke the company's success and integrity, the life insurance enterprise created a civic personae, a recognizable, tactile form through architecture and advertising. In many instances, architecture bore the entire load of iconographic presentation, and companies sited their large, opulent home offices prominently for maximum advertisement. Particularly in the wake of negative press coverage of the industry's quick and questionable expansion in the late nineteenth century, companies used their buildings to claim a spectrum of positive attributes: wealth tempered by conservative business practice; religious and secular morality; and allegiance to civic and family values. Companies reinforced their support of family and home by exploiting the domestic reference in "home office," claiming a familial relationship among policyholders ad agents, and reiterating their commitment to the nuclear family and its financial resources.[10]

Met Life, established in 1868 as a life insurance concern, was a newcomer to an industry already well established in New York City's financial markets. An industrial or working-class insurance program, introduced in 1879, produced phenomenal growth, and Met Life soon rivaled the size and public position of "The Big Three," industry giants Equitable Life Assurance Association, Mutual Life Insurance, and New York Life Insurance Companies.[11]

The physical world of New York City life insurance into which Met Life emerged was geographically clustered on Lower Broadway. A boom in the insurance industry following the Civil War gave rise to a series of home office buildings in the vicinity of City Hall Park. Equitable, Mutual, and New York Life built opulent home offices on Broadway between 1865 and 1870, and all three expanded these structures shortly after their completion. New York Life and Mutual expanded upward, adding floors, elevators, and mansard roofs. Equitable expanded laterally, and by 1887, filled nearly the full city block bounded by Broadway and Cedar, Pine, and Nassau Streets.[12]

In the years between the company's founding in 1868 and 1893, Met Life occupied three different offices: the first two were rental spaces in the four to five story storefront buildings that lined lower Broadway in the last half of the nineteenth century. In December 1875, the still-young company purchased the Constant Building, a five-story loft building on the southwest corner of Church Street and Park Place, just one block to the west of the 200 block of Broadway, City Hall Park, and the insurance strip. Architect Napoleon

LeBrun transformed the exterior with a mansard roof and domed corner tower, creating a scenographic design that asserted institutional and financial stability. It was also here that Met Life first touted its business headquarters as a symbol of permanence and responsibility, a "homestead" for the growing "Metropolitan family."[13]

By the late 1880s, undesirable changes to the area, and the northward drift of business prompted the company to consider an unprecedented move from the financial district. Seeking an uptown location with unobstructed views and expansion potential, Met Life looked northward along Broadway's angling spine to Madison Square Park, situated at the intersection of Fifth Avenue, Broadway, and Twenty-third Street.

Located at the northern edge of Ladies' Mile, Madison Square Park was a site of informal social mingling as well as a node on the route of organized outdoor events such as marches and political rallies. The park's eastern edge in the 1880s was lined with residences, interrupted only by the spiky gothic form of the Madison Square Presbyterian Church, famous as the home of Rev. Charles Parkhurst's war against crime and political corruption. Hotels, restaurants, and theaters gradually moved into this residential area, which was distinguished by another prominent social landmark: Madison Square Garden, a full-block sports and entertainment arena, whose towered roofscape, including a 340-foot tower topped with a statue of Diana, marked the square's northeastern corner.[14]

One Madison Avenue

In 1890, the company purchased a series of brownstones and broke ground for an office building at the southeastern edge of the square, on the northeast corner of Madison Avenue and Twenty-third Street. Architect LeBrun was charged with the design of a structure that would articulate both the company's primacy in the insurance field and its self-identification as both a civic and corporate entity. To the interior, the firm used spatial organization and aesthetics to delineate public circulation, rental offices, and home office workspaces that supported a sequential and highly systematized work flow.[15] Completed in 1893, Met Life's original Madison Square structure was designed in the Italian Renaissance style, a widely accepted aesthetic formula for the late-nineteenth-century office building. Faced in richly detailed white Tuckahoe marble and standing 11 stories and 168 feet high, the building struck a monumental pose in relationship to the adjoining brownstones to the east and the Madison Square Presbyterian Church to the north, its size rivaled only by the full-block Madison Square Garden two blocks to the north.[16]

The main entrance was placed at the center of the Madison Avenue facade, but LeBrun's design brought focus to the building's corner, much like his scenographic design on Park Place. This corner view, best gleaned from the intersection of Fifth Avenue, Broadway, and Twenty-third Street (a circulation node that would, a decade later, become the site of the Flatiron Building), lent the white palazzo a particularly monumental appearance across the green expanse of Madison Square. Commentary in the architectural and insurance press concurred that location was the structure's greatest financial and aesthetic asset. "There are other more solid structures," noted *Insurance World*, a trade publication,

> like unto the granite of the Equitable, or the grey stone of the Mutual, but they lack what the Metropolitan's new building enjoys, a magnificent location. Madison Square will forever remain an open space, and from any part of this square the new building can be seen to the utmost possible advantage . . .[17]

The public areas of the new building were spacious and detailed in rich materials. The main entrance opened onto a marble entrance court and a staircase fashioned after the famous Paris Opera staircase.[18] Upper floors of the building (floors two through five) were intended for company use, and the remaining space was divided into rental offices for professionals or small companies.[19]

However, by December 1893, less than six months after occupying the new building, Met Life needed additional space. Conserving its monumental corner building for publicity and rental income, Met Life constructed a substantial, but less ornate, addition diagonally behind the original building, and vacated the original home office except for the second floor, whose custom design for executive and cashiers' offices made it unsuitable for office rental. While the company continued to use its monumental corner building as a corporate symbol and income source, it eased complex management tasks by containing all employees within a single-use, purpose-built structure.[20]

From 1894 until 1906, the company engaged in land acquisition and building expansion, using the LeBrun firm to splice onto the original cube-like structure building segments identical in height, surface material, and articulation. In 1898, the company built a two-story taxpayer along much of the Twenty-third Street frontage, and in three building campaigns (1901, 1902, and 1905) the LeBrun firm extended the original structure around the Twenty-third Street corner, along the Fourth Avenue frontage, and along Twenty-fourth Street, finally meeting the 1896 addition. The result was an aesthetically seamless nearly full-block construction, a horizontal and vertical giant, whose uniform façade and cornice line increasingly placed the building at odds with its four to five story brownstone neighbors. Met Life also expanded on the northern side of Twenty-fourth Street, constructing a 16-story annex in 1905 to house the Printing Department, and other support services.

Within, the complex was linked by circulation spaces and communication technologies that served the work of insurance. Both insurance space and rental areas increased incrementally: in 1908, the company reported that it rented 50 percent of its space, primarily as individual offices looking onto the park and Twenty-third Street, to small businesses, professionals, and civic associations. At the same time that rental income helped to offset the costs of expansion and maintenance, the stature of the building's tenants, many of them small insurance companies and civic associations, added to the prestige of the address.[21]

Elaborate public spaces further anchored the building to its urban landscape, and conveyed the solidity and strength of the company. Running parallel to Twenty-third Street, a grand marble arcade lined with shops ran the full length of the building (425 feet), connecting the original block's grand stair hall and its main Madison Avenue entrance to its east entrance at Fourth Avenue (Park Avenue South). This interior sidewalk offered shelter and shopping to the passerby and a range of services to company employees and tenants.[22]

As Met Life worked with the LeBrun firm (the original home office architect, Napoleon LeBrun and his sons, Michel and Pierre) to shape a public face, the company interacted with its commercial and institutional neighbors, negotiating their moves and consuming their building sites. The company stated publicly two reasons for acquiring adjoining properties: to clear the way for future expansion, and to prevent the construction of structures "detrimental to the interests" of the company by virtue of function *or* appearance.[23] Both these motivations compelled Met Life to negotiate the purchase of the neighboring National Academy of Design (1863), a highly ornamented and polychromed studio and gallery building just east of the original home office at the corner of Twenty-third Street and Fourth Avenue.[24]

Displacement of another prominent institution, the Madison Square Presbyterian Church, made possible the final, most dramatic, and publicized addition to the office block, the 700-foot tower. The brownstone gothic sanctuary built in 1854 was the home of political reformer Rev. Charles Parkhurst, and was completely surrounded by the white monolith of the home office when the congregation agreed to relocate across the street, and build a new sanctuary on a site secured by Met Life. Aware that the home office had blocked the "fair share of light and air, and by force of contrast practically destroyed the architectural grace and dignity" of the Gothic structure, the congregation engaged architect Stanford White, designer of Madison Square Garden just two blocks to the north, to create a monumental design that would appear harmonious with its corporate surroundings. The new church was a domed structure, cross-shaped in plan, with walls of yellow buff brick and a portico of green granite columns. Just ten years later, this sanctuary fell to the same fate as its predecessor, consumed by another of Met Life's incremental additions.[25]

A Modern Campanile

Finally completing the building block bounded by Madison and Fourth Avenues, Twenty-third and Twenty-fourth Streets, the 50-story, 700-foot campanile, built between 1907 and 1909, fulfilled Company President Hegeman's long-standing wish for a home office tower. Using the Campanile of San Marco in Venice, a well-known civic monument, as their model, the LeBrun firm designed a tower that matched the materials and detailing of the existing office complex, carrying the line of the lower building's cornice with semi-octagonal balconies. Although part of the home office ensemble, the tower appeared from the park as an entity unto itself, rising from the sidewalk as an independent tower, unlike its contemporaries, such as the Singer Tower, which protruded from or were embedded in, an office block and were visible as "merely an emergence, a peak in a mountain chain."[26]

The tower provided office space for the company as well as for rental, but its primary task was to serve as a timely large-scale public declaration of civic stature and ethical responsibility. The collaboration between insurance executives and the LeBrun firm yielded a design in which aesthetics and functions served as specific symbols of a corporate message of civic engagement, traditional values, and modern accomplishment, writ large on the urban landscape.[27]

The Armstrong Commission Investigation of 1905, extensively covered in the trade and popular press, uncovered widespread corruption in the New York State life insurance industry. Met Life, relieved to have been found largely innocent, declared itself a public institution, and like many companies at this time, shifted from private stock to mutual ownership and embraced civic activities such as public health campaigns.

The tower was an emphatic and architectural demonstration of civic identity. Its formal reference to the San Marco Campanile in Venice, a historic monument of both religious and civic importance, reinforced the tower's ties to the public landscape. This and a more general reference to family towers of medieval Italian settlements such as San Gimingano, raised as assertions of dynastic and defensive strength, assured the tower's position in a rich cultural timeline of great urban masterpieces. This "modern campanile" was featured in the popular press, and visualized for the public on a 1909 cover of *Scientific American* (figure 9.2).[28]

The campanile type also provided features—large clock faces, chimes, a crowning beacon, and an observation balcony—that provided specific civic services, thus demonstrating corporate largesse. The LeBruns were praised by their design colleagues and the critics for their use of historic proportions and details to achieve a visually pleasing solution to "the skyscraper problem," and the New York Chapter of the American Institute of Architects recognized both building and designers with its 1909 award of merit.[29]

The tower's modern technological innovations were another detail laden with corporate symbolism. The company pointed to the new tower's structural steel, innovative windbracing, and fireproof construction as significant components of a virtual and symbolic "Tower of Strength."[30] At the ceremony celebrating the tower's completion and the accomplishments of its architects, company President Hegeman articulated the symbolism of structure, proclaiming

> may its massive steel and iron columns and beams and girders and braces typify the strength and solidity of the institution, and may the everlasting bedrock upon which it rests be emblematic of the sure foundation upon which its business shall forever and forever stand.[31]

SCIENTIFIC AMERICAN

(Entered at the Post Office of New York, N. Y., as Second Class Matter. Copyright, 1907, by Munn & Co.)

Vol. XCVI.—No. 13.
Established 1845.

NEW YORK, MARCH 30, 1907.

10 CENTS A COPY
$3.00 A YEAR.

Dr. Parkhurst's Church.   Cologne Cathedral.   Park Row Building.   The Metropolitan Life Campanile.   Washington Monument.   Dome of the Capitol.

This Stupendous Shaft of Pure White Marble Will Tower to a Height of 658 Feet Above the Sidewalk. The Topmost Office Floor Will Be 526 Feet Above the Ground.

A TWENTIETH CENTURY CAMPANILE IN NEW YORK.—[See page 270.]

Figure 9.2 "A Twentieth Century Campanile in New York" Cover, *Scientific American*, March 30, 1907. Surrounding the Met Life Tower are monumental structures, including Cologne Cathedral, the Washington Monument, and the dome of the Capitol

Claiming these accomplishments as part of a national advance in matters scientific, engineering journals published structural details and the popular *Scientific American* compared the tower to such modern marvels as zeppelins and ocean liners. Manufacturers like the Otis Elevator Company, whose products were used in the tower, featured it prominently in their advertisements, lending the tower additional public currency through details of elevator, framing, and flooring technologies.[32]

Most striking though, was the tower's sheer height. More than twice the height of the Madison Square Garden tower, the Met Life Tower captured, if only for a short four years, the title of world's tallest inhabited building.[33] Creating a swell of free publicity for Met Life, "the world's tallest inhabited building" was the centerpiece of advertisements by companies whose products were used in the tower, as well as an inexplicable collection of products ranging from cars to corn flakes and coffee beans. For example, Huyler's produced a chocolate bar called "Metropolitan Sweet Chocolate," whose wrapper bore an image of the tower, and an advertisement for Washington Crisps depicted a giant cereal box next to the tower, heralding "the two biggest things of their kind in the world." Stores that lined the arcade added the tower to their letterhead; and such varied products as the Flanders "20" Coupé and Coca-Cola used the Met Life office block and tower as the backdrop for their promotions, with Coca-Cola substituting a glass of soda for the tower's beacon.[34]

Also flooding the market were views of and from the tower, the property of commercial photographers and postcard companies, marketing the images as a part of an obsessive cultural interest in the skyscraper. The commercial work of the Byron Company, the Detroit Photographic Company, Underwood and Underwood, and the Keystone View Company, to name a few, captured the home office block and tower in varying stages of construction, from the street and from the dizzying heights of its steel skeleton. Through this outpouring of commercial imagery, as well as the pictorialist portraits of the tower, most notably those of Alfred Stieglitz and Alvin Langdon Coburn published in *Camera Work*, the tower permeated the urban everyday.[35]

Text coverage in the popular press chronicled process and product, documenting both the great cultural anxieties about modernism and pride in human achievement evoked by the skyscraper. As the newest of New York's skyscraper wonders, the tower served as a symbol, not only of the company, but also of the entire working world. In the words of one journalist, this "steeple of the business of this world," chimed "the religion of business—of the real and daily things, the seriousness of the mighty street, and the faces of the men and the women."[36]

The Light that Never Fails

Beyond public fascination with the skyscraper, and structural allusions to corporate strength and stability, the tower was successful in conveying a host of positive attributes: quasi-religious morality, civic and corporate responsibility, and the traditional values of home and family. This range of attributes and values were linked to the architecture of the home office through events and services, and through images and texts that specified the relationship between architectural form and ideology. Reinforcing this explicit message was the tower's presence on virtually all company publications—from policies, and correspondence to millions of health pamphlets rendered in a dozen languages. Known to staff, policyholders, and the public as "The Light that Never Fails," the image of the tower served as a non-textual shorthand of corporate ideology, spreading across North America Met Life's vision of the ideal family and its domestic and civic environments.

The use of symbols or logos to sell products and to convey desirable institutional qualities was a common practice among large life insurance companies. Prudential, a major player in the industrial insurance field acquired the Rock of Gibraltar logo in 1895, while New York Life and Equitable developed sculptural groupings for their home offices that summarized intentions and goals.[37] In contrast, Met Life used the actual architecture of its tower as an iconographic billboard that featured the company's overlapping religious, civic, and familial themes.[38]

The tower made possible a bountiful range of historical and religious references to church towers and the New Jerusalem. Company Vice-President Haley Fiske, a deeply religious man, made explicit the tower's religious aspect, likening its visual representation of Met Life's quasi-religious goals to the cross's symbolic embodiment of Christianity. The tower, pointing to Heaven, denoted righteousness, and its white surfaces bespoke honesty and openness of character. The clock represented the systemization that ensured policyholders fair treatment; and the chimes symbolized the harmony and respect that the company advocated internally and toward its policyholders. Finally, the evening beacon atop the tower, "the light that never fails," recalled that the company never failed in meeting its obligations, offering assistance to its policyholders and workers beyond its contractual requirements.[39]

Religious allusions to the company tower were used to cement public faith in the company, particularly in the post-Armstrong Investigation years. To this end, a series of ministers offered testimonials citing the common goals of religion and Met Life as a socially conscious business. In this construct, the tower was likened to a spiritual lighthouse, symbolic of the enlightenment and comfort the company offered through its welfare pamphlets and its "angel ministers of grace," the visiting nurses.[40]

Blending religious and civic identities, the tower identified Met Life as an institution providing "refuge" from the challenges of modern living. Policyholders, company literature claimed, could "fly to [the] Tower from the dangers of industrial life, from the enemies of civilization, disease, crime, from all the vicissitudes and uncertainties of life."[41] The flashing electric beacon that topped the tower and marked the time after dark, was a perpetual reminder that Met Life would never fail its policyholders, promising financial stability and comfort to policyholders, and free financial and health information for all.[42] The company also used the tower's observation deck to reinforce its programmatic links to the city below, inviting groups such as the Charity Organization Society to use its observation deck to introduce interns to the city where they would study social work.[43]

The completion of the tower coincided almost precisely with a major shift in the company's identity and allocation of its energies. In 1909, Fiske hired Lee K. Frankel, a scientist turned social scientist and reformer, to initiate for the company a welfare program to educate policyholders (a group that included all company employees) about preventable diseases. Fiske's claim that "Insurance, not merely as a business proposition, but as a social program, will be the future policy of the Company" was not exaggerated. Frankel and his assistant, statistician Louis I. Dublin directed the company's resources and promotions, quite visibly, to the areas of health and welfare, initially in support of the industrial program.[44]

Because they could prove statistically that these measures extended the life of policyholders, and thus profited the company, welfare initiatives were expanded to embrace the broader population, and to support large-scale environmental and social reform. Nationwide, Met Life collaborated with public health and welfare organizations such as the Red Cross and the American Tuberculosis Society to create research projects and exhibitions, educational campaigns and immunization efforts, and worked with municipalities to lobby for bond issues supporting infrastructures with public health benefits.

As an easily read symbol and the site of early welfare efforts, the home office and tower served as both the symbolic and programmatic cornerstone for Met Life's expansive welfare program. Well into the 1950s, line drawings of the tower with its beacon aglow marked policies and thousands of booklets on health, economics, and civics. The tower appeared on everything from coloring books to drinking cups, fly swatters to picture puzzles, and was emblazoned on the banners and membership pins of the company— sponsored Health and Happiness League for children (figure 9.3). Large tin models of the tower, some with elaborate electrification, accompanied exhibits to county fairs and international expositions. "The Light that Never Fails" was the ever-present reminder that Met Life, its value system, and its city building agenda were widespread and lasting.[45]

In a particularly complex overlay of themes, Met Life granted the "Light that Never Fails" yet another meaning. Invoking the themes of home and family so prevalent in life insurance advertising, Met Life asserted that the illuminated tower symbolized the "Metropolitan family," an imagined community that included all home office and agency workers and policyholders spread across North America.

Bound together in mutual ownership, and as subscribers to the corporate values of health, thrift, and civic responsibility, the Metropolitan family included the larger spread of policyholders (in 1920, one out of every five North Americans), the inner network of employees, the father figure of the company president, and of course, the benevolent and ever-protecting

Figure 9.3 Hygienic Drinking Cup, ca. 1920. These paper cups were distributed to Met Life policyholders, part of an extensive welfare campaign that sought to eradicate infectious disease and improve the urban environment. The tower logo appeared on millions of booklets on health, household management, and civic responsibility, as well as on children's games, fly swatters and puzzles, all of which carried messages to the far-flung Metropolitan family. Collection of the author

Mother Metropolitan. All company employees were regarded as "older siblings" to the larger family of policyholders. However, the overwhelmingly male agents were designated as "guardians of the light," a charge detailed in the company anthem, which was sung at all field conferences.[46]

Binding the agent yet closer to the company and its physical symbol, Fiske emphasized that each was not only a guardian, but was himself a human light, a small but essential part of the great symbolic beacon atop the tower. The assertion that the worker was literally *part* of the building was a particularly useful symbolic strategy to keep those in the field, primarily agents, connected to the home office and the goals of the corporation. With these suggestions, an agent on the west coast could visualize his relationship to fellow east coast agents and home office clerks, and to the ideals of honesty and service, which the tower beacon represented. In addition, the tower's symbolic aspect was extended to the individual employee, confirming in a tactile manner his role in the corporate effort.[47]

The Insurance Factory

Congruent with the complex symbolic functions of the home office was the operation of the insurance "factory," the network of elevators, corridors, and workrooms that served as a records processing center and repository, and the nerve center through which all communication flowed.[48] For hundreds of agencies dispersed throughout the country, the home office was also a supply warehouse, and the center from which company officers issued all decisions. In addition, it was a community in which men and women of varied ethnicities and economic classes worked and socialized.

For reasons of security and efficiency, most home office areas devoted to insurance work were tightly regulated and closed to the public. Yet there were two critical interfaces through which Met Life's internal work spaces and its culture carried the corporate message to the public. One linkage was through the workers themselves. The women and men of the home office brought social conventions about work and gender to their jobs, and in turn carried their work experiences, and the corporate values that shaped their environment, to the world beyond. The other link was through publications. Their images and texts described the home office buildings and the work within, presenting to millions of policyholders a model workplace configured by efficiencies of scientific management and new technologies, welfare initiatives, and traditional values of family and home.

The home office experienced by workers and captured in photographs was shaped largely by workflow related spatial organization and standardized procedures.[49] At the ground floor level of the 1909 full-block home office, the original stair hall and marble arcade provided access to elevator banks servicing the entire complex, all boundary streets, and the subway system. Beyond these areas, interior corridors, recreation spaces including the roof, elevators, and even ground-floor entrances were designated for use on the basis of workers' gender, floor, or division.[50]

On upper floors, with the exception of the ornately detailed second-floor executive suite of offices, library, and boardroom, open, simply finished spaces housed dozens of clerks. These workrooms placed a premium on natural light and ventilation, and permitted instruction and supervision of a large number of workers performing similar tasks. These systemized spaces were served by timesaving technologies, such as typewriters, telephones, and pneumatic tubes, always partnered with company-wide protocols. Departments were situated in relation to each other to facilitate the paper flow from one site to the next, and to provide workers with easy access to toilet facilities. This "factory layout," advocated by office management expert J. William Schulze, was used by many paper-intensive insurance companies at a time when smaller enclosures still characterized the clerical zone of other businesses.[51]

Home office space and activities were also substantially shaped by Met Life's employee welfare efforts. A lunchroom serving coffee and tea was provided for women as early as 1893, and between 1908 and 1994, the company supplied free lunches to all employees.[52] A library, auditorium, medical examination rooms, and a gymnasium offered space and services as an employee benefit. Workrooms were welfare-inflected as well: layout and seating met lighting and ventilation parameters, and desk-side five-minute exercise periods were conducted at mid-morning and afternoon, with open windows and gramophone. Other activities, such as after-hours classes in typing, sewing, and first aid changed employees' uses and perceptions of the building. Club meetings and organized social events placed the home office at the center of many young clerical workers' lives.[53]

After 1909, Met Life absorbed its employee welfare initiatives into a larger welfare program for policyholders and the general public. This connection brought the home office and its internal workings and culture in contact with the city beyond its walls, as health programs initiated within the home office and deemed successful were shared with policyholders and the public. Conversely, major projects and exhibitions for the public were previewed for staff in the home office.

In a more literal fashion, Met Life offered its operation as a model, a laboratory for the development of corporate best practices, through publications of the Policyholders' Service Bureau. A corporate subdivision, the Bureau undertook and published studies for group policyholders in office design, employee management, and benefits, safety measures, and community relations, frequently citing home office practices.[54]

Met Life's operations and internal culture were also inflected by the women and men of the insurance factory. Met Life moved 650 workers into its 1893 home office: by 1908, the staff of the expanded complex numbered just shy of 3,000, and grew to 14,500 by 1938. Replicating the social hierarchies and spatial borders of the city beyond the company's elaborate revolving doors, Met Life created and enforced separate spheres of immigrants, native-born women and upwardly-mobile white men. Service positions, such as elevator operator, custodian and commissary worker, were filled by immigrants and unschooled members of the working class. White-collar jobs, which included clerks, telephone operators, accountants, and actuarial assistants, were held by native-born, predominantly young men and women.[55]

Within the home office, the urban forces of economics and culture were supplemented by a corporate agenda that promoted personal health and education, and group cooperation. Immigrant service workers were nudged toward Americanization with free company-directed English and citizenship classes, women clerks toward better business and homemaking skills, and male white-collars toward a life insurance career. All clerks were encouraged to take the correspondence course, "The Principles of Life Insurance," a requirement for all agent trainees, so as to familiarize themselves with the fundamentals of the business in which they participated. Although Met Life's paternalistic social engineering urged self-improvement within and respect among groups of workers, the class system within the home office, and one's place in it, were largely unmovable.[56]

White-collar men and women were the largest work groups Met Life managed, and their job paths, social and spatial patterns were significant shapers of corporate culture.[57] Men were channeled into positions that required more technical and analytical skills, and were encouraged to engage in actuarial or other insurance studies that would enable advancement to supervisory, administrative, and perhaps executive roles. Women, who comprised fully 60 percent of the office staff, worked in clerical positions that required only limited training, performing tasks that were considered "feminine" by business manuals and women's career guides, and that would occupy them until they married.[58]

Spatially, the company managed their mixed-gender workforce with schedules, restrictions, and codes of conduct. Dining room and gymnasium use was gender specific, and actual workspaces were frequently single sex, although women were often overseen by a male supervisor. While spatial segregation was instituted in adherence to contemporary social norms, it was also the explicit and spatial expression of the gender-based hierarchy of jobs and salaries within the company: just as women and men rode on different elevators, so they moved on different career ladders.[59]

At the same time, company-sponsored and monitored recreational activities provided young women and men with interaction not always possible or permitted in the larger arena of the city.[60] Seeking primarily to uphold morality within the office, the company did not discourage romance or marriage within the ranks, and house organs record numerous "in-family" unions.[61]

While Met Life constructed guidelines for workers' conduct on and off the job, workers were not anonymous cogs in the insurance machine, bereft of power and desire. Workers formed clubs and organized social events and a cooperative buying club. Women and men alike brought their needs and interests to their workplace, and there were instances when their collective efforts shaped and at times reversed company policy. Office spittoons appear in photographs taken in years when the employee rulebook expressly forbade such masculine and unclean behavior in workrooms. And in a particularly striking instance of personal initiative and spatial ownership, women clerical workers defied company rules and decorated co-workers' desks to celebrate special occasions. These expressions of individuality on the small space that a worker could claim as her own were obviously compelling: within a decade, the company itself was creating such celebratory tableaux to mark personal milestones.[62]

Beyond the immediate zone where corporate and urban culture interacted, the company's home office spaces and practices were showcased to agents, policyholders, and the public through descriptive texts and photographs that took the form of postcards, pamphlets, magazine articles, and exhibitions. Central to the company's image making were three oversized monographs published by the company in 1897, 1908, and 1914, lavishly illustrated with photographs of the building, its interiors, and its staff. Collectively, these depictions formed the public face of the company, made possible largely by camera and photographer, but ultimately constructed by the corporation itself.[63]

Met Life presented the spaces and operation of its 1897 home office to its field staff in the oversized *Souvenir Number of the Weekly Bulletin, 1893–1897*. The volume contained a historical sketch of the company by actuary James M. Craig; a description of the two buildings by architects Napoleon LeBrun and Sons; and a lengthy account of the work carried on within by George B. Woodward, the vice-president in charge of home office activities. Photographs by Frank P. Jewett of Orange, New Jersey show the public spaces, the cashiers' department, and the executive offices of the 1893 building, and the workspaces of the Twenty-fourth Street annex.[64]

For a 1908 publication celebrating the company's fortieth anniversary and the near-completion of the tower, the prominent New York commercial photographic firm of Byron was commissioned to produce a series of photographs recording the home office. The resulting volume, *The Metropolitan Life Insurance Company* (a revised edition was issued in 1914) included exterior views and an extensive collection of interior photographs that depicted the ornate public areas, executive offices, and workrooms as well as auxiliary spaces such as gymnasium and dining rooms, and printing and supply divisions. History and symbolism were amply covered, but statistics and system prevailed: the textual and photographic tour of the building was not conducted floor by floor, but followed the efficiency-tested path of a policy from division to division.[65]

These images have achieved widespread currency in the field of business history as documentation of the nineteenth-century office building interior, neutral records of the inner mechanisms of the corporate world, and more specifically as evidence of Met Life's gendered corporate spaces. Confirming their documentary status, prominent photographer Edward Steichen characterized Byron's work as "objective," noting "the places, the things and the people photographed have a chance to speak for themselves without interference."[66]

If, however, the photographic effort was neutral and objective, it was not a candid or unobtrusive process: photographic processes required several minutes of posing for indoor shots. More importantly, these images of home office interiors were not used in a neutral way. They were systematically composed, collected, and disseminated by the subject/client, Met Life, to craft a corporate portrait that purposefully foregrounds certain features of the company while suppressing others. Images of office machinery, and of workrooms and lunchrooms populated by look-alike workers bespeak a modern and model work environment powered by the collective effort of what the company labeled "the Metropolitan Family." Documenting the company's financial and cultural stature are photographs of lavish executive quarters and board room, but absent are officers whose high salaries and personal business interests were a focus of state regulatory investigations. Perhaps the most "constructed" aspect of these photographs is their visual opening of spaces that were in reality closed to the public, granting to them a "publicness" that supported President Haley Fiske's declaration that Met Life was a "public institution."

The Byron photographs, and other images of the office interiors were made into postcards that were distributed by the home office and the field force: between 1906 and 1909 alone, the company purchased over eight million postcards. These postcards, like the welfare pamphlets emblazoned with the 1909 Tower, linked the business of insurance to a broader range of ideologies through architectural representation, and carried this promotional package into the homes of millions nationwide.[67]

Visible through company rulebooks, employee magazines, and photographs, life within the insurance factory expressed a corporate value system that blended the seemingly oppositional values of modernity (efficiency and profit) and of such conventional social frameworks as family, community, and country. As subject of the Byron camera, and as a laboratory for corporate welfare measures, office practices, and culture, the world within the monumental home office, like its monumental wrapper, served as visual and virtual interface between Met Life and the city.

*   *   *

Through its functional, visual, and symbolic qualities, the home office served as the site where Met Life engaged the challenge of reconciling sets of binaries at times in conflict: the human and social aspects of women and men; the efficiencies of modernity with the traditional values and roles of the family; and the profit-making initiatives of business with public welfare, benevolence, and civic responsibility. Each of these pairs was central to the life insurance enterprise and to Met Life in particular: the paper-intensive industry was early to introduce a female workforce to a male work environment; the family and home were primary objects of insurance protection; and Met Life, as an insurer of the working class, asserted that profitability was linked, in fact dependent upon, public health and welfare, and by extension, the design and use of home, work, and city spaces.

The Met Life Tower displayed in the landscape of the city in dramatic form the carefully constructed set of values and characteristics that the company sought to inculcate in its stakeholders—employees, policyholders, and ultimately the American everyman. Cleanliness and health, family cohesion and home ownership, civic responsibility and patriotism could be achieved and sustained, Met Life believed, through carefully directed environmental and behavioral practices. Thus, the company used architecture not only to symbolize its values and goals, it also relied heavily on architecture as a means by which these values and goals could be implemented.

Collectively, the reality and imagery of the home office knit together the work world of greater New York (which could view the tower as part of the skyline), the internal world of the company, and the millions of geographically dispersed policyholders, an imagined community unified by corporate beliefs cast in civic language. In this way, Met Life overlapped categories of public and private, civic and corporate. As a corporation, it defined space not simply by creating architectural boundaries that contained and controlled, but by ascribing meanings and values to spaces, rendering them at once public, because they were presented for popular consumption, and private, because they bore the imprimatur of the corporation and its specific agenda.

Architecture was central as well to the company's other major endeavors, in public welfare and housing, chapters of the Met Life story not detailed here. However, aesthetics were never a primary or independent focus in Met Life's enterprises: the company instead saw in architecture (and spatial practices) the potential to improve health, guide behavior, and inspire belief. Repeatedly, it turned to architectural and spatial design, and to education about the uses and care of domestic and urban/civic spaces, to enact its corporate ideology of service and reform. Quite simply, in architecture, Met Life found its single, most powerful means of shaping not only its corporate offices, but also the urban landscape and its public culture, which it so desired to configure in its own image.

Notes

I extend my appreciation to Dan May, MetLife Archivist, for his assistance in the corporate archives. Prof. Angel Kwolek-Folland and participants in the Hagley Research Seminar (February 2003) offered insightful comments on an earlier version of this essay. I also thank Prof. Edward K. Muller for his critical reading of the text.

1. Daniel Abramson, *Skyscraper Rivals: The AIG Building and the Architecture of Wall Street* (New York: Princeton Architectural Press, 2001). New York Life's advertising campaign entitled "Heritage" ran from September 2002 through 2003 and linked their Gothic home office to core values of financial strength, integrity, and humanity. This paper is drawn from a project entitled "Met Life's Metropolis," a revision of my dissertation, "Architecture as Cultural Design: The Architecture and Urbanism of the Metropolitan Life Insurance Company" (Ph.D. diss., Cornell University, 1995). A related essay focusing on the building as a moment in the rise of the American skyscraper is "The Corporate and the Civic: Met Life's Home Office Building," Ch. 6 in *The American*

Skyscraper: Cultural Histories, ed. Roberta Moudry (New York: Cambridge University Press, 2005).

2. An "imagined community" as defined by Benedict Anderson, is a group of individuals who may not know or see each other, but believe or are made to believe that they share common goals. Anderson believes this to be a factor in national identity, a construct promoted in particular by newspapers. Benedict Anderson, *Imagined Communities*, rev. ed. (London and New York: Verso, 1991), 33–36. For the application of this idea to a corporation and its architectural presence, see Katherine Solomonson, *The Chicago Tribune Tower Competition: Skyscraper Design and Cultural Change in the 1920s* (New York: Cambridge University Press, 2001), pp. 61–67.

3. For a general study of Met Life's corporate structure as well as the home office see Olivier Zunz, *Making America Corporate, 1870–1920* (Chicago: University of Chicago Press, 1990); and Gail Fenske and Deryck Holdsworth, "Corporate Identity and the New York Office Building: 1895–1915," in *The Landscape of Modernity: Essays on New York City, 1900–1940*, ed. Olivier Zunz and David Ward (New York: Russell Sage, 1992), 129–159. Gender theory and business history shape the extensive discussion of Met Life in Angel Kwolek-Folland, *Engendering Business: Men and Women in the Corporate Office, 1870–1930* (Baltimore: Johns Hopkins University Press, 1994).

4. Meir Wigoder, "The 'Solar Eye' of Vision: Emergence of the Skyscraper-Viewer in the Discourse on Heights in New York City, 1890–1920," *Journal of the Society of Architectural Historians* 61:2 (June 2002): 152–169; Sarah Watts, "Built Languages of Class: Skyscrapers and Labor Protest in Victorian Public Space," Ch. 9 in *The American Skyscraper: Cultural Histories*, ed. Roberta Moudry (New York: Cambridge University Press, 2005); Nick Yablon, "The Metropolitan Life in Ruins: Architectural and Fictional Speculations in New York, 1909–19," *American Quarterly* 56:2 (June 2004): 309–346.

5. See, for example, Daniel Bluestone, *Constructing Chicago* (New Haven: Yale University Press, 1991); Dolores Hayden, *The Power of Place: Urban Landscapes as Public History* (Cambridge, MA: MIT Press, 1995); Lauren M. O'Connell "Afterlives of the Tour Saint-Jacques: Plotting the Perceptual History of an Urban Fragment," *Journal of the Society of Architectural Historians* 60, no. 4 (December 2001): 450–473; Richard Pommer and Christian F. Otto, *Weissenhof 1927 and the Modern Movement in Architecture* (Chicago: University of Chicago Press, 1991); Katherine Solomonson, *The Chicago Tribune Tower Competition*, Dell Upton, "The Smell of Danger," Paper presented at the Society of Architectural Historians' Annual Meeting, April 1999, Houston, Texas; and Carol Willis, *Form Follows Finance: Skyscrapers and Skylines in New York and Chicago* (New York: Princeton Architectural Press, 1995). For a general framing of the question of architectural history's purview, see Dell Upton, "Architectural History or Landscape History?" *Journal of Architectural Education* 44, no. 4 (1991): 195–199.

6. See, for example, Thomas Bender, "The Modern City as Text and Context: The Public Culture of New York," *Rivista di studi Anglo-Americani* (*RSA*) 6 (1990): 15–34; Thomas Bender, *The Unfinished City: New York and the Metropolitan Idea* (New York: New Press, 2002); Richard Sennett, *The Conscience of the Eye: Design and Social Life of Cities* (New York: Knopf, 1990); Richard Sennett, *Flesh and Stone: The Body and the City in Western Civilization*

(New York: W.W. Norton, 1994); David Harvey, *The Urban Experience* (Baltimore: Johns Hopkins University Press, 1989).

7. The best general surveys of the American life insurance industry and culture are Burton J. Hendrick, *The Story of Life Insurance* (New York: McClure, Philips, 1907); Morton Keller, *The Life Insurance Enterprise, 1885–1910: A Story in the Limits of Corporate Power* (Cambridge: Belknap Press, 1963); and Viviana A. Rotman Zelizer, *Morals and Markets: The Development of Life Insurance in the United States* (New York: Columbia University Press, 1979).

8. Douglass North, "Capital Accumulation in Life Insurance between the Civil War and the Investigation of 1905," Chap. 9 in *Men in Business: Essays in the History of Entrepreneurship*, ed. William Miller (Cambridge: Harvard University Press, 1952); Kenneth Turney Gibbs, "Insurance Rivalry and Business Architecture," Chap. 3 in *Business Architectural Imagery in America, 1870–1930* (Ann Arbor: UMI Research Press, 1984), 21–40.

9. Companies thus bought large buildings as architectural billboards, using a small portion for office space as required by law, and renting the balance to smaller insurance companies and related businesses. New York State investigations in 1877 and 1905 indicated that this practice was a poor investment of policyholders' monies. New York State. Joint Committee of the Senate and Assembly, *Testimony Taken Before the Joint Committee of the Senate and Assembly of the State of New York to Investigate and Examine into the Business and Affairs of Life Insurance Companies Doing Business in the State of New York*, vol. 10 (Albany: The State, 1905–6), 383–384. This publication was also known as the *Armstrong Commission Report.* See also Harold Wayne Snider, *Life Insurance Investment in Commercial Real Estate* (University of Pennsylvania. S.S. Huebner Foundation for Insurance Education; Homewood, IL: Richard D. Irwin, 1956), 1–15; Hendrick, 120–125, 234–241.

10. Keller, 37–39; Gibbs, 21–40. For a full extension of the home metaphor in life insurance promotional literature, see Griffin M. Lovelace, *The House of Protection* (New York: Harper, 1921).

11. The standard corporate histories of Met Life are Louis I. Dublin, *A Family of Thirty Million: The Story of the Metropolitan Life Insurance Company* (New York: The Company, 1943); and Marquis James, *The Metropolitan Life: A Study in Business Growth* (New York: Viking Press, 1947).

12. In 1875, 22 of 29 life insurance companies active in New York City kept offices between 92 and 409 Broadway. *New York City Register, 1875* (New York: The Trow City Directory Co., 1875). North, "Capital Accumulation in Life Insurance"; Gibbs, 21–40. Both Equitable and New York Life used engravings of their buildings in advertisements: see *Insurance Times* 9, nos. 2, 3 (Feb., March 1876). Comparative analysis and view of nineteenth-century life insurance home offices may be found in "Life Insurance," in *King's Handbook of New York City*, ed. Moses King (Boston: Moses King, 1892), 615–634; and Sarah Bradford Landau and Carl W. Condit, *Rise of the New York Skyscraper, 1865–1913* (New Haven: Yale University Press, 1996), 62–67.

13. The interior accommodated large workrooms and officers' quarters for the insurance concern as well as rental floors: here the company initiated business practices, including work flow organization and the hiring of a female workforce that had spatial and organizational implications. *Plans of the New Building of the Metropolitan Life Insurance Co.* Oversized pamphlet

[1876]. MetLife Archives; Montgomery Schuyler, "The Work Of N. LeBrun and Sons," *Architectural Record* 27, no. 5 (May 1910): 365–381.

14. The area known as "Ladies Mile" was the strip of Broadway south of Madison Square, terminating at Union Square. See M. Christine Boyer, "Ladies Mile: The Rise of a Victorian Amusement District," Chap. 3 in *Manhattan Manners: Architecture and Style, 1850–1900* (New York: Rizzoli, 1985), 43–129; see esp. 43–56. See also David Scobey, "Anatomy of the promenade: the politics of bourgeois sociability in nineteenth-century New York," *Social History* 17, no. 2 (May 1992): 203–227; Charles Lockwood, *Bricks and Brownstones: The New York Row House, 1783–1929* (New York: McGraw Hill, 1972), 167–206; "Twenty-third Street District—East," in *25th Anniversary Journal* (New York: Twenty-third Street Assn., April 1954), 48; *Historical Sketch of Madison Square* (New York: Meriden Britannia Co., 1894), 21–31.

15. George B. Woodward, "The Home Office," in *Souvenir Number of the Weekly Bulletin, 1893–1897* (New York: The Company, 1897). Advertising, efficiency and uplift, as general goals of life insurance companies are explicitly discussed in a later paper, Benjamin Wistar Morris "The Home Office Building as the Expression of the Activities of the Life Insurance Company," *Proceedings of the Annual Conference of the Life Office Management Association (LOMA)*. First Annual Conference, 1924, 54–61.

16. Barnett Phillips, "A Mercantile Palace," *Harper's Weekly*, 38, no.1951 (May 12, 1894): 453. For a description of the original structure, see James M. Craig, "Historical Sketch"; George B. Woodward, "The Home Office"; and N. LeBrun & Sons, "Outline Description of the Metropolitan Building" in *Souvenir Number of the Weekly Bulletin, 1893–1897*. Sketch and plans were published in "The Metropolitan Life Insurance Building," *American Architect and Building News (AABN)* 38 (October 15, 1892): pl. 877.

17. *Insurance World* (January 1, 1893). Vertical File-Home Office, MetLife Archives. See also *Spectator* 50, no. 17 (April 27, 1893). For popular and architectural press coverage that note the advantage of the park site, see Phillips, "A Mercantile Palace" in *King's Handbook of New York City*, 629–631; and "The Metropolitan Life Insurance Building," *AABN*, 47, pl. 877. Phillips noted that "This building overlooks the whole area of Madison Square, plus the width of two broad streets . . . this gives the structure that exceptional visibility which crowded surroundings in great cities too often render impossible."

18. The staircase was more a theatrical set piece than a mode of circulation, as it led to the second floor cashiers' department and executive offices—richly detailed spaces much photographed for, but closed to, the public. "Main Staircase of Metropolitan Life Insurance Company," *AABN* 46, no. 991 (December 22, 1894); N. LeBrun & Sons, "Outline Description of the Metropolitan Building," and Woodward, "The Home Office," in *Souvenir Edition of the Weekly Bulletin, 1893–1897*, 23 and 24, respectively.

19. Early tenants included brick, glass and mosaic concerns, insurance and real estate companies, and the company architect, N. LeBrun & Sons. George Kellock Letterbook, ca.1893. MetLife Archives. *Physicians' Offices*, an advertising pamphlet distributed by the company ca.1896, stated that the company planned to reserve an entire floor for medical offices. Vertical File-Home Office. MetLife Archives.

20. The addition was begun in Spring 1894 and completed in October 1895. It is of note that when the company reoccupied the further extended home office building after 1902, they still reserved many offices fronting the park and Twenty-third Street for rental, using the less desirable and lower-rent offices facing the light court for company business.

21. *The Metropolitan Life Insurance Company* (New York: The Company, 1908), 28, 30; "Notice," *Daily Bulletin* (August 18, 1909). In 1913, rental space had decreased to 35 percent of home office square footage. Rental to 1,100 tenants indicates an average office size of 378 square feet. *The Metropolitan Life Insurance Company*, rev. ed. (New York: The Company, 1914), 49, 52, 58.

22. The arcade, a public thoroughfare between Fourth and Madison Avenues, also provided access to elevator banks, stairways up to workspaces, and after 1904, down to the subway. "The Metropolitan Building, New York City," *Architects' and Builders' Magazine* 6, no. 4 (January 1905): 145–156; *Architecture* 10, no. 58 (October 15, 1904): 152–157, pl. 76–80 (photographs and drawings only). See also N. LeBrun & Sons, "The Building," *The Metropolitan Life Insurance Company* (1908), 23–30. A recent historical and geographical analysis is provided by Fenske and Holdsworth, 139–143.

23. "National Academy's Sale," *New York Herald*, n.d. [1894]. Clipping Scrapbook, MetLife Archives. This quote, part of a statement released by the company, appeared widely in newspapers, the insurance, and real estate press.

24. Academy officers realized that the bulk of the adjacent home office had darkened their second floor studios, and that many members had moved further uptown, making relocation a reasonable choice. Folder #2: "Twenty-third St. Building Sale—NA's responses," and National Academy of Design President's Report, May 9, 1894 and October 15, 1895. National Academy of Design Archives; Eliot Clark, *History of the National Academy of Design, 1825–1953* (New York: Columbia University Press, 1954), 38–39. For a description of changes in the Madison Square area, see "Big Corporations Getting Control of Valuable Parcels," *New York Tribune*, n.d. [1894]; "Positive Evidence of Improvement," *New York Post*, n.d. [1894]. Clipping Scrapbook, MetLife Archives; and "Twenty-third Street—East," in *25th Anniversary Journal* (New York: Twenty-third Street Assn. 1954), 46–52.

25. *The Weekly Underwriter* 68, no. 6 (February 7, 1903): 92; Madison Square Presbyterian Church Trustee Minutes, January 1903–October 1906, esp. May 20, 1903. Concerning the aesthetics and style of the new sanctuary, see Madison Square Church. Report of Subcommittee on Selection of Architect &C. to the Building Committee. n.d.[1903?]; Stanford White, "The Madison Square Presbyterian Church," 2pp. Typescript; and Stanford White, 3pp. untitled typescript, all in the McKim, Mead & White Papers, The New-York Historical Society. See also Christian Brinton, "A Departure in Church Building," *Century Magazine* (September 1905): 718–719; and Rev. Charles H. Parkhurst, "The Erection of the New Church," *A Brief History of the Madison Square Presbyterian Church and Its Activities* (New York: Printed by request, 1906), 62.

26. The well-known campanile served as the prototype for other commercial interests: the Montgomery Ward Building (1897–1899) in Chicago had a campanile embedded in its facade, and a San Marco look-alike anchored the corner of Daniels and Fisher Department Store in Denver. The tower was generically described as continuing the early Italian Renaissance style of the

office block, "in its general design and outline, belonging to the type of the Italian Campanile of the period." Press release, "Description of the Tower Extension of the Home Office Building," n.d.[1906?]. Tower Scrapbook, MetLife Archives. The composition of the tower also drew from an earlier LeBrun tall building, the Home Life Insurance Building (1893–1894) on Lower Broadway. Schuyler, "The Work Of N. LeBrun and Sons," 378–380. Company president John Hegeman, who pasted a sketch of the Home Life Building next to an image of the home office, is credited with proposing the addition of a tower to the office block as early as 1893. The composite created by Hegeman is still held by the company, and is illustrated in *Tower 75* (New York: The Company, 1984).

27. The tower functioned as a multi-use structure. Rental office space was arranged on four sides of the tower around a circulation and utility core. The company retained space on the lower floors, but advertised office space from the fourteenth to the twenty-fourth floors, and above where room sizes were smaller and irregular in shape. The tower also accommodated an observation deck at the forty-fifth floor, clock, chimes and beacon, and a radio station. *The Metropolitan Life Building, New York.* Advertising booklet, 1910. Vertical File-Tower, MetLife Archives.

28. A wide range of clippings are collected in the Tower Scrapbook and the Vertical File-Tower, MetLife Archives. *Scientific American* frequently featured on their weekly covers comparative studies of large structures, including manmade constructions and natural wonders. It also presented illustrations comparing new and historic monuments, usually to gauge scale. See "A Twentieth Century Campanile in New York" Cover, *Scientific American* (March 30, 1907).

29. "The Metropolitan Life Building," *The New York Architect* 3, no. 7 (July 1909); "Architectural Criticism" *Architecture* 20, no. 3 (September 15, 1909): 129–130; Schuyler, "The Work of N. LeBrun & Sons," 365–381. See *The Weekly Underwriter*, 1906–1910, especially its coverage of the company's January 1910 banquet honoring the architects and celebrating the completion of the tower: "The Metropolitan Life Insurance Company Celebrates the Completion of Its Great Home Office Building," *The Weekly Underwriter* 82, no. 5 (January 29, 1910): 103–112.

30. For example, see the testimonial by Met Life booster, Rev. Dr. Elmer E. Helms, published as the pamphlet *Life From the Heights* (New York: The Company [1911]), 4: "With such a foundation, upon such a foundation, this greatest building in the world stands, and will ever stand straight. This is no Leaning Tower of Pisa; no tottering Campanile of Venice, after which this building was patterned, and which came crashing to the ground five years ago. This building stands straight, and looks the whole world in the face and says: 'Be like me. Stand like me—plumb, perpendicular, upright, straight, four-square.'" The San Marco campanile collapsed on July 14, 1902, and was rebuilt, reopening on April 25, 1912.

31. *Remarks of John R. Hegeman at the Banquet of the Metropolitan Life Insurance Company Given in Commemoration of the Completion of the Home Office Building.* Hotel Astor, January 22, 1910 (New York: The Company, 1910), 7. MetLife Archives.

32. "A New York Campanile 700 Feet High." Cover, *Scientific American* 98, no. 18 (May 2, 1908); "Metropolitan Tower Building," *Indicator*; "The Metropolitan Life Insurance Company: Its Wonderful History and Noble

Building," *United States Review* (December 24, 1908). All in Vertical File-Tower, MetLife Archives. Also "The Metropolitan Life Building," *New York Architect* 3, no. 7 (July 1909); "Architectural Criticism," *Architecture* 20, no. 3 (September 15, 1909): 129–130; Schuyler, "The Work of N. LeBrun & Sons," 365–381. See *The Weekly Underwriter*, 1906–1910, especially its coverage of the company's January 1910 banquet honoring the architects and celebrating the completion of the tower "The Metropolitan Life Insurance Company Celebrates the Completion of Its Great Home Office Building," *Weekly Underwriter* 82, no. 5 (January 29, 1910): 103–112. John L. Hall, "Description of the Structural Steel Framework for the Tower of the Metropolitan Life Insurance Building, New York City," *American Architect* 96, no. 1763 (October 6, 1909): 130–134; "Solving Problems in Tower Construction," *American Industries* (January 15, 1908). Tower Scrapbook, MetLife Archives.

33. N. LeBrun & Sons, "The Building," 25–26. Despite the company's efforts to hold the height record for at least a decade, Met Life's campanile was surpassed by the 760-foot Woolworth Building, completed in 1913.

34. "Tower Advertises Itself," *New York Herald* (August 4, 1907). Tower Scrapbook and Vertical File-Tower, MetLife Archives.

35. Most guidebooks after 1908, particularly through the 1930s, include the Met Life Tower in the constellation of great New York skyscrapers. The Detroit Publishing Company Collection in the Prints and Photographs Division, Library of Congress, the Byron Collection at the Museum of the City of New York, and the Keystone-Mast Collection at the Keystone-Mast Collection, at the UCR/California Museum of Photography, University of California, Riverside contain multiple images of the Met Life Tower and its environs. For the work of Alfred Stieglitz and Alfred Langdon Coburn, see Alfred Stieglitz, *Camera Work: The Complete Illustrations, 1903–1917*, ed. Simone Philippi and Ute Kieseyer (Köln: Taschen, 1997); and Alan Trachtenberg, "Camera Work/Social Work," Chap. 4 in *Reading American Photographs: Images as History, Mathew Brady to Walker Evans* (New York: Hill and Wang, 1989), 164–230. In 1911, art critic Sadakichi Hartmann, the literary voice for the pictorialists, commended "men who have preferred the city streets, the impressionism of life . . ." for their contributions of motifs and compositional strategies to photographic art, citing in particular "Stieglitz's skyscrapers and dock scenes, and some of Coburn's interpretations of city views." See Sadakichi Hartmann "What Remains," [1911] reprinted in *The Valiant Knights of Daguerre: Selected Critical Essays on Photography and Profiles of Photographic Pioneers by Sadakichi Hartmann*, ed. Harry W. Lawton and George Knox (Berkeley, CA: University of California Press, 1978), 149–153.

36. Gerald Stanley Lee, "The Metropolitan Tower," excerpted from *Everybody's Magazine* (February 1913), in *Intelligencer* (February 1, 1913). Vertical File-Tower, MetLife Archives.

37. Earl Chapin May and Will Oursler, *The Prudential: A Story of Human Security.* Garden City (NY: Doubleday, 1950), 119–121. Equitable's 11-foot high marble group, entitled "Protection," showed a widow and orphan under the protective shield of the allegorical figure of insurance, and New York Life chose a globe guarded by an eagle to portray its ambitions to both protect and expand. Buley, vol. 1, 106–109; Gibbs, 102.

38. *Tower 75*, which commemorated the tower's 75th anniversary, collects a number of images that indicate the range of materials on which the tower was emblazoned. It is of note that the tower was represented differently than other components of the company's physical plant. Company-published postcards and monographs depicted the monumental exterior, as well as work areas and machinery of the office block, but images of the tower represented not the mundane daily tasks of the clerical force but the larger, quasi-religious ideals of the life insurance industry.

39. Haley Fiske, "The Light That Never Fails," address given at the Triennial Conventions of 1909–1910, in *Addresses delivered at the Triennial Conventions and Managers' Annual Banquets of the Metropolitan Life Insurance Company*. vol. 1 (New York: The Company, 1923), 24–26.

40. Comments of Reverend Dr. F.G. Smith, Pastor, First Congregational Church, Kansas City, Mo., and Right Reverent Charles Fiske, Bishop-Coadjutor of Central New York in *Addresses delivered at the Triennial Conventions*, vol. 1, 188–193 and 280–286 respectively; William Henry Atherton, *The Metropolitan Tower: A Symbol of Refuge, Warning, Love, Inspiration, Beauty, Strength* (New York: The Company, 1915), 4–6.

41. Atherton, *The Metropolitan Tower*, 3–4.

42. "New York's Big Clock A Wonder," *New Jersey Guardian* (January 6, 1910). The *Herald Tribune* furthered the tower's civic position by flashing election returns from its pinnacle with a powerful searchlight beginning in 1908, when the tower was still partially skeletal. Tower Scrapbook, MetLife Archives. The religious and civic themes embodied in the tower are combined in the text of a full page ad entitled "The Light that Never Fails," *Metropolitan* 25, no. 5 (ca. 1910), back cover. MetLife Archives.

43. "College Juniors Visit Met Tower," *Home Office*, vol. 11, no. 2 (July 1929). The Charity Organization Society offered a one-month course in social work to select female college seniors beginning in 1917; they used the tower to introduce students to their "classroom," the city. Met Life officers Lee Frankel and Frederick Ecker were involved with the society.

44. Dublin, *A Family of Thirty Million*, 62. For a detailed account of the origins and expansion of Met Life's welfare program, see *An Epoch in Life Insurance: A Third of a Century of Achievement. Thirty-three Years of Administration of the Metropolitan Life Insurance Company*, 2nd ed. (New York: The Company, 1924), 204–266; and the quasi-autobiographical account by Louis I. Dublin, *After Eighty Years: The Impact of Life Insurance on the Public Health*, Gainesville, FL: University of Florida Press, 1966. See also Elizabeth Toon, "Managing the Conduct of the Individual Life: Public Health Education and American Public Health, 1910–1950" (Ph.D. diss., University of Pennsylvania, 1998).

45. "The Light That Never Fails," *Metropolitan* 25, no. 5 (ca. 1910) back cover. Also published as leaflet, ca. 1920. For additional information concerning the development of the tower logo and slogan see Internal Memorandum 3/10/39 in Vertical File-Slogans, MetLife Archives.

46. "We're the guardians of 'The Tower,'/ And the light which it enveils/ It's the symbol of our power/ To its height no other scales." For the origin of the company anthem, see "Company's Song Inspired by Kipling's 'Light That Failed,'" *Pacific Coaster* (July 1940). Vertical File-Songs, MetLife Archives.

47. The company had previously used this construct in "The Brick Contest of 1902," in which field employees who achieved sales goals had their names engraved on bricks that formed a wall in a home office meeting room. See the pamphlet *The Brick Contest in the Germantown District, October and November 1902* (New York: The Company [1903]). On another occasion, the agent had been described as "a stone . . . carefully chosen, unblemished, well-chiseled, cemented with devotion to a common cause, placed . . . to rear up a proud and noble organization founded on the corner-stones of loyalty and obedience." (Atherton, 7).

48. Met Life President John R. Hegeman referred to the home office as a factory, an allusion to insurance companies' use of large open workrooms to facilitate efficient processing of applications and claims.

49. Although the working interior of the home office, from its 1893 kernel to the massive complex of the 1920s, underwent spatial rearrangement roughly every five years, the interior form and function was consistently customized to accommodate these tasks by scientific office management, new technologies, and welfare imperatives. For a general discussion of office technologies and work, see Thomas J. Schlereth, "The World and Workers of the Paper Empire," Chap. 5 in *Cultural History & Material Culture: Everyday Life, Landscapes, Museums* (Charlottesville, VA: University Press of Virginia, 1990), 144–178.

50. At the time, restriction of office building access was not uncommon, and a 1895 guide to New York City noted that these structures "are like municipal-ities with laws of their own . . . [each] is a separate community with its own police, its own servants and with laws that must be respected . . . the duties of the guardians in ordinary times are confined to saving the tenants from annoy-ances and theft." *New York 1895 Illustrated*, 2nd ed. (New York: A.F. Parsons, 1895), 55. Various editions of the company's *Rules and Regulations*; the *Daily Bulletin*; and the memos of Third Vice-President George B. Woodward offer excellent documentation of daily life and problems in the home office. MetLife Archives.

51. A typical floor plan of the 1909 home office published in *American Architect* shows large workspaces located around light courts, and fronting Twenty-fifth Street. Smaller offices, presumably for rental, were located along Twenty-third Street, Madison and Fourth Avenue frontages, with the exception of space on the second floor, which was used by Met Life executive offices. See also *A Tour of the Home Office Building* (New York: The Company, 1914); *Rules and Regulations Governing the Office Employees of the Metropolitan Life Insurance Company* (1895), 3. Contemporary discussions concerning office layout include "Wasted Opportunities: A Critique on Planning and Construction," *Architectural Record* 3, no.1 (July–September 1893): 72–84, 169–174, 436–440; Barr Ferree, "The Modern Office Building," *Journal of the Franklin Institute* 141, nos. 1 and 2 (January and February 1896): 47–71, 115–140. For the "factory layout" prototype, see J. William Schultze, "Office Layout," Chap. 10 in *Office Administration* (New York: McGraw-Hill, 1919), 145–169. See esp. Fig. 21: "Detailed layout," 159. For a discussion of small office plans, see Carol Willis, *Form Follows Finance: Skyscrapers and Skylines in New York and Chicago* (New York: Princeton Architectural Press, 1995), 24–47.

52. Notice, *Daily Bulletin*, November 18, 1908; Dublin, *A Family of Thirty Million*, 246–247. Efficient use of segregated lunchrooms is described in *A Wonderful Village* (New York: The Company, n.d.[1911]), 3.

53. See *An Epoch in Life Insurance: A Third of a Century of Achievement. Thirty-three Years of Administration of the Metropolitan Life Insurance Company* (New York: The Company, 1914), 140–167 and *An Epoch in Life Insurance*, 2nd ed. (1924), 204–266; and Lee K. Frankel, "Welfare Work of the Metropolitan Life Insurance Company for its Employees," *New York State Journal of Medicine* (January 1917) for details of employee welfare. Met Life was of course not unique in its enactment of an employee welfare program. Various historical interpretations of welfare capitalism are summarized in Stuart D. Brandes, *Welfare Capitalism, 1880–1940* (Chicago: University of Chicago Press, 1970), 5–8, 135–140; Andrea Tone, *The Business of Benevolence* (Ithaca, NY: Cornell University Press, 1997) and Nikki Mandell, *The Corporation as Family: The Gendering of Corporate Welfare, 1890–1930* (Chapel Hill, NC: University of North Carolina Press, 2002). Zunz views the welfare activities of life insurance companies, and Met Life specifically, as closely related to philanthropic agencies. He calls Met Life a "reforming" corporate model. Zunz, *Making America Corporate*, 90–92, 100–101.

54. Vertical File-Policyholders Service Bureau, MetLife Archives. There is a large body of research and reports written by the PSB published or available in typescript form.

55. "An Echo From Sarajevo," *Home Office* 6, no. 9 (February 1925): 5–6. The 97 immigrants described in this article were all home office porters. The company overwhelmingly classified jobs by gender and ethnicity: native-born status presumed a facility with English that was essential for tasks of handling correspondence, filing and answering the telephone. Memo, JEM to D.E. Waid, architect, July 11, 1930, shows a breakdown of the maintenance staff by classification (job) and gender. See also Home Office Study, 1924 (looseleaf binder). Blacks were not hired in any capacity. The official explanation of exclusion of Blacks from the workforce was that it was "not because of any prejudice on the part of the company, but because there would be very serious objection on the part of our white employees." Statement of Met Life Vice President Leroy A. Lincoln in "Metropolitan Life Official Tells Why Company Does Not Hire Negroes," *New York Age* 43, no. 33 (April 26, 1930): 1.

56. *The Metropolitan Life Insurance Company* (1914), 142–151; "An Echo From Sarajevo," 5–6; "The Home Office 'Village'," *Home Office* 5, no. 11 (April 1924): 4. See also "The Carpenter Shop," *Home Office* 6, no. 11 (April 1925): 16–17; "There's Even A Modern Laundry To Be Found In This Home Office City of Ours" *Home Office* (October 1938); "The Work We Do: The Secretary," *Home Office* 41, no. 4 (October 1959): 1–4.

57. In 1893, at a time when women were just beginning to enter offices nation-wide, Met Life's office staff was 60 percent female, and rose to 66 percent by 1911, where it remained through the 1930s. Statistics calculated from *A Wonderful Village; The Metropolitan Life Insurance Company* (1908 and 1914), 33 and 66, respectively; *Number One Madison Avenue: The Business of a Life Insurance Company* (New York: The Company, 1927). For general information about women in the clerical force, see Elyce J. Rotella, *From Home to Office: U.S. Women at Work, 1870–1930* (Ann Arbor: UMI Research

Press, 1981), 2, 65–103; Sharon Hartman Strom, *Beyond the Typewriter: Gender, Class, and the Origins of Modern American Office Work, 1900–1930* (Urbana, IL: University of Illinois Press, 1992), 197 and passim.

58. For example, in the Actuarial Division, where women clerks outnumbered men six to one, the "male sections" collected data, operated multiplication and adding machines, and prepared "difficult classifications" and "detailed calculations," which demanded "not only technical knowledge, but often the most searching analysis." Women clerks in the division handled the cards on which information was recorded about each policy. *The Metropolitan Life Insurance Company* (1914), 66–67. There is no evidence of a written rule mandating that a female clerk resign upon marriage, although it appears it was either a verbal rule or that most did in the decades surrounding the turn of the century. However, there is evidence in the *Home Office* that by the late 1920s, some women did remain at Met Life after marriage. Policies at other insurance companies such as New York Life were not so liberal. See issues of the *Home Office*; D.M. Stevenson, "Some Social Aspects and Trends In Clerical Employment—Women vs. Men," *Proceedings of the Annual Conference of the Life Office Management Association* (1935), 90–97; *Special Report No.XIII, Life Office Management Association. Questionnaire Summaries: Personnel Policies. Part II: Employment of Married Women* (Fort Wayne, IN: LOMA, 1930).

59. See photographs in *The Metropolitan Life Insurance Company* (1908 and 1914). Etiquette books for the working girl cautioned clerical workers about improprieties that could occur within the office due to the unsupervised mixing of the sexes. Ruth Ashmore of the *Ladies' Home Journal* warned young working women to guard against sexual and financial temptation, to wear modest clothing, not to speak socially to male clerks, and to avoid familiarity with the boss. The intrigue of the mixed-gender office was further elaborated in office novels and short stories. See Lisa M. Fine, *The Souls of the Skyscraper: Female Clerical Workers in Chicago, 1870–1930* (Philadelphia: Temple University Press, 1990), 145–151.

60. *Rules and Regulations*, editions: 1895–1936, MetLife Archives; Angel Kwolek-Folland, "Gender, Self and Work in the Life Insurance Industry, 1880–1930," in *Work Engendered: Toward a New History of American Labor*, ed. Ava Baron (Ithaca: Cornell University Press, 1991), 168–190. Zunz, *Making America Corporate*, 120–121.

61. In 1930, the overwhelming majority of 139 life insurance companies surveyed stated that they did not discourage association between their female and male clerks. *Special Report No. 13*, LOMA, 24–25. The *Home Office* of June 1923 reported the marriage of two Statistical Bureau employees and noted that it was the fourth wedding of people within the Bureau. "Statistical Facts and Fancies," *Home Office* 5, no.1 (June 1923): 3.

62. An excellent, if fragmented, view of life at the home office is gleaned from the *Daily Bulletin*, published beginning in 1905, where company commentary, directives, and reprimands documented employees' daily activities, particularly those that diverged from the company's behavioral guidelines. The *Home Office*, published monthly beginning in 1919, featured longer articles about various divisions and their work, employee activities, and listed announcements of events, and of employee marriages, deaths, and other personal occasions. Although written by employees, the *Home Office* was published by the company and thus clearly reflects corporate policies and goals. The two house

organs provide a record, if selective, of everyday practices and issues within the home office and the company at large.

63. Pamphlets include *The Metropolitan Tower* (n.d.); *All in a Day's Work* (n.d.) and *Number One Madison Avenue: The Business of a Life Insurance Company,* rev. ed. (1927).

64. *Souvenir Number of the Weekly Bulletin, 1893–1897.*

65. *The Metropolitan Life Insurance Company* (1908; rev. ed., 1914). A number of the photographs of workrooms, dining room and machine shop from the 1908 and 1914 monographs are preserved as proofs and prints as part of the Byron archive at the Museum of the City of New York, as well as in the photographic files of the MetLife Archives.

66. Edward Steichen, "Foreword" in Grace M. Mayer. *Once Upon a City: New York from 1890 to 1910 as Photographed by Byron and Described by Grace Mayer* (New York: Macmillan, 1958), ix. See also Peter Simmons, *Gotham Comes of Age: New York Through the Lens of the Byron Company, 1892–1942* (New York: Pomegranate, 1999). The Jewett and Byron photographs have been used by a number of historians to make specific points about office practices and culture, frequently to document gender relations in the office. Surprisingly, these studies neither consider the photographs as corporate tools nor note that the Byron images were published in the company's lavish monographs and subsequently sent out by the millions as postcards.

67. Postcards were a major advertisement and canvassing tool. Between 1906 and 1909, the company ordered over eight million postcards, at a cost of approximately $17,000. "Metropolitan Calendars, Postcards," Bound volume. MetLife Archives. Also see the Postcard Collection, MetLife Archives.

Chapter 10

Architectures of Seduction: Intimate Apparel Trade Shows and Retail Department Design, 1920–1940

Jill Fields

In September 1921, *Corsets & Lingerie*, one of the nation's leading trade journals, reported to its wholesale and retail industry readers—manufacturers, store owners, buyers, and saleswomen—on the new interior design of "Molly Mayer's Beautiful Shop" in New York City.

> A green and gold salon of quiet magnificence and harmony, rich in its appointments, yet not ostentatious, colorful in decoration, and yet not garish. Soft tones, artistry everywhere in beauty of line and dignity of design. Modeled after the fashion of the court of Louis XVI, it breeds an atmosphere of old France. . . .

Describing the shop's carefully considered and lavish decor promoted the idea that attending to shop design in addition to keeping abreast of rapidly changing fashions in dress was a means to take advantage more fully of the booming consumer market emerging in the Post–World War I era. The article's persuasive question, "Why should not the corset, which plays such an important part in the role of a woman's wardrobe be as artistically displayed as a hat, shoes or gown," implied that the spaces devoted to corset sales lacked the appealing commercial aesthetic found elsewhere. According to this national trade journal, in order to seduce retail customers successfully, store owners and wholesale buyers would first need to be initiated into the art and science of modern sales techniques, including the look and atmosphere of intimate apparel departments and specialty shops.[1]

The rapid development in the mass production of clothing that took place in the United States at the turn of the twentieth century altered the way most Americans' wardrobes were manufactured. It also changed the way apparel was distributed, advertised, displayed, purchased, and worn. Yet, wholesale commerce and retail exchange have not often been examined together in studies of consumption, despite their significant structural relationship.

Considering the material culture of the objects produced, the built environment of the spaces where intimate apparel was sold, and the commercial practices engaged in by the industry reveals how changes in the culture of wholesaling and retailing were fundamental to the new landscape of retail work and consumption. Significantly, the tropes embedded both in interwar wholesale promotion and retail interior design relied upon and reworked prevailing constructions of feminine elegance, romance, and heterosexuality. The production and circulation of these tropes increased sales of corsets and lingerie, and promoted shopping and commerce itself as a pleasurable and sexually exciting, yet still respectable, arena. Furthermore, through their association with the powerful dynamics of gender, sex, and commerce, these retail and wholesale experiences disciplined female spectators to seek and take visual pleasure in the commodified display of women's bodies, while they also instructed female shoppers in the latest methods of constructing their own bodies as fashionable objects to-be-looked-at.[2]

Lingerie and corsetry, the first layers of clothing women put on when dressing, are integral to gendered self-construction through shaping and adornment of the body, particularly of those areas most closely associated with gender difference, sexuality, and femininity. The shopping environments created for female intimate apparel consumers in the early twentieth century therefore were critical locations for expanding women's skills and sensibilities in how to look for, locate, and purchase fashionable commodities, and in how to utilize those commodities to construct their bodies as fashionably feminine. These two pursuits echo and reinforce the dual position of female spectators outlined in the 1970s by feminist film theorist Laura Mulvey and explored by a range of scholars ever since. Looking at female bodies on display was central to the profitable development of twentieth-century commercial culture, but so also were active female spectators and consumers. Women shoppers, moviegoers, and flaneurs learned to view themselves through the "male gaze" in order to construct their bodies as objects of visual pleasure. Analyzing the sales arenas for intimate apparel during the interwar period shows how commercial concerns shaped the gendering of spectatorship.[3]

Designing retail space geared to enhance sales does not sound at all new to twenty-first-century consumers. Even by the 1920s, such innovations had been in the works for several decades, as growing use of electric lights, glass display cases, mirrors, elaborate window displays, and elegant interiors transformed department stores into "palaces of consumption."[4] But as those "big store" innovations became commonplace by the 1910s, personal attention to customers and departmental distinctions in merchandising slacked off. This made department stores vulnerable to growing competition offered by small specialty stores. In 1915, Wanamaker's, a leading Philadelphia retailer, responded to the intensified competition with newspaper advertisements declaring that it was "not a store made up of departments, but a store made up of specialized stores, each complete in itself."[5] Reorganization on that principle meant refurbishing store layout and department design, and retraining sales personnel.

A reexamination of corset display and marketing in particular was sparked in 1918 by the imposition of wartime restrictions on corset model forms and again when those restrictions were lifted in January 1919. By 1921, when the *Women's and Infant's Furnisher* reported that Harzfeld's, the top Kansas City, Missouri "high class exclusive women's wear store . . . has this spring been adding new touches to its merchandising and advertising and the most original touch of all has been that accorded the corset department," innovations were well underway.[6] Retailers' interest in upgrading corset departments stemmed from two important reasons. First, due to the complexities of corset fitting, successful purchase required an intensive degree of individual, specialized sales assistance. Second, from the 1920s through the 1940s, corset sections were the most profitable overall in department stores. The well-organized and very active Corset Manufacturers Association, formed in 1907, kept retailers and corset personnel aware of these critical points by publicizing sales statistics and providing trade publications endless copy on sales methods.[7]

Despite common assumptions held today that women wearing more figure-revealing flapper styles did not wear corsets, this was not always the case. Though distinct from corsets of earlier decades, figure-shaping garments were necessary for many women to achieve the slim, straight flapper line. Women's intensified preoccupation with slimness was also due to post–World War I era corset manufacturers who, feeling the heat of an overblown "corsetless fad," made extraordinary efforts to ensure that women and girls remained corseted. Their successful strategies facilitated corset sales while also maintaining a level of corset complexity in figure types and styles that kept women convinced that they needed to purchase and wear corset "wardrobes."[8]

In one such 1920s strategy, corset manufacturers sponsored well-attended training sessions for corset saleswomen and buyers in what they termed "scientific corset fitting." The training sessions enhanced familiarity, and thus wholesale distribution, of their brand and corset lines. Held in New York City and regional urban centers across the United States, these sessions also had the effect of promoting the status and prestige of corset saleswomen and buyers when they returned to work back home and deployed their new sales knowledge. By the 1930s, these women would also be invited en masse to Manhattan for "market week" activities that included meals, theatrical intimate apparel fashion shows set to music, and visits to well-appointed showrooms for closer scrutiny of foundation garments on live models.

The early twentieth-century marketing, design of retail environments, and wholesale promotion of intimate apparel contributed to post-Victorian gendered culture. Displaying women's bodies clothed in undergarments within respectable commercial contexts was particularly meaningful because of the larger framework of the consolidation of modern sexual mores in the 1920s. These changes bore special significance for women's expectations and experiences of romantic relationships and marriage, and also of work and leisure generally.[9] Retail interiors were designed to evoke romance and sexual experience, and to summon linkages with the re-imagined aristocratic past of corsetry. This imbued the experience of intimate apparel shopping with a sensuality heightened by the drama of encountering a vast array of beautiful objects for sale made of rich fabrics and striking colors. The industry also conceived of female wholesale buyers as sexualized consumers. The wholesale "market week" culture that emerged to address the growing presence of women buyers in the trade reformulated the long-held practice of treating out-of-town male wholesale customers to female companionship and sex. Drawing upon theatrical conventions of vaudeville revues, Broadway musicals, and illicit sexual entertainment, manufacturers created legitimate displays before mixed audiences—for commercial goals—of undressed female bodies.

*   *   *

"Molly Mayer's Beautiful Shop" explained the profitable benefits of installing elegant retail interiors by describing their effect upon her female clientele. The design provided an elegant, faux-aristocratic atmosphere so mesmerizing that the unpleasant aspects of corset fitting would be set aside by its upscale customers.

> On entering one almost forgets one's errand is to be fitted until two pleasing, smartly groomed women approach and conduct one to the rear. Here the same architecture and coloring are carried out in the small dressing rooms, the soft green blending beautifully with the flesh and pink corsets which are predominant. There is no suggestion of "stock." This is the day of clever corset artistry. . . .[10]

The rich fabrics and ornamentation of higher-priced corsets worked in a similar manner to overcome women's resistance to wearing confining garments. The enchanting furnishings, mirrored in the attractive look and feel of binding foundations made from silks and brocades, provided a captivating diversion from the actual discomforting purpose of the store visit and future wear of items purchased there. The shop interior elicited increased sales by evoking a seductive atmosphere of elite privilege. Retail consumers could transform their shopping experience and purchases into a means of constructing a sense of social prestige, one perpetuated when dressing in and wearing purchased garments.[11]

Associating lingerie shopping with social prestige provided retailers with an effective mechanism for infusing respectable status with a distinctly erotic charge. In 1925, *Corsets & Lingerie* noted that "not all shops that sell corsets are fashioned after a Madame Dubarry Boudoir, but [each] strives for that something intimate, personal . . . that will always attract the women buyer. The immediate and tremendous response that has been felt by these shops confirms what were formerly theories-viz. that atmosphere and a careful study of the woman's needs doubles the sales of corsets and brassieres."[12] The reference to Madame Dubarry worked to reconceptualize the lingerie department and shop as a pastiche of aristocratic status, sensuality, and respectable retailing carefully planned to promote intimate apparel consumption.

Saks & Co., several months later, was noted in *Women's Wear Daily* for "play[ing] up boudoir appeal" in their lingerie advertising.[13] Increased sales at the Saks Fifth Avenue shop was reported by *Corsets & Lingerie* to have "follow[ed] closely on the heels of beauty and privacy," though the journal found that "[n]owhere has this intimacy, this personal touch been better shown or developed than in the exquisite salon of Bonwit Teller."[14] At Marshall Field & Co. in Chicago, two "attractive rooms . . . one for the display of negligees, and the other for French undergarments" were "painted in old ivory touched at the edges with blue and pink. . . . with . . . furniture . . . of dark mahogany upholstered in damask which also makes the hangings, . . . the carpet . . . in a rich plum shade."[15]

In addition to lavish boudoir interiors, window displays invoking the aristocratic origins of the corset in Europe suffused contemporary corsetry with a romantic past. Harzfeld's of Kansas City ran a series of ads in 1921, coordinated with store displays, that provided a history of the corset "from the earliest known period." Illustrations of each period of women dressed "in the apparel of the day . . . show[ed] sufficient detail to indicate the 'torture' or the comfort—usually probably torture—to which wearers were subjected and the contrast is then drawn in text with the corsets of the present day which are scientifically planned for real comfort."[16] In this discourse, 1920s shoppers were encouraged to make and take pleasure in links between historic and contemporary corsetry, but also to read that history in terms of a narrative of progress that led to their greater comfort in current foundations.[17]

Upscale customers were not the only ones considered vulnerable to the appeal of corsetry's past. A Connecticut corset firm, George C. Batcheller Company, founded in 1857, distributed to various stores nationwide "antique corsets which have been used for window display purposes," and by 1933 had apparently done so for decades. A few years later, *Corsets & Brassieres* explained the "alchemy" of creating "magnetic" windows, pointing out the particular appeal of historical window displays in university towns. While noting that such displays had "been done before," the article suggested a fresh approach of arranging a "show with mannequins stepping through the pages of a history book and impersonating famous romantic characters."[18] In 1941, the journal proposed an "historical bra promotion" to capitalize on the fact that "the age of militarism into which we are going is resulting in a more feminine contour of the silhouette." To tie-in as well with the "resurgence of Medieval styles," and to enhance visual interest, the author recommended that "authentic Medieval costumes" be included in "window displays tracing the dramatic reflection of history in the changing bust contour" by showing "the latest and most modern V-cleft bras together with Medieval corsets." Such side-by-side display could tell a story of female progress, but one still suggestively charged with the narrative conventions and romantic images of knights and damsels-in-distress.[19]

Yet romance had its prosaic aspects as well. Intimate apparel companies utilized the frequently employed advertising strategy of provoking commodity purchase by appealing to, if not creating, women's anxieties about getting and keeping a husband. A "Success Story" printed in a 1931 issue of the *Maidenform Mirror*, a company newsletter distributed nationally to their wholesale customers, provides an unvarnished analysis of the stakes for women in conforming to fashion. "Wear Maiden Form and Get Your Man!" relays a purported conversation between a wholesale buyer and the royal *we* of the Company.

> "Do you know the sales argument I use?" she asked us with a twinkle in her eye.
> "No," we replied, innocent enough, though goodness knows, we could think of *many*.
> "Well—I tell the girls this—'Do you want to get a husband? Wear Maiden Form, then'".
> "And you're as frank as that?" we queried incredulously.
> "Oh yes," she said. "You see—I get to be very chummy with the girls—and the girls often tell me of their little personal affairs. So it's easy for me to advise them, and say what I really think. You'd be surprised how they respond to my suggestion."
> "You mean they actually come back with husbands, after wearing Maiden Form?"
> The buyers's eyes twinkled more merrily than ever as she looked at us. "Look at my order-blanks, if you don't believe me!"

Once married, women became even better customers, "buying Maiden Form foundations in double the quantity to be sure to hold" on to their husbands.[20]

Finding this strategy in a newsletter directed at buyers and saleswomen seems especially poignant, as the point is to persuade retail workers to exploit women's insecurities within fitting rooms when the female customer is most vulnerable to suggestion. Such ploys were not uncommon. Trade journals plainly show that the industry was keenly aware of the special relationship between corset saleswomen and their customers, and the power saleswomen wielded in the intimate environment of fitting rooms. Within this environment, saleswomen were in a unique position to deploy and reinforce dominant discourses of gender, wherein women were beholden to men, and valued in terms of their appearances.

The stimulation of desire was central to the reexamination of department store design and relocation of lingerie departments to areas of greater visibility. When the Russek Store opened in New York in 1924, the lingerie department was set up on the first floor, "a departure from the general custom" of more discrete placement on an upper floor. Organized around the "fundamental policy" of "value," a range of styles and prices of undergarments were visible to the customer in glass displays, so that she could "make her approach accordingly." However, *Women's Wear Daily* also noted that the location "places even more directly in the way of temptation apparel that has always been something of a temptation to the female mind—and purse." Thus, female customers in search of *value*, that is, lower priced goods, would do so in environments built to accommodate the imperative of *volume* in sales. In order to find and purchase less expensive lingerie, the female shopper would have to navigate departments designed to seduce her into buying additional items, and thus spend more than intended when she set out on her hunt for bargains.[21]

In similar large, mid-range priced stores, evoking privacy and intimacy was relegated to the fitting rooms. Corset fitting rooms were not a standard feature in department stores until after World War I. Their appointment, formulated in the midst of wider scale retail redesign, sparked great interest. The ever-inventive Wanamaker's was the first store to have special fitting rooms for "misses," in 1915. The industry immediately realized their value.

> One of the principle reasons that very few retail stores have the business that should come to them in misses' corsets is the failure of stores to take into consideration the natural reticence of girls to enter into any discussion of the individual corset problems with matrons and dowagers about. By providing a special demonstration and fitting room for misses, it is safe to say that any store so doing will reap the benefit of an immediate appreciation of this delicacy. And, since appreciation expresses itself in terms of dollars and cents, it can hardly be other than a profitable investment.[22]

The further development of the specialized "junior trade," as it would be dubbed in the 1920s, meant designing retail interiors geared to address potential reluctance by adolescents and young women in becoming corset customers.[23]

Gimbels' "young miss" section in the 1930s transformed stock display into a spectacle of abundance for junior shoppers (figure 10.1). Utilizing the tactic of excess overcame the disdain of upscale retailers like Molly Mayer for the pedestrian quality of "showing stock." The section featured "aisle after aisle" and "show case after show case of junior merchandise made to appeal to the eye of the discriminating youngster," which included not only "debutantes and society girls, but even working girls." Building upon the "insistent propaganda . . . [that] really aroused an interest on the part of the young girl, . . . buyers . . . succeeded in luring the girl into the department [and] are tireless in these efforts to keep her interest."[24] The evocative image conveyed by "luring" girls, language similar to that utilized for decades by moral reformers and social workers decrying the sexual dangers to which young women were vulnerable, became here a structure for their rationalized, profitable, and legitimate seduction as intimate apparel consumers.

*   *   *

All of the close scrutiny and revamping of corset and lingerie store interiors and sales tactics brought new attention to corset saleswomen, buyers, and

236

Figure 10.1 Marshall Field department store, *Women's & Infants' Furnisher*, July 1921, p. 29
Source: Courtesy of Special Collections, Gladys Marcus Library, Fashion Institute of Technology, New York City.

specialty shop owners. Their fitting skills, display artistry, knowledge of the trade, and keen sense of fashion's direction became recognized as important components in maintaining the high profits of corset and lingerie departments and shops. Advertising endorsements of, quotes by, and reports on experienced female buyers and owners such as Anna Ford, Mildred Tucker, and Clara Large in trade journals, and journal articles written by certified corset experts, such as the redoubtable Ethel Allen, provided wider acknowledgment of the expertise of these individual women.[25] Such national notice in print also augmented the prestige of women working in these capacities across the United States. By 1941, the industry assumed as common knowledge that a corset buyer was a "person of importance" whom "everyone treats . . . with respect."[26]

The inclusion of women in the usually male-dominated wholesale culture of "market weeks" formed another sort of recognition. Elizabeth Quinlan became "the first 'lady buyer' in the national apparel market . . . in the 1890s," representing her own Minneapolis store. She was also reported to be the first buyer to purchase a "ready-made dress in America, a brown woolen homespun lined with taffeta."[27] In 1904, go-getter Emily Keene became at age 18 assistant buyer of women's ready-to-wear for Stix, Daer & Fuller Dry Goods of St. Louis, and returned from "her first trip to the markets" with "six extravagantly expensive dresses of a type the store had never handled before." "Horrified" store officials were duly impressed when the dresses sold within six days. Keene soon became head buyer, en route to opening her own very successful department store with two male store managers as partners.[28]

Wholesale market week attractions as well as retail promotional events greatly expanded the use of "living models." English couturier Lady Duff Gordon claimed staging of the first "fashion parade" of outerwear as early as 1905, building upon the recently initiated Parisian custom of showing garments on live mannequins. Gordon stated in her 1932 autobiography, *Discretions & Indiscretions*, that Parisian mannequins were instructed not to exhibit any personality of their own and wore dresses over a "garment of rigid black satin, reaching from chin to feet, which were shod in unappetizing laced boots" to prevent anything "which might shock the susceptibilities of the *grandes dames* who visited the salons." Gordon developed what she termed the "social side of choosing clothes" by "serving tea and imitating the setting of a drawing room," assigning sensual titles to each ensemble, such as "When Passion's Thrall is 'o'er,'" "Give Me Your Heart," and "Do You Love Me," and choosing evocative new names such as "Gamela, 'Black Beauty' in Arabic. . . . Dolores. . . . [and] Hebe" for her "goddesses"—the "tall women with gracious curves" who worked as her mannequins. Six months after her first fashion parade, Gordon claimed she doubled her clientele and "nearly trebled" her turnover. When she opened a salon in New York City in 1910, naturally she brought the fashion parade with her.[29]

The stories Gordon tells in her autobiography about the fortuitous marriages her beautiful mannequins secured to rich bachelors echo the similar stories circulated about chorus girls, such as the highly publicized matches of the famous New York City Floradora Girls. Gordon further underscored this correspondence between fashion parades and the demi-monde of Broadway in recounting that Florenz Ziegfeld, after attending one of her parades, begged her to release one of her mannequins so that he could "take her in his Follies." (She did.) Gordon also describes her own successful work in costume design for Ziegfeld's Follies and creation of vignettes for the "show girl," a Ziegfeld innovation that reduced the chorus girl to her essence as specular object in that she would no longer be required to sing or dance, but merely "to look beautiful and wear beautiful clothes."[30] The growing presence of fashion parades consolidated this figure's reification.

By 1915, elaborate "style reviews" were being held at corset shops for customers, and at in-house shows that included entertainment for those working within the trade. The Kops Brothers corset manufacturing company held a ball that lasted until 4 a.m. for 2500 of their workers in December of 1915. The stageshow that followed dinner included minstrels, comedy, and songs such as "We All Wear Nemo Corsets," and "The Nemo Girl."[31] American Lady of Detroit held a convention for 50 of their salesmen in June 1921 that included informative speeches, morning and afternoon style shows, and a banquet. The style shows presented American Lady and Madame Lyra corsets "shown on live models."[32] A "private exhibition directed by Ned Wayburn, Stage Director of the Ziegfeld Follies on the New Amsterdam Roof" in July, 1922 provided a splashy debut for the Kops Brothers' "Netherall," a new garment combining "vest, bust confiner and hip confiner." *Corsets & Lingerie* reported on the event directed by Miss Cleaver of the Morton Advertising Agency and Miss Hoffman, designer of the Netherall.

> Several Ziegfeld favorites all of whom are celebrated for special features in the Follies demonstrated the good points of the garment and were photographed while performing various stunts which displayed . . . the marvelous adaptability of the Netherall and the complete freedom it accords the wearer. Among other athletic feats, Miss Hazel Jennings accomplished the "split" several times without displacing the garment in the least. . . . Florenz Ziegfeld . . . is delighted to have secured a garment that can be worn on the stage w/out restricting the movements of the girls and says that hereafter all Follies girls will wear a Netherall. The pictures taken will be shown by the Pathé News.[33]

All of these events describe an increasing intertwining of the practices of wholesale commerce with theatrical conventions, advertising images, and promotional journalism that offered views of unclad female bodies. Together, these usages reinforced the legitimacy and pleasure of displaying and looking at female bodies in a widening range of respectable locations.[34]

For the sixth annual review staged by the Wells Corset Shop over three days in April, 1921, proprietor Miss E. B. Wells sent out "1000 invitations, the majority of which were accepted and people brought along their friends."

For the review, the model first came on stage so that Wells could point out where she needed "protection or restraint." The model would then return in various styles of corsets to impress upon audience members the need for different corsets to be worn at different times of day and with different types of outfits. Trade journalist A. Pearl McPherson noted that "the models . . . also wore lovely pink satin teddies which were of the step-in sort, snapped across the crotch. This with the lovely silk stockings made the models look enticingly beautiful, and charmingly set off the finest of the corsets shown on their figures." The allure and pleasure for women of gazing upon "enticing" female bodies while receiving instruction in "correct corseting and daintiness" surely lent legitimacy and made respectable the staged display of undressed women as well as the pleasure taken in the experience by female audience members. Moreover, the staging and narration of these displays stimulated female spectators to enjoy identification with models as objects of approving gazes and also to relish their own viewing of models' bodies as specular objects.[35]

In the late 1920s, an increasing number of corset department buyers and managers were staging fashion parades in stores across the country, particularly in "large Western cities." Heartily endorsed by *Corsets & Brassieres*, the propriety of holding such shows was initially questioned. Corset buyers, facing "much opposition and criticism, staged fashion shows in which corsets were shown to the public in a more or less cautious manner, one or two garments just being shown incidentally, just glimpsed through some kind of transparent covering . . ." By the spring of 1930, New York City stores, described as "the last to succumb," were "staging corset fashion shows in an elaborate manner" to standing room only audiences. The corset fashion show held in the auditorium of Wanamaker's Manhattan store was reported to be "one of the biggest and most impressive." Attended by "hundreds of women of all ages and figures," the show featured "mannequins of various sizes [who] paraded around and around with the best and newest expressions of the foundation garment mode. . . . After a certain dress or suit was displayed, another model appeared with the foundation garment worn under it." The show also included a "brief address by Miss Virginia Wellwood, Fashion Coordinator of the store."

> The "nightgown" figure is gone, no longer does a woman follow the line of least resistance. Her figure, that has been allowed too much freedom, must now be reclaimed and as painlessly and as comfortably as possible. The Princess silhouette is here to stay, the experimental or hysterical period, when so many women said they'd have none of it, is over. There can be no doubt as to its permanence.[36]

Wellwood's comments reminded female audience members enjoying the spectacle of the fashion show to be actively attentive to fashionable standards and the methods of constructing them, but in the service of undermining "resistance" and securing compliance in stylish self-construction as objects to-be-looked-at.

A similar show was held at a department store in Hutchinson, Kansas six months later. Corset buyer and department manager Alice Warner staged her Corset Style Show at a local theater, "in connection with the regular film program." She distributed free tickets in her department, which produced a full house, got the store window display manager to design the stage set, and had a runway built out from the stage for a fashion parade. The four salesgirls who served as models, each representing a different "figure type"—small, slender miss, average, and the large woman—"appeared, one at a time, clad in the daintiest lingerie and corset, over which a silk dressing gown was worn. As each made her appearance the spotlight was turned on her. She walked out on to the runway, doffed the dressing gown, and went through several exercises, while the demonstrator explained the type of corset best suited to that particular figure." Business, Warner reported, picked up immediately after the show, and a month later corset customers were still talking about it.[37]

Apparently, no one in Hutchinson, Kansas questioned the propriety of local salesgirls appearing on stage and disrobing to reveal their bodies clad in dainty underwear. What the salesgirls themselves thought about it is hard to determine, but the fact that one model called in sick at the last minute may very well indicate a lack of full choice in the matter. Manager Warner stepped in to replace her as the average figure model in the show. Though outright refusal of their boss' request to appear in the show may have put their jobs at risk, a difficult prospect in the closing months of 1930, it is also possible that the salesgirls who participated enjoyed the opportunity to be on stage and engage in the somewhat risque behavior of displaying their undressed bodies before a crowd of strangers. Perhaps the experience echoed for them the frequent lingerie film scenes played by glamorous actresses or undergarment newsreel promotions that they saw on local movie screens, and thus allowed a rare opportunity for acting out a fantasy of sex appeal and stardom in public.[38]

The spectacular allure of viewing a range of female body sizes and shapes in corset style shows perhaps found its most extravagant expression in a 1933 show staged by Wanamaker's in Philadelphia: one corset model weighed 205 pounds. This woman's body was used as an extreme example to prove that anyone could benefit from corsetry, and as an appeal to the much sought after "stout" customer. Her presence, and the staging of this show, also evokes a carnivalesque reversal. Most models in this show had their hair styled and accessories coordinated for particular activities, ranging from a formal evening to tennis, but wore only the corset and undergarments promoted as appropriate for each occasion. Naturally, the "high spot" of the show took place when a bride, matron of honor, and bridesmaids paraded to "The Wedding March" in full wedding regalia, sans dresses.[39]

Corset school session group photographs of female attendees taken in the interwar period show that a growing number of women traveled to major urban centers to conduct the business of the intimate apparel trade and to receive career-enhancing training.[40] When major corset companies responded in the 1930s to the strong presence of women working in managerial retail capacities by staging lavish trade shows, they offered women in the corset trade new opportunities for travel and networking. Yet company shows also created new sites for the circulation of commercialized understandings about the female body and further imbued the arena of commerce itself with sexual excitement and glamour. Moreover, these shows reconfigured for the growing numbers of women wholesale customers the long-practiced tradition of pre-senting traveling salesmen with views of, if not access to, undressed female bodies (figure 10.2).[41]

Style shows staged by manufacturers for corset buyers who traveled from across the nation to New York during market week held each February evolved into even more extravagant stage productions in the mid-1930s. During this decade, the genre of Hollywood musicals formed, elaborating on the Broadway and vaudeville presentations of music, songs, romantic stories, and scantily-clad dancing girls. The La Resista company's 1935 *Period Promenade* combined several elements from this genre, and those utilized successfully in previous corset promotions. The show was described in the trades as "a picturesque and thoroughly enchanting presentation of the march of corsetry" from 1775 to the present. The hubbub generated by *Period Promenade* was such that it was filmed by RKO News Screen, and by the first week of March had already been shown at Radio City Music Hall and other RKO theaters in New York prior to being sent out to theaters nation-wide. The stageshow itself involved women removing their dresses to reveal their laughable old-fashioned, or laudable modern corsets. The movie ver-sion included a cinematic striptease, as a velvet negligee dissolved to reveal the all-in-one foundation garment the model wore beneath it.[42]

Gossard's presentation of fifty styles modeled by fourteen mannequins that same season produced a "glamorous affair" that clearly excited the anonymous trade journal reporter:

Colored spotlights! Fern-banked elevated runway! Music with a tantalizing lilt! A frequently changing picture book background! Good-looking mannequins! More than 1000 people jamming every nook and corner of the McAlpin Roof Ballroom and overflowing in the hall! Lots of applause! Dance numbers for entertainment during intermission![43]

Meanwhile, Formfit in Chicago went for the elegant approach, opening their style show with "The Three Graces." With 700 buyers, assistant buyers, and salespeople in attendance, each "Grace" first appeared on stage in an outfit suited to morning, afternoon, or evening and "then disrobed behind the silo-graph to show the outlines, and paraded." None other than the famous entertainer Irene Castle, dressed in an ankle-length, backless evening gown of chartreuse crepe that contrasted with her black satin gloves ornamented with feathers at the elbow, acted as hostess for the evening.[44]

The popularity of these productions encouraged ever more elaborate shows followed by lavish meals and entertainment, as companies tried to outdo their previous year's show and each other. The Gossard Promenade of

Figure 10.2 Corset fashion show of figure types organized by Miss MacKenzie, corset buyer for Gates Dry Goods Co., Fort Dodge, Iowa. *Corsets & Brassieres*, November 1935, p. 51

Source: Courtesy of Special Collections, Gladys Marcus Library, Fashion Institute of Technology, New York City.

1938 held in the Grand Ballroom of the Hotel Commodore, entitled "The Corsets of Tomorrow," was a two-act presentation of four scenes each separated "by an intermission during which the audience was entertained by a vocal solo." In one scene highlighting sports corsets, mannequins so attired played ping-pong. Warner's "Under Control" show that year created a sensation during its "perfect rendition" of a new dance, the "Big Apple," by professional Arthur Murray dancers and a mannequin in her Le Gant Veil of Youth corset.[45] Three years later, Warner's presented "The Corset Buyer's Dream" at the Astor Hotel in front of an audience of more than 1500. The show, which dramatized scenes from the corset buyer's work life, also included humorous depictions of shoppers, and a song and dance presentation of a corset line. Upon completion, the show was "broadcast to South America via short wave."[46]

In addition to attending entertaining trade shows, corset buyers could also visit manufacturers' well-appointed—and overtly sexualized—showrooms. Six hundred guests crammed into the new offices of the Fay-Miss Brassiere Company in 1938, which featured across the entryway a "photographic mural of a scene on the Island of Bali, showing a young woman with perfect breasts against an artistic background." At a Maiden Form cocktail party, guests were treated to what the company called a "peep show, through which [they] could see mannequins in miniature wearing the new Allo-ette brassiere" while mannequins "paraded through the showrooms" in the new spring line. More intimate showings on live models were also arranged at company offices for small groups of buyers and sales staff. Overall, market week showroom visits offered a mix of erotic images of pseudo-primitives, risqué peep show vistas, and up-close perusals of female bodies that evoked the visual world of disreputable commercialized sexual entertainment to engage the pleasure and win the favors of male and female wholesale consumers conducting legitimate business exchanges.[47]

* * *

From the late nineteenth century, display of the female body was central to the development and promotion of the new public commercial culture of print advertising, vaudeville and Broadway, movies, amusement parks, and department store windows. Female bodily display provided a means to coalesce—and thus make coherent for consumers—these disparate cultural experiences. As *Corsets & Brassieres* boasted in 1935,

> [r]etailers are merchandising brassieres and bandeaux with energy and vision. They "hammer away" at the public by constantly repeated newspaper advertising, by means of promotional window displays and printed notices in other departments of the store, by special fashion shows and by attractive contests.[48]

The passage from wholesale to retail was a critical juncture in fully realizing the aims of manufacturers and retailers through this process. Manufacturers' extensive efforts to make commerce entertaining for wholesale shoppers disciplined the gazes of female corset buyers, shop owners, and department managers in the profitable and therefore pleasurable practice of looking at half-dressed female bodies. Wholesale culture changed as a result. Back home, these women provided similar opportunities for their customers by mounting intimate apparel fashion shows, designing retail interiors, and creating in-store and window displays that expanded occasions for female retail consumers to learn to enjoy viewing nearly naked women's bodies in a new arena—the respectable and often homosocial world of shopping. Yet significantly, female consumers were also directed by fashion show narration, and induced by fashion show staging tactics, to simultaneously view "enticingly beautiful" intimate apparel mannequins with a critical eye provoked not so much by pleasurable looking but by the imperative to learn modern methods of constructing one's own body as an object to be looked at as well.

Concerns about the dynamics of female looking and being looked at permeate a report on The Ivy Corset Shop of Washington, D.C., investigated by trade journal writer A. Pearl McPherson because its goods were bestowed upon the first Miss America after her selection in 1921. In addition to describing the shop's new display of a corset model "christened 'Miss Washington' " after the city's victorious pageant participant, the story details the bandeau and other articles of underwear she wore and also her delight in doing so. Miss America elaborated that the entire experience of winning and wearing the beautiful garments "seemed [to her] like a dream." McPherson found that "as one looks about the little shop . . . it is not to be wondered that [she] felt still as though she was in a part of fairyland." McPherson was especially taken with the shop's window curtains.

> The windows are fitted, both inside the room and next to the outer glass, with curtains of the sheerest organdie; so that the passersby often gets a glimpse of the beautiful models through this sheer material. From the inside looking out there are these curtains which allow one to look out, yet they protect the customer from inquisitive eyes of passersby.[49]

McPherson's fascination with the possibilities for seeing into and out of The Ivy Corset shop through sheer curtains that somehow allowed glimpses of models, but prevented full exposure of customers, speaks to the tension between display and concealment central to women's fashion practices generally (figure 10.3). This tension is especially significant to the reliance upon figure-shaping foundation garments in creating a fashionable silhouette. In the interwar period, the directive to women, particularly younger women, to display their bodies in public meant display of a body appropriately molded to the shape in current fashion. The flattening brassiere and hip and bottom flattening girdle or combination corselette of the 1920s and the uplifting bra and pantie girdle of the 1930s shaped the female body in strikingly different ways. Yet while outerwear hides direct public viewing of these undergarments, they are indirectly visible because outer clothing

Figure 10.3 This award winning window design at Kerr Dry Goods Company, Oklahoma City, Oklahoma effectively plays upon themes of female spectatorship, undergarments' status as both seen and hidden, and women's self-display as "to-be-looked-at." *Corsets & Brassiers*, July 1930, p. 49

Source: Courtesy of Special Collections, Gladys Marcus Library, Fashion Institute of Technology, New York City.

conforms to the shape foundation garments produce, a shape clearly distinct from the wearer's unfettered body. In this sense, the divergently styled undergarments of these two periods produced a similar effect. Though they held the ever-present potential to reveal the constructed nature of this embodied femininity, conforming to fashion conventions by these visible and obscured dressing practices feminized and sexualized the wearer's body, producing the female body as a site for the instigation of desire. Investigating the sources and workings of such desire explains women's eagerness to comply with particular fashion practices, whether as consumers, retail workers, or shop owners.

Intimate apparel manufacturers and retailers, playing upon their participation in the production of multiple desires centered on the female body, employed promotional strategies to increase both wholesale and retail sales that drew upon and promoted gendered notions of romance, sexuality, and glamour. Retailers reshaped intimate apparel store interiors to create atmospheres designed to confer social prestige and sexual allure. They also sponsored fashion shows that made the display of undressed female bodies for female spectators a respectable form of pleasurable looking that was reinforced by the pleasure of consuming. At the wholesale level, the lavish intimate apparel trade shows, and the smaller presentations of new undergarment styles held in well-appointed company showrooms, created new spaces for the legitimate public display, performance, and viewing of the exposed, half-dressed female body for the enjoyment of large audiences of men *and* women. Aimed at enticing wholesale and retail shoppers to buy more of their goods, these design and marketing strategies doubled the meaning of these architectures of seduction, as they also commercialized understandings about female sexuality and erotic pleasure, and proliferated venues for the presentation of such understandings. Moreover the display of women's bodies in these retail and wholesale sites contributed to the historical construction of a distinct female gaze, characterized by duality created when women inhabit the heterosexual male gaze in order to successfully construct themselves as femininized objects-to-be-looked at. Wholesale and retail promotional strategies widened opportunities to rework and circulate representations of romance, glamour, and female sexuality, and promoted this particular trade, and shopping and commerce itself, as a sexually exciting, yet respectable arena for women.

Notes

1. "Molly Mayer's Beautiful Shop," *Corsets & Lingerie*, September 1921, p. 32.
2. A foundational theoretical text on the dual position of the female spectator is Laura Mulvey, "Visual Pleasure and Narrative Cinema," *Screen* 16:3 (Autumn 1975), 6–18. Mulvey later elaborated upon her analysis in "Afterthoughts on 'Visual Pleasure and Narrative Cinema'" inspired by King Vidor's *Duel in the Sun* (1946), *Framework* 10 (Spring 1979), 3–10. Linda Williams very helpfully assesses a range of significant pre- and post-Mulvey works on what she terms gaze theory in her introduction to *Viewing Positions: Ways of Seeing Film* (New Brunswick: Rutgers University Press, 1995), pp. 1–20.

3. Lauren Rabinovitz, for instance, analyzes movies, amusement parks, fairs, and department stores as essential locations for the early twentieth century emergence of new and overlapping locations for female gazing and being looked at. See Rabinovitz, *For the Love of Pleasure: Women, Movies and Culture in Turn-of-the-Century Chicago* (New Brunswick: Rutgers University Press, 1998). For an introductory overview and bibliography of gaze theory and scholarship, see Marita Sturken and Lisa Cartwright, *Practices of Looking: An Introduction to Visual Culture* (NY: Oxford University Press, 2003), chapter 3.

4. Susan Porter Benson, *Counter Cultures: Saleswomen, Managers, and Customers in American Department Stores, 1890–1940* (Chicago: University of Illinois Press, 1986); Elaine Abelson, *When Ladies Go A-Thieving: Middle-Clas Shoplifters in the Victorian Department Store* (New York: Oxford, 1989); and William Leach, *Land of Desire: Merchants, Power and the Rise of a New American Culture* (New York: Vintage, 1993).

5. *Women's & Infant's Furnisher*, November 11, 1915, p. 47.

6. *Women's & Infant's Furnisher*, April 1921, p. 28.

7. *Women's Wear Daily*, January 16, 1919. "The corset stock is one of the safest of all the stocks in the dry goods store." *Women's & Infants' Furnisher*, 1896 quoted in their 25th anniversary issue, January 1921, p. 61; "Corset Departments Lead in Store Profits!," Warner Brothers ad, *Corsets & Brassieres*, January 1933, p. 3; *Corsets & Brassieres*, February 1938, p. 25; *Corset Preview: The Bulletin of the National Retail Dry Goods Association*, July 1941, p. 13; *Corset & Underwear Review Sales Training Manual Issue*, August 1942, p. 122; "Corset Selling Is An Art," *Corsets & Brassieres*, February 1946, p. 34.

8. For more on the corsetless panic and manufacturers' intensified sales strategies, see Jill Fields, " 'Fighting the Corsetless Evil': Creating Corsets and Culture, 1900–1930," in Philip Scranton, editor, *Beauty and Business* (NY: Routledge, 2001), pp. 109–141.

9. See, for example, Ellen Rothman, *Hands and Hearts: A History of Courtship in America* (New York: Basic Books, 1984); John D'Emilio and Estelle B. Freedman, *Intimate Matters: A History of Sexuality in America* (New York: Harper & Row, 1988); Beth Bailey, *From Frontporch to Backseat: Courtship in Twentieth-Century America* (Baltimore: Johns Hopkins University Press, 1988); Steven Seidman, *Romantic Longings: Love in America, 1830–1980* (New York: Routledge, 1999). For a sociological study of romance and consumption, see Eva Illouz, *Consuming the Romantic Utopia: Love and the Cultural Contradictions of Capitalism* (Berkeley: University of California Press), 1997.

10. "Molly Mayer's Beautiful Shop," *Corsets & Lingerie*, September 1921, p. 32.

11. I never anticipated wanting to wear an extremely confining foundation garment myself, but in my initial foray into the costume collection held at the Los Angeles County Museum of Art, I found the exquisite 1920s peach silk and brocade binding brassieres extremely alluring—I wanted one. I felt that way also about some corsets and girdles I came across in other costume collections where I conducted research (Royal Ontario Museum, Smithsonian, NY Metropolitan Museum, NY Fashion Institute of Technology). Trade periodicals are also filled with descriptions of richly decorative foundations. See, for example, A. Pearl McPherson, "A Beautiful Small Shop," *Corsets & Lingerie*, October 1921, pp. 30–32.

12. *Corsets & Lingerie*, May 1925, p. 27.
13. *Women's Wear Daily*, December 1, 1921.
14. *Corsets & Lingerie*, May 1925, p. 27.
15. *Women's Wear Daily*, December 1, 1921.
16. *Women's & Infant's Furnisher*, April 1921, p. 28.
17. The history of corsets, and undergarments generally, was a topic that appeared from time to time in trade periodicals, including *Women's Wear Daily*. The fascination with recounting this fashion history also extended to the publications of organized labor from the 1930s on. New York City undergarment workers in the 1950s also performed the history of the garments they produced by staging a historical fashion show.
18. *Corsets & Brassieres*, February 1938, p. 26.
19. *Corsets & Brassieres*, February 1941, p. 27.
20. "Success Story," *The Maidenform Mirror*, June 1931, p. 4 (Smithsonian).
21. *Women's Wear Daily*, September 25, 1924.
22. *Women's & Infants' Furnisher*, February 1915, p. 49.
23. For more on the specialization of corset merchandising, see Fields, " 'Fighting the Corsetless Evil.' "
24. *Corsets & Brassieres*, July 1930, p. 43.
25. *Women's & Infant's Furnisher*, January 1910, p. 48; "Corsets Still in Vogue," *Corsets & Lingerie*, July 1921, pp. 37, 52; "The Junior Corset Department," *Corsets & Brassieres*, January 1930, p. 41; *Women's & Infant's Furnisher*, August 1921, p. 25; Ethel Allen, "Corset Fitting the Young Girl Figure," *Women's and Infants' Furnisher*, April 1921, p. 28; Ethel Allen, "Corset Fitting the Top-Heavy Figure," *Women's and Infants' Furnisher*, May 1921, p. 28; Ethel Allen, "Corset Fitting the Curved Back Figure," *Women's and Infants' Furnisher*, June 1921, p. 32; Ethel Allen, "Corset Fitting the Full Proportioned Figure," *Corsets & Lingerie*, p. 34; Ethel Allen, "Corset Fitting the Thigh Figure," *Corsets & Lingerie*, August 1921, p. 30; Ethel Allen, "Corset Fitting the Maternity Figure," *Corsets & Lingerie*, September 1921, p. 34. In 1921, Ethel Allen was the Supervisor of Instruction at the Kabo School of Corsetry.
26. "To Be A Successful Corset Buyer," *The Bulletin of the National Retail Dry Goods Association*, July 1941, p. 15.
27. *Women's Wear Daily*, March 20, 1944.
28. *Women's Wear Daily*, September 6, 1924.
29. Lady Duff Gordon, *Discretions & Indiscretions* (London: Jarrolds, 1932), pp. 56, 66–67, 70–71, 75–79, 134–135.
30. Ibid., pp. 214–216. See also Linda Mizejewski, *Ziegfeld Girl: Image and Icon in Culture and Cinema* (Durham: Duke University Press, 1999), pp. 21, 89, 93, 95.
31. "Kops Brothers Hold Entertainment and Ball," *Women's and Infant's Furnisher*, January 1916, p. 55.
32. "American Lady Sales Convention," *Corsets & Lingerie*, July 1921, p. 36.
33. "Introducing the 'Netherall,' " *Corsets & Lingerie*, August 1922, pp. 48–49.
34. On growing locations for female display and spectatorship at the turn-of-the-century, see Rabinovitz, *For the Love of Pleasure*.
35. A. Pearl McPherson, "The 1921 Style Review of the Wells Corset Shop," *Women's and Infant's Furnisher*, May 1921, p. 30.

36. "Corsets—The Spirit of Youth," *Corsets & Brassieres*, April 1930, pp. 24–25; "The New York Stores," ibid., p. 27.

37. "Corset Show Big Help," *Corsets & Brassieres*, December 1930, p. 33. For more on the development and deployment of "figure types," in the corset trade see Fields, " 'Fighting the Corsetless Evil.' "

38. Mary Ryan, "The Projection of a New Womanhood: The Movie Moderns in the 1920's," in Lois Scharf and Joan M. Jensen, *Decades of Discontent: The Women's Movement, 1920–1940* (Westport, Connecticut: Greenwood Press, 1983), pp. 113–130.

39. "Corset Fashion Review," *Corsets & Brassieres*, May 1933, p. 33. For more on the importance accorded the stout woman, see Fields, " 'Fighting the Corsetless Evil.' "

40. *Corsets & Brassieres*, July 1928, p. 41; *Corsets & Brassieres*, March 1930, p. 46.

41. See Patricia Cline Cohen, *The Murder of Helen Jewett* (New York: Vintage, 1998), chapter 4, for more on the treating of wholesale male customers to female companionship and sex in the antebellum era.

42. Elaborate trade shows were resumed after the war ended. "*A Period Promenade,*" *Corsets & Brassieres*, March 1935, p. 45; "*Period Promenade* on Screen," *Corsets & Brassieres*, April 1935, p. 37.

43. "Gossard Presentation," *Corsets & Brassieres*, March 1935, p. 48.

44. "Formfit Chicago Show," *Corsets & Brassieres*, March 1935, p. 55. See also "Warner's Show Spring Line," March 1935, pp. 46–47; "Gossard Chicago Show," ibid. p. 66; "Le Gant Fashion Show," *Corsets & Brassieres*, April 1935, p. 45.

45. "Gossard Promenade," *Corsets & Brassieres*, February 1938, p. 41; "Warner 'Under Control,' " ibid., p. 43.

46. "The Corset Buyer's Dream," *Corsets & Brassieres*, February 1941, p. 41.

47. "Coast to Coast Hook-Up," *Corsets & Brassieres*, February 1938, p. 52; "News," *Corsets & Brassieres*, February 1941, p. 51.

48. "Brassieres & Bandeaux," *Corsets & Brassieres*, November 1935, p. 29.

49. A. Pearl McPherson, "A Beautiful Small Shop," *Corsets & Lingerie*, October 1921, pp. 30–32.

Chapter 11

The Architecture of Mobility: Outdoor Advertising and the Birth of the Strip

Catherine Gudis

During the automobility boom of the 1920s, the billboard industry came to re-evaluate its assumptions about the distribution of audiences and the best placement of advertising. With the widespread use of cars, the market was no longer confined by geographic, political, or even business-district boundaries. The market now *moved*. Mobile audiences expanded outward from the compact urban market of yesteryear and seemed to draw no new market boundary in their wake. In effect, mobile traffic itself constituted the new marketplace. Recognizing this, advertisers predicted and promoted new commercial developments far from traditional business centers. They did this partly through an architecture of mobility that acclimated motorists to an ex-urban culture of spectacle and an auto-oriented consumer landscape, where drivers were encouraged to window shop right through the windshield. Moreover, outdoor advertisers helped develop fringe areas, laying the pavement for the birth of the commercial strip and the urban sprawl that came to the late twentieth and early twenty-first centuries. By recognizing a mobile market, charting its patterns, inscribing those patterns onto the landscape through an architecture of mobility, and promoting the commercial strip—the ideal space for mobile consumption—outdoor advertisers would help to define the shape of the decentralizing environment. Outdoor advertising emerges as a significant missing element in the story of commercial growth and urban deconcentration.

The Architecture of Mobility

The changed locations and relationships between buyers and sellers in the age of mass advertising and the automobile meant that advertisers, architects, merchants, and manufacturers had to develop techniques geared toward mobility. Trademarks and brand names had facilitated the job of advertisers by providing simple and identifiable imagery with which to represent nationally distributed goods. Strategies of "picturization" helped advertisers address mobile audiences without much use of text, and functioned to reorient viewers visually so that they could quickly recognize an abstract, massed, and iconic form as representing a product without much more than a side-window glance.[1]

Advertisers and retailers also had a vested interest in the spatial reorientation of mobile audiences, and created an architecture of mobility expressly suited to the decentralizing commercial arena. The structures, locations, and even animation of outdoor advertisements constituted a new physical organization of built forms aimed to acclimate motorists to mobile viewing and shopping. Utilizing elaborate and sometimes expensive devices of animation, the architecture of mobility called the attention of moving audiences to the advertising billboard. As retail shopping became increasingly dispersed and depersonalized (ads replacing salesmen, self-service markets replacing full-service shops) outdoor advertisers, perceiving themselves as conduits between consumers and merchants, needed more novel and eye-catching means of communicating to mobile audiences.[2] They often used visceral as well as visual cues to advertise new, unfamiliar, and difficult-to-represent goods and services.

Electrical companies sponsored perhaps the most architecturally dynamic and spectacular of all outdoor advertisements in the 1920s and 1930s. Electrical illumination had a long relationship with promotional enterprises of all sorts. For years, electrical "spectaculars" had turned night into day along New York's "Great White Way," so named for its fantastic quantity and illumination of electric bulb-adorned signs along the Broadway and 42nd Street theater district. New York's electrical displays were unique in their nationwide reputation. At the turn of the twentieth century, the Hotel Cumberland (later site of the Flatiron building) featured on its wall an incandescent-light emblazoned Heinz pickle in "57" Varieties. In 1917, Wrigley gum erected what was then the largest electrical display in the world, featuring six of its trademark "spear-men" doing acrobatics amid the extravagant plumage of a colossal peacock. By the 1930s, Times Square visitors thrilled at the eight-story-high and one-block-long Wrigley gum advertisement of brilliantly colored tropical fish (made up of 18,000 electric bulbs) gliding through waves of sea-green lights. The electricity it consumed could have served a city of 10,000. All of these campaigns (and others) were commented on internationally.[3]

These displays demanded high capital investment and maintenance costs and depended on the high circulation of urban throngs. Yet many small towns, inspired by Broadway, believed that electric devices would *bring* the crowds. Civic boosters across the country embarked on "Great White Way" campaigns throughout the 1910s and 1920s to make their towns the next New York City.[4] Even fictional Gopher Prairie, the setting of Sinclair Lewis's *Main Street*, participated, when "glory of glories, the town put in a White Way. White Ways were in fashion in the Middlewest. They were composed of ornamented posts with clusters of high-powered electric lights along two or three blocks on Main Street."[5]

Soon it became an accepted architectural principle to include electrical and structural requirements for rooftop, facade, and wall advertising signs in commercial buildings. There were multiple advantages to laying such plans. H. H. Magdsick, President of the Illuminating Engineering Society, reiterated this in a 1930 address to the Society titled "Building Prosperity Avenue." "Light has always been a fundamental in the work of the architect. But its general use as an architectural element in itself is something of recent growth." He urged that modern life, which brought people outdoors far more than in the past, demanded the use of light as "one of the architectural elements," particularly in commercial and public buildings, and "especially in the after-dark hours, when we are most impressionable and receptive."[6] The provision of diversified types of electrical decorative displays, he explained, "should form a part of every building on *Prosperity Avenue*."[7] Electric advertisements promised the transformation of ordinary byways into buyways.

Outdoor advertisers often promoted utility companies and appliances through the presentation of dramatic tableaux vivants that trained consumers in the use of new electrical products and the habit of driving to purchase them. Electrified billboard displays in the 1920s and 1930s proved to be as lavish as the show windows of the palatial department stores of the late nineteenth century, which had also indoctrinated shoppers in the excesses of conspicuous consumption.[8] The novel and spectacular displays created by outdoor advertisers operated along the same principles but with a different goal. Rather than luring the consumer into the structure on its site, they aimed to inspire audiences to drive further along the boulevard to fulfill their consumptive yearnings. Billboards thus became the showrooms of the new driving city. They defined the strip by offering a horizontal picture window of consumer delights to be enjoyed from the privacy of one's own vehicle and to be accessed through one's own power: power to drive to the shop, select the items, and carry them home with scarcely a jostle or a nudge from salesmen or fellow shoppers.

Billboards offered uniquely moving, visual displays and theatrical stagings of goods for sale and their domestic uses. While Maytag Aluminum Washer, Standard Plumbing Fixtures, and Remington Typewriter illuminated New York's Broadway district with their fifty-foot towers and waterfalls of flashing, moving lights, smaller versions lined Detroit's Michigan Avenue and Los Angeles' expanding shopping district on the edge of downtown.[9] But in these cities the show was also being presented at ground level. Horizontally stretching "special bulletins" as well as spotlighted and other illuminated billboards opened an entire nighttime market of advertising exclusively handled by outdoor companies. As one advocate put it: "After dark, a brilliantly illuminated poster, set against the blackness of the night, stands out like a diamond on black velvet."[10]

Regional "sign committees" of the electricity trade association worked with the Outdoor Advertising Association of America (OAAA) to promote electrical advertisements all over the country. They started with places such as

California, where, "on account of the favorable weather conditions and the many miles of highways close to power lines, illuminated billboards and painted signs have found almost unlimited use."[11] They also engineered new devices that helped outdoor ads to stand out more dramatically in areas already illuminated, and to bring the spectacle of light to those that were not. The electrical engineers also developed special equipment for different roadside uses. Reflective surfaces and lighting were designed to maximize their dramatic effect, but without blinding passing motorists.[12] Electric sign manufacturers became fascinated with the "increased speed of vision" that they believed would be obtained through the use of "higher intensities" of light. The pairing of light and quickly moving viewers promised an exponential increase in perceptual cognition.[13]

As lights needed to be both near power lines and within the private property lines of the area rented or owned by the outdoor company, illuminated billboards required a great deal of space. Consider, for instance, that the standard eleven-foot-high board required mounted lighting units approximately six feet out from the board; the higher the board, the greater the distance of the mounted lighting units.[14] These were electrified advertising spectacles that created not only a new temporal arena of fast nighttime commerce, but also a new spatial arena extending beyond the retail shop and boundaries of the cramped and congested business districts of years past. The retail arena in the age of the automobile went beyond the edge of the shop, moving into and along the arteries of traffic along with the mobile consumer.

Outdoor advertising companies recognized the physical changes to the city and the corresponding changes taking place in "current thought and trends" of their modern mobile audience. For this, the outdoor industry was increasingly recommending three-dimensional advertisements. As a sales manager for Foster and Kleiser Company explained in 1934, "Today's scene insofar as public life and thoughts are concerned is, to say the least, kaleidoscopic. . . . To catch the public mind with an advertising message is doubly difficult under such conditions; to hold the public mind is even more than doubly difficult." While previously advertisers seeking "animated effects" were confined to roof spectaculars (such as along the Great White Way), three-dimensional painted and poster bulletins could better compete in the kaleidoscope as an architectural representative of speed, animated by lights, colors, and forms.[15]

As illumination became more available and important in "increasing attention-value and often bringing light to streets otherwise practically dark," the "third dimension" of the billboard frame took the form of a larger stage on which cutout figures or actual objects—not just their pictorial representation—were presented. These displays were sold based on their "additional attention-factor of *Action*." It was a well-accepted design principle among outdoor advertisers that "moving objects, light, and color always catch the eye."[16]

A popular architectural device that used animation was the oversized, electrically powered and illuminated clock. It joined the usual advertising copy on the billboard structure. National advertisers such as Sunkist, Coca Cola, Anheuser-Busch, and Firestone used clocks, as did regional campaigns. Chevrolet became well known for theirs in Atlanta, Detroit, Los Angeles, and Minneapolis, among other places. Their billboard clocks measured between seven and twelve feet, were visible at great distances, and could be promoted in terms of the public service they provided. Practically speaking, these displays induced repeated and purposeful looks. They offered "a case where the outdoor display doesn't seek the public but the public seeks the outdoor display!"[17]

The clock supplied the requisite eye-catching elements of light and motion, and drew attention to the public and private uses of electricity and the products that would supply those services. A more abstract purpose is also possible. The clock on the billboard occupied an architectural place in the public arena along with the railway station, bank, and post office whose clock towers were traditional cornerstones of the communal space of the market or square. These were the timekeepers that calibrated activities of all strata of the population. The bank, in particular, represented both public exchange and private industry; the clock on its exterior literally embodied the principal that time is money. If outdoor advertising was to be established as an essential economic element and as a respectable architectural feature of the urban fabric, the association with banks and other public institutions, however negative the Depression might have made those affiliations, were legitimating. By associating the clock with advertised goods featured on the billboard, this form of display also communicated a sense of standardization, reliability, and efficiency. Other electrical animation devices of similar principles were the thermometer (which sometimes had a connection to the product advertised, like General Electric air conditioning or frosty cold Coca-Cola) and moving display lights that chased one another from one end of the board to the next. All sorts of other illusions were electrically produced, too, including burning houses, pouring bottles of beer, and moving locomotives.[18] These could be said to invert the usual architectural function of another downtown institution: the theater. Rather than house the entertainment, the moving imagery on the billboard screen brought the show to the street.

Animated effects more theatrically conceived than these were also staged in what were called "shadow-box" or "third-dimensional" presentations. One, used by the Los Angeles department store, J.W. Robinson Company, included a platform extending from the painted billboard of two cutout figures at the eighteenth hole of a golf course. Bullocks, also in Los Angeles, similarly oriented their third-dimensional bulletin toward selling men's apparel through a thematic lesson in style. The cutout figures extended in front of the billboard and above it too, breaking the outline of the frame while still keeping the suited and overcoated men tied to the outdoor domestic scene, which included a large automobile, a bicycle-delivery man (with a package of the long-stemmed variety), two boys being entertained with a newly purchased black-faced puppet, and a matronly nanny. In targeting the difficult-to-reach male consumer, Bullocks depicts a male-defined suburban vision of "masculine domesticity," calling forth imagery used as early as the turn of the twentieth century to illustrate the benefits of suburbia.[19] In the billboard tableaux, the men have contact with their children, shop, have a home of their own removed from the signs of urban congestion, and are assisted in it by servants.

It was a scenario with which people might be familiar or for which they might long, especially during the Depression. The billboard also allowed them to gaze upon the private domestic scene from within the similarly private space of their cars. The store featured in the advertisement promised a similar experience, one in which they could remain independent and free from the urban crowds. The male consumer courted by these ads (most likely assumed to be less interested than his wife and daughters in shopping) could drive up to Robinson's or Bullocks, park his car in the provided spaces, run into and out of the Men's Shop, with nothing to hinder the speed and economy with which he carried out his tasks. Both Bullocks and the outdoor advertiser had pitched self-serving messages in the pleasures and conveniences of the mobile shopping enterprise.

The third-dimensional bulletins frequently offered a view into other private domains of suburbanized life. Sometimes the startling contrast of the private context of domesticity in the public realm of the street enhanced their theatrical attraction. Quite popular were displays of bedroom, kitchen, and living room furniture sets, aimed at replacing the "monstrosities of the Mid-Victorian period, with its continual change and waste in home decorations" with "harmonious arrangement and setting such as have gone far toward making home more homelike with less foolish buying of things which were soon thrown away." This was "the renaissance of good taste,"[20] modern living displayed not through two-dimensional representations but through the third-dimension of the billboard as figurative display case and object lesson.

Lachman Brothers, self-proclaimed to be "one of America's largest home furnishers," used cutouts and a shadow box to create a realistic display of model bedrooms. "The room is recessed several feet from the face of the structure and is lighted from within at night." There was even a cutout figure of a woman "seated at a dressing table." Its realism was enhanced by the antics of a regular passerby who snuck into the box every morning. He was described by Herb Caen in the San Francisco *Chronicle*: "Gaily, he sits on the bed. Then he tiptoes over to the lady and tweaks her ear. Following this, he puts his arm around her waist and sits beside her, carrying on an exhibitionistic conversation."[21] Lachman continued to feature third-dimensionals in the 1940s, and passersby continued to step into the ad, as is documented in a photograph of another display featuring a cutout figure of a Marine carrying his bride over the threshold of their new house, cheered on by four real soldiers.[22] Again, like the Bullock's ad, this scene affirmed a masculine domestic bliss.

The presentation of entire rooms and lines of goods—the actual goods for sale, with price tags included—"taught consumers better buying habits."[23] In

Atlanta, Los Angeles, Milwaukee, and St. Louis, avenues and boulevards displayed electric-powered model kitchens, modern bathrooms, and gas appliances. The Georgia Power Company could tell Atlanta viewers: "You're right, it's a real model kitchen behind the plate glass window of this display."[24] Laclede Gas Light Company did this in St. Louis with a 14 × 48-foot billboard with two display windows, each eight-feet deep and nine-feet high. Behind one glass display window is "the beautiful new aristocrat of the kitchen, the Magic Chef range. In the other window is a gas radiant heater." A 1929 article that described this advertisement claimed that viewing the ad only required a few moments of attention from passing motorists. If so, then why was there a stone bench placed in front of the board? Its presence suggests that onlookers were encouraged to stay awhile. Though the display required some attention—these were not schematically silhouetted images for easy glimpsing—advertisers had contradictory expectations with the display. Aimed toward audiences in moving automobiles, these were spectacles demanding a closer look.[25]

Though these sorts of advertising spectacles seem contrary to the common sense of the outdoors medium, which sought to convey a message quickly to moving passersby—*not* to force them to stop and linger—they served a transitional purpose. They helped to decentralize shopping by presenting audiences with an opportunity for automotive windowshopping. Even if the car needed to stop and let out its passengers to see the sights within the billboard display, the ads did entertain and sometimes even train their consumers in the use of the products featured as well as the benefits of taking and parking the car for a shopping excursion.

Billboards that combined the real and the illusionary, the actual object for sale and the imagery that advertised it, acted out the steps consumers would need to take on their path from viewing to shopping. For instance, on multiple sites around Los Angeles, Pierce Arrow dealers featured actual automobiles—their 1926 model—behind the glass of an elaborately sculpted ornamental frame. Immediately adjacent was an even larger billboard poster whose bold colors, modern lettering, and Futurist design advertised the car and the car dealership where one could take a test drive. Lest the print ad serve too abstract a purpose in signaling modernity and high culture, the brand-new framed car embodied the message in three dimensions. Collapsing the lines between advertiser and seller entirely, an outdoor advertisement for Ford dealers in Indianapolis featured their 1935 model as part of an "outdoor salon," with additional cars displayed on the lawn around the billboard showroom (figure 11.1). In six days, fourteen cars were sold right off the billboard lot. The property was hardly small and modest, and the next year it was used again for a Ford ad, this one including a reflecting pool and landscaped grounds. The car was presented in an actual show window (complete with curtains), flanked by a procession of receding, curvilinear walls in the newly popular "streamline" fashion.[26] It was as elaborate as the swanky dealer showrooms of the 1920s that had created "automobile rows"—a new genre of the commercial strip—along main roads outside of towns.[27]

Figure 11.1 Promoting mobile window shopping, Ford placed real cars behind plate glass in deluxe "streamlined" billboards, some of which sold the cars right off the billboard "lot." Collection of the author

Even this was demure in comparison to the "super-spectacular" animated outdoor advertising structure built in Cleveland by the Central Outdoor Advertising Company. The tri-partite structure was 36 feet in height and 106 feet in length. The chandeliered central tower showroom featured the car on a revolving platform, flooded with intermittently changing colored lights. Flanking the tower were two wings with painted display messages reporting the "center-poise ride" and the "comfort zone" of the new Ford V8, with the name spelled out in neon.[28] Taking its visual cues from Ford's pavilion at the 1934 Century of Progress exhibition (the world's fair where the first stream-lined trains of the Burlington and Union Pacific railroads were on view), the deluxe display set off a flurry of talk among advertisers about the need to keep pace with their "modern-minded clients." "If outdoor advertising is to keep its foremost place among advertising mediums it must keep its foremost place in design, too," *Signs of the Times* reported. "It must have a physical appear-ance devoid of the old-fashioned." Lessons could be learned from the rail-roads, which had been "forced by streamlined competition to do something to save themselves, so they went streamlined, too." Just as many manufactur-ers and retailers had sought to open stagnant markets by revamping their products through modernized design and color, billboards needed to make that leap into the future, "to 'sell' a modern product in a modern way."[29]

Around Indianapolis, St. Louis, Atlanta, Kalamazoo, Portland, and Wheeling, Ohio, billboard companies felt the new streamline urge, and the OAAA adopted a new model of billboard beauty: the Streamliner.[30] In its most basic form, the Streamliner was white porcelain-enameled steel with stainless-steel trim and had rounded corners, streamlining stripes, and beveled edges. Its wide molded base rooted the structure to the ground (replacing the wooden latticed aprons of previous years). Variations included abstract and geometric forms bursting out from the borders of the frame or set askew, as if a cubist collage of elements aggressively dislodged the formal unity, jarring the otherwise stolid, oblong picture frame into visual action. It was an architectural framework that suggested speed and modernity, its rounded edges and streaming lines suggesting fluidity of movement, yet low-slung and with a weighty presence or stance that conveyed stability. In its gleaming, virile bulk, this was no flimsy fly-by-night construction; it had pure and solid architectural girth. In the midst of the social and economic dislocations of the Depression, such streamlined forms, as historian Jeffrey Meikle has written, served as a comforting expression of both security and fast, smooth progress, reflecting "the ease with which most people wished they could slide through the Depression."[31]

The new modernist design represented what the industry had been doing for years: streamlining their operation and their billboard displays. Advertisers evaluated the exposure or "space position" value of billboards (as well as window displays and retail building locations), and came up with "scientific" formulas for locating billboards with maximum viewing potential in relation to the street and highway. In Hugh Agnew's 1938 history, *Outdoor Advertising*, "before-and-after" photographs of the same billboard location made the point. Vertically reaching tiers of billboard structures holding numerous ads were consolidated into individual, larger, horizontally stretching boards. Orientation shifted also. Rather than paralleling the streetcar passengers' view, billboards catered to the motorists' forward-looking view.[32] The boards now imitated the lateral expansion of the city itself, from vertically oriented metropolis to horizontally sprawling strip and suburban developments. Simplified and modernized, the boards signaled efficiency, aiding the fluid movement of passersby and smoothing the road between production and consumption.

Each of these dramatically stylized billboards, from the shadow boxes to the Streamliner, transformed the two-dimensions of the poster into three-dimensional architectural space. They were not just signs, they were structures that housed goods for sale; they also served as stand-ins or models for the stores and shops that might eventually occupy the site, or accompany it on an adjacent lot. In some photographs, it is difficult to discern if the image is of a store or a billboard show-window display.[33] As both billboards and store fronts increasingly relied upon the use of neon embellishments in the 1930s to spell out the brand or store name and to activate the front of their structures, their visual similarities increased. The front of the store was a "living billboard," one journalist wrote of a Los Angeles drive-in market.

This same concept was embodied by retail shops, supermarkets, and gasoline stations whose one-story, horizontally stretching buildings included a high-reaching facade of stucco or porcelain-enameled sheet metal on which the cutout or painted letters were arranged, poster like. A&P supermarket, for instance, had a 100-foot-long façade of light-colored stucco that sported little more than a sign.[34] Industrial designer Walter Teague arranged all of the architectural features of one of his store fronts—from the doorway to windows to signage—as if they were visual elements of a "two-dimensional poster design," according to Jeffrey Meikle, creating a streamlined, unified façade that would read easily in one swift glance.[35] Teague's approach, integrating all elements of architecture and advertisement within one harmonious yet dramatically simple design, was advocated by many architects, industrial designers, and sign-makers, whose work was in great demand, given that between 1924 and 1938, according to a survey by *The Architectural Record*, "three-quarters of the nation's commercial establishments conducted face-lifting operations."[36] Teague's design for Standard Oil gasoline stations in 1934 also filled these prescriptions. It read as one unified plane of visual activity, the white oblong box mimicking the overall dimensions of a billboard; reproduced 10,000 times across the countryside, it served as an exemplary marketing campaign, the building as both billboard face and package design for the branded product.[37] In these ways the new architecture of mobility prodded both outdoor advertisements and the stores they announced to wear their functions on the outside, to hide nothing from view, and to blur the lines between indoors and out, private and public space, center and periphery.

The Strip

A constellation of factors including the activities of the outdoor advertising industry laid the groundwork for the commercial strip of the post–World War I period. By the mid-1920s, central business districts of small and big cities were overrun with automobiles, congesting streets designed to handle only a fraction of the demands put on them.[38] Real estate developers and merchants recognized the growing frustration of shoppers and, with and without the benefit of extensive market and traffic studies, they went to the fringes of the central city where land was less expensive, parking ample, and congestion not yet an issue. Businesses logically migrated toward arterial highways.

Since the nineteenth century, metropolitan areas had grown in this fashion, with trunk lines extending from the central city developing simple, inexpensive one-story structures that could be easily used for a variety of retail purposes. This provided the property owner with rental income while he waited for the land to appreciate in value. These lanes were called "taxpayers" and they stretched from several blocks to several miles, their range increasing with the growth of automobility.[39]

These linear corridors of commerce were not limited to the areas around downtowns or alongside streetcar routes. They extended far beyond the edge

of the incorporated city, persistently following the improving highways and
widened boulevards. In rural areas, "ribbon" and "shoe-string slums" of
commerce developed too.[40] One realtor was amazed that even the most
arbitrary and deserted areas sprouted successful businesses if they were on the
path between two destinations and accommodated the car. What mattered to
businesses, he added, was not the number of pedestrians and automobiles
passing a location, but their ability to stop. After all, traffic might be key to
trade, but parking was the only way to get those dollars in the door.[41]

In metropolitan areas other factors, such as zoning, contributed to the
formation of the strings of businesses along boulevards and thoroughfares.
Following the passage of the first comprehensive zoning codes in New York
in 1916, many cities established separate zones for residential, commercial,
and industrial property use (with a smattering of mixed residential-commercial
and commercial-industrial zones). Zoning prohibited billboards, filling
stations, and hot-dog stands from being planted next to homes.[42]
Although business was restricted from residential areas, planners tended to
over-accommodate it elsewhere, automatically allocating the property
fronting main roads for commercial use. Often, they dedicated far more land
than could ever be realistically used for that purpose, particularly since
commercial property tended to be more expensive than residential lots. In
Milwaukee, surveys revealed that due to this "shoe-string zoning" "only
39.88 per cent of all the area zoned for business was actually in business
use."[43] Often this meant there were long stretches of vacant lots lining streets
and boulevards. Moreover, acknowledged Harland Bartholomew, responsible
for over sixty comprehensive city plans during the period of 1912 to 1940,
the surplus of business property stimulated unreasonable speculation, created
problems of taxation, and oftentimes invited "blighting of large stretches of
property along our main thoroughfares."[44]

To the speculator-developer of these taxpayer blocks, the billboard
provided revenue by using the walls and roofs of the generic commercial
buildings for income. Inexpensive by comparison to other structures one
might erect on the land, billboards also became a popular use of otherwise
vacant lots. First, landowners completely covered their real estate taxes with
the profits from renting to billboard owners. This benefited both themselves
and the municipal agencies to which they paid taxes. Billboard owners who
leased from landowners could depreciate the posterboards on their taxes
(until 1934 they did not even need to supply supporting evidence), and
billboard owners who also owned the land could write off both. Considering
that billboards occupied otherwise neglected space, it was a good deal all
around.[45]

Billboards activated these areas economically and visually. Photographs of
commercial strips in many metropolitan areas reveal the omnipresence of
billboards as accouterments to single- and double-story commercial taxpayers,
adding vivid color, height, illumination, and multiplicity to the repetition of
similar storefronts. Images of Los Angeles in the 1920s and 1930s also show
how billboards served as physical and conceptual markers of the evolving

commercial strip. On boulevards that were originally planned as residential areas, but were arrested in their development and were now semi-commercial, billboards occupied vacant lots next to Victorian houses, presumably until other more lucrative uses arose. Along the east-west boulevards of Wilshire and Sunset and the north-south avenues of Vermont and Western, scattered rows of commercial development were interspersed with lots containing ornately columned billboards arranged in a broad V-shape, one facing each direction of traffic, whose individual proportions mimicked those of the shops nearby (figure 11.2).[46]

Marking the site for later commercial development, billboards, as one industry spokesman said, put "vacant lots to work carrying the pictorial messages that stimulate the traffic of the economic merchandising of goods. They spread and stabilize distribution," and cultivate the "spirit of growth, of development, [and] of economic progress" that "every city desires."[47] Despite the overblown language, the statement is plausible, especially given the large amounts of property that billboards occupied when they were properly positioned for long-range viewing and illuminated with high-powered floodlights to optimize night-time broadcasting. Done up according to OAAA guidelines—with well-maintained landscaping and freshly painted columns, frames, and lattice fringe—the structures surely activated the site, transforming otherwise desolate stretches into zones of commercial occupation.

Companies like Foster and Kleiser tried to procure ten-year leases of land and to purchase outright any property with actual or potential advertising value. Walter Foster explained: "If we can buy any property that will be paid for in ten years, we buy it."[48] Many outdoor companies were aggressive in their land acquisition, like Foster and Kleiser, which sent teams of trained men to travel the entire Pacific Coast to make "an actual count of all important cities, roads, and places" with vacant lots of potential advertising value. The task of the engineering assistant, armed with lists of ideal locations in and around every town, was to strike up relationships with local businessmen, the Mayor, members of the Chamber of Commerce, and the leading clubs with political or social influence, including "women's clubs which may have influence." He kept track of locations and, every thirty days, he or another company man checked with landowners previously unwilling to lease or sell to see if they had changed their minds.[49] The company leased and purchased at least one third more land than it needed. Industry leaders advised companies to safeguard themselves from space shortages by planning for 50 percent more sites than what they currently used at any one time, and to establish a "fund for protection" that enabled them to purchase extra land. These practices granted companies the advantage of both a real estate investment and the prevention of competitors from moving in. It also helped companies to expand into fringe areas at a low cost and to hold onto the land until it garnered a higher price. In short, it was a form of real estate speculation. Foster and Kleiser even purchased land along scenic highways in California as a means, they said, of preserving it from excess commercialism; the federal government saw this differently, as an attempt to hinder fair trade and competition.[50]

Figure 11.2   Billboards occupy the vacant lots along Wilshire Boulevard, Los Angeles, 1928.
Tom Zimmerman Collection

The serious concern outdoor advertisers paid to their real estate suggests
that billboards provided much more than a mere symbolic tool for building
automobile-oriented commercial strips. The purchase and lease of land and
other display space was an economic force that contributed to the diffusion
of the roadside strip. In this, billboards joined a host of other pioneers of the
roadside strip, from department stores that eased their way out from central

business districts in the 1920s, to chain stores, filling stations, drive-in markets, and food stands. They served as catalysts for further commercial development, whether on the urban fringe or more distant and rural thoroughfares.

Chain stores, for example, could afford to build on sites on the outskirts of commercial centers. They had numbers on their side, from research information on traffic compiled through their many branch offices, to bulk sales that could make up for branches that lost money. Other local and regional roadside businesses could afford to go even further afield, since they required lower investment. For instance, there were twenty Big Freezes—boldly painted white and red shops shaped like old-fashioned ice cream makers—erected on vacant lots around Los Angeles in the late 1920s, from Laguna Beach to the San Fernando Valley. Simple, inexpensive structures, easy to put up and take down, the stores could be packed up and moved down the road when the landlord decided to erect a more permanent building on the lot.[51] Indeed, such food stands served as good taxpayers, occupying vacant lots in urban areas, as well as marking the rural stretches where gas stations, motels, and other services aimed at recreational drivers tended to aggregate.[52]

The most numerous of roadside businesses to "colonize" the commercial strip were gasoline stations. They invaded the countryside in the 1920s, when oil companies vastly overdeveloped their fields, resulting in an immense glut of gasoline; flagging sales due to economic hard times in the Depression years led to the same result. The response of oil companies was to build filling stations devoted to their brand, to develop their market more intensively. As zoning restricted them from residential areas, companies like Standard Oil of New York established real estate departments devoted to acquiring sites in the ex-urban arena and on rural roads. While in 1920 there were 15,000 stations in the United States, by 1930 that number was 124,000. To put that in perspective, and to suggest that the 1920s were, in fact, the initial moment of the automobility and decentralization explosions, consider that in 1990 there were 111,657 stations.[53] Notably, where filling and service stations went, other businesses followed, inciting more development still.[54]

The outdoor advertising industry allied themselves with roadside businesses, emphasizing their "local service, nationally applied," in order to appeal to both chains and independents. Oil companies, needless to say, were among the biggest users of outdoor advertising. As oil companies consolidated and standardized their stations and national advertising campaigns, billboards became an especially important component of their marketing, since it put the brand name in front of the public where they had reason to look for it.

The outdoor advertising industry claimed it could do the same for a form of automobile-oriented commerce new to the 1930s, the supermarket. Growing out of drive-in markets and chain stores of the 1920s, supermarkets were a creation of the age of distribution.[55] They were huge warehouses (compared to contemporary markets) that stocked a wide variety of goods and counted on profits that would come through bulk sales at low prices. They saved money by being wholly self-service, and carried nationally branded items that people would know to look for and want to buy without clerk assistance. Supermarkets required a lot of space and demanded parking, since customers would be driving to do their buying in bulk, so they were located on cheaper land, far from established nodes of commercial activity (or even residential areas), and drew upon a larger trading area of mobile consumers. National branding strategies, which put the burden of advertising on manufacturers rather than the supermarket (in contrast to the chains, which were establishing their own private brands), the availability of the refrigerator, which allowed people to stock up on goods, and of course the automobile, helped bring the supermarket into being.[56]

Food and beverage manufacturers were second only to gasoline companies and automotive goods as clients for outdoor advertisers until the 1950s, when the astronomical growth in supermarkets put food products at the top of the list. As much as outdoor advertising serviced the supermarket, the relationship was reciprocal. For one, the supermarket represented an additional source of circulation of mobile consumers. As independent and chain supermarkets grew nationally in the 1940s and 1950s, they began to affect the traffic patterns upon which outdoor advertisers based their trade. Starting in 1938, Outdoor Advertising Incorporated (OAI) called upon OAAA members ("a veritable research army") and the Traffic Audit Bureau (TAB) to study supermarket sales volume and circulation in each of their regions, and to come up with a map of those locations and figures. OAI recognized that the travels of motorists to supermarkets represented a built-in, easy to locate secondary market for outdoor advertisers, one that would also be easy to sell to supermarkets and national manufacturers in addition to the usual coverage promised by outdoor advertisers. This, they thought, would give outdoor advertising an edge over other media, all of whom (especially radio) were being employed by big food manufacturers for their national branding campaigns.[57]

Able to target mobile consumers precisely, OAI could thus claim: "Outdoor Advertising is Made-to-Measure for the demands of Self-Service." Why worry about "inferior shelf position" when you can reach "*all* of America's food market" through billboards? Customer selection in the age of self-service is entirely visual, one publicist wrote, giving outdoor advertising the extra advantage of "appetite appeal," picturing the product larger than life, in four color, with packaging and trademark intact (figure 11.3). He added that billboards offer the extra ingredient of "recency," providing the "last word," as a "point of purchase" display before the shopper goes into the store.[58]

With the benefit of TAB studies, supermarkets were thus able to target audiences at just the right places, to the extent that Oscar Meyer could claim that their ads were within 3-1/2 minutes of most metropolitan shopping centers. The national and local coverage of outdoor advertising by the 1950s was indeed a science, tailored to reach not only specific retail areas or

Figure 11.3 Larger than ever before, and more realistic, too, billboards for food products began to mark the way to the supermarkets of the commercial strip. Collection of the author

shopping centers but also specific occupational, language, and social groups.[59] In this sense, outdoor advertising was not only targeting audiences, but inscribing the landscape itself with social, cultural, and class distinctions.

In the post–World War II years, the streets and highways of the decentral-izing urban landscape became more crowded showrooms for a consumer culture of renewed vigor, where not one but two cars in the ranch-house garage were the best way to keep up with the Joneses. During the war, rationing of gasoline and tires and restrictions on unnecessary building construction and travel had slowed roadside development. Highway construction halted, too, and did not resume again until the mid-1950s. Car production, on the other hand, started right up again after the war, and by 1955 reached an all-time peak.[60] As a result, the arterial highways formerly seen as the endless, frictionless frontier for auto-friendly commercial expansion became a congested morass.

The cacophony of the commercial strip escalated in proportion to the growth in automobility and lack of adequate roads to handle the flow. The more businesses and signs there were, the greater the competition to gain the attention of mobile consumers. Shop signs, often standing separate from the building, became bigger and more glaring. Billboards increased in size (a 30-sheet poster of 115" by 259" becoming an alternative to the 24-sheet standard of 104" by 234"), height, and animation too. Objects and cutouts made from molded plastics and acrylics as well as borderless Fiberglass board allowed the advertising content to explode off of the billboard surface, while new reflective paints and super-real painting techniques gave two-dimensional art an enhanced sense of verisimilitude.[61] Efforts to compete with the new advertising medium of television also led to the innovation of rotating tripanels, which offered three changing scenes on one billboard. OAAA members continued to follow the trends in industrial design, and hired Raymond Loewy, one of the innovators of streamlining, in 1946 to create an aerodynamic billboard frame that became the new industry standard (barely changed for decades thereafter), with its slender beveled 19-inch molding, border of pearl gray, angled gold stripe, and white enameled surface.[62] By the 1950s, the frame was lifted high in the sky on aircraft-grade alloy legs. New "boom" trucks, which held racked-up sections of billboards and a crane to lift them up to the frame, allowed signs to be placed at greater heights where they could be more visible to the strip-driving public.[63] As the strip increased in density and length, it also rose in height, a concrete jungle forested by signs.

For many, the fanfare of signs, shops, and billboards stretching out in linear fashion was an uncoordinated mess of crass, tacky grotesqueries, a honky-tonk. To regional planners like Clarence Stein and Catherine Bauer and Wilderness Society founder Benton Mackaye, this unplanned arterial growth forecasted nothing less than an endless "roadtown" based on the prioritization of the automobile and commerce over social and communal facilities. The public arena was being forsaken by such dispersion. For Stein and Bauer, the shopping center emerged as the somewhat improbable solution to the problem. They thought that planned centers, where all retail could be gathered in one place and all the signs clustered onto one standardized unit, would reduce the proliferation of linear commercialism.[64] Unfortunately, though, the shopping centers merely became another form of roadside architecture contributing to the automotive way of life. Other urban planners and highway officials thought that building bypass roads would free up highways that had become cluttered with commerce. Of course, those bypasses eventually faced the same plight as the trafficked ones they were built to alleviate. For Mackaye, planned towns that were separate from highways, and highways that were clear of the residences and commerce of towns, were the answer. Decentralization, he and others such as Lewis Mumford believed, held great potential for humanizing urban life and bringing people in contact with nature. Unchecked and uncoordinated commercial growth along the highways did little to achieve this. As metropolitan regions grew into the countryside, and highways connecting rural settlements developed into linear corridors of consumption, the distinctions between city and country seemed lost. Commerce was colonizing the natural environment. And the strip was paving the way. Though strip growth reached a frenzy in the decades after World War II, its roots, and a good deal of its trunk, grew in the 1920s and 1930s.

The influence of outdoor advertising and the architecture of mobility thus resonates on several levels, but allow me here to conclude with just one—the fostering of our present sense of placelessness and the meandering of the market beyond geographic boundaries. The nationally standardized billboard structures, advertisements, and featured goods created a web of recognizable material similarities that served to connect, visibly, different people and places, while it marked and encouraged highway lanes as commercial strips. This diffused and spread the market, leveled regionally specific place characteristics, and standardized spaces dedicated to advertising and selling. As national chains and franchises revolutionized retail, restaurant, and hotel industries by the 1960s and 1970s, their signs, structures, and billboard advertisements served as another means by which local distinctions diminished. As a regional and local medium, increasingly adept at targeting mobile audiences with greater and greater specificity from the 1950s forth, outdoor advertising did offer local variations on the national themes. Mostly, however, the specificity they provided was not regional. Ironically, the successful charting of diffuse markets had led right back to a kind of fixing of market boundaries, not by geography but according to social delineations related to presumed patterns of travel and buying. Traffic had acquired distinguishing contours, while places lost theirs. It had been this realization of the outdoor advertising industry—that traffic itself, wherever it went, now comprised the market—that had helped make places as diverse as Houston, Minneapolis, Oklahoma City, Atlanta, and Los Angeles, come to resemble one another as the same sprawling commercial buyway.

Notes

1. See my book *Buyways: Automobility, Billboards and the American Cultural Landscape* (New York: Routledge, 2004), from which this essay is drawn. See also "Advertising & Selling Presents Tribute to Progress of Medium," *Outdoor Advertising Association News* 31, no. 2 (February 1941): 7, (hereafter, *OAA News*). This visual training included showing "the customer a picture of his package, so he will know what to look for in the store."
2. Self-service shopping was significantly different from prior experiences, as there was no clerk to ask about or suggest a product. This made the package and the brand all the more important. Kerwin H. Fulton, "Advertising Today," *OAA News* 30, no. 4 (April 1940): 1.
3. The Wrigley tropical fish spectacular cost $8,000 per month on an eight-year contract. Some advertisers felt the signs in Times Square had limited impact on actual sales, since visitors to the site were tourists, and were not aiming to buy the gum or washing machines advertised. They acknowledged, however, that these spectaculars did bring the manufacturer great attention nevertheless. "Representatives' Meeting—Friday, July 6, 1928," 15, J. Walter Thompson Staff Meeting Minutes, Hartman Center, Duke University; "World's Largest Electrical Unit Begins Operation," *OAA News* 26, no. 4 (April 1936): 1; "The World's Largest Spectacular," *Signs of the Times* 82, no. 4 (April 1936): 7–9; "A Brief History of Electric Advertising Displays," *Printers' Ink Monthly*, March 1931, 94–96. See William Taylor, ed., *Inventing Times Square: Commerce and Culture at the Crossroads of the World* (New York: Russell Sage Foundation, 1991); David Nye, *Electrifying America: Social Meanings of a New Technology* (Cambridge, Mass., and London: The MIT Press, 1990), 73–84; William Leach, *Land of Desire: Merchants, Money, and the Rise of a New American Culture* (New York: Vintage, 1993), 340–348; Tama Starr and Edward Hayman, *Signs and Wonders* (New York: Currency-Doubleday, 1998), 88–131.

4. Paul S. Clapp, "Electric Power Transforms Main Street," *The Magazine of Wall Street*, June 29, 1929, 422–423; Nye, 54–57.

5. Sinclair Lewis, *Main Street* (New York: The New American Library, 1961 [1920]), 400.

6. H. H. Magdsick, "Building Prosperity Avenue," *Transactions of the Illuminating Engineering Society*, May 1930, 451–453.

7. Magdsick, "Building Prosperity Avenue" (Italics are mine). To fulfill this goal, some urged that companies lobby for the standardization of ordinances governing the extent to which light could be projected. Tracy Simpson, "Advertising Value of Electric Signs and Billboards," *Journal of Electricity*, 1 June 1924, 414.

8. Leach, *Land of Desire*, 39–41, 55–70.

9. See *The Poster* 17, no. 11 (November 1927): 4; *The Poster* 17, no. 2 (February 1927): 3; *The Poster* 16, no. 10 (October 1926): 4.

10. Kerwin Fulton, "Advertising Today," *OAA News* 30, no. 4 (April 1940): 10.

11. Simpson, "Advertising Value," 413.

12. "Electricity for Publicity," *The Electrician*, February 15, 1924, 197.

13. Toward this, sign manufacturers marketed special projectors and reflectors to be mounted on the billboards or on adjacent buildings. They found that "the best results are obtained by the use of specially built, porcelain enameled, steel, angle reflectors well out in front and above the board." These became the standard for the OAAA and were marketed through their trade journals and promotional materials. Simpson, "Advertising Value," 413. Psychologists suggested that advertisements using pictures were like film, able to hit the mind direct through the eye. Electricity made the outdoor advertisement even more filmic.

14. Simpson, "Advertising Value," 413.

15. "Brown Says Third Dimensional Bulletins Are Here to Stay," *OAA News* 24, no. 10 (October 1934): 4.

16. *Outdoor Advertising—the Modern Marketing Force* (Chicago: OAAA, 1928), 9, 47.

17. "Chevrolet Places Clock Bulletins," *OAA News* 26, no. 10 (October 1936): 10; and *Chevrolet: Enterprising and Consistent* (New York: Outdoor Advertising Inc., n.d.); R. S. Fulton, "Advertising Clocks," *Signs of the Times* 82, no. 1 (January 1936): 24–25; P. E. Van Horn, "Tools for Painted Display," *Signs of the Times* 76, no. 3 (March 1934): 21; "The Complete Story About the New Sunkist Campaign," *Signs of the Times* 75, no. 4 (December 1933): 12; Augusta Leinard, "Electric Clocks Mark S&W Time," *Advertising Outdoors*, May 1931, 7. Leinard was talking about another clock campaign by S & W Coffee which used the slogan "S & W Time is all the time." Only a few ads actually incorporated the clock into their advertising content in this way. S & W advertised on billboards from Canada to Mexico. In fact, their only advertising media were radio and outdoors (7–8).

18. Special Scotchlite and other reflectorized materials added to the impact of the electrified ads. P. E. Van Horn, "Tools for Painted Displays," 21. Also see "Bulletin Reports Stock Trend Out of Doors," *OAA News* 26, no. 8 (August 1936): 12.

19. Margaret Marsh, *Suburban Lives* (New Brunswick and London: Rutgers University Press, 1990,), xiii–xiv.

20. Lee S. Arthur, "Advertising That Has Taught Consumers Better Buying Habits," *Printers' Ink Monthly*, December 1923, 24.

21. Quoted in "Model Bedrooms In Streamliners Prove Effective," *OAA News* 28, no. 12 (December 1938): 12.

22. *OAA News* 28, no. 5 (May 1938).

23. Arthur, "Advertising That Has Taught Consumers," 24.

24. *OAA News* 26, no. 2 (February 1936): 3.

25. Norman B. Terry, "Display Windows in Billboards Produce Results," *Gas Age-Record*, December 28, 1929, 957–958.

26. "Show-case Bulletin Scores a Hit for Indianapolis Ford Dealers," *OAA News* 25, no. 12 (December 1935): 10.

27. Chester Liebs, *Main Street to Miracle Mile: American Roadside Architecture* (Baltimore and London: The Johns Hopkins University Press, 1985), 82–86.

28. "Views in the News" *Signs of the Times* 79, no. 3 (March 1935): 57; "Super Structure," *Signs of the Times* 79, no. 4 (April 1935): 66; advertisement, *Signs of the Times* 79, no. 4 (April 1935): 37.

29. Jeffrey L. Meikle, *Twentieth Century Limited: Industrial Design in America* (Philadelphia: Temple University Press, 1979), 4; "That Growing Demand Among Advertisers and Agencies For Streamlined Structures," *Signs of the Times* 81, no. 4 (December 1935): 12; "Streamlined Outdoor Structures," *Signs of the Times* 82, no. 3 (March 1936): 10; advertisement for streamline designed bulletin by Dick & Anderson, Knoxville, Tennessee, *Signs of the Times* 79, no. 7 (July 1935): 29.

30. See, for instance, Foster and Kleiser streamliners in "Modern Painted Bulletins," *Signs of the Times* 89, no. 3 (July 1938): 22–23.

31. Meikle, *Twentieth-Century Limited*, 154.

32. Hugh E. Agnew, *Outdoor Advertising* (New York and London: McGraw-Hill Book Company, Inc., 1938), 28; J. M. Jones, "Walker and Co. Celebrates Its Golden Anniversary," *OAA News* May 1935, 7.

33. See, for instance, the images of the Minneapolis-area display for Bouttells department store, "Two Windows Featured," *Signs of the Times* 74, no. 4 (August 1933): 46–47.

34. Richard Longstreth, *The Drive-in, the Supermarket, and the Transformation of Commercial Space in Los Angeles, 1914–1941* (Cambridge, Mass., and London: The MIT Press, 1999), 48, 62–63, 105–106; M. Jeffrey Hardwick, *Mall Maker: Victor Gruen, Architect of an American Dream* (Philadelphia: University of Pennsylvania Press, 2004), 62–65; John A. Jakle and Keith A. Sculle, *The Gas Station in America* (Baltimore and London: The Johns Hopkins University Press, 1994), 146.

35. Meikle, *Twentieth-Century Limited*, 119.

36. "Main Street, U.S.A.," *The Architectural Forum* 70 (February 1939): 85; Horace Ginsbern, "In Store-Front Displays," *Signs of the Times* 77, no. 3 (July 1934): 11; Morris Lapidus, "Where the Sign Begins . . . ," *Signs of the Times* 78, no. 1 (September 1934): 11; William F. Rooney, "Electrical Displays," *Signs of the Times* 73, no. 2 (February 1933): 10.

37. Jakle and Sculle, *The Gas Station*, 146.

38. J. C. Nichols, "The Planning and Control of Outlying Shopping Centers," *Journal of Land and Public Utility Economics*, January 1926, 17; John Ihlder, "The Automobile and Community Planning," *Annals of the American Academy of Political and Social Sciences* 116 (November 1924): 199–205.

39. My use of "strip" is consistent with what Chester Liebs has traced to the turn-of-the-century "taxpayer strips." These were linear commercial corridors

comprised of single rows of one-story shop fronts that were conceived as temporary structures to produce enough revenue to pay taxes and retain the property for more profitable development at a later time. Chester Liebs, *Main Street to Miracle Mile* (Boston: Little, Brown and Company, 1985), 12–16ff, 229. Also see Michael Ebner, "Re-reading Suburban America," in Howard Gillete, Jr. and Zane L. Miller, eds., *American Urbanism* (New York: Greenwood Press, 1987). Richard Longstreth's detailed studies of Los Angeles in *City Center to Regional Mall: Architecture, the Automobile, and Retailing in Los Angeles, 1920–1950* (Cambridge, Mass.: The MIT Press, 1997) have been useful in understanding the birth of the commercial strip too. Other scholarly works that address decentralization, though as a post–World War II phenomenon, are Brian Berry and Yehoshua Cohen, "Decentralization of Commerce and Industry: The Restructuring of Metropolitan America," in Louis Masotti and Jeffrey Hadden, eds., *The Urbanization of the Suburbs* (Beverly Hills: Sage Publications, 1973), 431–455; John A. Jakle and Richard L. Mattson, "The Evolution of a Commercial Strip," *Journal of Cultural Geography* (Spring-Summer 1981): 12–25; Brian J. L. Berry, "Ribbon Developments in the Urban Business Pattern," *Annals, Association of American Geographers* 49 (March 1959): 145–155; F. N. Boal and D. B. Johnson, "The Functions of Retail and Service Establishments on Commercial Ribbons," in Larry S. Bourne, ed., *International Structure of the City* (New York: Oxford University Press, 1971), 368–379.

40. See, for instance, the use of phrases "shoe-string" and "ribbon" slums in: "Well done, California!" *Sunset*, August 1939, 14; *The National Committee for Restriction of Outdoor Advertising: What It Is and What It Seeks to Do* (New York: National Committee for Restriction of Outdoor Advertising, n.d.), unpag.; Albert S. Bard, "Progress in Billboard Control," in Harlean James, ed., *American Civic Annual*, vol. 3 (Washington, D.C.: American Civic Association, 1931), 196; "Shoe string building," Alfred Bettman, Robert Whitten, E. P. Goodrich, "Roadside Improvement: A Report of the American City Planning Institute," *City Planning* 9, no. 4 (October 1933): 181–186.

41. Longstreth, *The Drive-In, the Supermarket*, 37–38, 72; Clarence S. Stein and Catherine Bauer, "Store Buildings and Neighborhood Shopping Centers," *Architectural Record*, February 1934, 184.

42. Green Bay, Wis., is one example of zoning to keep auto-related and grocery store business from residential districts in 1925; Champaign, Ill., sought to use excess commercial zoning to stabilize property values, and implemented commercial zoning in 1926. Jakle and Sculle, *Gas Station in America*, 187, 215.

43. Stein and Bauer, "Store Buildings," 187.

44. Bartholomew quoted in Stein and Bauer, "Store Buildings," 187. Also see Harland Bartholomew, "Business Zoning," *Annals of the American Academy of Political and Social Science* 155 (May 1931): 101–102; Bartholomew, *Urban Land Uses* (Cambridge: Harvard University Press, 1932), A list of Bartholomew's urban plans appears in Eldridge Lovelace, *Harland Bartholomew: His Contributions to American Urban Planning* (Urbana: University of Illinois, Department of Urban and Regional Planning, 1993), A-20. On his city planning see Marina Moskowitz, *Standards of Living: The Measure of the Middle Class in Modern America* (Baltimore and London: The Johns Hopkins University Press, 2004).

45. F. T. Hopkins, "The Roadside Advertising Controversy" (New York: National Outdoor Advertising Bureau, 1938), unpag., OAAA Collection, Fairleigh Dickinson University, Madison, N.J. After I completed my research, this collection was transferred to the John W. Hartman Center for Sales, Advertising, and Marketing History, Duke University, Durham, N.C., where it is organized under the general title of Outdoor Advertising Archives. Hereafter, materials from Fairleigh Dickinson as well as those subsequently acquired by Duke University will be referred to as OAA/Duke.

46. Longstreth, "The Forgotten Arterial Landscape," 439, 454; Longstreth, *City Center to Regional Mall*, figs. 45, 66, 94. See Wilshire, Vermont, Western, and Sunset street scenes in Photograph Collection, History Department, Los Angeles Public Library and in the Dick Whittington and Title Insurance and Trust Company photograph collections, Regional History Center, University of Southern California, Los Angeles. (In the Dick Whittington collection, see, for instance, photographs numbered 8-75-22, 3-54-5, 811-127-1, A10-17-4; in the Title Insurance collection, see 1-1-1-424, 1-1-1-425, 1-1-1-430.)

47. "Economic Utility of Poster Panels," *OAA News* 15, no. 4 (April 1924): 17.

48. Walter Foster, "Leasing and Maintenance of Poster Advertising," *OAA News* 14, no. 1 (January 1923): 9.

49. Foster, "Leasing and Maintenance."

50. Walter Foster explained his practice of leasing but not using space as "protection to keep anyone else from leasing it or building on it. . . . we set up a fund for protection." Ibid., 8; "Outdoor Advertising Company Takes the Count," *Civic Comment*, March–April 1931, 13, OAA/Duke.

51. Jim Heimann, *California Crazy & Beyond: Roadside Vernacular Architecture* (San Francisco: Chronicle Books, 2001), 50.

52. Heimann, *California Crazy*, 45, 50; Longstreth, *The Drive-In, the Supermarket*, 69.

53. Jakle and Sculle, *Gas Station in America*, 55, 58, 183.

54. Jakle and Sculle, *Gas Station in America*, 135–136, 209, 227; Longstreth, *The Drive-In, the Supermarket*, 69.

55. Richard S. Tedlow, *New and Improved: The Story of Mass Marketing in America* (New York: Basic Books, 1990), 238; Longstreth, *The Drive-in, the Supermarket*, 78, 92.

56. Tedlow, *New and Improved*, 238; Longstreth, *The Drive-In, the Supermarket*, 110.

57. Reprint of Donald Curtiss, "Super Markets and Self-Service Stores," *Advertising and Selling*, June 1940, OAA/Duke.

58. Curtiss, "Super Markets"; reprint of Edward Pachuta, "Building Brand Identification Through Outdoor Advertising," *Quick Frozen Foods*, March 1958, OAA/Duke; Press Release from Vincent V. Van Beuren, OAI, "The Outdoor Supermarket Alliance: How Outdoor Serves Advertisers in the Self-Service Field," January 27, 1958, 2, OAA/Duke.

59. "Outdoor vies for more sales, fewer curbs," *Printers' Ink*, June 5, 1959, 50.

60. Liebs, *Main Street to Miracle Mile*, 60, 90.

61. W.C. Wall, "A 'New Look' for Signs, Too," *Signs of the Times*, September 1948, 26; "Outdoor vies for more sales," 50; "Highlights in the Poster and Painted Display Medium (By Decades)," n.d., 2–4, Clear Channel Archive. Many issues of *Signs of the Times* in this period document the technological advances in plastics, such as the use of backlit Plexiglas boxes.

62. C. D. McCormick, *Advertising and Selling* 40 (February 1947): 60; see blueprints and patent applications for the Loewy billboard frame, OAA/Duke. Gannett Outdoor Advertising Company made one of the first notable changes to the Loewy panel, introducing the "Trim Panel," which replaced the foot-wide curved frame with a mere 1-1/2-inch border. James Fraser, *The American Billboard: 100 Years* (New York: Harry N. Abrams, 1991), 157.

63. The ease with which billboards could be installed, dismantled, and moved around with the boom truck also led to the practice of sign rotation; advertisers could move and reuse the same signs all over town, guaranteeing the kinds of saturation that traffic and trade surveys had proven necessary. *Outdoor 101* (New York: The Institute of Outdoor Advertising, n.d.), 12; Sally Henderson, *Billboard Art* (San Francisco: Chronicle Books, 1980), 54.

64. Stein and Bauer, "Store Buildings and Neighborhood Shopping Centers, 175–183; Longstreth," *The Drive-in, the Supermarket*, 156; Hardwick, *Mall Maker*, 77–78.

Part IV

Representation and Organizational Culture in Post–World War II United States

Chapter 12

Postwar Sign, Symbol, and Symptom: "The Man in the Gray Flannel Suit"

Anna Creadick

The Suit as Sign—A Contest for Meaning

Everett himself was a man about Tom's age and was also dressed in a gray flannel suit. The uniform of the day, Tom thought. Somebody must have put out an order.
—Sloan Wilson, *The Man in the Gray Flannel Suit*

The cover image for Sloan Wilson's best-selling 1955 novel *The Man in the Gray Flannel Suit* features a slim, suited man, striking what looks like a military "at ease" stance. Shoulders squared, feet apart, hands clasped behind him, this dark-gray silhouette is clever in its combination of legibility and illegibility. In the original image, which I am unable to reproduce here, one can clearly make out the suit, the straight edge of a white handkerchief, the white collar.[1] But beyond a vaguely stern, upward glance, the man's face remains indecipherable beneath its fedora. Who is this "Man in the Gray Flannel Suit?," the mystery of the title and illustration beg us to discover. But the tag line above the image on the 1956 paperback edition suggests that readers of the 1950s *already* knew him: "The superb best seller America is taking to its heart. . . . A touching, powerful novel about men and women you know, live with, and love!"[2]

Postwar cultural discourse reveals conflicting emotions about the gray flannel suit, and postwar suits themselves carried multiple meanings. While the somber men's business suit certainly predates the Post–World War II period, in specific ways, the suit itself did become a *subject* at this time. Was this suit an example of "inconspicuous consumption" or "non-fashion"—a kind of erasure of the body, a desexualized, equalizing disguise?[3] Or was the suit, like the military uniforms that preceded it, "sexually potent, and more than a little menacing."[4] Was the postwar suit confining, or did it have a democratizing function, collecting fractured identities into a new middle class? Was it a threat to individualism, or was it marked with enough specific accents to be an expression of one's tastes, of one's shape, or even one's type? To some degree, the evidence suggests all of these interpretations. The gray flannel suit, in all its contradictions, came to function as a sign, symbol, and symptom of a culture of "normality" in the decades immediately following World War II, and a closer look at the discourse surrounding it reveals complicated questions about the instability of middle-class identity, the gender of corporate culture, and new anxieties over a perceived social uniformity in postwar culture.

World War II marked a watershed moment of transformation for the United States, from more than a decade of New Deal liberalism—largely focused on and driven by the interests of the poor or working class—toward a Postwar liberalism, characterized by anti-union legislation, the buildup of a military–industrial complex, an increase in white-collar workers, and a shift toward the interests of a reinvigorated "middle." Lennard Davis makes the convincing claim that the rise of the category of "normal" coincided with an earlier rise of bourgeois hegemony in the late nineteenth century: "The average man, the body of the man in the middle, becomes the exemplar of the middle way of life . . . [and] the bourgeoisie [becomes] rationally placed in the mean position in the great order of things."[5] Post–World War II America saw the re-inscription of "normality," because these years mark another period of rapid growth and renewed hegemonic claims by the middle class. The postwar consolidation of the middle class is thus concomitant with an epistemological category that defines, circumscribes, and celebrates the "norm," casting it as both average and ideal. The exterior gray-flannel uniform could effectively disguise the inconsistencies and inequalities of the people beneath it, so that the postwar middle class could be perceived—and could perceive itself—as normal, as unified, as uniform.[6]

The cover of the June 16, 1945 *New Yorker* featured a tongue-in-cheek illustration of a World War II paper-doll soldier, surrounded by his various postwar apparel choices. The image effectively links the returning GI and the postwar white-collar businessman by inviting us, at least mentally, to place the clothing of one upon the other. In fact, the paper-doll's original, permanent clothes are not tasteful white skivvies, but his wool army uniform. Under all his new postwar fashions, it seemed this smiling American male would always be a soldier. The artist's use of the paper-doll image reveals the conscious parody of an apparently amusing sameness in the millions of American men demobilizing *en masse* from military to civilian life, and from one uniform to another.

One month later, Oscar E. Schoeffler, fashion editor of *Esquire* and *Apparel Arts* magazines, warned a gathering of the International Association of Clothing Designers to anticipate "mass fashions" in order to aid the industry in retaining its wartime volume. He even forecast a new uniformity of body: "Broadening of shoulders and slimming of waists in Army training will have an effect upon the men's fashion silhouette," he predicted, and returning veterans will demand clothes "as comfortable and utilitarian as those supplied by the military."[7] Soldiers did return eager to shed their uniforms for civilian clothes. In fact, the immediate postwar years of 1945 and 1946 saw a national suit shortage, experienced, briefly, even by President Truman himself.[8]

By late 1945, veterans were given precedence, according to the *New York Times*: "Some retailers are refusing to sell to casual customers, with the exception of those wearing a service emblem."[9] On a visit to Kansas City in June, 1945, Truman tried to order three white shirts from his former haberdashery partner, but was told none were available. When the President's shirt shortage made the press, "three dozen shirts, the correct size . . . arrived from store owners and individuals in St. Joseph, Wichita, and Oklahoma City."[10] Six months later, with white shirts still in short supply, President Truman again made news by offering to share his own shirts with a needy reporter, but "could give no assurances when shirts or two-pants suits might be generally available."[11] A September 1945 *New York Times* feature, entitled "New Plumage for the Male Animal," focused explicitly on the tensions over the postwar man's fashion transition. The article's cartoon illustration shows a panicky, uniformed GI, trapped between two mirrors reflecting competing images of himself, the first showing him in a conservative dark suit, the alternative sporting a wild polka-dot and checkered ensemble; the caption reads, "GI dilemma—Blue serge or all the colors of a rainbow?" Author Edith Efron cites some fashion designers' predictions that "in the shiny new post-war world, . . . men are going to want things different . . . Color!" Meanwhile other designers, "hot for the status quo, . . . can't think of anything nattier than a nice gray suit with a dark blue tie." Despite hopes that postwar men would take some new wardrobe chances, most designers were not fooling themselves. Efron interviews men on the street to find the consensus that "It all depends on what everyone else is wearing." "I still don't think it will happen," stated ex-serviceman and editor of *Men's Modes* Merrill Mitchell. "I'm an average man, I think, and I sure wouldn't want to dress up in a lot of colors."[12]

He was right. Postwar men chose the more somber suit precisely because "everyone else" was wearing it. What, then, does the nondescript gray flannel suit reveal about *itself*, as an object of postwar material culture? Admittedly, postwar suits in and of themselves are un-remarkable, but according to market research, that was the point. As early as 1948, a *Fortune* magazine feature on "The Business Suit" was able to pin down the "one category of business suit" that was always "wholly acceptable": "The S.E. [Standard Executive] or N.A.M. [National Association of Manufacturers] is most commonly a neutral-colored, double-breasted affair, remarkable neither for trimness nor for premeditated illness of fit. It is usually worn with a soft shirt and a necktie either deadly sober or dully bright." The writer concludes, unequivocally, that this suit is "The safest garb. . . . That may be, profoundly, why so many people wear it. Uniforms still matter."[13] The homogenous features of the postwar suit,—those qualities that made it "uniform"—also made it "safe." It was desirable, then, to look like everyone else, to blend in, to be inconspicuous.

In the 1951 sci-fi film *The Day the Earth Stood Still*, an alien visitor named Klaatu is able to "pass" as a mild-mannered businessman throughout the film simply by donning a gray flannel suit. In the 1952 Hitchcock thriller

I Confess, a Catholic priest played by Montgomery Clift, falsely suspected of murder and tormented over whether to give up the priesthood to save himself, walks frantically through the town contemplating his dilemma. He stops, suddenly, in front of a menswear shop window and notices a gray flannel suit, on display, complete with white shirt and bowtie. Immediately, he turns, walks to the police station, and turns himself in. Then there is the moment in *Rear Window* (1954) when the marriage-minded socialite played by Grace Kelly tries to tempt her rough-edged, free-spirited photojournalist boyfriend (Jimmy Stewart) by suggesting how easily he could slip into a New York magazine job, and how handsome he would look in a "nice, dark blue, flannel suit": Kelly literally seems to be dressing the pajama-clad Stewart with her eyes. Finally, there is the decision, for the 1957 film version of *The Man in the Gray Flannel Suit*, to cast hulking cowboy actor Gregory Peck in the lead, so that on his body, the business suits seem more like straight-jackets.[14]

In all of these film moments, the suit functions to erase prior identities, allowing the wearer—whether alien, priest, outlaw or cowboy—to pass for "normal." Presumably, there was some comfort in dressing alike, as men had done for years in the Armed services. But as a sign, the suit itself could be a disguise or a threat, could mean success or entrapment. A new discomfort was emerging in the continuation of uniformity after the war's end, and in the implications of it.

The Suit as Symbol: Sloan Wilson's (Wife's) Metaphor

Sloan Wilson's 1955 work *The Man in the Gray Flannel Suit* was an extremely popular novel. Despite its status as "middlebrow" fiction, critics praised the novel for the resonance of its novel's subject matter. Columnist Orville Prescott featured *The Man in the Gray Flannel Suit* as one of his "Books of the Times": "This is a good novel—neat, smooth, and reportorially exact in its account of the pressures, problems and tribal customs of the men in gray flannel suits. . . ."[15] The novel was a "Literary Guild" choice before it landed on the shelves, and became a big-budget Twentieth-Century Fox motion picture less than two years after its debut.[16] Author Sloan Wilson had tapped into the issues of his day, and by suggesting "The Man in the Gray Flannel Suit" as the title, Wilson's wife Elise Pickhardt Wilson provided a powerful metaphor at a pivotal moment.[17]

The shadow of World War II dominates this text, over ten years later. More than anything, *The Man in the Gray Flannel Suit* is a novel about demobilization—about how to survive in a postwar world. The story centers on protagonist Tom Rath's half-hearted attempt to move up professionally, in order to get his wife and three small children out of their "dull" suburban home "small, ugly, and almost precisely like the houses on all sides of it" (p. 3). Disenchanted with his meaningful job at a nonprofit organization, Tom decides to apply for a higher-paying public relations job at the

"United Broadcasting Corporation":

> The next morning, Tom put on his best suit, a freshly cleaned and pressed gray
> flannel . . . . On his way to work he stopped in at Grand Central Station to buy
> a clean white handkerchief and to have his shoes shined. (p. 7)

In Tom's mind, the crisp, clean gray flannel is the "best suit," and the details
of his appearance would be important factors in this corporate environment.
After showing some healthy resistance to authority in his interview "test,"
Tom is hired by UBC and put in the high-pressure position of assisting the
corporation president.

From this point, the novel features a back-and-forth between Tom's tribu-
lations in his new job and flashbacks of his service as a paratrooper in World
War II. Tom's wartime secrets literally come back to haunt him: he killed
seventeen men, one in cold blood just to take his warm jacket; he accidentally
killed his best friend with a grenade; and in his most hopeless hour, he had an
affair and fathered a child with a young woman in Italy. Tom's new job in the
cutthroat corporation unearths these disturbing memories of the war: his
own dishonesty playing the corporate "yes-man" reminds him that he is also
lying every day to his wife. He realizes that the very nihilism that helped him
survive combat also helps him adapt to the humiliations and immoralities of
big business. Tom pretends to be "adjusted" but the war is always just a
flashback away, triggered by a passer-by's leather jacket, the familiar face of an
elevator operator, or the captivity of a train ride to work—a little too similar
to his plane trips as a paratrooper. Like so many others, Tom Rath has gone
from the uniformed positions on slate-gray troopships to the uniformity of
gray flannel suits and the "opaque-glass-brick-partitioned world" of the
corporation, looking for comfort again in routine (23). But the world of
the corporation is nearly as threatening and unfamiliar to him as the world of
combat had been.

In Tom Rath's case, the hierarchies of his work are even more dangerously
complicated by gender, as female secretaries often know more than their male
bosses, and male workers like himself often feel positioned as secretaries. In
1951 C. Wright Mills wrote that,

> . . . the white-collar girl dominates our idea of the office. She *is* the office,
> [according to] the editors of *Fortune*: "The male is the name on the door, the
> hat on the coat rack, and the smoke in the corner room. But the male is not
> the office. The office is the competent woman at the other end of his buzzer,
> the two young ladies chanting his name . . . pecking out his initials with pink
> fingernails on the keyboards of . . . machines . . . ."[18]

The move toward office jobs could be unfamiliar and seem feminized for
men whose fathers had been farmers, entrepreneurs or unionized laborers.
Similarly, the focus on "gray flannel suits" or the "white collars" or "organization *men*" within the cultural discourse of the times serves to recast this
new class of workers as unquestionably male in the face of this insecurity.

In Sloan Wilson's novel, female office workers are either banal extensions of machines, or extremely sexualized, and references to them pop up incongruously in the novel:

> A secretary in a tight pink sweater told Tom . . . a pert brown-haired secretary sat at a small desk copying letters . . . the door to his office opened and a distinguished and statuesque blond girl in a dark-green blouse and expensive-looking tweed skirt came in. "You buzzed, sir?" (102).

After this parade of secretaries, Tom looks at his intercom buttons and thinks, "Maybe the second one's for a redhead and the third one's for a brunette . . ." (102).

In several other scenes, Tom Rath finds himself acting like a secretary, or—more precisely—like a woman:

> "Hello!" Walker said as Tom entered his office. "You're right on time!"
> Tom smiled. "I try to be punctual" he said primly, and felt absurd. (41)

Wilson's use of the word "primly" feminizes the role, and Tom's anxiety emphasizes this move into the corporation as a kind of gendered boundary-crossing that feels "absurd." In other moments, he is being treated as a secretary by his immediate superior, Bill Ogden, a man he describes as "handsome . . . slender . . . well dressed and in a position of at least a little authority" (p. 41):

> "Take notes," Ogden hissed at Tom.
> Tom quickly took a pad from his pocket and sat with pencil poised. (108)

Rath's humiliations (combined with the author's regular gratuitous references to buxom secretaries) have the effect of emphasizing gender *difference* in a realm where "men's work" and "women's work" have become indistinguishable.

In all of Tom Rath's interactions—whether at work or at home—he constantly thinks one thing and says another. This doubleness, which Wilson represents by contrasting internal and external dialogue, strikes at the performance at the heart of the novel, and emphasizes its theme of keeping up appearances. Tom says what he thinks people want to hear, what he thinks he is expected to say.

In one climactic scene, Tom realizes that he must not expect to know himself or to find meaning in his work—he must simply keep his gray flannel suit "neatly pressed," as if it were a costume in a play:

> The trick is to learn to believe that it's a disconnected world, a lunatic world, where what is true now was not true then . . . . for now is the time to raise legitimate children, and make money, and dress properly, and be kind to one's wife, and admire one's boss, and learn not to worry—I'm just a man in a gray flannel suit. I must keep my suit neatly pressed like anyone else, for I am a very respectable young man. (101)

In a postwar context, then, what was important was to remember his lines, to raise children, work hard, dress well, and try not to think about who he was under his gray-flannel uniform.

With the help of his clear-sighted wife, Betsy, who criticizes his cynical approach to his job, and the working-class elevator operator Caesar Gardella, who—having served with Tom in the war—reminds him to do the right thing for the woman and child he left behind in Italy, Tom eventually recovers his integrity. He levels with both his wife and his boss, and in the end is able to enjoy the two things he thought incompatible: honesty and financial reward. He reflects on his experience in a way that takes this individual's story back to a more collective one:

> . . . when I got back from the war . . . all I could see was a lot of bright young men in gray flannel suits rushing around New York in a frantic parade to nowhere. They seemed to me to be pursuing neither ideals nor happiness—they were pursuing a routine. For a long while I thought I was on the sidelines watching that parade, and it was quite a shock to glance down and see that I too was wearing a gray flannel suit. . . . (283)

The novel's resolution only comes about when Tom unifies his worlds, integrating the past with the present, and being "honest" both at home and at work. Throughout *The Man in the Gray Flannel Suit*, the suit itself functions to symbolize the protagonist's conflict as he passes into the new postwar middle class. The suit itself was the driving metaphor for Tom Rath's story, according to Mrs. Wilson, the publishers, and the consuming public who made a catch phrase out of it that continues to the present day. But beyond its symbolic value, Wilson's text also articulated some of the real troubles of his readers: the lingering impact of the war, the discomfort with corporate white-collar work, and the pressures to "keep up appearances" in an unstable postwar milieu.

If before World War II, as Anne Hollander argues, there still existed "huge visible divisions between the classes" in apparel, the postwar suit helped to disguise those differences, as suburbanites—importantly, *white* suburbanites—worked to "assimilate one another" into a kind of middle-"classlessness."[19] But working against the democratizing potential of the suit itself was the anxious discourse surrounding it. The first line of C. Wright Mills' 1951 study *White Collar* sounds nearly like *Invasion of the Body Snatchers* in its echo of this idea of the suit as a disguise: "The white-collar people slipped quietly into modern society" (ix). Poor, nonwhite, or working-class people could use the suit to pass into the middle class to some degree, and this notion of class passing was palpable. William Whyte named it explicitly in his 1956 text, *The Organization Man*: Of the newest suburbanite who has just barely escaped the "city wards," Whyte writes, "It is not stretching the sense of the word too much to say that he has not made it so much, but that he is passing. Still fundamentally urban and lower class in his reflexes, he has a long acculturation ahead of him . . ."[20] But the discourses surrounding men in suits most often

revealed deep anxieties over social uniformity. As Fred Miller Robinson suggests, "the fear that people will look like one another . . . is fundamentally
alarm . . . over the blurring of class boundaries . . . the sartorial assimilation
of all classes."[21]

The Suit As Symptom—The Sociological Critique

*I began to notice that every applicant wore a dark-blue suit and a conservative tie
and had ready and right answers for most of my questions.*
          —corporate recruiter, in William H. Whyte, *The Organization Man*, 123

*In Germany, the "black-coated worker" was one of the harps that Hitler played on
his way to power.*
                                        —C. Wright Mills, *White Collar*, xvii

In June of 1953, *Fortune* magazine ran a now-familiar photograph showing
a throng of commuters crowding off the train platform in the new Chicago
suburb of Park Forest.[22] Nearly one hundred men—and a few women—inch
along the platform toward the camera, descending down stairs at the front of
the frame. They present a curious combination of uniformity and specificity.
Nearly every man wears a somber topcoat and hat, white shirt, and tie. Nearly
every man whose arms are visible clutches a newspaper, and nearly all their
faces seem tight, nervous, or tired. This is the classic image of the "organization men," the "white collar" workers of the urban centers, retiring to their
suburban ranchers at the end of a day. But the photograph invites closer
inspection.

Some men don't wear hats. One man's tie is strikingly different from the
others, with its unusual horizontal stripes of varied widths. A few men wear
glasses; several wear very dark topcoats, which stand out against the crowds
of gray. One wears a bowtie, another a white hat. One man smiles directly
into the camera; another seems to smile to himself, knowing he is being
photographed. None of the women look into the camera, but look far down
or away from the photographer, as if hoping not to be captured on film. One
woman, scarved and downcast under the camera's gaze, ironically clutches a
Look magazine to her chest.

In fact, the longer one looks, the more differences emerge. No two hats
are *precisely* alike: brim up, brim down, curled brim, wide brim; thin ribbon,
wide ribbon, very wide ribbon; worn straight, worn askance, worn high on
the head, worn low over the eyes. Even the gray topcoats differ in pattern,
material, and width of lapel. And the men's bodies, at first so homogenous,
begin to distinguish themselves: narrow shoulders here, round face there;
dark features, hollowed cheeks, deep-set eyes; a thin, older-looking man
walks stiffly up front; a lummox of a man looms above others in the back.

Two of the most prominent observers of these postwar men (and
occasionally women) in suits were Colombia sociologist C. Wright Mills
and *Fortune* editor William H. Whyte.[23] In his 1951 study *White*

Collar: The American Middle Classes, Mills not only uses the sartorial "white collar" to define his subjects, but then claims that these workers in particular constitute the "new middle class," and, further, that this new middle class is "symptom and symbol of modern society as a whole" (xx). William H. Whyte's popular 1956 text *The Organization Man* took a more anthropological approach to the corporate employee, studying him in school, at work, and cavorting in his natural habitat of suburbia, concluding that corporations and social institutions should emphasize individualist thinking in order to keep the new "Social Ethic" of "group-mindedness" in check (p. 435).

Writing from their respective positions at Columbia and *Fortune*, Mills and Whyte *were* the white-collar organization men they wrote about. Mills places professors in his categorization of white-collar workers, and some of his most impassioned writing comes during his critique of the incorporation of the intellectual: "The political intellectual is, increasingly, an employee living off the communication machineries which are based on the very opposite of what he would like to stand for" (pp. 129, 159). Whyte thanks his managing editor at *Fortune* in his acknowledgments page, "and not merely because I am a good organization man," he adds. Such positionality lent an urgency to their texts: they knew whereof they spoke. But it also created a tendency for them to generalize out from where they stood, to normalize what they saw around them.[24] These works became a sociological critique of something that may not have been as real as they felt it to be. Was the "new middle class" of "organization men" the postwar male's version of "the problem with no name," or was it more of a name with no problem?[25] It may, in fact, have been something very *un*real that these two social observers helped to create:

> . . . the moral problem of social control in America today is less the explicit domination of men than their manipulation into self-coordinated and altogether cheerful subordinates.[26]

René Magritte's famous 1953 painting *Golconde* contains echoes of the *Fortune* magazine photograph published the same year. In the *Golconde*, briefcase-clutching, suited workers rain down upon their own middle-class suburban homes; in the *Fortune* photograph, the suited Park Forest commuters seem to have puddled at the station.

As early as 1946, C. Wright Mills was addressing the postwar "middle classes" and their "competitive" society.[27] By 1951, in *White Collar*, Mills argued that "Images of white-collar types are now part of the literature of every major industrial nation" (x). Belgian surrealist painter René Magritte completed twenty-one paintings of black-suited businessmen in bowler hats between 1948 and 1966, representing what one Magritte scholar called "the strikingly unstriking figure singled out from the crowd without which he is inconceivable."[28] Magritte explained that he liked to remove and paint objects in order to recover them, so that their "subversive effect" might again exist "in the real world."[29] And this was the move Sloan Wilson made when he turned the mass-man—the gray-flannel office worker—into a protagonist. Both Mills and Whyte, on the other hand, participate in his collectivization by imagining him as a "class" or a "type."

Both Mills and Whyte indulge in hand wringing over a generational shift. Mills is a frustrated Marxist, looking for language to describe this "new" group's "drift" away from union-based, organized worker politics. He keeps the bourgeois origins of fascism in the back of his mind, and makes regular reference to Weimar Germany, totalitarianism, fascism or authoritarianism. Never very good at hiding his loathing, Mills describes white-collar workers as "morally defenseless as individuals and politically impotent as a group" (xvi). Whyte is more the liberal humanist, anxious over what the overly-managed hierarchies of organization life mean for American individualism: "it is all very well to say one should belong. But how much? Where is the line between co-operation and surrender?" (387).

Generally, Whyte's work is descriptive. What most disturbs him about the "Social Ethic" replacing the "Protestant Ethic" is the endangerment of the individual in the face of a corporation that asks men to hand over their "souls," and the endangerment of individuality in organization families—men, women, and children—ensnared in "webs" of friendship and mandatory "tolerance" in suburban communities (440–441; 365, 405). Although William Whyte swears he is not writing The Organization Man about the exteriors—the seeming conformity of suits, ramblers, model homes—he invokes these "surface uniformities" constantly in order to then explore them (12). He criticizes the "scientism" of communications research, and yet regularly turns to a quick sociological survey himself to illustrate a point: "A study we made at Fortune of nine hundred top executives . . ." (179).

Whyte's text is full of such slippages. Purporting to write about men "owned" by the organizations they work for, Whyte constantly turns to writing about "suburbanites" in general, the "middle class," the "main stream." By the end, he is writing about bridge parties, church-going, and child-rearing. Whyte seems to want to have both sides of the argument—to claim homogeneity, but also difference; to show distress, but also contentment; to illustrate the importance of "appearances," but also of realities. He begins to explore the significant shades of difference within suburban homogeneity, especially that lower rung of suburbanites, who are effectively passing as middle class, with a lot at stake if they lose any prestige. His conclusions—that belongingness and conformity are closely related, and that the new social ethic is both a moral imperative and a counterproductive turn—do, however, make peace with the contradictions he finds. He is an organization man, and he is writing, largely, for other organization men. He is not so quick, therefore, to size up the "group" from a distance. He carefully conducts his door-to-door research like the salesmen he describes.

Both writers employ the new sociological research at the same time that they critique its dominance in American life. What can explain Whyte's decision to plot out the patterns of bridge, cocktail, and Christmas parties in a suburban neighborhood? In contradictory ways, Whyte was both critiquing "scientism" and promoting/distributing it to a broader audience. Mills thanks Paul Lazarsfeld for sharing 128 of his "intensive interviews" with white-collar workers taken in 1946 (356). What else did these sociological studies do, then, if not "normalize" their subjects? With the moral and intellectual authority of the postwar "expert," these writers helped to construct boundaries and typologies of middle-class identity, gendered typologies.

How does the suit figure into these texts? For Mills, exterior appearance is one of the only ways he can collect these workers together and conceptualize them as a class. The color of the collar is the dominant metaphor; wearing a "white collar" to work becomes the sign, the "accent" of belonging to a "new middle class." In his appendices, Mills relies on a Bureau of Labor Statistics paper on the "Problem of Definition" to define white-collar workers:

> The Labor Economics Staff of the Bureau of Labor Statistics ("White-Collar Workers: The Problem of Definition," unpublished) uses, along with "fixed payment by the day, week, or month," two other criteria which I found helpful: "A well-groomed appearance" and "the wearing of street clothes at work." (359)

In a postwar context, he turns to surfaces, to uniforms to demarcate class. Although Mills does refer to white-collar "men and women" regularly, and acknowledges the presence of women in the "white-collar pyramids" with seven pages devoted to the "Office Girl," his conception remains largely male. The suit—the white-collared "street clothes"—is the visible symptom that enables him to define and diagnose the disorder of the "new middle classes." Extending the metaphor of physical or spiritual sickness, Horace M. Kallen, in his review of *White Collar*, predicted that Mills' book "would alert [white-collar workers] to their condition for their better salvation."[30]

In *Organization Man*, Whyte pointedly refuses to discuss the suit as a symptom. Actually, he does protest too much:

> I am not . . . addressing myself to the surface uniformities of U.S. life. There will be no strictures in this book against "Mass Man" . . . against ranch wagons, or television sets, or gray flannel suits. They are irrelevant to the main problem, and furthermore, there's no harm in them . . . . Unless one believes poverty ennobling, it is difficult to see the three-button suit as more of a straitjacket than overalls, or the ranch-type house than old law tenements.
>
> And how important, really, are these uniformities to the central issue of individualism? . . . . The man who drives a Buick Special and lives in a ranch-type house can assert himself as effectively and courageously against his particular society as the bohemian against his particular society. He usually does not, it is true, but if he does, the surface uniformities can serve quite well as protective coloration. (11–12)

Whyte's invocation of the "gray flannel suits" attests that the suit was a subject for what seemed to him tiresome debate. *The Organization Man* was put out only a year after Sloan Wilson's *Man in the Gray Flannel Suit*, and by the same publisher. Whyte's argument is that the suit could function as a kind of camouflage; since "surface uniformities" are "disarming," he suggests, clever organization men can look one way, and act another. More precisely, they can *look* like conformists but *act* like individuals. Given Whyte's prescription, it is confusing that he so clearly despised Wilson's novel, in which a "yes man" finds even more success by tapping into his individualism and integrity. In his occasional references to *The Man in the Gray Flannel Suit*, Whyte criticizes the "sanctimonious materialism" of Tom and Betsy Rath: "In [their] self-ennobling hedonism . . . they don't see why they shouldn't have the good life and good money both" (146). Faulty logic operates in Whyte's advice to use the suit as "protective coloration" in order to act more individualistic. Similarly, he concludes by proposing that the Organization Man can "turn the future away from the dehumanized collective" first by learning, through his appendix, "How to Cheat on Personality Tests." Whyte's mixed messages were well perceived in 1956 by his *New York Times* book reviewer: ". . . such deception as he recommends is quite in line with the ethos that already prevails in much of the corporate world . . . . Wouldn't it be better to refuse—if possible as a group—to take the silly things?" The book reviewer? C. Wright Mills. And—perfectly pointing to the distinction between his own approach and Whyte's, he concludes, "wouldn't it be still better if Mr. Whyte would shelve his earnest optimism just long enough to explore the economic basis and the political meaning of the white-collar ideologies he so intelligently describes?"[31] Instead, Whyte sticks to his man-against-the-boss-but-protect-the-system approach, and concludes with the tongue-in-cheek promise: "In all of us there is a streak of normalcy" (456).

Both authors confess a lack of clarity about their own subjects. Mills admits the group may be heterogeneous, but that it can be distinguished by what it is not—namely, neither "entrepreneur class" nor "manual laborers." Effectively, Mills is "other-directed" in his conceptualization of this new middle class: he only understands them in relation to others. Even the organization of his text reveals this, as he begins with a section on the "Old Middle Classes" in order for his "New Middle Class" to become visibly different. He's not sure who is middle, but he knows they're neither propertied entrepreneurs nor unionized workers.

William Whyte states up front that he has a subject, but that he's not certain about how to tackle it: "This book is about the organization man. If the term is vague, it is because I can think of no other way to describe the people I am talking about" (p. 3). Whyte's suburban interviewees show similar confusion in trying to define their "Eastgate" neighbors: "No one can bring himself to say 'working-class people'; the phrases are more likely to be 'people who work with their hands more than their heads,' 'artisans,' or, at worst, 'blue collar' " (340). He acknowledges that Park Forest residents protect "pretensions of classlessness" that "strain" under the proximity of working-class "newcomers," yet continues to collect together "suburbanites" as a class himself.

Despite the vagaries, both Whyte and Mills wax generic about the white-collar masses, and in so doing help to reify them as a subject, and—further—to gender that subject male. Mills labels the white-collar worker the "little man." But this is not the "little man" one should stick up for. Mills calls this little man "[t]he hero as victim, the small creature who is acted upon but who does not act, who works along unnoticed in somebody's office or store, never talking loud, never talking back, never taking a stand" (p. xii). Here, Mills tries to establish the white-collar workers as "political eunuchs" (p. xviii). Yet, these are strikingly *feminine* qualities: "works along unnoticed," quiet, obedient— he might as well be describing a female office secretary. White-collar workers are conceptualized male ("little man" or "organization man"), then gendered female, and "costumed" in gray business suits. What a difference, therefore, a suit makes.

Whyte's discussions of "keeping *down* with the Joneses," "inconspicuous consumption" and "belongingness" are the philosophies that underlie the importance of the gray flannel suit (346). His analysis of the suffering of "the deviate" and the simultaneous control and warmth of "the group" illuminate the contradictions in a culture where the suit could be both a mark of security—literally "fitting in"—and a mark of conformity—looking just like all the rest (397–401). Most importantly, Whyte gives insight into the ambiguities of "middle class" status—in a way that reveals it to be a problematic engine to attach to normality. His section on "How to Cheat on Personality Tests," along with discussions of "façades" and the "mutual deception" of trying to be "normal" (449, 216) illustrates both the dominance of normality in discourse at this time, and the fact that normality as an homogenizing concept could be both produced and critiqued at the same time: even in the postwar period, a critique of normality had emerged. In Whyte's view, the resistance to conformity resided in an awareness, or self-consciousness about one's own conformity.

The whiteness of these "new" middle classes and "organization men" is so much a part of the definition that the two sociologists barely acknowledge it. Such realities as racism in suburbia—mentioned only in passing as "segregation problems" by Whyte (325)—or hiring of only "native-born" workers for white-collar jobs—what Mills calls "status by descent" (74)—are mentioned only once or twice in these studies of four- and five-hundred pages in length. Not only, then, do the authors gender this new middle class in subtle ways, but they also presume its whiteness.

For postwar men who were already securely middle class, the suit may well have symbolized the entrapment which "imprisoned [him] in brotherhood" at the office (Whyte 404). But for those who were *newly* middle class, especially previously poor or working-class whites, blacks and other "minorities," and first- or second-generation immigrants, the suit—like the military garb that preceded it—could be an equalizing uniform of respectability. Both C. Wright Mills and William Whyte acknowledge this fact:

> For two generations sons and daughters of the poor have looked forward eagerly to becoming even 'mere' clerks. (Mills, xiii)
>
> . . . for many a resident the curving superblocks of suburbia are the end of a long road from the city wards to middle-class respectability. (Whyte, 295)

Both men understate the phenomenon, however. The end of World War II and the prosperity that eventually followed, as historian Perry Duis argues, enabled the embrace of a "dream deferred" for many. Duis argues that the postwar "return to the home" was a "popular movement . . . based on need for privacy, 'normal' domesticity, personal freedom for millions of people who had been living with social, economic, and emotional upheaval for two decades of depression and war."[32] A move into the middle class meant a move into the "main stream." The suburban dwellers William Whyte found "keeping *down* with the Joneses" had a sense of what was at stake in postwar communities where construction of a large new middle class meant downplaying lingering class differences.

Horace Kallen saw Mills' white-collar worker as "only a unit in an aggregation, mass-man incapable of organic action, seeking refuge from anxiety and futility in a struggle to keep up appearances."[33] A 1959 Ned Hilton cartoon in *Look* magazine shows that "middle-class" Americans were still struggling to understand their status.[34]

A white, suburban housewife, sits on a couch reading a sociological text, and asks her pipe-smoking husband, "Are we in the uppermost upper part of the lower middle class, or the mid-lower part of the *upper* middle class?" Hilton both illustrates and ridicules the fact that people had to read the sociological critique in order to understand the subtleties of their class position. Yet, the assumption of the comic is that everyone (especially everyone who reads *Look* magazine) is *somewhere* in the middle class.

A 1956 Bureau of Labor Statistics essay on White-Collar Employment and Income concludes by casually dividing laborers into only two groups: "office" workers and "factory" workers.[35] Was this to be the new simplified manifestation of class after World War II? The spatializing division of workers by their place of work, and by the colors of their collars?[36] If so, the sociological critics were in fact supporting or constituting the same culture of conformity that they were critiquing, by allowing white collars or suits to collect a "type" of American worker into a "new middle class." In effect, Mills and Whyte did reify a postwar white-collar "middle class" first, by naming it as a "new" object of study. They then "define" their object through such external markers as the suit, the space of the office, their gender, and their race. Although in their studies they may have disagreed over the politics and meanings of this "new middle class," by making it a subject for scrutiny, they both cooperated in its construction. None of these postwar attempts to "normalize" the middle class, however, would ever fully overcome its instability as a subject.

In 1951, C. Wright Mills wrote that "In America, unlike Europe, the fate of white-collar types is not yet clear" (p. xi). But it would be. The 1955 metaphor of "The Man in the Gray Flannel Suit" helped further define the white-collar "type," and in 1956 *The Organization Man* charted his fate. But interestingly, as early as 1957, films like *Will Success Spoil Rock Hunter?* were already turning the white-collar office worker into a parody of himself. In Frank Tashlin's farcical comedy, Rockwell Hunter (played by the importantly effeminate Tony Randall) nearly ends up dead in his panicked attempt to get ahead in the firm with an ad campaign featuring the ultimate in comically exaggerated femininity, Jayne Mansfield. In the end, he is rewarded, literally, with a set of keys to the executive washroom.[37]

The gray flannel suit has been understood as a mark of inconspicuous consumption in postwar consumerist culture. Ironically enough, its very drab sameness was cause for a lot of attention. The uniformity of the suit contradicted newly potent ideologies of individualism, while it also satisfied a perceived need for a return to what Wendy Kozol calls a "normality that never existed."[38] Tensions arose over the vagaries of a large "new middle class," and over the importance of "fitting in" to that class. Often the suit itself, or the "white collar" of the shirt beneath it, became the site for such tensions. The suit itself became a tautological sign of normative middle-class identity: wearing a suit meant being middle class; being middle class meant wearing a suit.

Anxieties around the suit suggest that "normality" was only suit-deep, not only for those "passing" for the first time into a middle-class identity, but also for those members of American postwar society who supposedly embodied it most: white, (heterosexual, married) middle-class (able-bodied, employed) men. By 1960, a photograph in *Look* magazine took the parody of the gray flannel suit one final step. Comic actor Art Carney, clothed in "sincere grey flannel," clutching a copy of Vance Packard's *The Status Seekers*, and surrounded by the "essentials for the hard life of the soft sell"—a martini, briefcase, pedestal furniture, and tranquilizers—seems to have forgotten his pants.[39] At first described as a "uniform," the suit was now exposed as a put-on, a performance, a gray projection always more appearance than reality.

Notes

1. Regrettably, the high fees charged by some copyright holders to publish images, even within academic works, means I am unable to reproduce the images I discuss in this essay here.
2. Sloan Wilson, *The Man in the Gray Flannel Suit* (1955; rpt. New York: Cardinal/Pocket Books, 1956), front cover. All future references are to the Cardinal edition and will be cited in the text by page number.
3. This term *inconspicuous consumption* is used in William Whyte's *Organization Man* (New York: Doubleday, 1956), and is derived from Thorstein Veblen's concept of "conspicuous consumption" in his *Theory of the Leisure Class* (New York: Macmillan, 1899). The phrase "non-fashion" is from Anne Hollander, *Sex and Suits: The Evolution of Modern Dress* (New York: Kodansha, 1994), 17. Hollander writes that non-fashion "creates its visual projections primarily to illustrate the confirmation of an established custom, and to embody the desire for stable meaning even if custom changes—it is normative." She argues, however, that the suit does not qualify as "non-fashion."
4. Hollander, *Sex and Suits*, 55.
5. Lennard J. Davis, *Enforcing Normalcy: Disability, Deafness, and the Body* (London and New York: Verso, 1995), 6–27.
6. Eventually, that perceived uniformity would make the gray flannel suit the locus for parody and critique of what was by then understood to be a homogenized

middle class of "status seekers" or, later, "the Establishment." According to the *Oxford English Dictionary*, the *locus classicus* for the phrase "the Establishment" as it came to be used in the counter-culture movements of the 1960s is actually 1955, "though earlier usages have been recorded." An *OED* source from 1957 describes "the Establishment" as "a term generally taken to denote those elements in society and politics which are self-satisfied and opposed to all radical change." See "Establishment," *OED online*, 2nd ed., 1989, Oxford University Press, 2002.

7. "Schoeffler Warns Men's Wear Trades," *New York Times*, July, 17, 1945, 16.
8. "Vets Happy to Discard Uniforms," *New York Times*, November 11, 1945, 39.
9. "Veterans Favored in Apparel Pinch," *New York Times*, October 29, 1945, 24, 26; DePinna clothing advertisement targeting veterans, *New York Times*, April 10, 1946, 16.
10. "White Shirts Found for Truman," *New York Times*, July 1, 1945, 10.
11. "President Offers Shirt, 15 1/2 by 33, to Reporter," *New York Times*, April 4, 1946, 29.
12. Edith Efron, "New Plumage for the Male Animal," *New York Times*, September 9, 1945, VI, 16, 44.
13. Wilder Hobson [J. K. Galbraith], "The Business Suit: A Short and Possibly Tactless Essay on the Costuming of American Enterprise," *Fortune*, July 1948, 104, 126. Thanks to Kevin S. Reilly for sharing this resource.
14. *The Day the Earth Stood Still*, Dir. Robert Wise, screenplay Edmund H. North, with Michael Rennie and Patricia Neal (Twentieth Century Fox, 1951); *I Confess*, Dir. Alfred Hitchcock, with Montgomery Clift and Anne Baxter (Warner Brothers, 1953); *Rear Window*, Dir. Alfred Hitchcock, with James Stewart and Grace Kelly (Paramount, 1954); *Man in the Gray Flannel Suit*, Dir. Nunnally Johnson, with Gregory Peck and Jennifer Jones (Twentieth Century Fox, 1956).
15. See John McNulty, "Tom Rath, Commuter," rev. of *The Man in the Gray Flannel Suit*, *New York Times*, September 16, 1955, VII, 18; Orville Prescott, "Books of the Times" rev. of *The Man in the Gray Flannel Suit*, *NYT*, July 18, 1955, 19.
16. *The Man in the Gray Flannel Suit* [film] (20th Century Fox, 1957); "Man in a Gray Flannel Trap: Peck fights high-pressure life in a movie version of the best seller" [photo-essay] *Life*, 111–116.
17. Significantly, Wilson begins his acknowledgments by thanking his wife for her role: "She mowed the lawn, took care of the children, and managed the family finances so that I could find time to write. She never made me feel that writing is justifiable only if it is successful . . . . Many of the thoughts on which this book is based are hers." The penultimate "About the Author" page reveals that "the publisher wishes to add that it was Mrs. Wilson who so ably summarized the theme of her husband's book by suggesting the title" (289).
18. C. Wright Mills, *White Collar: The American Middle Classes* (New York: Oxford University Press, 1951), 200. All future references are to this edition and will be cited in the text by page number.
19. Hollander, *Sex and Suits*, 153; see also Whyte, *Organization Man*, 299.
20. William H. Whyte, Jr. *Organization Man* (New York: Doubleday, 1956), 338, emphasis in original. All future references are to this edition and will be cited in the text by page number.
21. Robinson, *The Man in the Bowler Hat* (Chapel Hill and London: University of North Carolina Press, 1993), 26.

22. "Archive: Just Passing Through," rpt. in *Fortune*, September 18, 1995, 248.
23. Along with sociologist David Riesman, Mills and Whyte effectively gendered the phenomenon of the rising postwar middle class in distorting ways. Kevin S. Reilly has unearthed interesting data on the almost entirely female research staff behind much of the social criticism in the pages of *Fortune* magazine. See his dissertation "Corporate Stories: *Fortune* Magazine and the Making of a Modern Managerial Culture," Department of History, University of Massachusetts-Amherst, 2004.
24. Roland Marchand, *Advertising the American Dream: Making Way for Modernity, 1920–1940* (Berkeley: University of California Press, 1985). Marchand argues that modern ad-men designed advertisements according to the motivations of themselves and others of their rank, class, and profession. The difference here, ostensibly, is the explosion of sociological research that both C. Wright Mills and William Whyte employ in analyzing the white-collar environment. A similar tendency seems to be at work nonetheless.
25. "The problem with no name" comes from Betty Friedan's expression for the ennui and frustration of postwar middle-class suburban women in *The Feminine Mystique* (New York: Dell, 1963).
26. C. Wright Mills, "Crawling to the Top," Rev. of *The Organization Man* by William H. Whyte, Jr. *New York Time*, December 9, 1956, VII, 26.
27. "The Middle Classes in Middle-Sized Cities," *American Sociological Review*, October 1946; "The Competitive Personality," *Partisan Review*, September–October 1946; cited in *White Collar*, 356.
28. Hammacher, qtd. in Robinson, *Man in the Bowler Hat*, 126.
29. Robinson, *The Man in the Bowler Hat*, 127.
30. Horace M. Kallen, "The Hollow Men: A Portrayal to Ponder," rev. of *White Collar* by C. Wright Mills, *New York Times*, September 16, 1951, VII, 4.
31. C. Wright Mills, "Crawling To the Top."
32. See Perry Duis "No Time for Privacy: WWII & Chicago's Families," in Lewis A. Erenberg and Susan Hirsch, eds., *The War in American Culture: Society & Consciousness During World War II* (Chicago and London: Chicago University Press, 1996).
33. Kallen, "The Hollow Men," 4.
34. Ned Hilton cartoon, *Look*, August 1959. Rpt. in Daniel Horowitz, *Vance Packard and American Social Criticism* (Chapel Hill and London: University of North Carolina Press, 1994), 167.
35. Jean A. Flexner and Anna-Stina Ericson, "White-Collar Employment and Income: Trends and Current Status of Employment and Income for a Large but Diverse Group of Workers," *Monthly Labor Review*, Washington, D.C.: U.S. Dept. of Labor/Bureau of Labor Statistics, 79:4 (April 1956), 401–409.
36. See Mirra Komarovsky, with Jane H. Philips, *Blue-Collar Marriage* (1962) (New York: Vintage, 1967).
37. By 1960, making the arguments even more accessible in a pulp paperback formula, Vance Packard's *Status Seekers* helped make the sociological critique itself "mainstream": See Horowitz, *Vance Packard*, 1994.
38. Wendy Kozol, *Life's America: Family And Nation In Postwar Photojournalism* (Philadelphia: Temple University Press, 1994).
39. Art Carney in "sincere gray flannel" photograph, *Look*, February 1960. Rpt. in Horowitz, *Vance Packard*, 216.

Chapter 13

"Girls in Gray Flannel Suits": White Career Women in Postwar American Culture

Clark Davis

Women on certain jobs are every bit as good as men. We wouldn't think of having a man selling brassieres. But women will be stepping into top management spots. It's just an evolutionary thing.

—Montgomery Ward Vice President, 1956[1]

In 1949, *Life* magazine ran a profile of the Daly family's four daughters, all bright young professional women who were earning a combined annual salary of more than $100,000. Ten years later, the magazine's editors decided to re-visit the "career sisters" to see what had happened. Their finding: "The four sisters said they would and . . . they all made good." After a decade that one sister summarized as "hard work, babies, and fun," the women had all married, collectively had nine children, and were now pulling in over $200,000 combined in their four thriving careers. Marguerite, age 41, had progressed from modeling to producing television fashion shows. Kathleen, 39, had climbed up the ladder to the vice presidency of a New York advertising agency. Maureen, 37, had continued her career as an author. Sheila John, 31, had gone from being a newspaper writer to working as a feature columnist for the *Chicago Tribune*. Her articles now appeared in fifty newspapers nationwide.[2]

The Daly sisters seemed to be superwomen, enjoying happy families alongside thriving careers. If family, social networks, money, and status meant success, then they were indeed living the American dream. In this, they were not alone. Thousands of American women during the 1950s engaged in professional careers that their mothers and grandmothers could not have imagined. Indeed, *Good Housekeeping*, hardly a magazine noted for challenging traditional gender roles, began featuring a column in the early 1950s entitled "American Career Girls" that touted women with notable careers. Later in the decade, *U. S. News & World Report*, also no mouthpiece for radical social change, urged young women to obtain professional and technical skills so they could have a place in the booming postwar economy and job market.[3]

For nearly a century and a half of U.S. history, entrenched beliefs about women's difference operated through social, cultural, political, and legal structures to limit their access to jobs of status and power in the public sphere. White men held almost exclusive claim to the powerful, prestigious, and lucrative positions in business and the professions. White women held these jobs only in rare circumstances, and women of color faced almost impenetrable barriers. In the first half of the twentieth century, however, a number of revolutions in American life, including urbanization, the rise of big business, the passage of women's suffrage, a devastating Depression, and World War II widened women's possibilities in the nation's occupational landscape. For the first time, white, middle-class American women began to enter the paid labor force in significant numbers. Whereas paid work had long been a central fact of life for American women of color and those in the laboring classes, the proportion of white women working for wages during this period reached 34 percent, almost double that in the early twentieth century, while the number of married white women working surged from 3 percent to over 30 percent.[4]

The hundreds of thousands of white, middle-class women who entered the labor force in the postwar years did so with the hope that they could access "respectable," salaried middle-class jobs.[5] In the postwar years, popular culture presented sporadic images of women holding status and power within the business and professional world, suggesting to audiences that perhaps openings did exist in the nation's corridors of power. Notable in this regard was *Adam's Rib*, the 1949 film that showcased Katharine Hepburn and Spencer Tracy as married lawyers on opposing sides of an attempted murder trial. Hepburn, a very successful private attorney, proved herself to be Tracy's professional superior in a sharp courtroom duel. Magazine features on "career women" added to the picture. In 1958, for example, *Coronet* ran a feature on Nan Marquand, a once prominent actress who now served as casting director for the nation's fourth largest advertising agency. Readers learned that New York's Madison Avenue had "its girls in gray flannel suits too," who every day "prove that creativity and efficiency under pressure are not masculine monopolies." Indeed, none less than the chairman of RCA announced in 1956 that "the discovery that women are people is being extended and opportunity for women should expand with it."[6]

Popular images of the 1950s, drawing on both postwar television images as well as Betty Friedan's *The Feminine Mystique*, have often emphasized the demonization of professional women and the glorification of feminine domesticity. While some historians, such as Elaine Tyler May in her work *Homeward Bound*, have underscored the postwar years as a time of "domestic containment," others, like Joanne Meyerowitz, have sought to complicate the June Cleaver stereotype by pointing attention to women's dramatic increase in labor force participation during this era.[7] Even as American industry, returning veterans, and much of popular culture told the millions of working war-time women to return to the home, the half-century long rise in female labor force participation continued. In the late 1940s and early 1950s, most American firms abandoned the long-standing marriage bar that had dominated corporate hiring practices for decades, as well as the widespread thirty-five year old age limit for hiring female office workers. These developments opened up vast numbers of new jobs that appealed to white middle-class women, particularly married women in this demographic who previously would not have considered working. By 1950, one in every four married women held a job outside the home; by 1960, one in three. At the dawn of the 1960s, 20 percent of all women with a child age six or younger and 39 percent of all mothers with school-age children worked outside the home. And a great many of these middle-class women increasingly looked not just to temporary "jobs" but to long-term "careers," promising them more meaning and identity.[8]

So how do we wrestle with these contrasting images of the 1950s? How do we resolve the tension between the postwar domestic ideal and the reality of growing labor force participation on the part of American women? This essay argues that this very contradiction is key to understanding both the experience of postwar "career" women and the often pervasive conservative reaction against them. The entrance of hundreds of thousands of white, married women into the labor force during the 1950s, many in search of not just jobs but careers, generated a powerful backlash of male fears and resentment, as well as an often vitriolic cultural response to the destabilization of traditional gender roles.[9]

This essay explores the contradictory mix of new career opportunities and possibilities alongside powerful pressures to abide by codes of feminine domesticity that pervaded the lives of occupationally ambitious white middle-class women in the postwar years. Whereas scholarship on women's experiences in the 1950s has often emphasized the decade as a time of extreme conservatism with respect to gender roles, newer interpretations by historians such as Joanne Meyerowitz have revealed a wide diversity of gender norms in postwar popular culture.[10] My analysis of white women's place in the postwar labor market alongside a survey of popular cinema in this era supports and furthers these more complex understandings. While conservative views ultimately took a leading place in middle-class rhetoric about women's status and place, the period's reactionary impulses must be understood as a response to women's real labor and economic gains, advances that were a significant part of the cultural dialogue about working women in the 1950s.

The Subtle Revolution

When I ask undergraduates about life for American women in the 1950s, they often respond by discussing the image of Marion Cunningham in the 1970s television series, *Happy Days*. In this popular and long-running television program, set in the 1950s, Marion Ross played "Mrs. C," a ditzy but warm suburban housewife. Though hardly a documentary, the portrayal of women in *Happy Days*, in fact, paralleled the representations of white women that dominated American television in the 1950s. Idealized portraits of the nuclear family, such as *The Donna Reed Show, Leave it to Beaver,* and *Ozzie and Harriet,* filled living rooms during prime time and cemented a vision of the nurturing and maternal female homemaker that would dominate images of the "real" American family to the present day. Even the character Lucy Ricardo from *I Love Lucy,* whose antics and aspirations defied the convention of the dutiful and submissive housewife, became essentially just that at the end of every episode.[11]

Such television images were not mere fiction. When Betty Friedan castigated the smothering ideology of feminine domesticity in her 1963 book, *The Feminine Mystique,* millions of white American housewives nodded in exasperation over their confining lives.[12] While World War II is sometimes described as a "watershed" in American women's history for greatly increasing women's employment opportunities, the war's end ushered in an often hostile ideological climate for working women.[13] Leaders in American society from every stratum promoted marriage and motherhood as women's cherished lot; long-standing middle-class tenets of feminine domesticity hardened and grew into a near national religion. Popular magazine articles routinely praised women who cherished the role of mother as key to the nation's strength and virtue, dubbing this profession with labels such as "the greatest occupation of mankind," the job "most girls are dreaming of," and a "higher career" than that held by women who worked outside the home.[14]

The pervasive rhetoric of feminine domesticity in postwar culture certainly shaped white women's place and experience in the workforce, but even as many forces exhorted female workers to return to the home following World War II, and even as more and more women married younger and had more babies, the fifty year-long rise in female labor force participation continued.[15] In early 1947, when postwar employment hit its nadir, dropping 14 percent from the wartime high, seventeen million working women remained, a 17 percent increase over 1940, and a number that would rise steadily thereafter. A Department of Labor survey found that 80 percent of women working during the war wished to retain their jobs, and despite some major postwar layoffs, growing numbers of women did find work. Between 1940 and 1960, the total proportion of women in the labor force rose from 25 percent to 35 percent.[16] Clearly, the images of domestic bliss that pervaded postwar American culture and dominated popular historical memory of the era obscure much about the experience of white women in the 1950s.

Historian Angel Kwolek-Folland has argued that four general factors nudged upward the number and percent of working women during the twentieth century. First, the general growth of American business made more jobs available. Second, increasing numbers of women took advantage of the expansion of higher education and the opportunities found therein. Third, economic crises, wars, and rising divorce rates continually forced women into the workforce. And finally, the nation's gender stereotyping of work has in some ways actually helped women as the growth in the economy has come largely in the service sector. The evolution in the practice and ideology of working women reflected the pull of a rapidly changing economy on rigid but ultimately malleable gender roles. All of these forces collided sharply in the immediate postwar years. Historian Susan Hartmann notes: "The war had broken down some of the resistance of employers to married women, and their postwar need for labor led them to accept, even seek, women whom they would not previously employ." It is this turbulent social and economic context women faced when entering the postwar job market.[17]

Ultimately, raw economic needs and consumer desires contributed to the rising number of white and married women working in the postwar years. The combination of a higher level of skill and experience among the adult female population along with higher labor needs within American business created growing opportunities for female labor force participation. The average American family felt a slight decrease in purchasing power between 1944 and 1950, which, when combined with intensifying consumerist pressures, led many to seek greater incomes. Broad sectors of American women in the 1950s found themselves at least partly responsible for dependents. A survey of the largely white and middle-class membership of the General Federation of Business and Professional Women's Clubs in 1952 found that one third of members contributed financially to the support of their dependants.[18] And with memories of Depression-era and wartime security concerns still much in mind, postwar advice literature often urged women to be prepared to work should financial crises arise. An article in *Today's Health* summarized the prevailing concern: "It is wise for most girls to choose a career that will train them for marriage, homemaking and childrearing and at the same time provide a satisfying means of gainful employment in the event that it becomes necessary to earn their living and perhaps that of dependants."[19]

National debates about the fate of the postwar economy often made women's employment a central concern. In many quarters of American government and business, euphoria over the war's end quickly turned to concerns about a possible postwar recession. Such fears did not bode well for working women. If jobs became scarce, then women in the labor force would again face critical eyes. In fact, however, following some minor bumps, the postwar economy boomed. By 1950, fears of unemployment had turned into widespread discussion about how to satisfy the economy's ravenous demand for labor, and some suggested American women would rise to fill this need. None less than President Truman, in a joint session to Congress in 1951, declared that "in the expanding labor force the most important source is women." A *New York Times* piece in 1954 declared that "this may be a man's world generally, but when it comes to getting a first job in the 'white collar field,' the young women have a decided edge."[20] Indeed, women's job prospects were good through the decade. A study of women college graduates from 1956, for instance, found that eighty-one out of every one hundred found a job within six months of graduation. Roughly three quarters of these jobs were in professional fields, with teaching the leading choice.[21]

The entry of married women into the paid labor force became the single most important change in the postwar labor market. Once virtually absent from the ranks of wage-earners, married white women, working part- and full-time, became one of the largest sectors of the female labor force by the mid-1950s. In part, they were pulled into the workforce by the financial carrots offered in a rapidly expanding economy and through aggressive business recruiting practices. Some firms, for instance, gained attention through public efforts to combat "wolfism" at the workplace and by founding day care centers in a bid to lure married women. *Fortune* magazine noted the shift in a 1956 article which declared, "Today a girl who announces that she is being married is asked, 'are you taking a trip, or will you be back on Monday?' It is becoming increasingly rare that she does not return at all." Some employment data seem to confirm this trend. A survey of 1955 women college graduates one year after graduation found that of the one third who were married, 70 percent also worked.[22]

The greatest number of married women entering the workforce, however, were not those who stayed on upon marriage but those who returned to work after their children had grown. Though many ended up doing so, young, middle-class white women generally did not anticipate working after marriage. The same survey of women college graduates from 1955 found that only 25 percent were planning to "have a career," a phrase which typically meant not a certain type of vocation, but rather, a job which one continued in even after marriage or as one aged. Almost half expected paid employment to be a temporary activity between college and marriage.[23] The married women who joined the labor force in the late 1940s and 1950s were usually older women, part of a generational cohort who as single women in the 1910s and 1920s broke norms by entering the white-collar clerical workforce prior to marriage. With their children largely raised, they were returning to work. Indeed, while only 10 percent of married white women between the ages of 45 and 54 worked in 1940, 38 percent did so by 1960. These women had some skills and experience, and with home pressures lessened and consumer temptations rising, returning to work offered important personal and financial perks. *Fortune* described this as a "new life pattern" for the American woman: "She works when young, married or not, and returns to her job when her children are grown up." The magazine, *National Parent-Teacher* lauded the newfound opportunities for women to re-enter the workforce when their children were older. One article asked, "Is your teen-ager dreaming of a home and babies or of a career studded with paychecks?," and responded, "Chances are she'll have both." Women were fortunate, the magazine proclaimed, because "opportunity knocks twice."[24]

Amidst the postwar emphasis on women's domestic duties, working women became an increasingly common feature of the middle-class landscape. Vocational counseling and placement centers which had catered to young men for many years began in the late 1940s and 1950s to devote more and more energy to women, and to focus increasingly on middle-class youth. The opening of the Spitalny All-Girl Job Center in Chicago in 1951 typified trends. At the end of its first year, the Center employed a staff of 29 who had placed nearly half of its 15,000 customers. Major national news magazines came to routinely address and report on women. If Depression-era reporting looked at "women taking men's jobs" critically, 1950s publications more often accepted that women played a valuable role in the nation's business and professional offices. By the early 1950s, popular newspaper and magazine reports about job opportunities and career possibilities regularly devoted significant attention to both male and female prospects. Though most reports clearly differentiated between the two, all assumed that many if not most white and middle-class women would spend at least part of their lives in the workforce.[25]

Glass Ceilings and Iron Gates

While the number of working women increased dramatically in the postwar years, and became a more common feature of the nation's occupational landscape, these women confronted a painful and troubling paradox. Even as their presence in the workforce grew, as the number of college-educated women rose, and as more and more middle-class women pursued professional careers, the doors to the country's most powerful and lucrative jobs remained largely closed to women, and those who pressed for access met intense cultural ridicule and abuse.

Despite the growing entrance of middle-class white women into the paid labor force, and despite the celebration of women in significant professional careers, the doors to the nation's real corridors of occupational power remained barely ajar and hard to find. In 1960, women still comprised a minuscule 3 percent of lawyers and judges and less than 7 percent of American physicians and surgeons, most of whom practiced in the "suitable" and segregated fields of pediatrics, obstetrics, or gynecology. Women in 1960 represented just 13 percent of the nation's managers, officials, and proprietors, and most women in this category were in tenuous small retail businesses, not corporate management. Women were 21.9 percent of those employed as college presidents, professors, and instructors, but the latter comprised the majority of that figure, and the total percentage had been declining since earlier in the century.[26]

The vast gap between the growing proportion of working women and their access to the nation's most desired jobs resulted not only from explicit sex discrimination in graduate and professional school admissions offices, and by employers themselves, but also from more subtle social and cultural forces that acted on girls and young women to dissuade them from pursuing such careers. Typical of this, a 1949 *Ladies Home Journal* article "New Careers for College Girls," declared that "housework is becoming one of the highest-paid, most-privileged occupations for girls with intelligence and taste." It alleged that fashionable families paid their housekeepers as much as teachers made, and additionally offered free room and board. Lest a young college-educated woman have ambivalence about the value of such work, the author implored that "her college education would be something which never could be taken away from her. She would not need to feel she was wasting it, for she would find she needs brains and managerial ability to be a good housekeeper, and she would be able to develop many of her latent abilities." In fact, readers learned that the transition from "campus belle" to paid housekeeper had already come about with the emergence of the "student baby sitter."[27]

Of course, most young college-educated women, as well as older women re-entering the workforce, desired to become more than paid housekeepers. They, no different than men, wanted jobs that not only paid well, but also offered status, interesting opportunities and challenges, and the ability for advancement and growth. Yet securing such work proved extremely difficult. The magazine, *Independent Woman*, drawing on the discourse of "women adrift," wrote at length about the difficulties professional women encountered. One essay described corporate women as "free-floating," without the support of families, friends, social institutions, and society at large that working men enjoyed. In articles and editorials, magazine editors continually decried the hiring and promotion barriers working women faced and called on the National Federation of Business and Professional Women's Clubs to sponsor and support women in the white-collar workplace. The journal *Occupations* further noted that even when women obtained professional positions in traditionally male-dominated fields, they faced continual doubts about their qualifications and rightful claim to such work. One essay noted that women in higher-level positions found themselves challenged on two fronts. First, they must prove themselves capable in the face of assumptions of women's inferiority. And second, they must fight continually management's tendency to generalize: "Women, more than men, must bear in mind that their job performance at any level, however routine, affects management's attitudes toward women who aspire to higher-level jobs."[28]

The sharp rise in working women accompanied heightened rhetoric aimed at limiting their opportunities within the workforce. Traditionally female-dominated lines of work, such as elementary teaching, nursing, and clerical work, offered welcome sites for women workers in the 1950s, but few were encouraged to pursue careers in more "manly fields." Young women preparing to enter the workforce encountered many initiatives and cultural messages encouraging their labor force participation that simultaneously limited the range of their employment options. In one survey of 4500 films between 1930 and 1975, for instance, women appeared as airline stewardesses in twenty-one films, but as pilots in only thirteen, and as nurses in 177 movies, but as doctors in only seventy-three, and lawyers in only twenty-eight. The Cleaton Vocational Interest Inventory, widely used in American high schools to measure students' occupational interests, for instance, clearly differentiated between careers for men and women. In 1947, the categories appeared as follows:

Male Career Fields	Female Career Fields
Physician, biological sciences	Clerk, stenographer, office worker
Specialized selling	Sales clerk, selling trades
Technologist, physician scientist	Nurse, bacteriologist, natural sciences
Teacher, minister, social worker	Social worker, lawyer, social service

Continued

Continued

Male Career Fields	Female Career Fields
Business manager, lawyer, journalist, legal and literary occupations	Artist, writer, composer
Skilled mechanical occupations	Grade school teacher
Accountant, statistician, and other financial occupations	High school or college teacher
Actor, musician, artist, and other performance occupations	Manicurist, actress, dancer, personal service occupations
	Housekeeper, factory worker, mechanical and household work[29]

The list speaks volumes about the gendered division of occupational opportunities in the postwar years. Not only did men and women have different
rosters of potential jobs, but the same occupations also appeared in different
categories for each, clearly signifying that a woman lawyer did not really have
the same type of job as a male lawyer, and that teaching was a very different
career for men than women.

A widely varying combination of parental and peer pressures, school
vocational messages, media images, as well as points of fairly overt discrimination in applying for jobs, nudged young, career-minded women into
traditionally female occupations. One typical advice article in *Woman's Home
Companion* urged young women to do volunteer work during high school in
order to determine what line of work to pursue. The article provided three
examples of young women who had done just that and based on their
experiences had settled on the fields of nursing, medical secretary, and teaching. *Good Housekeeping* similarly enticed young women with the promise that
"there is a big demand for women in the health field," but then defined such
positions as "helpers" for doctors, dentists, and research assistants. The list of
potential jobs for women included dental assistant, medical record techni-
cian, laboratory help, and a variety of other aids and clerical types in the allied
health professions. One advice columnist bluntly told mothers: "Don't
encourage your daughter to set her heart on a career in a typically man's field
or one that will not combine with marriage, should she want to continue her
work after marriage. Surgery, diplomacy, or engineering, for instance, are not
particularly good bets."[30] While perhaps offered as a realistic assessment of
the labor market, the constant repetition of such messages over time
dissuaded women from seeking to upset the gendered order of occupations
and further entrenched occupational sex segregation.

Just as career counseling for young women channeled their range of
options, cultural texts reified occupational differences between men and
women by showcasing them in distinctly gendered occupations, and by highlighting career women's domestic incompetence. The 1957 film, *Designing
Woman*, for instance, chronicled the relationship of "man's man" sports
reporter Michael Hagan, played by Gregory Peck, and fashion designer
Mirella Brown, played by Lauren Bacall. Despite their traditionally masculine
and feminine careers, respectively, the film opens on an egalitarian note.
Hagan meets Brown while in southern California covering a golf tournament. The meeting is fortuitous for the night he is to write and wire the golf

tournament story to his New York newspaper is also the night of a drunken binge. Brown saves the day by helping to write the article and sending it herself. The attractive and ambitious couple fall quickly in love and marry before returning home to New York City. Once in New York, however, the two learn distressing things about each other. She finds he lives in a "shoe-box" and fraternizes with a rather rough crowd, while he learns, to his disappointment, that she is a high-powered businesswoman, and one who changes clothes "nine times a day." Their interests, friends, and lifestyle prove worlds apart, with he in the masculine and aggressive world of sports reporting, and she in the feminine world of fashion design. Fitting the stereotype of the aggressive career women, she is hopelessly lacking in domestic skills. When one night she tries to prepare him dinner, she helplessly burns the ravioli. *Designing Woman* reifies traditional gender roles by emphasizing men and women's supposed fundamentally contrasting natures. In doing so, it offers a particularly biting critique of career women, for even though Brown appears the paragon of femininity, and works in a distinctly feminine line of work, she still evidences utter domestic incompetence.[31]

Ladies Home Journal also underscored the gendering of the workforce by offering different career tips for men and women. A 1950 article presenting career advice counseled men to walk a fine line between being shy and over-selling themselves, to know all about their prospective job ahead of time, and to take their work seriously. As a motivational device, the author presented biographies of four men who had started at the bottom but made it to the top. Women readers received very different advice. The essay presented nursing, teaching, and fashion designing as the exemplary careers, and urged women to avoid being a "femme fatale," an "eager beaver," a mess, or a know-it-all. In giving examples of successful women, the article closed by telling of four employees who had ultimately married their boss.[32]

With each surge in female labor force participation, it seemed that the media paid more attention to defining differences between male and female employees.[33] An emphasis on typecasting working women, in particular, pervaded much reporting in the 1950s. The most simple of these described women in infantalizing, objectifying, or pejorative ways, such as a 1958 *Newsweek* article that labeled the growing numbers of women bank executives as "honey in the bank."[34] More significant were the frequent "research investigations" into the differences between male and female employees. The *Saturday Evening Post*, for instance, ran an article in 1958 on the Klein Institute for Aptitude Testing which found that while there were "few significant psychological differences between men and women in business," women were more likely to switch positions because their "ultimate objective is marriage, not job tenure." The report noted, however, that women's "flightiness" was balanced by "her superior capacity for keeping personal crises, such as divorce and death in the family, out of her work." Finally, the report concluded that the most successful career women tend to be "more self-sufficient and aggressive than men," but only because those are the traits needed to overcome the prejudice against them.[35]

Common in postwar magazines were glib analyses that caricatured women in the workplace as aggressive, emotional, and often unstable. Typical of these was a 1954 piece in *Look* that told of the Research Institute of America's efforts to study how supervisors and foremen managed women. Unable to find anything conclusive, presumably because of women's "confusing nature," the institute decided to abandon the project. At that point, however, a woman editor in the human-relations division, Phyllis Brown, offered to reveal the secrets of her sex. "You want to know how to handle women," she declared, "let us tell you." Brown warned, "you can't work with women without running into special problems from time to time," but, counseled that when managed effectively, women could make excellent office workers. The key, she claimed, was to recognize that all working women fell into one of five categories. Old maids, mature married women, teenagers, and those waiting for "Mr. Right" comprised the first four. For women in each group, work played a secondary role in their lives. Only the "old maids" took their jobs seriously, but, bored and depressed because they had been unable to marry, often took their work too seriously and bothered or harassed their coworkers. "Career women" made up the fifth category of employees. According to Brown, the typical career woman wanted to "get ahead on her own," and would be "the first to deny that she needs a man's help." The problem for supervisors, Brown warned, lay in that fact that career women refused to ask for help even when they needed assistance, and that they evoked a sense of independence when they really desired affirmation and praise. To handle career women properly, Brown advised, employers should praise them regularly, give them simple and achievable tasks, and when they make the inevitable errors, be gentle with corrections for they are stung by rebuke. In a final piece of advice, Brown urged employers not to castigate male workers for making "off-color" jokes. Women employees, she believed, would "resent the assumption that they can't protect their own dignity—or that they can't take a risqué joke."[36]

Even in small business, the allegedly open frontier of the American economy, white women faced a range of subtle barriers and constraints. The sheer number of women entrepreneurs grew steadily throughout mid-century, rising from 650,000 in 1944 to one million in 1960, but the types of businesses in which most were involved remained in traditionally "feminized" areas. American men, at least those white and native born, often entered business through formal education and personal networks, but women were typically more isolated in their occupational quests and faced a more daunting task. Women business owners were more concentrated than their male counterparts in small retail ventures, often the most difficult and competitive of economic sectors. Historically, American women's business activities had often originated in making a product at home, and that remained true of many endeavors in the postwar period.[37] Stories of such women filled the pages of women's magazines in the 1950s. In one issue of *Women's Home Companion*, for instance, readers learned about Laura Schuler from Los Angeles who carved swans or goldfish from orange peels and suspended them in jars of orange jelly, and Helen Gibbons of Westwood, New Jersey, who sewed chamois skin moccasins for babies who kicked their booties off. Both women earned money by signing contracts with local department stores who sold their wares. Another, Cynthia Richardson of Doylestown, Pennsylvania, had started a business that charged three dollars for a series of encouraging letters to sick children from her fox terrier, Susie Cucumber. This genre of articles continually urged woman to think of skills they had that might be of use in their local communities. One article illustrated this entrepreneurial mindset by discussing a woman who had sat beside a department store manager at a dinner party and complained about the lackluster nature of his store's displays. He ended up hiring her to help out with them.[38]

Popular magazines found numerous ways to demean and poke fun at career women. One common trope was the assertion that many women worked simply to find a husband and were hardly serious about their jobs. One such article in *Colliers* in 1949 offered advice to women about what kinds of husbands they would find in various jobs. The author opened by stating that all of the jobs available to women had "great drawbacks," but "every business or professional career can be short for an attractive girl, perhaps only a few months, perhaps even less than that." The bulk of the article analyzed various careers, how to dress and act in such positions, and the kinds of men one would meet in those jobs. The article singled out teaching as a particularly poor field for finding a husband because the men one would meet would not be highly paid. Jobs in civil service and in the scientific field were also bad bets for finding men, while secretarial and receptionist positions offered the most contact with desirable potential husbands.[39]

The pervasive structural and cultural barriers women entering the American workforce faced significantly affected their hopes and aspirations, as numerous postwar surveys and polls revealed. In 1954, for instance, the University of Washington asked its seniors about their career preferences. The greatest number of women, 27 percent, sought a future in teaching, compared with only 7.4 percent of men. The next largest segment, 16.7 percent, hoped for careers in business, though this was only half the percent of men pursuing business careers. Nursing came in a close third as the desired career of 14.5 percent of the women; only 0.1 percent of men sought nursing jobs. Whereas nearly 20 percent of the male seniors expressed a desire to enter engineering or the natural sciences, only 3 percent of women joined them. Similar results from other studies clearly revealed the power of prevailing gender norms in shaping young women's occupational plans, norms particularly evident in cinematic depictions of career women.[40]

The Career Woman in Postwar Cinema

If the 1950s proved an era of enormous gains for and much reaction against working women, nowhere did the stinging paradoxes, ironies, and misogynistic jabs appear more vividly than in American cinema. Working women were strikingly absent from the era's blockbusters. The highest grossing films in the years from 1946 to 1959 featured male doctors (*Welcome Stranger*), resort operators (*White Christmas*), military personnel (*The Bridge over the River Kwai* and *South Pacific*), and numerous famous male figures from biblical history. Women, however, garnered lead roles only in animation (*Cinderella*) or in the 1949 smash *Samson and Delilah* (and the role of Delilah was hardly an encouraging text for ambitious women). The era's highest grossing films portrayed virtually no women working in elite occupations. In a process media critic Ella Taylor calls "domesticating the television workplace," popular sitcoms and dramas in this era similarly present the working world as almost wholly masculine.[41]

Though largely absent from the nation's select blockbusters, career women appeared in a broad swath of postwar films that poignantly captured their situation and plight, and more often than not put them in "their place." The contradictions and ambivalence surrounding "women's place" within postwar films have been well recognized by numerous film scholars. Jeanine Basinger, for instance, notes that "watching hundreds of women's films reveals how cleverly they contradicted themselves, how easily they reaffirmed the status quo for the woman's life while providing little releases, small victories—or even big releases, big victories. From movie to movie or within one single movie, opposing attitudes were voiced and demonstrated."[42] We see these tensions in the 1959 film *Pillow Talk*, for instance, which opened with songwriter Brad Allen, played by Rock Hudson, and interior decorator Jan Morrow, played by Doris Day, fighting over the use of the telephone party line they shared. Morrow comes across as a smart and successful woman with her own business, and it is hard not to empathize with her when she bemoans her inability to obtain a private telephone line for her work. She struggles to obtain a line because in the crowded New York market, pregnant women received priority. But audience empathy is soon cut short when after a conversation in which Morrow protests Allen's claim that her anger stemmed from her lack of male companionship, her maid declares, "If there's anything worse than a woman living alone, it is a woman saying she likes it." Morrow responds, "I do like it. I have a good job, a lovely apartment, I go out with very nice men to the best places. What am I missing?" Her maid then retorts: "When you have to ask, believe me, you're missing it." *Pillow Talk* ultimately showcased the pathetic plight of the independent career woman who is made content and well rounded only when paired with a man.[43]

In the mass of cinematic representations of white women in postwar popular culture, we can sense both the new worlds opening up, and the lingering conservatism and ferocious backlash career-minded women faced. My survey of postwar films finds a significant number of "working women's films," most of which offer one of four different interpretations of women's experience and status in the workplace: plots that present at least relatively positive representations of career women; plots that emphasize young working women's quest for husbands; plots that offer critical images of women who put career over marriage; and finally, plots that suggest women's role in the business world lay in being corporate spouses. Taken together, these films illustrate the broad spectrum of attitudes about career women and illuminate the gender complexities of this era.[44]

In the first, and distinctly smallest, category, Hollywood showcased working women in sometimes laudatory and in others at least partially sympathetic ways. Most notable in this regard among American films was *Adam's Rib*, discussed earlier, which in 1949 showcased Katharine Hepburn and Spencer Tracy as married lawyers who find themselves on opposing sides of an attempted murder case. Though Hepburn's emotions are ridiculed later in the film, her abilities are never questioned. She proves herself a successful private attorney, every bit his professional equal.

The 1949 film, *Miss Grant Takes Richmond*, chronicled the fortunes of a less sophisticated and successful woman, and unwittingly showed the kinds of office harassment many clerical workers faced. Lucille Ball plays Miss Grant, a dim but aspiring secretary. Her aunt tries to persuade her to get married, but Grant, determined to become a secretary, declares, "it just might be the first rung on the ladder." Unfortunately, she proves a typing-school failure. Grant flunks the final exam in disastrous fashion, but then to both her and the instructor's surprise, is chosen above the others by an evaluator from the Woodruff Realty Company who had stared at her legs during the test. "Frankly," he remarked, "I liked your looks." As it turns out, the real estate office is simply a front for a gambling syndicate, whose owner is played by William Holden. His operatives continually harass and belittle Grant with remarks such as, "nice eyes, nice hair, and nothing under." Though hired for her good looks and feeble mind, Grant ultimately not only exposes the gambling syndicate and drives the crooks out of town, but develops a program to provide the town desperately needed low-income housing. Though a "success story" in the end, the plot's humor rests on the irony of a "dumb secretary" enjoying considerable success. Ultimately, her talents and successes are understood as a humorous aberration from the mass of such working women who are unlikely to ever enter much less succeed in masculine careers.[45]

The 1957 film *Desk Set* combined positive and demeaning portrayals of working women in showcasing the travails of the all-female reference office at the fictitious Federal Broadcasting Company. Katharine Hepburn plays office director Bunny Watson, a smart and professional middle-aged librarian. She is clearly as far up the ladder as she could go, but not as far as she is capable of going. Her brains and insight become the fuel for her boyfriend, another employee, who with Watson's help becomes vice president of the entire company. Several other women work for Watson. One is a smart and professional thirty-something woman who commiserates with Watson's desire to get married by exposing her own feelings of worthlessness: "You go along thinking tomorrow something wonderful is going to happen, you're not going to be alone anymore, and then one day you realize it's all over, you are out of circulation. It all happened and you don't even know when it happened." Young single women who spend most of their days fretting about dates and clothes comprise the rest of the staff.[46] *Desk Set* thus offered contradictory visions of women in the labor force, reifying the image of women workers as silly girls aspiring only to marriage, and yet, in a rare move, positively presenting a career woman whose talents clearly equal or surpass her male superiors.

A second category of Hollywood "working women's" films focused on the very theme of young working women seeking husbands. This much larger category of films hammered home the message that a job is fine and career success is even noble, but only when the ultimate pursuit is marriage. The angst of working women unable to snare husbands appeared often on the postwar silver screen. In the 1950 film *A Life of Her Own*, for instance, Lana Turner plays a young Midwestern girl, Lily James, who comes to New York City to pursue a modeling career. She enjoys spectacular success, but proves a loser in the world of relationships. Steeped in personal turmoil, she declares: "I told myself if I had money, if I was important, if people knew my name and who I was, then I'd be happy, then it'd be worth it, but it was never true, it was never true." Actress Celeste Holm echoes this theme in 1955's *The Tender Trap* in which she plays a talented violinist who struggles with loneliness. In one scene, she recounts how she could have gotten married in her home town, but came to New York instead to find glamour and excitement. She found what she sought, but all of the sudden, she and her friends realize: "We are 33 years old and we don't have a man." Debbie Reynolds co-stars in the film as an aspiring singer who has her priorities better set. She emphatically announces: "A career is just fine, but it is no substitute for marriage . . . A woman isn't really a woman at all unless she's been married and has had three children."[47] Hollywood's fixation on working women's desire to quit and marry consistently undercut the rare idealistic visions of postwar career women by etching into American popular culture notions of all women as family-, not career-, bound.

The highly celebrated 1950 Joseph Mankiewicz-directed *All About Eve*, which garnered fourteen Academy Award nominations and six Oscars, including Best Picture, painfully probed the inner fears of women in a society that ultimately reduced them to wives. Bette Davis received a Best Actress nomination for her performance as aging theater queen Margo Channing, who is hounded by a young upstart, Eve Harrington, played by Anne Baxter. As Channing fights desperately to stay at the top while steadily succumbing to the inevitable menace of age, she confides to a friend that amidst all her successes and career achievements, the lack of a husband continually stood as a gaping hole in her life:

> One career all females have in common, whether we like it or not—being a woman. Sooner or later we've got to work at it, no matter how many other careers we've had to wanted. And in the last analysis, nothing is any good unless you can look up just before dinner or turn around in bed and there he is. Without that you are not a woman.

Channing reveals her feelings of personal failure to friend Karen Richards, played by Celeste Holm. Whereas Margo Channing had sacrificed much for her career, Richards stands as the model wife. Her steadfast devotion to marriage has left her immensely vulnerable, however. Eve Harrington threatened Channing's career and Richards' marriage. Fearing she would lose her husband to the young actress, Richards laments: "It seemed to me I had known always that it would happen, and here it was. I felt helpless. That lifelessness you feel when you have no talent to offer outside of your love to your husband." In other words, *All About Eve* presented the portrait of a lose-lose world for women. Women who worked abandoned hopes for a happy family life. Those who devoted themselves to the family life risked having nothing if the family should dissolve. This devastating message thus not only re-emphasized the frequent attacks on independent career women as social losers, but also suggested that women who sacrificed careers for the allegedly "right" career path of homemaker also risked personal failure. *All About Eve* thus presented for women the ultimate double bind.[48]

A third category of Hollywood films exuberantly mocked and demeaned women who put career over marriage. Postwar popular culture caricatured many powerful and ambitious women in ways that underscored their marginalization in the nation's pathways of success.[49] In the 1948 Frank Capra film, *State of the Union*, Angela Lansbury plays Kay Thorndyke, a powerful newspaper publisher with grand ambitions. Her aspirations are fueled by the words of her late father, a politician, who on his deathbed told her that he used to hate her because she was a girl and thus could not fill his ambitions. Having watched her strength and determination, however, he had concluded that she had a "woman's body with a man's brains." "Use them," he declared, "and you'll make the White House, one way or another." That way turned out to be as a mistress for a powerful, married industrialist whom she persuades to run for the presidency. Her carefully crafted plan, and her relationship with him, falls apart when the industrialist, played by Spencer Tracy, renounces her corrupt political tactics. At the film's conclusion he chooses to realign his life and campaign with the morality and integrity of his wife, played by Katharine Hepburn. *State of the Union* captures well the tensions in the world of working middle-class women during the early postwar years. The film presented a powerful and successful career woman, yet one whose sex thwarted her professional ambitions. And rather than lauding the professional accomplishments she did enjoy, the film presented Kay Thorndyke as mean spirited, power hungry, and ruthless in her ambition, in direct opposition to the politician's wife, a housewife who stood as the paragon of moral integrity.[50]

As in *State of the Union*, cinematic attacks on career women usually represented them as distastefully masculine. None did so more comedically but viciously than the 1950 film, *A Woman of Distinction*. Rosalind Russell played Susan Middlecott, a New England women's college dean who had garnered a national reputation as a brilliant educator. Spinsterhood proves to be the price of Middlecott's success. She continually tells friends and reporters that "there is no room for romance in my career," though she did find room for a daughter whom she adopted from Europe during the war.

The film's plot revolves around a media-driven rumor about an affair between Middlecott and a visiting British astronomer, played by Ray Milland. In her efforts to halt the embarrassing rumors, Middlecott continually lands in a series of humiliating incidents of madcap physicality, such as getting stuck in a beauty parlor fan, and becoming drenched by a hose while trying to break into a house. Despite Middlecott's annoyance with the professor, her father encourages him to pursue her, promising that "just because there is snow on the roof doesn't mean there isn't a fire in the house." Middlecott's daughter lobbies her mother: "all the little girls I know have dads. I wish I had one." Near the film's end, Middlecott and her father have an emotional confrontation in which he chides her for giving up her opportunity to "be a woman." When she responds, "I am a woman," he retorts, "No, you look like a woman but that is where the resemblance ends. You talk like an encyclopedia. You think like a dictionary." Nearly in tears, Middlecott counters that she became the kind of woman her father wanted her to. He denies this, however, and explains that his investment in her was not for her career: "I gave you every possible advantage. The best schools, Europe in the summer, because I like spoiled women, I like them. They are more feminine, and I thought that with education, clothes, reasonably good looks, and my money, you'd bring home a man, but did you? Oh no, you brought home degrees, diplomas, and uniforms. Instead of coming home with a man, you came home with stripes on your arm." The words stung at first but upon reflection, Susan has a change of heart. At the film's conclusion she resigns her position and rushes into the professor's arms and declares her love. He embraces her and coos: "That is the first sensible thing I've heard you say. It's time you realized you need a man in your life." Dean Middlecott who once appeared on the cover of *Time* magazine for her achievements was first humiliated and then finally tamed, a process that required a smothering of her "masculine" nature and the rebirth of her inner femininity.[51]

A final category of Hollywood films pursued a pervasive postwar argument that one of women's most likely routes to corporate leadership during the early postwar years lay in the job of "business wife." The significant role a wife could play in a male executive's career became an established part of corporate lore by the 1950s. William H. Whyte Jr., in the *The Organization Man*, wrote about an executive and his wife as a two-person single career. *Time* magazine even went so far as to label a corporate wife a "Goddess of Success." The article noted that corporate wives could assure their husband's success by doing all of the onerous chores at home and the childrearing, and thus securing his "base of operations." Ideally, however, the corporate wife was to not only handle the "home front," but also to take part in the community and local charities: "Her participation can be a direct stepping stone in getting to know the right people."[52] Many firms, such as the Carnation Company, made spousal quality a factor in hiring decisions. In a 1954 article advising young men on how to secure the best jobs, the company's personnel director stated that before his department made a recommendation for a hire, they tried to meet the applicant's fiancée or wife, for "her job is a big one. She must inspire him, keep the home setting harmonious, be congenial with the wives of his associates and supervisors, and be an asset when he entertains and is entertained for business reasons."[53]

The 1954 Twentieth-Century Fox Film, *Woman's World*, focused on the place of wives in corporate hiring decisions. In this story, adapted from a Mona Williams novel, the president of a New York City-based automobile company, Gifford Motors, seeks a new general manager. He selects three candidates for the job based on their exceptional records. Because all three were fully qualified to perform the job well, the president decides to focus on the quality of their wives in order to make his final decision. Gifford hosts the three couples for a weekend in New York City, during which time his society sister advises them on the roles of a corporate wife. The essential rules included "saying nice things you didn't mean to people who didn't believe you," and allowing husbands to not feel guilty for never being at home. After careful observation of the three couples, Gifford realizes that the man he preferred had an unacceptable wife. Lauren Bacall plays the ideal company spouse, an elegant woman with tremendous poise and social graces, but job pressures had impaired the health of her husband, played by Fred MacMurray, and she fears the promotion would ultimately kill him. On the opposite end of the spectrum stands June Allyson who plays a Kansas City simpleton, completely devoted to her husband and children but horrified about living in New York City and unable to make it through a conversation without committing disastrous social *faux pas*. The best man for the job proves to be a modest and unassuming but talented figure played by Van Heflin. Unfortunately, Gifford cannot stand his wife, played by Arlene Dahl. Beautiful, charming, and ambitious, she superficially seems an ideal person to fill the role of corporate spouse, but in her assertiveness and quest for power, she crosses the line of acceptable womanly behavior. Her conniving tactics to secure her husband's career ultimately include a willingness to romance his superiors. When he learns of the extent of her tactics, he declares: "I'll get to the top, but I'll get there on what I've got, not what you've got." At the film's conclusion he receives the job upon leaving his shamed and shameful wife. *Women's World* not only reified traditional images of working husbands and homebound wives, but its vicious depiction of the one woman who seemed most ambitious offered a subtle jab at career women themselves.[54]

Conclusion

The nation's collective perceptions of women's experience during the 1950s have remained heavily influenced by the decade's television moms. Loving mothers, doting wives, and calm, efficient homemakers—the June Cleaver ideal—have epitomized postwar womanhood for many in the generations since. Far from an era of maternal domestic tranquility, however, the 1950s proved a decade of enormous transition in the gendering of the nation's labor force. Middle-class white women entered the white-collar workforce in steadily swelling numbers and work became an increasingly standard part of life for married women. By the dawn of the 1960s, a career beyond their duties as wife and mother became both possible and desirable for millions of young white women who only a generation or two before would have been dissuaded from such aspirations.

Perhaps these realities were one reason Twentieth-Century Fox decided to make Rona Jaffe's 1958 novel, *The Best of Everything*, into a film almost as soon as the book appeared. Jaffe wrote the best-selling novel, which chronicled the experiences of five young women seeking both "great jobs and great husbands" in New York City after speaking with many "career girls" in California and New York. *The Best of Everything* hardly proved a documentary of women's experiences, but it was a powerful window into the real social and cultural pressures postwar career women encountered.

Joan Crawford stars in the film as Amanda Farrow, a powerful, cold, and calculating editor in a New York City publishing house. Farrow's successful career has required the repression of her maternal instincts and feminine impulses; indeed, her career effectively replaced marriage. The film's plot revolves largely around the life of Carolyn Bender, a beautiful, young Radcliffe graduate, played by Hope Lange, who becomes Farrow's typist. Early in the film, a senior editor named Mike Price counsels Bender: "Work six months or a year, prove whatever you have to prove, then marry the med student or law student and love happily ever after." Bender responds that this was indeed exactly what she intends to do, and after confirming to him that she had no real career ambition, he smiles and says, "How wonderful."

Bender's future plans are soon dealt a blow, however, when her fiancée suddenly marries another. She deals with the loss by focusing on her work and quickly earning a major promotion and the shot at becoming an editor. Amidst her success, Mike Price dampens Bender's mood when, during a conversation at a company picnic, he criticizes her ambition, charging her with wanting to become a "ruthless, calculating woman." When Bender responds that she just might be very good in such a career, he derides her talent by saying she is only interested in a career because of the recent breakup: "Being a woman is too painful so you are not going to be one. Men aren't lovers, they're competition, so let's not join 'em let's lick 'em." Stung by the criticism, Bender lashes out at Price and redoubles her efforts to climb the company ladder.

Meanwhile, Bender's boss, Amanda Farrow, starts to have second thoughts about her own choice of career over marriage when a young typist, quitting to be married over Farrow's objections, retorts that Farrow had no business giving love advice: "You remind me of something somebody once said about love: Those who can, do, those who can't, teach." The criticism touches a hidden longing within Amanda Farrow and she decides to abandon her career and move to a midwestern farm to marry a father of two with whom she had long ago had an affair. In telling Bender of her decision to quit, Farrow becomes soft and gentle for the first time in the film and notes: "He treats me as if he believes I am the gentlest softest woman in the world. And maybe with enough time and tenderness, if it is not too late, maybe I can get to believe it myself."

Farrow's departure opens up the editorship for Bender who grabs the opportunity. In the weeks that follow, Bender immerses herself into the editorship and evolves into the dreaded hardheaded single career woman. She adopts not only Amanda Farrow's cruel, aggressive, temperament, but even her hair style. Suddenly, however, Farrow returns to New York City, abandoning her effort to assume the roles of wife and mother. She confides to Bender: "It was too late for me. A lonely man, two children, they needed too much. I found I had nothing to give. I had forgotten how."

In a major twist, Bender, instead of viewing Farrow's return as threatening, welcomes Farrow back and willingly gives up her office, saying, "I never really belonged in it anyway." The film then closes with Bender strolling wistfully out of the office, where she takes off her business-like hat and glides into the arms of Price. Arm in arm and with much joy, they stroll off together.

The film's title did not end up meaning that young college-educated women could have the "best of everything" if that implied both work *and* marriage. Rather, it meant that despite opportunities for women in the working world, marriage was ultimately the best option. Lest viewers miss the subtlety in the film's conclusion, lyrics to the closing song blared: "Romance is still the best of everything, that sudden thrill, the best of everything, that one little sigh is treasure you cannot buy, or measure, love can be all or nothing, but even when, it is nothing, it is still the best, the best of everything." Bender had clearly learned what Farrow had not. A real career precluded a real marriage. And even if a woman made that choice, as Price reminded Bender, it reflected not a love or desire for one's job, but simple "hot ambition." To her credit, Bender learned the lesson before it was too late.[55]

Hope Lange may have walked off with a smile but millions of American women were not so happy with this pervasive construction of womanhood. The challenges to career women transcended social and cultural pressures to prioritize family over work. Even if a woman was willing to break the social norms and assume the personal costs, rewards were simply not forthcoming. Glass ceilings prevented women from advancing as high up corporate ladders as men; discriminatory admissions policies and procedures prevented women from accessing many of the professional sector's most lucrative jobs, and even in cases where men and women stood on an equal footing, women were usually paid less. Study after study documented that while college degrees tremendously boosted men's salaries, women did not gain as much. In a study of 1947 college graduates, 86 percent of men made over $3,000 compared with only 36 percent of women. Only 1 percent of working women graduates made over $7,500 while 23 percent of men did so. The study's authors stated bluntly: "Our former coeds are much more successful than the average working woman . . . But compared with the Old Grads, they were nowhere." This inequality had changed little ten years later when a national survey of women college graduates from 1956 found that most all who had wanted jobs, roughly 80 percent, had found them, but of these 60 percent were teachers, 11 percent were secretaries or clerical workers, and 5 percent were nurses. The average salary of the entire female cohort stood at just over $3,000, substantially below the norm for male college graduates.[56]

The 1950s proved a decade of considerable change for the nation's labor force as millions of white, middle-class women left home and entered offices, schools, and professional suites all across the country. Their numbers, however, did not dilute long-standing prejudices against working women. To the contrary, postwar career women encountered an often fiercely negative cultural reaction to their achievements. This transitional generation's frustrations would provide the fuel for the women's rights movement that would explode in the next.[57]

Notes

1. "American Women at Work," *Newsweek* (February 27, 1956): 76.
2. "Career Sisters," *Life* 27 (November 7, 1949): 75–79; "The Four Sisters Said They Would and . . . They All Made Good," *Life* 46 (May 11, 1959): 93.
3. "More Jobs for Skilled Women," *U.S. News and World Report* 45 (October 17, 1958): 98–101.
4. The proportion of women of color employed held relatively steady at about 40 percent between 1890 and 1960. Stephanie Coontz notes that the oft-cited figures for the number of women working, in general, under-report the numbers of working women as the census did not count much paid work, such as working at home for wages, and that census figures did not count women working less than fifteen hours a week. Whatever calculations are used, however, the percent of white and married women in the labor force was quite low in the early part of the twentieth century. See Stephanie Coontz, *The Way We Never Were: American Families and the Nostalgia Trap* (New York: Basic Books, 1992), 156; Claudia Goldin, *Understanding the Gender Gap: An Economic History of American Women* (New York: Oxford University Press, 1990), 17; Brett Harvey, *The Fifties: A Women's Oral History* (New York: Harper Collins, 1953), 137.
5. One 1956 survey showed that 74 percent of working women would work even if they received huge inheritances. Daniel Bell, "The Big Parade of Women to Work," *Reader's Digest* 69 (September 1956): 25, reprinted from *Fortune* (July 1956).
6. James Skardon, "Madison Avenue Career Girl," *Coronet* 44 (October 1958): 146–153; "American Women at Work," 76. On the general history of women's representations in postwar cinema, see Molly Haskell, *From Reverence to Rape: The Treatment of Women in the Movies* (Chicago: University of Chicago Press, 2nd edn, 1987).
7. Elaine Tyler May, *Homeward Bound: American Families in the Cold War Era* (New York: Basic Books, 1988); Betty Friedan, *The Feminine Mystique* (New York: Norton, 1963); Joanne Meyerowitz, ed., *Not June Cleaver: Women and Gender in Postwar America, 1945–1960* (Philadelphia: Temple University Press, 1994).
8. "Job Projects Aid Mature Women," *New York Times* (December 23, 1948); "Record Labor Force Makes Industry Hum," *New York Times* (August 21, 1955); "Older Group Seen as Job Leaders in '65," *New York Times* (December 26, 1956); Susan M. Hartmann, *The Homefront and Beyond: American Women in the 1940s* (Boston: Twayne Publishers, 1982), 91–93, 164–165; Goldin,

Understanding the Gender Gap, 17; Susan J. Douglas, *Where the Girls Are: Growing up Female with the Mass Media* (New York: Times Books, 1994), 43.

9. For a general survey of postwar U.S. Women's History, see Ruth Rosen, *The World Split Open: How the Modern Women's Movement Changed America* (New York: Penguin Books, 2000), 3–64; Rosalind Rosenberg, *Divided Lives: American Women in the Twentieth Century* (New York: Noonday Press, 1992), chapter 5; Lois Banner, *Women in Modern America: A Brief History* (New York: International Thomson Publishing, 1994).

10. Joanne Meyerowitz, "Beyond the Feminine Mystique: A Reassessment of Postwar Mass Culture, 1946–1958," *Journal of American History* 79 (March 1993): 145–148.

11. On women and gender roles in postwar television, see Lynn Spigel, *Make Room for TV: Television and the Family Ideal in Postwar America* (Chicago: University of Chicago Press, 1992); and Ella Taylor, *Prime Time Families: Television Culture in Postwar America* (Berkeley: University of California Press, 1989), chapter 2.

12. The public emphasis on family and motherhood in the 1950s reflected a real social transformation in the lives and experiences of American women. One recalled, "There was much to be afraid of in the postwar era, or so we thought." Indeed, for those who had survived a devastating economic crisis and a world war, a secure home seemed an enticing environment. Between 1945 and 1960, the average age of marriage for American women plunged, dropping to the lowest level anywhere in the western world. The birthrate correspondingly soared among all classes; for the first time college-educated women had as many children as the poorest sectors of women. Harvey, *The Fifties*, xii; Barbara J. Harris, *Beyond Her Sphere: Women and the Professions in American History* (Westport, CT: Greenwood Press, 1978), 165.

13. Susan Hartmann writes that after the war, social stability "replaced military victory as the national goal and women were needed as wives and mothers rather than as workers." Elaine Tyler May adds, "the short-lived affirmation of women's independence gave way to a pervasive endorsement of female subordination and domesticity." Hartmann, *The Homefront* 24–25; May, Homeward Bound, 89.

14. Susan M. Hartmann, *The Homefront*, 24–25. Edward Prager, "Just a Housewife," *Coronet* 28 (May 1950): 97; Ruth Imler, "It's Your Move," *Ladies Home Journal* (June 1954): 28; Harford Powel, "Good Jobs for Good Girls," *Colliers* 124 (September 3, 1949): 16–17, 56; Brett Harvey, *The Fifties*, 73.

15. Growing rates of married women working occurred as an international trend during these years in advanced capitalist nations. Coontz, *The Way We Never Were*, 157; Andrew Cherlin, *Marriage, Divorce, Remarriage* (Cambridge: Harvard University Press, 1981), 65–66; Goldin, *Understanding the Gender Gap*, 17, 70.

16. Susan M. Hartmann, *The Homefront*, 91–93, 164–165; Barbara J. Harris, *Beyond Her Sphere*, 155; Goldin, *The Gender Gap*, 17; Susan M. Hartmann, "Women's Employment and the Domestic Ideal in the Early Cold War Years," in *Not June Cleaver*, 86; Coontz, *Way We Never Were*, 156–162.

17. Angel Kwolek-Folland, *Incorporating Women: A History of Women and Business in the United States* (New York: Twayne Publishers, 1998), 138; Hartmann, *Homefront*, 92–93.

18. A 1952 survey of women union members found that approximately 70 percent worked to help "support their families," though most had more than mere survival in mind. Many cited a desire for home ownership, automobiles, furniture, or children's education as a key need. "The Older Woman Goes to Work," *Occupations* 30 (May 1952): 593; Hartmann, *Homefront*, 93; "Business Women Carry Heavy Dependent Support Load," *Independent Woman* 32 (January 1953): 20–21.

19. "Helping Your Child Choose a Career," *Today's Health* 34 (April 1956): 38–41; Elsie McCormick, "Every Woman Should Learn a Trade," *Good Housekeeping* 134 (April 1952): 51, 154.

20. Bernard, "Counting on the women," 110–112; "Girls Fare Better Hunting For First Job," *New York Times* (January 18, 1954); "Plan Aims to Fill Need for Typists," *New York Times* (March 24, 1952); "Women Workers Needed in Offices," *American Magazine* (June 5, 1955): 127.

21. "Most Women Get Into Professional Fields," *New York Times* (June 1958). The connection between an expanding economy and growing numbers of working women became a common theme of labor reports and prognostications in the 1950s. One 1956 study declared that during the next decade industry will need to turn out 40 percent more goods and services while the labor force will grow by only 14 percent. The solution: A growing proportion of the nation's workforce will "have to wear skirts." A *Newsweek* article in 1958 reported that the country would need ten million more workers in the next ten years and half of those would have to be women. This was, in fact, a matter of fundamental national security: "Nothing less than the fate of America's standard of living rests on the well-manicured hands and well-coifed heads of its women." "American Women at Work," 76; "The Ladies are Getting Ahead," *Newsweek* 52 (September 22, 1958): 93–95.

22. "Married Women Top Single in Jobs," *New York Times*, (December 23, 1948): Daniel Bell, "The Big Parade," 23–25; Alice Leopold, "1955's Women College Graduates in 1956," *Personnel and Guidance Journal* 35 (February 1957): 346.

23. Alice Leopold, "1955's Women College Graduates in 1956," *Personnel and Guidance Journal* 35 (February 1957): 346; Susan Hartmann, "Women's Employment and the Domestic Ideal in the Early Cold War Years," in *Not June Cleaver*, 90.

24. Goldin, *Understanding the Gender Gap*, 17–22, chapter 5; Daniel Bell, "Parade of Women," 23–24; Alice K. Leopold, "Homemaker—Money Maker," *National Parent-Teacher* 52 (May 1958): 8–10.

25. For examples, see "Employment: Something For the Girls," *Newsweek* 40 (September 22, 1952): 91–92; "Where Youths Can Find the Best Job," *U. S. News and World Report* 40 (June 15, 1956): 56–60.

26. United States Department of Commerce, Bureau of the Census, *Statistical Abstract of the United States*, 1965 (Washington, D.C.: U.S. Government Printing Office, 1965), 230–235.

27. Dorothy Entwistle Swenson, "New Careers for College Girls," *Ladies Home Journal* 66 (May 1949): 109, 111. The politics and cultural significance of women's magazines have attracted much scholarly attention. See, for instance, John Tebbel and Mary Ellen Zuckerman, *The Magazine in America, 1741–1990* (New York: Oxford University Press, 1991), chapter 19. For an analysis of more recent publications, see Ellen McCracken, *Decoding Women's*

Magazines: From Mademoiselle to Ms. (New York: St. Martin's Press, 1993); Susan Alexander, "Messages to Women on Love and Marriage From Women's Magazines," in Marian Meyers, ed., *Mediated Women: Representations in Popular Culture* (Cresskill, NJ: Hampton Press, 1999), 25–38.

28. Helen G. Hurd, "Leadership Problems of the White Collar Woman Worker," *Independent Woman* (May 1956): 2–3; "The Challenge to the Career-Minded Woman," *Occupation* 29 (January 1951): 273.

29. Jeanine Basinger, *A Woman's View: Holy Hollywood Spoke to Women, 1930–1960* (New York: Alfred Knopf, 1995), 450. T. Kopp and L. Tussing, "The Vocational Choices of High School Students as Related to Scores on Vocational Interest Inventory," *Occupations* 25 (March 1947): 336.

30. "How to Choose a Career," *Woman's Home Companion* 81 (December 1954): 85–86; "Good Jobs for Women as Medical Helpers," *Good Housekeeping* 151 (April 1960): 125; Elizabeth B. Hurlock, "Your Child's Career in Life," *Today's Health* 29 (September 1951): 68.

31. *Designing Woman*, Vincente Minelli, director (MGM, 1957). Fox's 1949 *A Letter to Three Wives* offered another portrait of career women's domestic incompetence. In this case, the token career woman forgets her husband's birthday and instead makes him attend terribly boring dinner parties on her behalf.

32. "What Do You Know about Earning a Living?" *Ladies Home Journal* (June 1950): 48–49.

33. On how such distinctions became critical to corporate cultures, see Clark Davis, *Company Men: White Collar Life and Corporate Cultures in Los Angeles, 1892–1941* (Baltimore: The Johns Hopkins University Press, 2000), 144–146.

34. "Ladies are Getting Ahead," 95; "Can They Get Away With More than Men?" *Newsweek* 52 (September 22, 1958), 93.

35. Stanley Frank, "Too Smart for Your Job?" *Saturday Evening Post* 230 (May 3 1958): 100.

36. "How to Handle Women," *Look* 17 (March 24, 1954): 96.

37. Kwolek-Folland, *Incorporating Women*, 13, 132–133, 159.

38. Robert Froman, "Cash for Your Ideas," *Woman's Home Companion* 78 (December 1951): 4–6; Priscilla Jaqueth, "Money Making at Home," *Women's Home Companion* (December 1950): 8; Berta Crone Horrock, "Perhaps There's a Paying Job for You," *Woman's Home Companion* 80 (January 1953): 46.

39. Harford Powel, "Good Jobs for Good Girls," *Colliers* 124 (September 3, 1949): 16–17, 56.

40. A survey of high school national merit semi-finalists two years later came up with similar findings. Careers in engineering and science attracted 56 percent of the boys and only 16 percent of the girls. Similar numbers of boys and girls expressed interest in the health fields and in business, but a whopping 36 percent of all girls planned on a career in teaching. A national 1957 survey of college students underscored these earlier studies. Only 5 percent of women anticipated careers in law, engineering, farming, or business, compared with half of the male students surveyed. Conversely, half of the women queried sought careers in social work, teaching, art, journalism, drama, or secretarial work, compared with only 1/7 of male respondents. Carl Dickinson, "How College Seniors Preferences Compare with Employment and Enrollment Data,"

Personnel and Guidance Journal 32 (April 1954): 485–488; "Gifted American Youth Prefer the Professional Careers," *School and Society* 83 (May 26, 1956): 192; "College Students' Career Choices," *School and Society* 85 (October 26, 1957): 314.

41. Molly Haskell writes of the 1950s as a transitional decade for women in cinema as the disintegration of the Hollywood studio system and the industry's sweeping decline meant both fewer roles for women and fewer social realism films. MollyHaskell, *From Reverence to Rape*, 231–276. See also Haskell's more recent work, *Holding My Own in No Man's Land: Women and Men and Film and Feminists* (New York: Oxford University Press, 1997). Useful sources of feminist film criticism include E. Anne Kaplan, ed., *Feminism and Film* (New York: Oxford University Press, 2000); Constance Penley, *Feminism and Film Theory* (New York: Routledge, 1988); and Annette Kuhn, *Women's Pictures: Feminism and Cinema* (Boston: Routledge & Kegan Paul, 1982). On images of work in television, see Taylor, *Prime Time Families*, 32–41.

42. Jeanine Basinger, *Woman's View: How Hollywood Spoke to Women, 1930–1960* (New York: Alfred A. Knopf, 1995), 10. Susan Douglas writes of these contradictions as leading to a "media-induced schizophrenia" that produced "tension, anger, and uncertainty in everyday women" of this era. Douglas, *Where the Girls Are*, 20. On this topic in later Hollywood films, see Philip Green, *Cracks in the Pedestal: Ideology and Gender in Hollywood* (Amherst: The University of Massachusetts Press, 1998).

43. *Pillow Talk*, Michael Gordon, director (Universal, 1959). For an excellent discussion of Doris Day's importance for women's images in postwar films, see Molly Haskell, who describes Day as "one of the few movie heroines (and one of the last) who had to *work* for a living." In *Holding My Own*, 26; Haskell, *Reverence to Rape*, 262–265.

44. Excellent studies of postwar cinema include Peter Biskind, *Seeing is Believing: How Hollywood Taught us to Stop Worrying and Love the Fifties* (New York: Henry Holt and Company, 2000); Lary May, *The Big Tomorrow: Hollywood and the Politics of the American Way* (Chicago: University of Chicago Press, 2000), chapter 5. For a discussion of more recent working women's films, see Yvonne Tasker, *Working Girls: Gender and Sexuality in Popular Cinema* (New York: Routledge, 1998).

45. *Miss Grant Takes Richmond*, Lloyd Bacon, director (Columbia Pictures, 1949).

46. *Desk Set*, Walter Lang, director (Twentieth Century Fox, 1957).

47. *A Life of Her Own*, George Cukor, director, (MGM: 1950); *The Tender Trap*, Charles Walter, director (MGM, 1955).

48. *All About Eve*, Joseph L. Mankiewicz, director (Twentieth-Century Fox, 1950). For an excellent analysis of this film, see Haskell, *From Reverence to Rape*, 244–248.

49. On motherhood and film, see Lucy Fischer, *Cinematernity: Film, Motherhood, Genre* (Princeton, New Jersey: Princeton University Press, 1996).

50. *State of the Union*, Frank Capra, director (MGM, Liberty Films, 1948).

51. *A Woman of Distinction*, Edward Buzzell, director (Columbia: 1950). On this pervasive theme in American popular culture, see Judith Halberstam, *Female Masculinity* (Durham: Duke University Press, 1998); Biskind, *Seeing is Believing*, 274, 298–303.

52. Kwolek-Folland, *Incorporating Women*, 161; "Goddess of Success," *Time* 67 (March 26, 1956): 100–101.
53. Wallace Jamie, "Wanted: Young Men for Top-Salary Jobs," *American Magazine* 157 (June 1954): 93.
54. *Woman's World*, Jean Negulesco, director (20th Century Fox, 1954).
55. *The Best of Everything*, Jean Negulesco, director (20th Century Fox, 1959).
56. Helen Lefkowitz Horowitz, *Campus Life: Undergraduate Cultures from the End of the Eighteenth Century to the Present* (Chicago: University of Chicago Press, 1987), 219; "Employment of June 1956 Women College Graduates," *Monthly Labor Review* 81 (July 1958): 752–756; "Employment of June 1957 Women College Graduates," *Monthly Labor Review* 82 (June 1959): 663–666.
57. On how the workplace frustration of working women in the 1950s would lead to struggles for more rights and opportunities, see Alice Kessler-Harris, *In Pursuit of Equality: Women, Men, and the Quest for Economic Citizenship in 20th Century America* (New York: Oxford University Press, 2001).

Chapter 14

Ayn Rand and the Politics of Property[1]

Andrew Hoberek

It wasn't too long ago that Ayn Rand, despite her enormous and ongoing popularity, was all but invisible in the criticism and history of twentieth-century American fiction, although that has begun to change. Sharon Stockton and Michael Szalay have recently demonstrated Rand's engagement with conceptions of brainwork central to the Depression era in which she wrote her first bestselling novel, *The Fountainhead* (1943).[2] In what follows I use Rand's 1957 novel *Atlas Shrugged* to argue that she plays an even more central and active role in discussions of mental labor following World War II, when such labor became central to both the US economy and the work of the American middle class. *Atlas Shrugged*, like Rand's oeuvre more generally, participates in the voluminous postwar discourse dedicated to describing and criticizing the transformation of the American middle class from "independent entrepreneurs" to "managers and white-collar workers."[3] This process was already well under way during the first half of the twentieth century, but it became a central focus of American social criticism during the 1950s. *Atlas Shrugged*, published just one year after white-collar workers surpassed blue-collar workers as the largest segment of the non-farm workforce,[4] shares many of the preoccupations of such non-fiction works as William H. Whyte's 1956 *The Organization Man*. Whyte's book, like other works of postwar social criticism, argues that white-collar work for large organizations has caused the middle class to abandon its forebears' individuality and creativity in exchange for a disempowering emphasis on consensus in the workplace.[5] *Atlas Shrugged* concurs with this analysis, although as a work of fiction it goes Whyte and other observers one better, offering not just a diagnosis of but an imaginative solution to the problem of middle-class deindividuation. This solution has two parts. First, Rand obscures the connection between the rise of the new middle class and the increasing concentration of capital in the US economy[6] by rewriting the traditional American conflict between small and large capital—in which the middle class had historically belonged to the former camp—as one between business and government. In doing so, she anticipates the now all too common understanding of the corporate world as the site not of alienated labor and self-commodification but, on the contrary, of all the agency denied by government bureaucracies. Less obviously but perhaps even more importantly, Rand presciently depicts mental labor not as paid employment for large corporations but rather as the exchange of intellectual property. In this way she helps uphold the American middle class's commitment to property as such—and, secondarily, to the large corporations that increasingly controlled it in the 1950s—despite this class's loss of its own once defining control over decentralized forms of small property. These strategies, as even this brief resume should suggest, have since proven incredibly foresighted in anticipating the ways in which capital has maintained the allegiance of the American middle class in a period when this class otherwise might have been forced to understand its economic role in very different terms, as a form of structurally (and increasingly materially) proletarianized labor for large corporations.

Atlas Shrugged invokes the problem of middle-class downward mobility through its motif of a group of industrialists, inventors, and sympathetic artists who go on strike—the working title of the novel was "The Strike"[7]—to demonstrate to the world what happens when they withdraw the productive energies that politicians, intellectuals, and ungrateful employees simultaneously denounce and exploit. As I will discuss at greater length below, however, Rand's account of this strike ultimately works not to reveal but to deny the transformation of the American middle class from property owners into mental laborers. Rand's heroes proudly define themselves as producers and traders, in contrast to villains who reproduce the picture of white-collar self-abdication central to books like *The Organization Man*. Mr. Thompson, the Head of State in the totalitarian government that coalesces as the strikers withdraw, is no jackbooted führer, but on the contrary "a man who possessed the quality of never being noticed":

> In any group of three, his person became indistinguishable, and when seen alone it seemed to evoke a group of its own, composed of the countless persons he resembled. The country had no clear image of what he looked like: his photographs had appeared on the covers of magazines as frequently as those of his predecessors in office, but people could never be quite certain which photographs were his and which were pictures of "*a* mail clerk" or "*a* white-collar worker," accompanying articles about the daily life of the undifferentiated—except that Mr. Thompson's collars were usually wilted.[8]

Literally embodying the triumph of the group over the individual central to Whyte's analysis of postwar business, the "undifferentiated" and explicitly white-collar Thompson likewise shares the organization man's lack of ambition: "Holding enormous official powers, he schemed ceaselessly to expand them, because it was expected of him by those who had pushed him into office. . . . The sole secret of his rise in life was the fact that he was a product of chance and knew it and aspired to nothing else" (494). Whereas the strikers are self-contained, self-starting prime movers symbolized by their leader John Galt's invention of a motor that runs on atmospheric electricity, their opponents are mere conduits for an impersonal and purely negative evil. Rand's villains, she insists, do not reveal their true natures when they stop casting their motives in terms of altruistic service and instead declare a will to power or profit. Rather, their professed greed no less than their professed altruism obscures the true horror behind their actions, a thanatopic "lust to destroy whatever was living, for the sake of whatever was not" (1052).

If Rand's villains thus epitomize the transformation of middle-class identity central to the work of Whyte and other postwar social critics, her heroes represent precisely the forms of agency traditionally identified with the American middle class. The symbol of her strikers, stamped on their own personal brand of cigarettes and cast in a three-foot gold statue suspended on a granite column in their Rocky Mountain hideaway, is the dollar sign. As one of these renegades explains to Dagny Taggart, the railroad executive who shares their values but who resists joining them until the final pages of the novel, they have adopted the dollar sign as their ensign in defiance of its common use as "the one sure-fire brand of evil," preferring instead to understand it as a badge of "achievement, . . . success, . . . ability, [and] man's creative power" (630). They do so in tribute to the United States' role as "the only country in history where wealth was not acquired by looting, but by production, not by force, but by trade, the only country whose money was the symbol of man's right to his own mind, to his work, to his life, to his happiness, to himself" (630). The ancestral exemplar of American capitalism within the novel is Dagny's forebear Nat Taggart, the founder of the once enormously successful railroad now being held together only through her unremitting exertions. Where Dagny must continually deal with a company whose executives—exemplified by Taggart's president, her brother Jim—are timid, hyperconscious of bureaucratic restraints, and more interested in engineering profitable government regulations than in running trains, her predecessor worked blessedly alone:

> He was a man who had never accepted the creed that others had the right to stop him. He set his goal and moved toward it, his way as straight as one of his rails. He never sought any loans, bonds, subsidies, land grants or legislative favors from the government. He obtained money from the men who owned it, going from door to door—from the mahogany doors of bankers to the clapboard doors of lonely farmhouses. He never talked about the public good. He merely told people that they would make big profits on his railroad, he told them why he expected the profits and he gave his reasons. He had good reasons. Through all the generations that followed, Taggart Transcontinental was one of the few railroads that never went bankrupt and the only one whose controlling stock remained in the hands of the founder's descendants. (62)

Rumored to have murdered a state legislator who tried to use regulatory chicanery to make a profit on his failure, Nat Taggart is his successor's antisocial *beau ideal*. Passing his statue in the concourse of the Taggart station she feels "a moment's rest . . . as if a burden she could not name were lightened and as if a faint current of air were touching her forehead" (63).

Galt makes clear the connection between Dagny's reverence for her ancestor and the strikers' ideals when he tells her that she can signal her willingness to join them by "chalk[ing] a dollar sign on the pedestal of Nat Taggart's statue—where it belongs" (884–885).

In part then, *Atlas Shrugged* understands its capitalist ideal in explicitly nostalgic terms. Rand notes of Galt's home in the strikers' refuge of Atlantis that it has "the primitive simplicity of a frontiersman's cabin, reduced to essential necessities . . . with a super-modern skill" (655); likewise, one of his lieutenants lives in a home "like a frontiersman's shanty thrown together to serve as a mere springboard for a long flight into the future" (710). Like many postwar texts, from novels to Western films to the new works of American Studies scholarship, *Atlas Shrugged* celebrates the nation's heritage of frontier individualism. At the same time, one of the novel's last scenes consists of a nightmarish depiction of stranded rail passengers rescued by a wagon train. For Rand, the pioneer only serves as a metaphor for her true hero, the robber baron. The moment of declension in her mythos is not the closing of the frontier that preoccupied Frederick Jackson Turner's heirs, but rather the moment when, say, Andrew Carnegie sells out to US Steel or Thomas Edison's workshops institute team research—the moment, that is, when the individual owner or inventor cedes control to the collaborative organization of management and mental labor characteristic of the modern corporation. This explains *Atlas Shrugged*'s characteristic investment in such anachronisms, from the perspective of business history, as a family-owned railroad system or the head of a steel company who personally invents a revolutionary new alloy.

But although *Atlas Shrugged*'s plot focuses on the eventual conversion of Dagny Taggart and mill owner Hank Rearden, and spends a lot of time theorizing the natural aristocracy that links heirs like Taggart and copper magnate Francisco D'Anconia to self-made men like Galt and Rearden, its actual historical referent is not the American ruling class but the middle class concerned, as the popularity of books like *The Organization Man* attest, about the loss of agency incumbent upon the transition to white-collar employment for large organizations.

Among postwar social critics, C. Wright Mills most forcefully and directly linked this loss of agency to "The centralization of small properties" that undermined the traditional basis of American middle-class identity.[9] If, for Mills, the new middle-class white-collar worker is the deindividuated "cog and . . . beltline of the bureaucratic machinery" (80), this is because he lacks the old middle class's defining relationship to small capital. The possession of such capital made the middle-class entrepreneur, in Mills's most hyperbolic formulation, into "an 'absolute individual,' linked into a system with no author-itarian center, but held together by countless, free, shrewd transactions" (9). It is of course the case that this account of American economic history obscures significant disparities in who could own property, not to mention the fact that for much of this period some Americans were owned *as* property. Mills's investment in this version of the American past might, moreover, seem even more suspect when placed alongside Rand's strikingly similar sense of the market as matrix for the ideal social system. Consider, for instance, the following passage from *Atlas Shrugged*, another of the novel's rhetorical set pieces about money:

> Money rests on the axiom that every man is the owner of his mind and his effort. Money allows no power to prescribe the value of your effort except the voluntary choice of the man who is willing to trade you his effort in return. . . . Money permits no deals except those to mutual benefit by the unforced judgment of the traders. Money demands of you the recognition that men must work for their own benefit, not for their own injury, for their gain, not their loss—the recognition that they are not beasts of burden, born to carry the weight of your misery—that you must offer them values, not wounds—that the common bond among men is not the exchange of suffering, but the exchange of *goods*. . . . And when men live by trade—with reason, not force, as their final arbiter—it is the best product that wins, the best performance, the man of best judgment and highest ability—and the degree of a man's productiveness is the degree of his reward. (383; Rand's emphasis)

For Rand, the market is not the source of social inequality but the mechanism for eliminating hierarchical relationships, the basis for what is in effect a functioning anarchy. In the strikers' haven, there are "no laws . . . , no rules, no formal organization of any kind," other than the "custom[ ]" that forbids "the word '*give*' " (659; Rand's emphasis). On this basis, the strikers erect a perfectly functioning social system that for the first time fulfills man's nature as "a social being" (690). Despite the vast gulf separating their politics, then, Rand shares Mills's vision of a society structured not around an "authoritarian center" but through a multiplicity of "free, shrewd" exchanges.

Whereas Rand sees this system as the ideal and heretofore unrealized fulfillment of human history, however, Mills sees it as a moment now irretrievably lost to the centralization of property and the resulting concentration of economic control. The process of middle-class expropriation that culminated in the mid-twentieth-century United States, as a factor in the ongoing centralization of property, helps to explain *Atlas Shrugged*'s anachronistic investment in the managerial revolution that began in the mid-nineteenth-century, and was more or less a *fait accompli* by World War II. The idea of a railroad still owned and managed by its founder's descendants completely belies the railroad industry's historical participation in this revolution, as those familiar with Alfred Chandler's *The Visible Hand* (1977) will recognize. Railroads, Chandler argues, played a central role in the shift from "small, personally owned and managed enterprises . . . coordinated and monitored by market price mechanisms" to large, vertically integrated organizations "monitored and coordinated by salaried employees" because they were, along with telegraph companies, the first businesses "to require a large number of full-time managers to coordinate, control, and evaluate the activities of a number of widely scattered operating units."[10] The extent and complexity of railroads' operations, drove the development of precisely the forms of bureaucratic administration by professional managers that rendered owner-managers like Nat Taggart obsolete. Dagny Taggart thus fights a battle that, in a more historically accurate account, Nat Taggart would already have lost. Or perhaps even more accurately, she fights a battle against forces that Nat Taggart himself would have set in motion.

Rand's celebration of owner-managers like Taggart and Rearden might make sense, however, if we see them not as a belated generation of robber barons but rather as outsized representatives of the middle-class entrepreneur whose historical twilight had occurred more recently. And, in fact, the novel itself suggests this connection insofar as the strikers give up the giant industries they are unable to run in the modern world for the life of middle-class proprietors. Dagny, having stumbled prematurely on their mountain hideaway, finds the oilman Ellis Wyatt, for instance, supervising just two workers (665), while "Calvin Atwood of the Atwood Light and Power Company of New York is making the shoes" (668) and others have opened small shops on "the valley's single street" (670) among them a former automaker whom Dagny spies "weighing a chunk of butter" at his new grocery store (670). This transformation of captains of industry into shopkeepers, while meant to highlight the dignity of free trade, suggests the historical dilemma behind Rand's simultaneous love and fear of the nineteenth-century past. Recognizing that her trader's utopia is unfeasible in the contemporary world, and able to realize it only in the terms of a nostalgic regression, Rand cannot depict the new world of large industry *and* individual trade that the strikers promise to build after the old system's failure. The novel ends with Galt announcing "We are going back to the world" (1074), unable actually to show what happens when they do.

In its form, then, *Atlas Shrugged* reveals the problem inherent in its own celebration of the capitalist producer and trader: the way in which capitalism itself, by continually concentrating property in larger and more complex forms, leads to the disenfranchisement of individuals that Rand abhors. Ever more centralized property, and not external controls, undermine the market of free individuals that can only be restored through an artificial return to smaller-scale capitalism. This is not, however, to suggest that Rand's investment in a by mid-century largely residual mode of property ownership likewise marks her politics as residual. On the contrary, Mills for one stressed the durability of "the ideology suitable for the nation of small capitalists" in a United States "transformed from a nation of small capitalists into a nation of hired employees" (34). For Mills, the persistence of the politics of small capital, "as if that small-propertied world were still a going concern" (34), ironically served the big business interests responsible for small capital's difficulties:

> at the same time that small firms are being driven to the wall, they are being used by the big firms with which they publicly identify themselves. This fact underlies the ideology and the frustration of the small urban capitalist; it is the reason why his aggression is directed at labor and government. (51)

Big business, Mills argued, uses "small businessmen [as] shock troops in the battle against labor unions and government controls," thereby "exploit[ing] in its own interests the very anxieties it has created for small business" (53). *Atlas Shrugged* exemplifies this process, blurring the distinction between small and large capital by stressing what Rand sees as their shared conflict with government.[11]

Rand's decision to make Dagny Taggart a railroad executive makes sense insofar as by 1957 the railroad industry exemplified the industrial decline that *Atlas Shrugged* imputes to the economy as a whole. Here too, though, Rand fails to get her business history exactly right. At one point during a press conference held to discuss the opening of a new rail line, Dagny tells the assembled reporters that "the average profit of railroads has been two percent of the capital invested" (220). Assuming that *Atlas Shrugged* does in fact take place in a parallel universe version of the late 1950s, this statistic slightly undershoots the actual figure, even for what had been lean years for the industry. According to John F. Stover's 1961 *American Railroads*, "the four largest railroads had a net income of only 2.9 percent" in 1957, although the figure for the industry as a whole since 1945 had "ranged from 2.76 per cent to 4.31 per cent" and "averaged . . . 3.64 per cent."[12] More important than the actual figure, however, is the way in which Rand implicitly poses this particular industry as a representative of the postwar economy more generally. There is no doubt that the railroads were in trouble in the late 1950s, and in fact had been in decline since rail mileage had peaked in 1916.[13] In *Atlas Shrugged*, however, the progressive decline of Taggart Transcontinental emblematizes an economy more like that of the Depression thirties than the boom fifties. The reader's introduction to Dagny, riding a Taggart train diverted by a broken switch and halted by a faulty signal light, anticipates a world in which—even before the total collapse that sets wagon trains in motion—goods are scarce, machines are breaking down and can't be fixed, and streets are filled with empty storefronts.[14] But of course the railroad industry's difficulties were not typical of the postwar economy. In the same year, for instance, airlines posted a 7.75 per cent return on their investments,[15] and much of the railroads' troubles in these years was the result of competition from both the airlines and the equally well off trucking industry.

This is not to endorse the market-based analysis of the railroads' vicissitudes that has governed the most recent round of attacks on what is left of US rail service, however. As Amtrak's proponents have pointed out in response to criticisms of its inefficiency, the carrier receives only a small percentage of the government funding devoted to highways and the infrastructure of the aviation industry.[16] This pattern was already established by the late 1950s, belying Rand's sense—which, of course, remains central to conservative rhetoric—of government as the purely negative enemy of business. In the postwar period, railroads were, to some degree, victims of aggressive government regulation left over from their glory days in the late nineteenth century.[17] At the same time, however, the industry's competitors benefited not only from the absence of similar regulation but also from positive government action, including massive direct funding for highways, airports, and other facilities.[18] As Kim McQuaid has pointed out, World War II and the cold war led to a new symbiosis between government and big business, with the state more and more exerting its financial, regulatory, and even diplomatic and military powers in the interests of business.[19]

On one hand, *Atlas Shrugged* fully acknowledges this new corporate–state intimacy through its depiction of executives like Jim Taggart and the steel maker Orren Boyle, who devote their time to engineering government regulations that allow them to ruin their competitors and steal their products. Indeed, Rand's description of Boyle reads, in the post-Enron world, like a left indictment of corporate welfare and the CEO star culture:

> Orren Boyle had appeared from nowhere, five years ago, and had since made the cover of every national news magazine. He had started out with a hundred thousand dollars of his own and a two-hundred-million-dollar loan from the government. Now he headed an enormous concern which had swallowed many smaller companies. This proved, he liked to say, that individual ability still had a chance to succeed in the world. (49)

Here Rand's novel seems to dramatize Mills's sardonic comment six years earlier that "Nobody talks more of free enterprise and competition and of the best man winning than the man who inherited his father's store or farm" (36). *Atlas Shrugged* is filled with similar critiques of businessmen who spend their time "running to Washington" rather than "running . . . mills" (283). Such depictions at times make it seem as though the novel is as opposed to big business as it is to Rand's more expected government and union targets.

But this is not the case, insofar as Rand sees men like Taggart and Boyle as aberrations from capitalist business practice rather than its norm. Rand's insistence, driven home by Taggart's final breakdown, that such men act out of a perverse death drive rather than self-interest highlights her flawed picture of postwar capitalism. In her world, as we have seen, steel companies prosper because their owners invent new metals, not because Taft-Hartley and other legislation weakens the labor movement or because the Korean War generates sharp demand for steel while accelerated depreciation encourages steel companies to expand.[20] Likewise, oil companies succeed because the young "prodig[ies]" who run them discover "rich new oil field[s], at a time when the pumps were stopping in one famous field after another" (16–17), not because the US government exerts its power to open up Middle Eastern oil fields to American companies.[21] This is not to say that the federal government, after World War II, became simply the tool of big business. In fact, both big oil and big steel endured regulatory incursions from antimonopolist legislators from the South and West. Even these legislators were operating, however, not in the interests of public service but rather in those of small producers in the same field who briefly managed to swing the ideology of small capital in their favor.[22] In *Atlas Shrugged*, by contrast, government action is only inimical to business, and companies thrive best in an atmosphere where, as one character says of the temporarily booming state of Colorado, government "does nothing . . . outside of keeping law courts and a police department" (254).

Rand's own brief history of the railroads, first published two years after *Atlas Shrugged*, demonstrates how she obscures the conflict between large and small capital by stressing instead the conflict between business and government. In "Notes on the History of American Free Enterprise" (1959), Rand reduces the early history of the railroads to a battle between individual-istic capitalists and coercive government regulations, arguing that "The evils, popularly ascribed to big industrialists, were not the result of an unregulated industry, but of government power over industry."[23] This argument is most convincing when she contends that Cornelius Vanderbilt only engaged in stock market manipulation because city and state politicians reneged on promises of favorable action, hoping to make a profit by selling Vanderbilt stock short (105–106). Elsewhere, however, the lines between business and government get blurrier, and can only be maintained by the same problematic distinction that she makes in *Atlas Shrugged* between proper and improper businessmen—or, as she calls them in "Notes on the History of American Free Enterprise," "free enterprisers" and those who "achieve[ ] power by legislative intervention in business" (104). As in the novel, Rand's investment in the free market leads her to claim not just the moral but the strategic high ground for businesses that go it alone, arguing that "The degree of government help received by any one railroad, stood in direct proportion to that railroad's troubles and failures. The railroads with the worst histories of scandal, double-dealing, and bankruptcy were the ones that had received the greatest amount of help from the government" (103). Yet Rand's own description of the eminently successful Central Pacific on the subsequent page belies her claim not to have discovered any "exceptions to this rule" (103):

> The Central Pacific—which was built by the "Big Four" of California, on federal subsidies—was the railroad which was guilty of all the evils popularly held against railroads. For almost thirty years, the Central Pacific controlled California, held a monopoly, and permitted no competitor to enter the state. It charged disastrous rates, changed them every year, and took virtually the entire profit of the California farmers or shippers, who had no other railroad to turn to. What made this possible? It was done through the power of the California legislature. The Big Four controlled the legislature and held the state closed to competitors by legal restrictions—such as, for instance, a legislative act which gave the Big Four exclu-sive control of the entire coastline of California and forbade any other railroad to enter any port. During these thirty years, many attempts were made by private interests to build competing railroads in California and break the monopoly of the Central Pacific. These attempts were defeated—not by methods of free trade and free competition, but by *legislative action*. (104; Rand's emphasis)

What is most interesting here is not that Rand contradicts her assertion that recourse to government leads inevitably to business failure, although that is certainly the case. Rather, it is the way in which she does this: by implying that the Central Pacific's manipulation of the legislature originates not with the railroad but with the legislature itself—that it is legislative and not corporate "action" that is at issue here. This sleight of hand enables Rand to transform what might otherwise be described as a conflict between small and large capital—with the latter employing legislative action among its weapons against "competing railroads"—into a conflict between business *per se* and government *per se*. Lining up the sides in this way obscures the distinction between big and small capital.

If there is no distinction between big and small capital, then the conflict "between holders of small property . . . and holders of larger property" (Mills, *White* 55) that Mills saw as central to pre-twentieth-century US history likewise disappears. The ills of small business, many of them caused in both the long and short term by big business, become the imagined ills of big business; the defense of big business against the very state that it just as often employs to its own ends becomes small business's duty. No longer anchored in actual socioeconomic conditions as they had been through the Progressive Era, the politics of small capital became more powerful than ever following the war, when they were pressed into the service of the large capital that had been small capital's historic enemy.

It makes sense that the politics of small capital would continue to appeal to the remnants of the *petit bourgeoisie*, even if they were being manipulated in the interests of another class. Less logical is why they would appeal to the structurally proletarianized—*and therefore no longer really middle class*—mass of white-collar workers for whom a more traditional class politics might make more sense. One obvious answer is the enormous political pressure deployed against class politics throughout US history, and particularly in the cold war era. Another is the fear of downward mobility through being identified with the working classes that Mills notes in his discussion of why white-collar workers don't unionize (301–323). Finally, less obviously, capital continues to seduce the "disappearing middle"[24] with things like home and stock ownership that blur the distinction between property and capital, or between capital and capital that matters, thereby keeping white-collar workers invested in the ideology of property as such.[25]

But Rand suggests an additional avenue whereby white-collar workers are kept affectively routed into a politics of small capital that no longer serves their interests. Fatally attached to market exchange as the only possible basis for desirable social relations, Rand denigrates all other forms of social relatedness as inherently deindividualizing and alienating. The question is, to what end? One possible answer is that Rand provides a kind of Walter Mitty-esque fantasy for white-collar workers who can eat shit at the office while imagining themselves as steadfast Hank Reardens. David Riesman suggests as much when he argues in *The Lonely Crowd* (1950)—a book with its own suspicions of the social—that *The Fountainhead*'s Howard Roark is "the very apotheosis of the lonely success, to be admired perhaps . . . but too stagey to be imitated," a figure who allows readers to feel superior to others while remaining "quite unaware of [their] own tendencies to submission in the small, undramatic situations of daily life."[26] But to figure Rand in this way would be to confine her influence to a few lonely fans (precisely our stereotype of Rand), and to ignore the similarities between her worldview and that of postwar white-collar workers more generally—not excluding those of us who work in the academy. Rand depicts a world in which people experience intensely passionate relationships with their work, and secondarily with people who are valued, and in turn value others, on the basis of work. That is, she presents something much like Stefano Harney and Frederick Moten's description of academic work, in which academics, approaching their work through both "a nostalgic and historically inaccurate view of craftwork" and an equally misguided model of "liberal individualism and market exchanges," misread their place in the social relations of production defined by capitalism.[27] If, as Andrew Ross has recently argued, academic labor provides a model for labor exploitation more generally in the new knowledge economy,[28] then we might say that capitalism has finally caught up with Rand. For Rand's novels do not simply project a fantasy of old middle-class property ownership for white-collar employees. They also struggle to reimagine white-collar work as itself a form of property ownership and exchange—a move that requires refiguring all property as intellectual property.

Central to this reconceptualization of property is the selfsame motif of the strike that might seem to reveal, as I earlier suggested, the contemporary middle class's new status as workers. Rand's protagonists' strike exemplifies not their transformation into workers organizing to better negotiate the terms of their labor's sale, however, but rather their ur-capitalist ability to choose how to dispose of the property now understood precisely as their non-physical ideas. As the mine owner Ken Dannager says just before he joins the strike, "Why should I leave a deed or a will? I don't want to help the looters to pretend that private property still exists. I am complying with the system which they have established. They do not need me, they say, they only need my coal. Let them take it" (415–416). Likewise, Dagny is initially put on Galt's trail when she and Rearden find the remains of Galt's motor sitting on a junk pile in the now abandoned factory where Galt built it, before leaving in protest of the employees' decision to run the factory on the principle of "from each according to his ability, to each according to his need." As Galt explains his decision,

> I looked at my motor for the last time, before I left. I thought of the men who claim that wealth is a matter of natural resources—and of the men who claim that wealth is a matter of seizing the factories—and of the men who claim that machines condition their brains. Well, *there* was the motor to condition them, and there it remained as just exactly what it is without man's mind—as a pile of metal scraps and wires, going to rust. (688)

Dannager and Galt can leave their physical property behind because their true property is intellectual property, a point Rand reinforces by including artists as well as industrialists in the strikers' hidden colony. For Rand, artists practicing what Michael Szalay has called the "politics of textual integrity"—the privileging of artistic products over the processes that generate them[29]—exemplify the recondensation of mental labor more generally into property. The artists who live in Atlantis are there not simply to offer aesthetic representations of the strikers' worldview—symphonies that "embody every human act and thought that had ascent as its motive" (20); plays about "human greatness" (723)—but because they ultimately perform the same activity as the inventors and businessmen. All three groups exchange (or refuse to exchange, where the outside world is concerned) the products of their mind. Thus the other activity, besides shopkeeping, in which the strikers most frequently and fervently participate is performance: not the performance-as-process opposed by Szalay's late modernist proponents of textual integrity, but discrete performances for pay that reaffirm the ability of ideas to serve as alienable property. When Dagny is shocked to discover that Galt has been spending his evenings in Atlantis lecturing on physics, he tells her that the strikers, committed to denying the outside world the fruits of their intellects by working only menial jobs, spend their time together "trad[ing] the achievements of our real professions. Richard Halley is to give concerts, Kay Ludlow is to appear in two plays written by authors who do not write for the outside world—and I give lectures, reporting on the work I've done during the year [at] ten dollars per person for the course" (714). Here it is not their minds that the strikers take off the market, but the products of their minds—a crucial distinction, as it reverses the historical trajectory of the middle class by transforming them from mental laborers to owners and sellers of intangible but nonetheless real property.

Rand makes the logic behind this move explicit in her 1964 essay "Patents and Copyrights," arguing that

> Every type of productive work involves a combination of mental and physical effort: of thought and of physical action to translate that thought into a material form. The proportion of these two elements varies in different types of work. At the lowest end of the scale, the mental effort required to perform unskilled manual labor is minimal. At the other end, what the patent and copyright laws acknowledge is the paramount role of mental effort in the production of material values; these laws protect the mind's contribution in its purest form: the orgination of an *idea*. The subject of patents and copyrights is *intellectual* property. (*Capitalism* 130; Rand's emphases)

Rand here affirms the superiority of mental labor, which lies in its counter-intuitively greater productivity. By preventing the "unauthorized reproduction of the object," she goes on to note, intellectual property "law declares, in effect, that the physical labor of copying is not the source of the object's value" (*Capitalism* 130). Physical labor does not create, but only reproduces; only mental labor, contra Mills and other theorists of white-collar work, actually does make things. Rearden, refusing the government's offer of "an impressive profit, an immediate profit, much larger than you could hope to realize from the sale of the metal for the next twenty years" (171) in exchange for not producing it, tells his puzzled interlocutor, "Because it's *mine*. Do you understand that word?" (172; Rand's emphasis). Because it is his—because, that is, its formula is his—he and he alone can make and sell the metal whose status as property lies not in its physical instantiations but in his ownership of an idea.

Rand's reconfiguration of property as ideas rather than things reveals how mainstream—if not in fact prescient—her economic thinking was. In particular, this move anticipates the key concept of Gary Becker's influential 1964 study *Human Capital*. Citing "a realization that the growth of physical capital, at least as conventionally measured, [now] explains a relatively small part of the growth of income in most countries," Becker focuses his study on "activities that influence future monetary and physical income by increasing the resources in people," especially education.[30] Becker's argument quite legitimately attempts to take into account the shift from industrial capitalism to the new form—variously called, among other things, post-industrialism, post-Fordism, network capitalism, and informatization—"in which providing services and manipulating information are at the heart of economic production."[31] But Becker's model of human capital also implicitly elides the difference between this change in the relations of production and the less tenable assertion that the binary class system no longer applies to capitalism. It does so by fudging the definition of "capital." Insofar as he focuses on "monetary and physical income," Becker ignores the distinction—fundamental to the Marxist understanding of class—between those who own capital and those who must sell their labor to its owners. The concept of human capital thus fails to distinguish between intellectual property (an idea that one can sell for profit) and skills (abilities that one can use to bargain for a better income from one's employer). It is no doubt true, as Becker's successor Pierre Bourdieu argued in 1984, that "a growing proportion of the ruling fraction derives, if not its power, at least the legitimacy of its power from educational capital acquired in formally pure and perfect academic competition, rather than directly from economic capital."[32] Of course, the Bush administration has reminded us that old-fashioned economic capital still goes a long way, just as Bush's Yale degree suggests the limits of Daniel Bell's 1973 assertion that "the university, which once reflected the status system of the society, has now become the arbiter of class position."[33] But more importantly, concepts such as human capital and Bourdieu's cultural capital are problematic in that—precisely through their focus on education—they make it possible to understand employed mental laborers as entrepreneurs. They do, that is, precisely what Rand's novels do.

Bourdieu himself suggests the limits of the concept of cultural capital when he notes that:

> Although executives and engineers have the monopoly of the means of symbolic
> appropriation of the cultural capital objectified in the form of instruments,

machines and so forth which are essential to the exercise of the power of economic capital over this equipment, and derive from their monopoly a real managerial power and relative privileges within the firm, the profits accruing from their cultural capital are at least partially appropriated by those who have power over this capital, i.e., those who possess the economic capital needed to ensure the concentration and utilization of cultural capital.[34]

The possessors of even high-level cultural capital, that is, remain beholden as employees to those who own economic capital. If this is a problem for those at the top of white-collar pyramids, it is even more so for those lower down, for whom curtailed autonomy can translate directly into the loss of money and job security. The recent trend among downsizing companies of firing experienced white-collar workers in favor of younger, cheaper ones, for instance,[35] provides a sharp rebuke to the more celebratory accounts of human capital. Such downsized workers are free to trade their human capital precisely as workers are free to trade their labor: largely at the will of those who can purchase it. In this respect, the idea of the mental laborer as entrepreneur—which arose at a time when stable jobs were equated with ennui—now provides a fantasy of agency within an economy in which job security is increasingly tenuous. Witness, for instance, the *Wall Street Journal*'s CareerJournal.com article "Should You Stay Energized by Changing Your Job Frequently?"[36]

Such romanticized—and deeply Randian—notions of craftsmanship and liberal exchange prevent contemporary white-collar workers from understanding themselves as workers. Harney and Moten provide an example close to home for academics when they suggest that one reason tenure-track faculty are so willing to participate in the exploitation of casual adjunct labor is that they view their work through the lens of "liberal individualism and market exchanges" rather than paid employment.[37] Academics' sense that some kinds of intellectual labor (research) are superior to others because, in Randian terms, they are solitary and thus creative forestalls more collective (if less glamorous) ways of conceiving the labor done in universities. In this respect some tenure-track academics' resistance to academic unions no doubt bears out Mills's argument that the "status psychology of white-collar employees" is a major impediment to white-collar unionism (312, 301–323 passim). Academics thus prove themselves to be prototypical white-collar workers at precisely the moment when, Andrew Ross argues, white-collar workers are becoming more like academics, translating the characteristically academic / artististic investment in "nonmonetary rewards—mental or creative gratification—as compensation for work" into things like the dotcomers' heroic cult of overwork.[38] Rand's characters would be totally at home in this structure of feeling; which they would recognize depends not so much upon the Romantic conception that "*The artist cannot afford to be rewarded well*"[39] as upon the more characteristically American notion that the artist cannot afford to be rewarded well *except by the market*.

Rand's, at the time, relatively novel understanding of mental labor as entrepreneurship depended upon the same free market fundamentalism, and the same shift of focus from big capital to big government, as her nostalgia for nineteenth-century small property. The villains of *Atlas Shrugged*, for instance, include the following language outlawing intellectual property as part of a government directive:

> Point Three. All patents and copyrights, pertaining to any devices, inventions, formulas, processes and works of any nature whatsoever, shall be turned over to the nation as a patriotic emergency gift . . . . The Unification Board shall then license the use of such patents and copyrights to all applicants, equally and without discrimination, for the purpose of eliminating monopolistic practices, discarding obsolete products and making the best available to the whole nation. No trademarks, brand names or copyrighted titles shall be used. . . . All private trademarks and brand names are hereby abolished. (499–500)

Here, predictably, it is the regulative state that seeks to undermine by fiat the property rights—in this case, intellectual property rights—of individuals.

The more recent history of intellectual property suggests, however, that Rand once again misses how capitalism itself undermines these rights in its relentless drive toward centralization. For Rand, as we have seen, property becomes property through the process whereby an individual realizes his or her productivity. Hence she asserts, elsewhere in her essay on patents and copyrights, that "a *discovery* cannot be patented, only an *invention*" (*Capitalism* 130; Rand's emphases). As anyone familiar with debates over the property status of the human genome will recognize, however, it is precisely the transformation of "discoveries" into property to which capitalism has turned in its latest phase. Global capital is currently reorganizing itself around what Caren Irr calls a "virtual land grab," a return to the stage of primitive accumulation whose object this time around is "the sudden and immensely profitable treatment of a vast array of existing relations as property relations":

> In this enclosure of the global textual commons, Disney has seized monopolistic hold over the folk and fairy tales of a Brothers Grimm-type European heritage; Time-Warner aims to acquire exclusive access to recent history in the form of the Zapruder tapes; pharmaceuticals companies lay claim to the biological commons of the rainforests; and corporate-funded geneticists race to see who will decode and patent the information contained in the human genome. By converting existing natural and cultural resources into certain kinds of texts, corporations are now able to claim monopolistic ownership in a range of potentially supervaluable intellectual commodities.[40]

Just as the original phase of primitive accumulation freed the lower classes from feudalism by rendering them landless laborers, so this new phase transforms knowledge and information previously held in common into the site of corporate employees' mental labor. The profits from this labor accrue not to the individual creator claiming his "right to the product of his mind" (Rand, *Capitalism* 130), but rather to the large corporations that manipulate the law to transform found materials into their property.

Within this framework, the notion that mental laborers are entrepreneurs encourages white-collar employees to identify with the corporate owners of intellectual property, just as home ownership encourages the members of the middle class to identify with the owners of property as such. In both cases, big capital benefits from confusion between what it owns—the means of production—and what the members of the middle class own—their labor and (if they are lucky) non-productive personal property. Just because capital has been severed from individual producers and vested in corporate entities does not mean, of course, that it has ceased to exist, or that individuals no longer benefit from it. On the contrary, as Mills argued in 1951, the fact "That the power of property has been bureaucratized in the corporation does not diminish that power; indeed, bureaucracy increases the use and the protection of property power" (111). In this regard, Rand's mistake—which I have been arguing is her failure to distinguish between an earlier model of middle-class small property and property as such—has been an enormously productive one for the last half century of capitalism. Intellectual property law as it has been codified in recent decisions, Irr argues, promotes corporate ownership of texts not only "over public interest in the distribution of knowledge" but also over a largely residual notion of authorship: "in the late twentieth century, the author can be construed as an almost entirely anonymous creature—faceless, factual, dispersed into the events in which he was an integral but somehow also impersonal player."[41] If the author now sounds like a classic postwar organization man, this suggests the extent to which Mills's account of white-collar expropriation has been fulfilled in the new era of intellectual property, in which ideas rather than things have become the characteristic object of production. The academic left has been talking for some time now about how universities are becoming more like businesses, although for the purposes of critiquing contemporary capitalism the larger and more pressing problem may be the fact that businesses are becoming more like universities.

Within this rapidly coalescing regime, academics' understanding of their research work as both craft labor and personal property does not just reflect a general white-collar worldview with its origins in the postwar era and authors like Rand. It also limns the shape of much more profitable sectors of the economy. Take, for instance, the recent debates over music piracy, in which the members of Metallica and other celebrity musicians argued that file sharing abrogated their property rights. At the same time, some artists lower down the record-label food chain argued that they actually profited from file sharing, insofar as most of their income came not from publishing but from touring, for which the dissemination of their music provided publicity.[42] In Mills's terms, we might see artists like Metallica as well-paid employees taking on the mantle of small-property owners for the benefit of big corporations, to the detriment of other artists who are either more exploited employees of the labels or actual small business people. In this case, the nostalgia for the market that we have tracked through Rand's work becomes the basis for the extraction of surplus value from mental laborers carrying on their backs the corpse of what we used to call the middle class.

Notes

1. A somewhat longer version of this essay appears as Chapter One of my book *The Twilight of The Middle Class: Post–World War II American Fiction and White-Collar Work* (Princeton: Princeton University Press, 2005).

2. Sharon Stockton, "Engineering Power: Hoover, Rand, Pound, and the Heroic Architect," *American Literature* 72.4 (December 2000): 813–841; Michael Szalay, *New Deal Modernism: American Literature and the Invention of the Welfare State* (Durham: Duke University Press, 2000), 75–119.

3. Olivier Zunz, "Class," *Encyclopedia of the United States in the Twentieth Century*, ed. Stanley Kutler, Vol. I (New York: Scribner's, 1996), 198.

4. Carol A. Barry, "White-Collar Employment: I—Trends and Structures," *Monthly Labor Review* (January 1961): 11.

5. William H. Whyte, *The Organization Man* (1956; Garden City: Anchor, 1957). For a summary of other arguments in this vein see Richard H. Pells, *The Liberal Mind in a Conservative Age: American Intellectuals in the 1940s and 1950s* (New York: Harper, 1985), 188–216.

6. As Zunz notes, by "1948, the corporate sector held almost 60 percent of national income-producing wealth"(197).

7. Leonard Peikoff, "Introduction to the 35th Anniversary Edition," Ayn Rand, *Atlas Shrugged* (1957; New York: Signet, 1992), 1.

8. Rand, *Atlas Shrugged* 494; Rand's emphases. Hereafter cited parenthetically.

9. C. Wright Mills, *White Collar: The American Middle Classes* (1951; New York: Oxford University Press, 2002), xiv; hereafter cited parenthetically.

10. Alfred Chandler, *The Visible Hand: The Managerial Revolution in American Business* (Cambridge: Harvard University Press, 1977), 3, 79.

11. Jennifer Burns is currently writing a groundbreaking dissertation in the Berkeley history department on the complexities of Rand's reception, including her appeal among small businessmen. See Burns's essay "Godless Capitalism: Ayn Rand and the Conservative Movement," *Modern Intellectual History* 1.3 (November 2004): 1–27.

12. John F. Stover, *American Railroads* (Chicago: University of Chicago Press, 1961), 211.

13. Stover, *American* 210.

14. This is in New York City. Things are even worse in the countryside: "They drove through small towns, through obscure side roads, through the kind of places they had not seen for years. She felt uneasiness at the sight of the towns. Days passed before she realized what it was that she missed most: a glimpse of fresh paint. The houses stood like men in unpressed suits, who had lost the desire to stand straight: the cornices were like sagging shoulders, the crooked porch steps like torn hem lines, the broken windows like patches, mended with clapboard. The people in the streets stared at the new car, not as one stares at a rare sight, but as if the glittering black shape were an impossible vision from another world. There were few vehicles in the streets and too many of them were horsedrawn. She had forgotten the literal shape and usage of horsepower; she did not like to see its return" (263).

15. Stover, *American* 210.

16. Sylvia de Leon, "No Way to Run a Railroad: A Bailout Won't Solve Amtrak's Fundamental Problem," *The Washington Post*, 24 June 2002, http://web. lexis-nexis.com/universe (accessed August 28, 2004).

17. Stover, *American* 252–253.
18. Stover, *American* 217.
19. Kim McQuaid, *Uneasy Partners: Big Business in American Politics, 1945–1990* (Baltimore: Johns Hopkins University Press, 1994).
20. Judith Stein, *Running Steel, Running America: Race, Economic Policy, and the Decline of Liberalism* (Chapel Hill: University of North Carolina Press, 1998), 17, 14.
21. McQuaid, *Uneasy* 48–58; David S. Painter, *Oil and the American Century: The Political Economy of U.S. Foreign Oil Policy, 1941–1945* (Baltimore: Johns Hopkins University Press, 1986).
22. McQuaid 52–54; Stein, *Running* 21.
23. Ayn Rand, *Capitalism: The Unknown Ideal* (New York: Signet, 1967), 102; hereafter cited parenthetically.
24. Paul Krugman, "For Richer," *The New York Times Magazine* (October 20, 2002): 62.
25. See Randy Martin, *On Your Marx: Relinking Socialism and the Left* (Minneapolis: University of Minnesota Press, 2002), 159–183.
26. David Riesman, with Nathan Glazer and Reuel Denney, *The Lonely Crowd: A Study of the Changing American Character* (1950; New Haven: Yale University Press, 1969), 156.
27. Stefano Harney and Frederick Moten, "Doing Academic Work," *Chalk Lines: The Politics of Work in the Managed University*, ed. Randy Martin (Durham: Duke University Press, 1998), 157, 171.
28. Andrew Ross, "The Mental Labor Problem," *Social Text* 18.2 (2000): 2, passim.
29. Szalay, *New Deal* 6, 75–119.
30. Gary S. Becker, *Human Capital: A Theoretical and Empirical Analysis with Special Reference to Education* (New York: National Bureau of Economic Research, 1964), 1.
31. Alain Touraine, *The Post-Industrial Society; Tomorrow's Social History: Classes, Conflicts and Culture in the Programmed Society*, trans. Leonard F. X. Mayhew (1969; New York: Random House, 1971); Daniel Bell, *The Coming of Post-Industrial Society: A Venture in Social Forecasting* (1973; New York: Basic, 1976); David Harvey, *The Condition of Postmodernity: An Inquiry into the Origins of Cultural Change* (Cambridge; Blackwell, 1989); Manuel Castells, *The Rise of the Network Society* (Cambridge; Blackwell, 1996); Michael Hardt and Antonio Negri, *Empire* (Cambridge: Harvard University Press, 2000). The quote is from Hardt and Negri 280.
32. Pierre Bourdieu, *Distinction: A Social Critique of the Judgement of Taste*, trans. Richard Nice (1979; Cambridge: Harvard University Press, 1984), 315.
33. Bell, *Post-Industrial* 410.
34. Bourdieu, *Distinction* 301–303.
35. Stephanie Armour, "Higher Pay May Be Layoff Target," *USA Today*, June 23, 2003, Money, 1B.
36. Tony Lee, "Should You Stay Energized by Changing Your Job Frequently?" CareerJournal.com, http://www.careerjournal.com/jobhunting/strategies/19980111-reisberg.html.
37. Harney and Moten, "Doing" 171, 154–180 passim.
38. Ross, "Mental Labor" 22.
39. Ross, "Mental Labor" 15; Ross's emphasis.

40. Caren Irr, "Literature as Proleptic Globalization, or a Prehistory of the New Intellectual Property," *South Atlantic Quarterly* 100.3 (Summer 2001): 797–798.

41. Irr, "Literature" 795.

42. Brian Mansfield, "When Free Is Profitable," *USA Today*, May 21, 2004, http://web.lexis-nexis.com/universe (accessed August 28, 2004). See also the excellent website www.downhillbattle.org.

Afterword

Chapter 15

Advertisements for Ourselves: Being and Time in a Promotional Economy

Jean-Christophe Agnew

What is your archetypal image of commerce? Is it a seventeenth-century Flemish fair? An eighteenth-century London coffeehouse? A nineteenth-century Moroccan souk? A twentieth-century commodities pit? Fill in the blank. As twenty-first-century commerce slips—click by click—into the placeless void of on-line transactions, nostalgia prods us to remember, or to invent, the intimacies of the arms-length transaction: the cries of street-hawkers, the boasts of market-day vendors, the piles of fresh produce, and the jingle of coin; the higgling, haggling, and handshakes of the open market. Consider for a moment just how many economic textbooks preface their graphs and equations with quaint images of the agora or the bourse. Images that animate the abstractions to follow; images that give life and heft—action and architecture—to the weightless equilibria of supply and demand. Images that naturalize what may seem altogether denatured on paper or flat panel screen.

Not for nothing does Stanford Economics Professor John McMillan title his recent "natural history of the market" *Reinventing the Bazaar*.[1] The bazaar is iconic, aesthetic, photogenic. Its mix of crowds and clientalism—of sociability and negotiability—sets "commerce" aside as an intensely visible and audible form of social action. Neither solidarity as such nor competition as such, commerce has always seemed to economists to be a hybrid of its own—a form of sociability that set humans apart from all other animals.[2] Dogs may hunt in packs and race in packs, but, as Adam Smith once put it, "Nobody ever saw a dog make a fair and deliberate exchange of one bone for another with another dog." To Smith as to the countless economists who have taken their inspiration from him, the free and open commerce of the marketplace dramatizes "a certain propensity in human nature . . . to truck, barter, and exchange one thing for another."[3] It is an axiom that has been endlessly repeated, and endlessly paraphrased. "Man has been defined as a tool-making animal," one recent, illustrated history of financial markets observes. "He could just as well be described as an animal that makes bargains."[4] Our *ur*-image of commerce, it seems, is the point of purchase.

Yet there is something odd here. For if the struck bargain is a stock image of commercial practice, how is it that we encounter these images only in their historical or exotic versions—the bourse and the bazaar again? Why are pictures of contemporary commercial transactions such scarce commodities in the visual culture of our own time? Outside the introductory economics textbook, the proprietary sales training manual, or the occasional caricature, the market transaction—the actual exchange of promises or of goods for money—is a visual taboo, something to be seen only in its soft-core versions, as when smiling sales or service personnel are filmed greeting customers or bidding them good-bye. Even odder, the same euphemistic delicacy toward the crude facts of exchange governs the general business press, where the visual order confines itself for the most part to images of conference rooms, laboratories, hard-hat sites, production facilities, and assembly and distribution areas.[5] It is not so much commerce that is on view in this imagery as it is the division of labor, which Adam Smith theorized as the unintended *consequence* of commerce. Somehow, the camera never seems to catch sight of the coin.

Why does Atlas blink? Why would a market culture devoted to the dream of making the sale, of closing the deal, of getting to "yes," not treat these contractual climaxes as so many Kodak Moments? Where, one might well ask, is the money shot?

One answer would return us to the on-line world where the click of the camera gives way to the click of the keyboard. Commerce relentlessly seeks to reduce its transaction costs, the economic sociologists tell us, so we should not be startled to see handshakes yield to keystrokes, paper money to plastic, and M1 to M2 and M3. By this account, the virtualization of the market is a shortcut—a fast-forward—*to* the transaction, not a jump-cut over it. The split-second quality of contemporary exchange bespeaks the drive to multiply such moments rather than the wish to put them out of sight. Efficiency, not anxiety, is its engine, and any effort (by, say, a historian) to interpret the low public profile of the transactional "moment" as a meaningful cultural puzzle would be dismissed, like the handshake, as a quaint and ultimately superfluous gloss on an otherwise self-evident and self-justifying price-making market process.[6] Yet for all these assurances—and maybe just because of them—the puzzle remains.

Everywhere one looks today, one sees a culture—a world—awash in images of commerce, images produced by and for commerce. This flood has been some time in the making, having begun some two centuries ago as a mere trickle of hoardings, wall posters, and trade cards. Most of this imagery was advertising, some of which fell into the category of institutional or goodwill advertising: a corporation's advertisements for itself. Beginning in the 1920s, however, a small but noticeable fraction of institutional advertising began to be taken out by advertising or public relations agencies themselves in the hope of persuading prospective clients of the necessity of "representing" them. Their message to budget-conscious manufacturers was—and remains today—a simple one: *imaging* business is a cost of *doing* business; it is not just a rational transaction cost, it is an indispensable one. And though historians and social scientists alike have never been able to prove the commercial efficacy of a particular advertising or public relations campaign, the advertising agencies' message has never wavered through the years.[7] To the skeptic who would point to any given advertisement and ask "is this not the sound of one hand clapping," the agency—like so many Zen masters—extends its own hand, pats the client on the shoulder, and assures him that, after all, it is not logic that seals the deal.

Advertising *is* the visible hand of modern commerce. It might even be called its prosthetic arm, reaching out as it does in virtual space to hold a product and its imagined consumer in the best possible light: the light of satisfied ownership. That in doing so, the arm also reaches around and beyond the transactional *moment* should really come as no surprise. As marketing's targeted customer is always a hypothetical and often a composite figure, an advertisement has no other hand to shake but its own.[8] Neither Zen koans nor market research can wish away the fundamental solipsism built into the rhetorical and pictorial conventions of modern advertising.

* * *

It has taken some three decades of work by historians, sociologists, and anthropologists to appreciate how long and how hard the advertising industry has labored to open up this closed circuit of self-referentiality, to reach out and touch someone besides itself. On the other hand, it has taken almost as long for scholars to appreciate what consumers have made of the world of goods pictured for them—how often, for example, consumers have tapped into, without buying into, the advertising's imagery of commerce. A part of that delay may be traced to the problems of the sources themselves: rich as they are on the supply side (ads, agency records, surveys, etc.) and thin and scattered as they are on the demand side (interviews, diaries, letters, oral histories, protests). But it is also the case that in the 1970s and early 1980s the new social history was just coming to maturity, while the new cultural history was busy being born. Historians were in effect customizing theoretical models of the "culture industry" that had been first introduced by the Frankfurt School and the mid-cult critics of the postwar period: fitting these models, in turn, to the "corporate liberal" chassis designed by New Left historians Martin Sklar and James Weinstein and piloting them with members of what Barbara and John Ehrenreich termed the professional-managerial class.[9]

Thirty years ago, Stuart Ewen published *Captains of Consciousness*, a perfect example of this emerging historiographical consensus and a book that, in its own right, launched consumer culture studies on this side of the Atlantic.[10] As much a provocation as an inspiration, Ewen's book took the promotional copy and professional manuals of the advertising industry at their word. What ad agencies and their academic allies promised the corporate liberal leadership of the capitalist class, Ewen argued, was a blueprint for "manufacturing" consumers to the specifications of mass production. As members of the "ideological vanguard of the business community" advertising experts expanded the businessman's vision of social control by shifting the weight of social and cultural citizenship from a work-based to a goods-based footing.[11] Accordingly, images of business as manufacturing—images of labor, machinery, and production—gave way to images of business as commerce: images of the products and services on offer.

Ewen encapsulated this displacement perfectly on the cover of *Captains of Consciousness*, which featured a marvelous 1880s Ivory Soap ad of mustachioed workers washing themselves up after work. Only later was it revealed that Proctor and Gamble had appropriated Thomas Anschutz's austerely classicist painting of an ironworkers' noontime and converted it from a heroic republican frieze to a workaday soap opera. Anschutz's painting was bought by the Rockefellers; the Ivory Soap ad was posted on billboards across the country.[12]

Whether one dates the modernization and professionalization of advertising to the 1920s—as Stuart Ewen's and Roland Marchand's work suggested—or to the turn of the century, as Richard Ohmann's, William Leach's, and Pamela Laird's work argued, there is no mistaking its eventual impact on business's mode of address to the consumer—from "let's talk about me" to "let's talk about you."[13] Look over the color lithographs of advertisements inserted into Laird's book, *Advertising Progress*, and you can immediately see these baby steps away from the familiar entrepreneurial territory of conspicuous production. The images begin with smoking factories as emblematic testimonies to the health and stability of the business enterprise, but they end with Woodbury Soap's celebration of the radiance of the consumer—"the skin you love to touch." True, Ivory's spotless factory workers may not have been the target of Woodbury's (or, for that matter, Ivory's) appeal, but their mere presence in a soap advertisement previewed another of Stuart Ewen's historical themes: namely the story of corporate liberalism's accommodation after 1919 to the labor movement's drive for shorter hours as firms willingly or grudgingly accepted the claim that reduced hours would liberate the waged worker to consume.

As Lawrence Glickman has reminded us, the Ira Stewards and George Guntons of the American labor movement had been making this same argument for years in their campaign for the eight-hour day and the "living wage."[14] But it took decades of class warfare, overproduction, and cyclic depressions to persuade businessmen—most of them in the consumer goods and retail investment sectors—that "Eight hours for what we will" could be translated into "Eight hours for what we sell." Leisure time now figured as prominently as labor time in the corporate profit picture and, correspondingly, in the Ivory Soap advertisement. What Thomas Anschutz had painted as a conspicuously *noontime* scene—the symbolic apex of a producerist's day—Proctor & Gamble turned into a quitting-time scenario, with Anschutz's proud iron puddlers now posing as poster-children for cleanliness. As posters, billboards, and other imagery of commerce multiplied in the years that followed, Americans would discover that time was no less commodified for its being "free," for its being lived outside the work discipline of the office or factory.

*   *   *

Now it goes without saying that time remains one of the critical divisors by which capitalist productivity is calculated—and experienced. Marx was the first to theorize this point when writing of the struggle over the working day in the first volume of *Capital*. But historians, sociologists, economists, and anthropologists (not to mention physicists) have enlarged the topic beyond anything Marx might have imagined in 1867.[15] Shortly after the appearance of *Capital*, neoclassical or so-called "marginalist" economists refined an older, scarcity postulate and made it the foundation for a subjective, time-bound, choice-driven theory of labor, capital investment, and (for the first time) private consumption.[16] Radical as this theoretical shift of focus toward consumption was, marginalists did not at first lose sight of the labor theory of value. A vaguely Dickensian form of the concept lingered in the early work of economist William Stanley Jevons, who calculated the cost of labor as the pain or "negative utility" for which wages were offered in compensation. Subjective as these valuations of labor now were, the final prices of goods that labor produced were—in Jevons's account—still warm with the sweat equity invested in them.[17] A perspirational calculus had yet to become an aspirational one.

What made the difference was the so-called Austrian School of economics, which brought time fully into the neoclassical calculus and which, like Ivory Soap, washed away the last traces of the labor theory of value. Carl Menger and Eugen von Boehm-Bawerk embraced time as an economic category because it was scarce, or rather their commitment to the scarcity postulate converted time itself into a rare commodity: one haunted by the number of other uses (investments, employments, allocations) to which it might have been put. The Austrians calculated the value of labor—indeed the value of any expenditure of energy or resources—by the returns that would have accrued from the unventured alternatives.

From this methodologically individualist perspective, the wage-bargain soon lost any connection to class struggle, even in the faint, residual form that Jevons had given it when he wrote of the wage as compensation for the irksomeness of labor. Labor-*time* became something even less than a negative utility in marginalist theory. Like the images of factories and chimney smoke (and like the images of marketplace transactions), labor as such disappeared from the scene of economic theory. The quality of work, the expectations brought to work, the satisfactions taken from it—all of these yielded pride of place (quite literally) to the expectations that consumers brought to the marketplace and to the utilities they derived from it. Labor-*time* became little more than a black hole, an absence or forfeiture of pleasures whose measure the laborer calibrated introspectively—as a matter of private preferences or trade-offs—rather than collectively, as a matter of shared social claims.[18]

By the turn of the century, then, neoclassical economists had quietly moved the theoretical site of the wage-bargain off the shop-floor, away from the factory gates, and into the "free" space of the box office, the retail counter, and the credit union. The worker had become, by default, a consumer who bargained with and at times against himself, calculating the value of his or her labor-time as the opportunity costs of the leisure alternatives foregone. At least that was the way it was supposed to work on paper, and marginalist theory was nothing if not an effort to move beyond the relatively simple arithmetical formulations of classical and Marxist economics. But mathematically abstract as the marginalist move might have been, it did not occur in a vacuum but rather (as we have seen) at the very moment that the American labor movement was making its own "consumerist turn" toward the politics of the living wage.

Images of labor returned to the foreground of public culture during the crisis of the Great Depression, only to retreat again—where they were not deliberately repressed—in the postwar period.[19] During the 1950s and 1960s, the question of mass leisure that had been first raised during the 1920s became once again a matter of public debate. The irony was that by mid-century, free time—time off the clock, so to speak—was no longer expanding for American workingmen and women. To the contrary, the mid-1940s marked the last, sputtering breath of the movement for a shorter workweek in the United States. UAW leader, Walter Reuther, abandoned the thirty-hour cause in 1945, for instance, arguing instead for "a balanced economy—full production—full consumption."[20] Faced with a choice between higher wages and shorter hours, workers were consistently choosing the former. The trend defied the vision of "democratic" and "distributed leisure" once championed by progressives and the labor Left, but it also flew in the face of conventional neoclassical theory, which had assumed that in full employment economies, workers would invariably trade higher wages for fewer hours.[21]

To resolve this conundrum rational-choice economist Gary Becker wrote a memorable-article in 1965 titled "A Theory of the Allocation of Time" and premised on the characteristically postwar assumption that wage-earning householders controlled far more capital at home than they did where they worked. By Becker's lights, the postwar proliferation of homebuilding, furnishings, cars, appliances, and entertainment technology entitled him to treat the household as if it were a "small factory" maximizing the returns—the utilities or "commodities" as he called them—to its domestic investments. Becker reasoned that big-ticket, more-bang-for-your-buck items reduced the "indirect" or opportunity costs of forgone income imposed on an earners' leisure time by the mere fact of a secular rise in real wages. Rising incomes raised the ante on leisure time, thus inducing breadwinners to choose moonlighting and overtime on one side and "goods-intensive" consumption on the other in lieu of a shorter workday and more time-consuming ("earnings-intensive") recreation.

On the surface, Becker's model appeared to invert the neoclassical labor/leisure indifference curve. Now wages, not leisure, formed the index against which workers weighed the opportunity costs of their "free" time. But Becker was taking his cues from the upward movement of *wages*, not from any improvement in the experience of work itself. His model did nothing to redeem wage-work—its pleasures or its pains—from marginalism's traditional condescension. What it did do was to expand the scene, if not the image, of business to the household by translating and transposing the ideological co-ordinates of labor-time to the time spent and the experiential "commodities" (or utilities) produced *outside* the waged workplace. "[O]ur theory," Becker remarked parenthetically, "emphatically cautions against calling such time 'free.' "[22]

*   *   *

At first glance it might seem that Thorstein Veblen had made much the same point more than a half-century earlier when he theorized the time-savings the Leisure Class gained by trading the *longueurs* of conspicuous leisure for the symbolic efficiencies of goods-intensive or conspicuous consumption.[23] A walking stick telegraphed so much more about status, after all, than the walk itself. And indeed one could hear distinct echoes of the Veblenian critique of an accelerated, emulative consumption drive throughout the 1950s and 1960s—in works like David Potter's *People of Plenty* (1954), John Kenneth Galbraith's *The Affluent Society* (1958), and Vance Packard's *The Status Seekers* (1959). A 1964 collection of essays by David Riesman asked the question *Abundance for What?* As if in reply, Tibor Scitovsky wrote *The Joyless Economy*, published in the same year as Stuart Ewen's *Captains of Consciousness*.[24] The titles alone signaled the ethical, aesthetic, or cultural inflection of the postwar critique—its preoccupation with the psychic and cultural impoverishment of materialism, manipulation, emulation, waste, vulgarization, and embourgeoisement.[25] A member of the New Left, Ewen alone kept faith with Marx. For their part, Potter, Galbraith, and others, inspired as they were by economic institutionalists like Veblen, Wesley Mitchell, and Max Weber, steered clear of the Marxist tradition. And neither they nor Ewen bothered to address the arcana of marginalist theory, much less the "human capital" approach of a Gary Becker.[26]

   Yet in its odd, single-minded way, Becker's economism offered an unexpected consumerist parallel to Marx's producerist account of the trajectory of capitalist enterprise, with its relentless substitution of fixed for variable capital and, of course, its falling rate of profit. Even odder: one of the only, mid-century cultural critics to wrestle with this parallel was Norman Mailer, in a very brief, anecdotal passage from his aptly titled collection, *Advertisements for Myself* (1959). "From Surplus Value to Mass Media" was the title the aging hipster gave his meditation, and in it he pondered a supermarket riddle—a "trivial discrepancy" he called it. Why was it, he asked, that a carton of fresh orange juice cost fifteen cents more than a can of frozen, when the production and distribution costs of fresh juice accounted (by his calculation) for no more than a few cents of the difference? Odds are that the high mark-up reflected the power of an oligopolistic, Florida citrus industry to name its price, but Mailer still wanted to know why the processors thought the ten-cent increment for fresh orange juice would not drive consumers to the concentrate.[27]

To answer his own question, Mailer began by performing what might be called a "Becker." Imagining a generic wage worker who earned $3 an hour but who valued his leisure at $6 an hour *or ten cents a minute*, Mailer hypothesized "that a covert set of values in the consumer" equated the "three or four minutes assembly time" saved by buying fresh juice at a "ten-cent mark-up" as equivalent to a "saving of 30 to 40 ideal cents of his pleasure time." The dime pocketed by the "entrepreneur," Mailer concluded (abruptly leaving the world of opportunity costs for the world of surplus value) amounted to a "secondary exploitation" extracted from "the consumer's at-home working time" and driven by the consumer's own desire to protect his discretionary leisure. To Mailer this trade-off marked the arrival of a new political and psychic economy in which profit was extracted *outside* the waged workplace by ransoming the consumer's private "pleasure time" from the clutches of household obligations. "Over the economy as a whole," Mailer added, "this particular germ of profit . . . is not at all trivial."[28]

For those who suspect that Norman Mailer never thawed, much less made, a quart of frozen orange juice in his life, his effort to duplicate the classic opening paragraphs of *Capital* may seem a tad disingenuous. But, for that matter, one may reasonably doubt that Marx ever squeezed a fresh orange in his life. And, as Mailer himself acknowledged elsewhere in *Advertisements*, there was as much marijuana as Marx in his mind at the time of these ruminations. Nowhere in his calculations had Mailer considered, for example, the savings afforded the manufacturer and distributor by the concentrate's extended shelf life: a savings passed through to the consumer. A corporate food-processor's ability to finesse the seasons and to slow even entropy itself by turning perishables into near-durables had its parallel in the price-conscious homemaker looking to synchronize shopping and freshness to a weekly schedule of family meals, a homemaker ready—or resigned—to assembling and redistributing the final product. What Mailer discovered in *her* place was the price he would have to pay for *his* convenience, namely the pleasure of finding fresh-squeezed orange juice in his refrigerator.

Convenience is what advertisers touted in 1959, and convenience is presumably what consumers wanted, as convenience refers by definition to that which is quick, suitable, and accessible to the user.[29] Yet we should not be too quick to dismiss Mailer's lunge at political economy because he ignored the gendered aspects of frozen and fresh in the 1950s. For a good part of that decade, the frozen food industry did as well.[30] The word "convenience" may draw upon the lexicon of freedom, it may promise the reduction of effort, it may accent the discretion in discretionary income, but it is for all that a thoroughly contextualized term: unthinkable except in relation to the established habits—the *habitus*—of social life and social time. As the anthropologist Sidney Mintz demonstrated brilliantly years ago, sugar may have begun its commodity life as a status or positional good, but it came into its own as a convenience food in the political economy of industrialized England. There it served as a quick, suitable, and accessible stimulant for the new factory workers—more pick-me-up for the pence, so to speak; a trans-Atlantic balancing, as Mintz, put it, of the industrial revolution's caloric accounts.[31]

A balancing, let us add, keyed to the availability of wages *and* to the constraints of industrialism capitalism's new workday. By "provisioning, sating—and, indeed, drugging—farm and factory workers," Mintz concluded, "sugar and other drug foods . . . sharply reduced the overall cost of creating and reproducing the metropolitan proletariat."[32] We should take special note of this historical example of externally scheduled preferences, Mintz added, because it predates and prefigures our own situation; one in which the extraordinary growth of convenience foods—often packaged in an outer skin of sugar and fat—occurs in tandem with a workday whose length and "flexibility" depends in considerable part upon the "convenience" of the snack-form. Setting aside Mintz's comments on the dietary and social costs of this liberatory regime—namely, the loss of nutrition and commensality—consider only what he calls the "time-formula" in which the new consumption is implicated:

> One of the effects [Mintz writes] of changing the time formula is that it subtly recasts people's images of their lives and of themselves. How much time people actually have for different pursuits, how much time they believe they have, and the relationship between these are aspects of daily life shaped by externalities and, in particular in the modern world, by the reorganization of the workday. What seems visible to the worker, however, are the changed conditions of work. These new conditions shape in turn what is left of his time; yet how much time one 'has' may be only fleetingly perceived as dependent, ultimately, on the work regime. People live inside the time they think they have; they may experience subjective changes in their moods, conditioned by their ability to live up to (or, often, not to live up to) their own standards of performance; but only now and then do they conceive of their performance as affected by alterations that give and take away time, or their will to feel they are controlling the use of time.[33]

"Only now and then do they conceive." Mintz's hint of the occasional economic and political epiphany returns us to Norman Mailer's kitchen as an image of commerce, a setting for marginalist *and* Marxist computations. There we see the Author, gazing balefully at the package of Minute Maid as it unaccountably melts in his hand, wondering to himself on whose time-card is to be credited the contemplated labor of "opening [the] can, mixing the frozen muddle with three cans of water, and shaking."[34] Not an idle question for a stoned freelance writer, nor for a sober homemaker; nor for that matter for the Imagineers of retail.

Self-service and do-it-yourself may be unwaged labor, but they are no less labor for that. And according to those who have researched the so-called "service encounter," the customer who walks into a store, selects a good (say, frozen concentrated orange juice), brings it home, and assembles it should be considered a "partial employee" for the unpaid labor that would otherwise be the store's responsibility.[35] That the wage "earned" by this "employee" takes the form of a putative price-savings only underscores the arbitrariness of the boundary separating the work of selling from the work of buying.

Why, then, should this particular scene of business—the "servicescape" as it is currently called—stop arbitrarily at the doors of the store, or its parking lot? Why should our image of commerce not include the home where the big-ticket freezer sits keeping the "inputs" on ice while the "partial employee" recalculates the earnings forgone, the leisure forfeited, or the surplus value lost by assembling the product? And which index, which metric, which *numéraire*, should the "partial employee" use to arbitrage the opportunity costs of, say, an afternoon at the mall? Compelled as they are to shuttle daily, sometimes hourly, across an intricate servicescape of incommensurable labor time zones, is it any wonder that "every now and then" consumers should feel themselves, like the befuddled Norman Mailer, thrust outside the "time they live inside?"

*   *   *

But wait, a skeptic might reply. Such questions are largely rhetorical in that they assume what needs to be proved: that consumers actually lose sleep, or heart, from the pressures to perform this kind of mental accounting. Yes, the skeptic admits, a shop steward might compute such labor-leisure trade-offs for his union membership, but only sociologists and market researchers would care enough to press *consumers* about the order or transitivity of their time-preferences—what Mailer called their "covert set of values."[36] Leave it to the talking cure of the focus group to coax such epiphanies about personal "time formulas" out of the average consumer.

Focus groups are familiar instruments of market research, just as market research is an adjunct of advertising and advertising is, in turn, the main subject of focus groups. Consumer surveys, questionnaires, even "cool-hunting" feed a running cultural commentary that advertising performs upon itself. It is these questions that are rhetorical, for by couching them in the language of choice, rank, and preference, market research invites the consumer to live, if not love, the drama of opportunity costs. Any answer implicitly enacts and endorses the marginalist theoretical protocols that frame the questions. When it comes to market research, we are all seasoned test-takers: we know what will be on the exam.

And so we find ourselves once again within mass marketing's self-referential circuit, yet this time we may take our cue from Norman Mailer himself, who in his little essay of 1959 concluded that "[s]o soon . . . as the surplus labor of the proletariat comes to be replaced by the leisure-value given up by the consumer, *the real expropriator of the wage-earner has to become the mass-media. . . .*"[37] Suggestive as the line was, Mailer's economic imagination

failed him at that point in the essay, and he lapsed into a conventional 1950s
screed about mass-mediated and manipulated needs. It was thus left to later
writers to follow up on the inferences to be drawn from Mailer's—and
Becker's—thoughts on the allocation and assessment of time in postwar
consumer culture: thoughts that converged on the view that, as a matter of
time-budgets and cost-accounting, the scene of business now included the
household itself. One short but critical step in this logic remained: to see
advertising—or more precisely, the attention given by a household to ads and
commercials—as itself a claim upon the "partial employee's" labor time.

It was during the 1920s—salad days for the advertising industry—that
marketing and merchandising professionals stumbled upon the problem of
the consumer's limited attention. Even with shorter workweeks, potential
customers were subject to competing and burdensome claims upon their
unwaged time, and these importunities inevitably slowed consumption
down. First, there was the explosion of advertising itself, which, operating as
a form of psychic clutter, threatened to distract consumers from any particular
merchandising appeal. Beyond that, as Catherine Gudis has shown,
marketers of the 1920s faced a population in movement, easily diverted by
what they saw passing outside the trolley, the elevated, or the automobile
window.[38] At the very moment, then, that market researchers had the
consumer squared up in their sights, the moment itself threatened to shrink
to nothing. To be sure, most of the marketing science of this period was, as
I have suggested, an advertisement for itself: pseudoscience aimed at potential corporate clients. But the numbers game did capture—symptomatically at
least—the dawning realization among marketing professionals that
consumers' leisure time or, more specifically, their isolatable units of
consumer attention, were themselves scarce commodities that could be
"purchased" (or sold), first as a matter of media access and second as a matter
of eye-catching promotional strategies.

Call this principle the Tinker Bell Effect insofar as it treats the value of ads,
things, and people as rising and falling in proportion to the attention "paid"
to them or the recognition "earned" by them. Or, following Roland
Marchand, call it the "parable of the first impression," in keeping with the
interwar advertising campaigns that warned consumers of the make-or-break
impact of their personal appearance in a world afflicted by attention-deficit
disorder. For copywriters and commercial artists, Marchand suggested, the
parable of the first impression had both its origin and its validation in the
nerve-wracking experience of pitching ad campaigns to corporate clients—
another instance, if we need one, of advertising's self-referentiality.[39]

We can never know whether this new notion of commodifiable units of
attention span was experientially or experimentally generated—whether it
was the product of autobiography or automobility. A little of both, no doubt.
But that said, it is still possible to look at the charts and graphs of twentieth-
century marketing manuals and make out, however dimly, the silhouette of
what the communications theorist, Dallas Smythe, would later call the
"audience commodity." By that he meant the labor power of spectatorship

that media-audiences exercised in exchange for the so-called "free lunch" of programming—a labor power (or time) that the media could then turn around and sell to advertisers.[40]

Writing at roughly the same moment as *Captains of Consciousness* and three decades after the advent of television, Smythe argued that the effort to make one's way through the cognitive and affective clutter of the advertising mindscape was *labor* for both consumer and advertiser. To grasp that point was also to appreciate advertising's tendency to speed-up, to compress, to contrive some form of visual hieroglyphic or audio hook as a tactical response to the consumer's inclination to soldier, to fall into a fugue state, or to zap commercials. In this give-and-take emerged a parallel, however muted, to the familiar Taylorist battles of the factory floor. But it was a parallel, Smythe added, that had so far passed unremarked by Marxists. Even Mailer, as we have seen, failed to realize that his calculations of the earnings-intensive assembly-time of Minute Maid orange juice could be just as easily applied to the earnings-intensive audience-time of Minute Maid commercials on radio or television. Western Marxists' stubborn loyalty to a nineteenth-century labor metaphysic, Smythe concluded, had blinded them to the presence of this new "job front," this new "leisured" frontier of effort, value, and struggle. Transfixed by the brawny ironworker, Marxists had overlooked the soft soap.[41]

And the soft sell as well. It is a long way from Ivory soap to Woodbury soap, or from the soap that floats to the skin you want to touch, and class conflict alone will not get one there. Race and gender figure in that odyssey as well, but I shall set those categories to the side for the moment so as not to lose sight of the free-labor commodity of a consumer's attention. Take the former domestic science pioneer, Christine Frederick, for example. When Frederick turned her interest in scientific management from household engineering to her husband's field of advertising and in 1929 published her classic, *Selling Mrs. Consumer*, she wrote of enhancing the power of women as domestic "purchasing agents." But the absence of the preposition—Selling *to* Mrs. Consumer—quietly acknowledged the operative if not fully avowable presence of the audience commodity that Frederick's book was likewise marketing to advertisers: namely Mrs. Consumer's attention span.[42] As more and more women like Frederick moved in and out of the waged workplace after 1929, this traffic could only amplify the commodification of personal or so-called leisure time as a private and familial opportunity cost. Postwar boycotts of soap and other household items in response to aggressive radio advertising speak—as Kathy Newman has recently pointed out—to the growing conviction among homemakers that they were being sold, not just sold *to*.[43]

*　*　*

Commodity epiphanies of this order are rare and easily dismissed by (male) authorities as trivial or domestic.[44] But if Norman Mailer's Marxist illumination amid the orange juice cans in his kitchen lacks the grandeur of, say, Perry

Miller's Calvinist revelation amid the oil drums in Africa, it can still be sufficiently jarring to thrust contemporary readers momentarily outside the "time we live inside." Mailer's and Becker's use of metaphorical commodification, their almost insouciant and incongruous mixing of traditionally incommensurable life-worlds, can still elicit the slight but palpable *frisson* of the surreal.[45] On the other hand, when these "perspectives by incongruity" turn out to be the musings of a moralist or the modelings of an economist, there is a palpable sense of relief, of things falling back into place.[46] As with the missing imagery of the commercial transaction, an elaborate and largely unexamined etiquette governs what we say and what we show as we toggle between market and non-market moments and settings.

Most marketing manuals today display an over-riding anxiety about the mere appearance of commodification. "There is no such thing as a commodity," one marketing expert assures his professional readers. "All goods and services can be differentiated. . ."[47] The nightmare on Elm Street or Madison Avenue (they are both equally fictional places) is the fear that the consumer will be made to feel herself, her time, or her preferences to be in one way or another fungible. To deflect and defeat these anxieties, marketing theorists write with an enthusiasm bordering on hysteria of the need for "customer intimacy" and "permission marketing"—of tailoring, fitting, coaching, and partnering one's customers—all of which begins to sound suspiciously like the *Joy of Sex*: as if Walter Dill Scott, the founder of advertising psychology, had returned as Alex Comfort.

Seduction has long been a part of the appeal—and the critique—of advertising, but the ideal customer relationship imagined in contemporary marketing literature more closely resembles a companionate marriage than a courtship—a relation calibrated, perhaps, to the imagined community of full and "partial" employees. "The goal," one recent marketing manual offers, "is to draw the customer into the process of designing, producing, packaging and/or delivering the item." Thus arises "the great feeling with which new Saturn car owners leave the lot after every employee in the place gathers round to clap and celebrate their purchase."[48] Tinker Bell on the car lot; neither Updike nor Mamet could imagine the amount of theater-work incorporated into such retail strategies.[49]

What manuals like these invariably gloss over, however, are the labor theories guiding the employees in their performances: Should they be consulting Stanislavsky? Strasberg? Grotowski? To write of these matters would be more than a little awkward, as it would inevitably bring up the undebited costs to retail workers of what the sociologist Arlie Hochschild has called the "emotional labor" of a service economy, an economy, that is, in which the goods on offer are increasingly "experiential" ones.[50] What, after all, is the shelf-life of a frozen smile? How long should it take to thaw, and whose labor time is that? Were someone to paint a "Service-Worker's Noontime," would we be watching employees wiping the smiles off their faces?

The question may (again) be regarded as rhetorical, but it should be clear by now that the rhetoric of the market—metaphorical commodification, for example—is (like the imagery of commerce) of a piece with the calculative behavior and feeling rules it licenses. Sociologist Michel Callon contends that the language of the market is itself a self-fulfilling protocol, that it helps frame, format, and fit commercial behavior within the flow and entanglements of any particular culture.[51] Some two and a half centuries before Callon, however, Adam Smith went even farther, treating the "propensity . . . to truck and barter and exchange" not as the prime mover of social life but as "founded," in turn, on "the natural inclination everyone has to persuade." "The offering of a shilling," Smith went on, "is in reality offering an argument to persuade one to do so and so as it is for his interest. Men always endeavor to persuade others to be of their opinion even when the matter is of no consequence to them . . . ."[52] When these thoughts are joined to Smith's ideas on society, sympathy, and self-presentation in *The Theory of Moral Sentiments* (1759), the image of business turns inside out. Advertising no longer appears as the prosthetic arm of commerce; to the contrary, commerce appears as the prosthetic arm of self-advertising. From this perspective, the stability and flow of social life—and commerce—hang on the mutual exchange of attention to the advertisements that we make for ourselves.[53] Attention must be paid. We are all Tinker Bells.

Persuasion is hard work, all the more so if the advertisements for ourselves are offered on behalf of others. At the end of the day, as Arlie Hochschild and others have observed, retail and service employees are repeatedly left wondering which feelings belong to them and which to their employers; or, in other words, how far and how deep their bodies and their minds have been incorporated into a packaged consumer experience. Not surprisingly, we are told, employees devise defenses that imagine a "real" or "core" gestalt of feeling that is then jealously concealed and guarded from the "quality assurance" teams of the company—an intriguing wage-work parallel to Norman Mailer's concept of the consumer's wish to protect his "private, productive time."[54]

Service unions at first lagged behind market researchers in their response to these unrecorded levies upon the selves of their members. A 1985 *Journal of Marketing* article, for example, briefly pondered the "legal and ethical issues" that might "arise from organizations' attempts to 'package' their employees." Should every moment of the service encounter be "tightly scripted," the authors asked, "or should individual actors be allowed to ad-lib by improvising unique identities on the service stage?"[55] Fifteen years later, Verizon settled a strike with the Communications Workers of America, which had called for more improvisatory control over the telephone scripts the company had required its customer representatives to follow. The company script, one striker was quoted as saying, "fights with the inner part of me."[56] Phrased in this way, such poignantly existential formulations may strike a discordant note to the postmodern ear, but at minimum they represent a strategic essentialism pitted against the corporate expectation that full (and partial) employees may be drafted into the rites of retail performativity: that for minimum wage and less they must become walking emoticons, animatronic faces, or "communicative containers" for the "experiential commodities" on sale.[57]

Once, long ago, unions fought over company stores and company scrip. Today they fight over company stages and company scripts. But in a sense the contest remains the same: the struggle over labor time and the labor commodity. When, then, does that work-time begin and when does it end? How expansive is the place, the "scene," of business, and how much of the employee's self is for sale? Finally, by what (and whose) metric should it all be calculated? In the new marketplace—the site of flex time, free agency, portfolio careers, and the "company of one"—there is no single, Archimedean point from which to pry open and audit the secrets of surplus value, opportunity costs, or even productivity.[58] Mailer, then, is scarcely alone in his confusions. Accounting as a practice, the sociologists tell us, is "riven with tensions as to its identity and its boundaries," tensions induced in part by accounting's gradual incorporation of Gary Becker's (and Ronald Coase's) version of the opportunity cost. Bottom line: accounting is most appropriately seen as a "form of bricolage, an activity whose tools are largely improvised and adapted to the tasks and materials at hand"—adapted sometimes quite "aggressively," as Enron and other disasters have taught us.[59]

So Atlas is not the only titan to have blinked. For all the paperwork, the audits, the contracts, the stock quotes, the indexes—the stream of market data that "crawls" under the news of the day—we hardly ever see represented the consummatory moment of commerce: the bargain, the handshake, the meeting of minds, the name on the check. (Checks are enlarged and displayed only when they are donated to charities.) This is so, as I have intimated, not just because of commerce's entry into the virtual world of on-line, microsecond transactions. Long before the arrival of digital technology, Americans already inhabited a commercial culture whose central visual and performative practice—advertising—had framed, formatted, and fitted experience to the virtual, "as if" matrix of the opportunity cost. In such a life-world of imagined transactions, internal trade-offs, and hypothetical returns, the actual bargain, when struck, arrives already hedged by the regret of forgone "earnings." Keatsian as this moment may seem, American literature has been as leery of such moments as American visual culture. As Adam Smith once observed, "No one ever made a Bargain in verse."[60]

Prose is another matter, and in this respect, economic theory as—in Smith's phrase—a "language of Business" has occupied a large place in my story of lost bargains. Theory has operated as a charter for commercial practice, as a model of commercial experience, and, occasionally, as a perspective by incongruity. For all its abstraction, theory furnishes images of business and models of commerce, and like literature, it makes visible social and material relationships that would otherwise go unremarked. But its epiphanies are balanced by its blindspots, so what economic theory can deliver in the end may—like accounting—come closer to translucence than transparency.

Still, for all the failings of economic theory—Marxist and marginalist, institutional and neo-institutional—it has kept its eye, and ours, on time: work hours, investment terms, attention spans, lived time. Cultural historians have written a good deal about time-formulas in other epochs and other modes of production—early modern, early industrial, slave, and so on—but very little about the time of late capitalism.[61] But as the workday continues to be reparceled and redistributed, the definition of labor time and its compensation may again be an issue of hot dispute. And in that event, the movers and shakers may well be the part-time and the "partial" employees: the corporals of consciousness.

Notes

1. John McMillan, *Reinventing the Bazaar: A Natural History of the Market* (New York: Norton, 2002); as it happens, there are very few studies of the images and artifacts of commerce, see, for example, Elizabeth A. Honig, *Painting and the Market in Early Modern Antwerp* (New Haven: Yale University Press, 1998); Michael Augsberger, *An Economy of Abundant Beauty: Fortune Magazine and Depression America* (Ithaca: Cornell University Press, 2004); Elspeth H. Brown, *The Corporate Eye: Photography and the Rationalization of American Commercial Culture* (Baltimore: Johns Hopkins University Press, 2005); otherwise one is left to coffee-table books designed for business gifts, such as Daniel Okrent, ed., *Fortune: The Art of Covering Business* (New York: Gibbs Smith, 1999).

2. See, for example, Clifford Geertz, "Suq: The Bazaar Economy of Sefrou," in *Meaning and Order in Moroccan Society*, Clifford Geertz, Hildren Geertz, and Lawrence Rosen, eds. (New York: Columbia University Press, 1979); Lawrence Rosen, *Bargaining for Reality: The Construction of Social Relations in a Muslim Community* (Chicago: University of Chicago Press, 1984).

3. Adam Smith, *An Inquiry into the Nature and Causes of the Wealth of Nations* (New York: Modern Library, 1965), 13.

4. Christopher Finch, *In the Market: The Illustrated History of the Financial Markets* (New York: Abbeville Press, 2001), 14.

5. An exception to this rule are retail trade journals, which of necessity must address the visual dimension of commerce in precise detail; see also Dan Weiner, *America Worked: The 1950s' Photography of Dan Weiner*, William A. Ewing, ed. (New York: Abrams, 1989) and, for a surreal example, Tim B. Wride, *Retail Fictions: The Commercial Photography of Ralph Bartholomew, Jr.* (Los Angeles: L.A. Museum of Art, 1998).

6. See, for example, the views of one of the leading exponents of the New Institutionalist Economics, Oliver Williamson: "The legal philosopher Lon Fuller distinguished between 'essentials' and 'tosh,' where the former involves an examination of the 'rational core' and 'tosh' is preoccupied with 'superfluous rituals, rules of procedure without clear purpose, [and] needless precautions preserved through habit. . . . a place should be made for 'tosh,' but 'tosh' should be kept in its place. . . . 'Tosh' is arguably more important in non-commercial circumstances—state, family, religion—than in the commercial sector. . . . 'Tosh' is a source of interesting variety and adds to the spice of life. Core features of the institutional environment . . . are arguably more important, however, to the study of comparative economic organizations"; "Transaction Cost Economics and Organization Theory," in *The Handbook of Economic Sociology*, Neil J. Smelser and Richard Swedborg, eds. (Princeton: Princeton University Press, 1994), 97–98.

7. See, for example, Michael Schudson, *Advertising, the Uneasy Persuasion: Its Dubious Impact on American Society* (New York: Basic Books, 1984); Roland Marchand, *Creating the Corporate Soul: The Rise of Corporate Public Relations and Corporate Imagery in American Big Business* (Berkeley: University of California Press, 1998).

8. The closer one gets to commerce of local provisioning—high periodicity consumption, in Mary Douglas's and Baron Isherwood's phrase—the less these observations apply to the corresponding advertising, which will tend to foreground bargains, as in the bazaar. That said, advertising's mode of address to, say, the supermarket shopper may be at some distance from the actual ritual processes at play in the shopping experience itself, as Daniel Miller has argued in *A Theory of Shopping* (Ithaca: Cornell University Press, 1998); cf. also Mary Douglas and Baron Isherwood, *The World of Goods: Towards an Anthropology of Consumption* (New York: Norton, 1979), chapter 6.

9. Sklar, James Weinstein, *The Corporate Ideal in the Liberal State, 1900–1918* (Boston: Beacon Press, 1968); Barbara and John Ehrenreich, "The Professional-Managerial Class," *Radical America* 11 (April 1977), 7–22; Jean-Christophe Agnew, "A Touch of Class: The Professional-Managerial Debate," *Democracy* 3 (Spring 1983), 59–72; Val Burns, "The Discovery of the New Middle Class," *Theory and Society* 15 (1986), 317–349.

10. Stuart Ewen, *Captains of Consciousness: Advertising and the Social Roots of the Consumer Culture* (New York: McGraw-Hill, 1976); Daniel J. Boorstin's book, *The Americans: the Democratic Experience* (New York: Random House, 1973), had appeared three years before and had taken a quite different tack toward the chronology and impact of American consumer culture; interestingly, it did not appear in Ewen's bibliography, and it was Ewen's argument, not Boorstin's that served initially as both model and foil for the first generation of consumer culture historians.

11. Ewen, *Captains of Consciousness*, 33, 53, 28.

12. Anschutz's painting was given to the de Young Museum in San Francisco by Mr. and Mrs. John D. Rockefeller, III in 1979, roughly a century after it was made; see Frank H. Goodyear, Jr., "Ironworkers: Noontime" *American Art Review* 1 (January–February 1974).

13. Roland Marchand, *Advertising the American Dream: Making Way for Modernity, 1920–1940* (Berkeley: University of California Press, 1985); Richard M. Ohmann, *Selling Culture: Magazines, Markets and Class at the Turn of the Century* (New York: Verso, 1996); William Leach, *Land of Desire: Merchants, Power, and the Rise of a New American Culture* (New York: Pantheon, 1993); Pamela Laird, *Advertising Progress: American Business and the Rise of Consumer Marketing* (Baltimore: Johns Hopkins University Press, 1998).

14. Lawrence B. Glickman, *A Living Wage: American Workers and the Making of a Consumer Society* (Ithaca: Cornell University Press, 1997).

15. See, for example, E.P. Thompson, "Time, Work-Discipline, and Industrial Capitalism," *Past & Present* 38 (December 1967), 56–97; Daniel T. Rodgers, *The Work Ethic in Industrial America, 1850–1920* (Chicago: University of Chicago Press, 1978); David S. Landes, *Revolution in Time: Clocks and the Making of the Modern World* (Cambridge, Mass: Harvard University Press, 1983); Lawrence O'Malley, *Keeping Watch: A History of American Time* (New York: Viking Penguin, 1990); Mark M. Smith, *Mastered by the Clock: Time, Slavery, and Freedom in the American South* (Chapel Hill: University of North Carolina Press, 1997).

16. Nicholas Xenos, *Scarcity and Modernity* (London: Routledge, 1989); Simon Clarke *Marx, Marginalism and Modern Sociology: From Adam Smith to Max Weber* (London: Macmillan, 1982), 152–154; the classic formulation of the scarcity postulate is to be found in Lionel Robbins, *An Essay on the Nature and Significance of Economic Science* [1932] 3rd edition (London: Macmillan, 1984), 16.

17. William Stanley Jevons, *The Theory of Political Economy* [1871] (Harmondsworth, U.K.: Penguin, 1970), 190–198.

18. David A. Spencer, "From Pain Cost to Opportunity Cost: The Eclipse of the Quality of Work as a Factor in Economic Theory," *History of Political Economy* 36 (Summer 2004): 387–400.

19. See Marlene Park and Gerald E. Markowitz, *Democratic Vistas: Post Offices and Public Art in the New Deal* (Philadelphia: Temple University Press, 1984); Barbara Melosh, *Engendering Culture: Manhood and Womanhood in New Deal Public Art and Theater* (Washington, D.C.: Smithsonian Press, 1991); Michael Denning, *The Cultural Front: The Laboring of American Culture in the Twentieth Century* (New York: Verso, 1997).

20. Reuther quoted in Gary Cross, *Time and Money: The Making of Consumer Culture* (London: Routledge, 1993), 190.

21. The end of the shorter-hours movement in the United States (in contrast to continental Europe) is a complex one and is well told in Cross and Benjamin Kline Hunnicutt, *Work Without End: Abandoning Shorter Hours for the Right to Work* (Philadelphia: Temple University Press, 1988); Hunnicutt (pp. 142–143) sees the 1920s as the moment when leisure was widely redefined as an alternative to (rather than a recreational enhancement of) work; some researchers have suggested a correlation between the intensification of advertising and the freezing of the industrial work week at forty hours; John Brack and Keith Cowling, "Advertising and Labour Supply: Workweek and Workyear in U.S. Manufacturing Industries, 1919–76," *Kyklos* 36 (1983), 285–303.

22. Gary S. Becker, "A Theory of the Allocation of Time," *Economic Journal,* LXXV (September 1965), 493–517; see also the discussion in Cross, 195; Alfred Gill, *The Anthropology of Time: Cultural Constructions of Temporal Maps and Images* (Oxford: Berg, 1992), chapter 21.

23. Thorstein Veblen, *The Theory of the Leisure Class: An Economic Study of Institutions* [1899] (New York: New American Library, 1953), chapter 4.

24. David M. Potter, *People of Plenty: Abundance and the American Character* (Chicago: University of Chicago Press, 1954); John Kenneth Galbraith, *The Affluent Society* (Boston: Houghton, Mifflin, 1948); Vance Packard, *The Status Seekers: An Exploration of Class Behavior in America and the Hidden Barriers that Affect You, Your Community, Your Future* (New York: D. McKay, 1959); David Riesman, *Abundance for What?* (Garden City: Doubleday, 1964); Tibor Scitovsky, *The Joyless Economy: An Inquiry into Human Satisfaction and Consumer Dissatisfaction* (New York: Oxford University Press, 1976); see also Daniel Horowitz, *Vance Packard and American Social Criticism* (Chapel Hill: University of North Carolina Press, 1994) and *The Anxieties of Affluence: Critiques of American Consumer Culture, 1939–1979* (Amherst: University of Massachusetts Press, 2004).

25. The critique continues in the work of Robert H. Frank, *Choosing the Right Pond: Human Behavior and the Quest for Status* (Oxford: Oxford University

Press, 1985) and *Luxury Fever: Why Money Fails to Satisfy in an Era of Excess* (New York: Free Press, 1999); Juliet B. Schor, *The Overspent American: Upscaling, Downshifting, and the New Consumer* (New York: Basic Books, 1998); Robert E. Lane, *The Loss of Happiness in Market Democracies* (New Haven: Yale University Press, 2000); John De Graef, David Wann, Thomas H. Naylor, *Affluenza: The All-Consuming Epidemic* (San Francisco: Barrett Koehler, 2001); Jane Hammerslough, *Dematerializing: Taming the Power of Possessions* (New York: Perseus Press, 2002); Tim Kasser, *The High Price of Materialism* (Cambridge: MIT Press, 2002); Peter C. Whybrow, *American Mania: When More is Not Enough* (New York: W.W. Norton, 2005). James Twitchell has mounted a spirited defense of emulative materialism in a number of recent books, including *Lead Us Into Temptation: The Triumph of American Materialism* (New York: Columbia University Press, 1999) and Pierre Bourdieu has reformulated Veblen and redeemed a flamboyant working-class consumer aesthetic in his influential *Distinction: A Social Critique of the Judgment of Taste* (Cambridge: Harvard University Press, 1984); see also Shelley Nickles, "More is Better: Mass Consumption, Gender, and Class Identity in Postwar America," *American Quarterly* 54 (December, 2002): 581–622; neither Bourdieu's nor Nickles' arguments, it should be said, are at odds with Becker's.

26. Two important exceptions were Fred Hirsch, *Social Limits to Growth* (Cambridge: Harvard University Press, 1976), especially chapter 6, and Staffan Linder's short and witty critique, *The Harried Leisure Class* (New York: Columbia University Press, 1970).

27. Shane Hamilton discovered that in the case of frozen concentrated orange juice—a wartime creation of government researchers—Florida growers did not use technology to even out seasonal supplies but instead used their market position to profit from bumper crops and damaged crops alike, thus mocking both rational-choice and Maileresque models; see "Cold Capitalism: The Political Ecology of Frozen Concentrated Orange Juice," *Agricultural History* 77 (Fall 2003), 557–581; "The Economies and Conveniences of Modern-Day Living: Frozen Foods and Mass Marketing, 1945–1965," *Business History Review* 77 (Spring 2003), 33–60.

28. Norman Mailer, "From Surplus Value to the Mass Media," *Advertisements for Myself* (New York: G.P. Putnam's, 1959), 398–401.

29. The meanings of "convenience" and "commodity" have historically overlapped: "advantage," "expediency," etc. Commodification is the critical "convenience" of a market economy, of course.

30. Shane Hamilton points out that the frozen food industry first marketed their products as luxury goods ("built-in maid service" was the slogan), then as high quality, low price goods for white suburban homemakers, and finally (late 1950s) as niche-products for a segmented market. Just as Mailer characteristically ignored the women who actually "assembled" the frozen orange juice in most households, so the frozen food industry (Hamilton observes) ignored working women as customers until the late 1950s; "The Economies and Conveniences of Modern-Day Living." Jeanne Boydston's *Home and Work: Housework, Wages, and the Ideology of Labor in the Early Republic* (New York: Oxford University Press, 1990) shows how the emergence of wage labor as an ideological system rendered women's housework invisible in the ledger of the larger economy; Mailer's marxisant musings left it, unwittingly, a bit more discernible.

31. Sidney Mintz, *Sweetness and Power: The Place of Sugar in Modern History* (New York: Viking, 1985).

32. Mintz, *Sweetness and Power*, 180.

33. Mintz, *Sweetness and Power*, 204.

34. Mailer, *Advertisements*, 398.

35. See, for example, Peter K. Mills and James H. Morris, "Clients as 'Partial' Employees of Service Organizations: Role Development in Client Participation," *Academy of Management Review* 11 (October 1986), 726–735; Mary Jo Bitner, "Servicescapes: The Impact of Physical Surroundings and Employee Responses on Customers and Employees," *Journal of Marketing* 56 (April 1992), 57–71; Chris Manolis, Laurie A. Meamber, Robert D. Winsor, Charles M. Brooks, "Partial Employees and Consumers: A Postmodern Meta-Theoretical Perspective for Services Marketing," *Marketing Theory* 1 (2001): 225–243; and John A. Czepiel, Michael R. Solomon, Carol F. Surprenant, eds., *The Service Encounter: Managing Employee/Customer Interaction in Service Businesses* (Lexington, Mass: Lexington Books 1985).

36. See, for instance, Frances Leclerc, Bernd H. Schmitt, Laurette Dube, "Waiting Time and Decision Making: Is Time Like Money?" *Journal of Consumer Research* 22 (June 1995), 110–119; A. Peter McGraw, Philip E. Tetlock, Orie V. Kristel, "The Limits of Fungibility: Relational Schemata and the Value of Things," *Journal of Consumer Research* 30 (September 2003), 219–229; see also the useful overview in Wendy Nelson Espeland and Mitchell L. Stevens, "Commensuration as a Social Process," *Annual Review of Sociology* 24 (1998), 313–364, and Barry Schwartz, *The Paradox of Choice: Why More is Less* (New York: HarperCollins, 2004).

37. Mailer, *Advertisements*, 400; emphasis added.

38. Catherine Gudis, *Buyways: Billboards, Automobiles, and the American Landscape* (New York: Routledge, 2004), chapters 2 and 4.

39. Roland Marchand, *Advertising the American Dream: Making Way for Modernity, 1920–1940* (Berkeley: University of California Press, 1985), 233–234; Marchand also points to the tradition of self-help literature as a source of the first-impression theme.

40. Dallas Smythe, "Communications: Blindspot of Western Marxism," *Canadian Journal of Political and Social Theory* 2 (1977) and Bill Livant, "The Audience Commodity: On the 'Blindspot Debate'," *Canadian Journal of Political and Social Theory* 3 (1975).

41. The "blindspot" argument has had a long but erratic afterlife; see Graham Murdock, "Blindspots about Western Marxism: A Reply to Dallas Smythe," *Canadian Journal of Political and Social Theory* 2 (1978) and Smythe's response in the same issue, "Rejoinder to Graham Murdock;" Sut Jhally, "Probing the Blindspot: The Audience Commodity," *Canadian Journal of Political and Social Theory* 6 (Spring 1982), 204–210 and Bill Livant, "Working at Watching: A Reply to Sut Jhally," in the same issue; Sut Jhally and Bill Livant, "Watching as Working: The Valorization of Audience Consciousness," *Journal of Communication* 36 (Summer 1986) 124–143; also, Sut Jhally, *The Codes of Advertising: Fetishism and the Political Economy of Meaning in the Consumer Society* (New York: St. Martin's Press, 1987), chapter 3 (with Bill Livant).

42. Christine Frederick, *Selling Mrs. Consumer* (New York: Business Bourse, 1929); Janice Williams Rutherford titles her chapter on the book, "Selling

Out Mrs. Consumer," *Selling Mrs. Consumer: Christine Frederick and the Rise of Household Efficiency* (Athens, Ga: University of Georgia Press, 2003), chapter 12.

43. Kathy M. Newman, *Radio Active: Advertising and Consumer Activism, 1935–1947* (Berkeley: University of California Press, 2004); Newman draws heavily on Smythe's model; see 4–5 and *passim*.

44. See Lizabeth Cohen, *A Consumers' Republic: The Politics of Mass Consumption in Postwar America* (New York: Knopf, 2003), chapter 3; Amy Bentley, *Eating for Victory: Food Rationing and the Politics of Domesticity* (Chicago: University of Chicago Press, 1998), chapter 6; Meg Jacobs, *Pocketbook Politics: Economic Citizenship in Twentieth-Century America* (Princeton: Princeton University Press, 2004), chapter 6.

45. Contemporary culture-jammers and ad-busters regularly use these strategies to satirize and ironize brand advertising; Art Spiegelman's *New Yorker* cover (April 17, 1995) of the Easter Bunny crucified on an income tax form stirred not just a frisson but a furor.

46. The phrase is taken from Kenneth Burke, *Permanence and Change: An Anatomy of Purpose* [1935] rev. ed. (Indianapolis: Bobbs Merrill, 1954) Part II.

47. Theodore Levitt, *The Marketing Imagination* (New York: Free Press, 1983), 72.

48. Joseph Pine II and James H. Gilmore, *The Experience Economy: Work Is Theatre & Every Business a Stage* (Boston: Harvard Business School Press, 1999), 20.

49. See, for example, Steven J. Grove and Raymond P. Fisk, "The Dramaturgy of Services Exchange: An Analytical Framework for Services Marketing," in Christopher H. Lovelock, ed., *Services Marketing*, 2nd edn. (Englewood Cliffs, NJ: Prentice Hall, 1991), 59–68; see also David Mamet's astute observations on billboards, time, and casino gambling in *True and False: Heresy and Common Sense for the Actor* (New York: Knopf, 1997), 53.

50. Arlie Russell Hochschild, *The Managed Heart: Commercialization of Human Feeling* (New York: W.W. Norton, 1983).

51. Michel Callon, "Introduction: The Embeddedness of Economic Markets in Economics," in *The Laws of the Markets*, Michel Callon, ed. (Oxford: Blackwell, 1998), 19–25, 34–43; see also Michel Callon, Cecile Medel, and Vololona Rabeharisoa, "The Economy of Qualities," *Economy and Society* 31 (May 2002), 194–217, where the authors highlight what they regard as the collaborative and performative relationship between economic theorists and economic actors in the service industry; it should be said that Callon sees the embedding of markets in culture—the formatting of spheres and spans of market calculability—as subject to "overflow" and new social entanglements and attachments.

52. Adam Smith, *Lectures on Jurisprudence*, R.L. Meek, D.D. Raphael, P.G. Stein, eds. ([1762–63] Indianapolis, In: Liberty Press, 1982), 352.

53. Self-promotion should not be confused here with tooting-one's own horn; it can take, and given Smith's vaguely Stoic sensibility, often did take the form of the soft sell. Part of my argument is developed at greater length in my *Worlds Apart: The Market and the Theater in Anglo-American Thought, 1550–1750* (Cambridge: Cambridge University Press, 1986), 177–185; for different views of the role of rhetoric in Smith, see Charles L. Griswold, Jr., *Adam Smith and the Virtues of Enlightenment* (Cambridge: Cambridge University Press, 1999), 297 and Emma Rothschild, *Economic Sentiments: Adam Smith, Condorcet, and the Enlightenment* (Cambridge, Mass: Harvard

University Press, 2001), 242–244; the most developed alternative view may be found in Andreas Kalyvas and Ira Katznelson, "The Rhetoric of the Market: Adam Smith on Recognition, Speech, and Exchange," *Review of Politics* 63 (2001), 549–579; they translate Smith's concept of sympathy into "a modern theory of recognition" (554) while ignoring Smith's comments on the effects of the limited fund of sympathy itself; see, in this regard, a neo-Beckerian view of social control through the exchange of "esteem-services," in Geoffrey Brennan and Philip Pettit, "The Hidden Economy of Esteem," *Economics and Philosophy* 16 (April 2000): 77–98 and *The Economy of Esteem: An Essay on Civil and Political Society* (New York: Oxford University Press, 2004).

54. Hochschild, *Managed Heart*, 186–189; Robin Leidner, *Fast Food, Fast Talk: Service Work and the Routinization of Everyday Life* (Berkeley: University of California Press, 1993), 194–197.

55. Michael R. Soloman, Carol Surprenant, John A. Czepiel, and Evelyn G. Gutman, "A Role Theory Perspective on Dyadic Interactions: The Service Encounter," *Journal of Marketing* 49 (Winter 1985), 103.

56. *New York Times*, August 12, 2000.

57. Some market researchers might prefer "back-stage" or "back-region" selves to "inner selves," in keeping with the theatrical vocabulary used by Erving Goffman in his pathbreaking *The Presentation of Self in Everyday Life* (Garden City, NY: Doubleday, 1959), published in the United States the same year as Mailer's essay; the phrase "strategic essentialism" is borrowed from the work of Gayatri Chakravorty Spivak.

58. See Thomas Frank, *One Market Under God: Extreme Capitalism, Market Populism, and the End of Market Democracy* (New York: Anchor, 2001).

59. Peter Miller, "The Margins of Accounting," in Callon, ed., *Laws of the Markets*, 190; see also the essays in Marilyn Strathern, ed. *Audit Culture: Anthropological Studies in Accountability, Ethics and the Academy* (New York: Routledge, 2000).

60. Adam Smith, *Lectures on Rhetoric and Belles Lettres*, J.C. Bryce, ed. ([1762–63] Indianapolis, In: Liberty, 1985), 137.

61. One interesting exception is Thomas Hylland Eriksen, *Tyranny of the Moment: Fast and Slow Time in the Information Age* (London: Pluto Press, 2001).

Index

Note: Page numbers in italics refer to illustrations

A&P stores, 31, 260
academia, 331, 334, 336
activism, political, 144, 157–158, 162
Adam's Rib, 296, 308
Advertisements for Myself, 349–352
advertising, 4, 5, 10, 15, 21, 27, 34–35,
   40, 55, 61, 63, 67, 75–79, 82,
   84–86, 92, 102, 104–107, 126,
   161, 175, 200, 208, 237–238,
   243, 344–346, 353–355, 357
   outdoor, 251–268
Aeolian Company, 82, *83*, 84, *85*
aesthetics, 31, 35–36, 43, 63, 67, 84,
   201, 203, 206
   modern aesthetics, 51–52, 54, 61,
   64–65
African Americans, 121, 143–163
agriculture, 18–21
All About Eve, 309–310
American Advertising Guild, 52, 61, 63,
   64
American Museum of Natural History,
   123, 133
anti-immigration campaigns, 117, 122,
   127, 129, 133
anti-modernism, 52
anti-Semitism, 119, 120, 124, 129
Architectural Record: 59, 260
architecture, 4, 5, 40, 57, 60, 199–217,
   260
art, 23–24, 28, 52–53, 57, 59, 60, 76, 79
   commercial, 5, 17–18, 61, 63, 67,
   91–109
   modern, 52, 53, 59, 65, 91–95
Art Directors' Club: 85, 106
Art Students League, 34, 54
assimilation, 130–131

Atlas Shrugged, 5, 321–336
automobiles, 27–30, 32, 34–37, 41, 125,
   251–252, 257–258, 261, 263–266
Ayer, N.W., Company, 97, 100, 102, 104

Babbitt, 44, 119, 130
Barnum, P.T., 174
Barthes, Roland, 77
Bauhaus, 52, 54, 56–57, 59, 63–64
Bayer, Herbert, 59, 63, *64*, 66
beauty culture, 143, 145–146, 148,
   151, 155, 156, 159–160, 163
beauty industry, 144, 146, 148,
   150–151, 154–155, 157–163
Becker, Gary, 333, 348–349, 355, 357
Bel Geddes, Norman, 55, 58, 60
The Best of Everything, 313–314
billboards, 251–268
Blanc, A., 12, 166
Book and Magazine Guild, 52, 59,
   61–63, 65
boosterism, 4, 126, 133–134
Bourdieu, Pierre, 333
Briggs Brothers & Company, 11, *12*,
   15, 17, 22, 23
Buick, 27, 29, 39, 43, 44
Bullock's Department Store, 255–256
Bureau of Labor Statistics, 287, 290
Burpee Company, 12–13, *14*, 15–17,
   19, 21–24
Burroughs, Nannie Helen, 145, 151, 154
business sector, 1, 9, 27–28, 159–160,
   296, 321, 328–329, 356
Byron Company, 208, 215–216

Cadillac, 29, 30, 34, 44
Cahill, Holger, 54, 56, 57

Camera Work, 93, 99, 208
capital, 321
   cultural, 333, 334
   human, 333, 334
Capital, 347
capitalism, 51, 65, 176, 335, 323–324,
   326, 331, 336, 347
Capra, Frank, 310
Carter, Ezella Mathis, 149–150
catalogues, 9, 11, 13, 16, 19, 22
Century of Progress, 258
Cheney Brothers Silk Manufacturing
   Company, 32, 40, 41, 44
Chevrolet, 30, 44, 255
childhood, 173, 175, 181–182, 184,
   186
chromolithography, 11, 17, 22–23, 31
class, 29, 51, 52, 54, 61, 173, 333, *see*
   also middle classes, working classes,
   elites
Cold War, 52, 67
Colliers, 127, *128*, 306
color, 27–45
   psychology of, 31, 34
   revolution, 27–28, 31, 37, 40, 43
   system, 31, 42
   theory, 31, 45
commerce, 1, 3, 5, 32, 40, 160, 230,
   343–344, 352, 356–357
commodification, 9–10, 18, 22, 133,
   255
commodities, 3, 9, 10, 22, 24, 28, 66,
   75, 125, 186, 189, 230, 351
Communism, 57, 121
Congress of Industrial Organizations,
   51, 53, 61, 62
consumerism, 64, 67, 299
consumers, 18–19, 28, 34, 39, 41,
   43–44, 56, 66, 75, 77, 79–80, 130,
   144, 161–162, 232–233, 243, 253,
   256, 265, 345–348, 350, 352–354
Consumers Union, 58
consumption, 1, 2, 5, 19, 67, 75, 82,
   126, 129, 173–176, 183,
   189, 252–253, 256, 291,
   347–349, 353
Container Corporation of America, 52,
   64, 66
conformity, 5, 278
consumers, women as, 229–246
Coolidge, Calvin, 127

corporations, 66, 281, 321, 322, 324,
   see under specific names
Corsets and Brassieres, 233, 239, 243
Corsets and Lingerie, 229, 232–233, 238
Corsi, Edward, 130–131
Creange, Henry, 40, 43
Creel, George, 127, *128*
Cubism, 61, 95, 98
culture, 1, 5, 39, 66, 123
   business, 1, 43, 45, 53, 77
   commercial, 28, 175, 243, 357
   consumer, 73, 83, 163, 291, 353
   corporate, 215, 278
   market, 1, 344
   mass, 1, 2, 51, 53, 61, 67
   national, 117, 119
   popular, 31, 297
   see also beauty culture
   see also industry—culture industries
   see also material culture

demobilization, 278, 280
department stores, 175–176, 179, 230,
   243, *see under* specific store names
Depression (1930s), 51–53, 55, 67,
   255, 257, 348
design, 3, 5, 11, 19, 22–23, 28–29, 34,
   40, 44, 52–54, 56–57, 59–60,
   65–67, 233–234, 257, *see also*
   industrial design
Design Laboratory (later known as
   Laboratory School of Industrial
   Design), 51, 53–54, *55*, 56–58, 65
distribution, 1–2, 5, 15, 18–19, 21, 56,
   59, 66, 75, 125
domesticity, 296, 298
   masculine domesticity, 256
Dreyfuss, Henry, 55, 58, 60
Du Pont Company, 3, 27–29, 32,
   34–35, 38, 40–45
Duco Color Advisory Service, 27–28,
   34–35, 38, 40–42
Duco Finish, 27, 29–30, 34–35, 42, 44

Earl, Harley, 27, 38–39, 44
Earl, Wheeler, 32, 39
economics, 347–349, 351–352
education, 298, 333
   beauty, 146, 155
   consumer, 79
   design, 51, 53–54, 57–58, 61, 63–66

electrotypography, 15–17
elites, 122–123
Erector Toys, 178, 186–188
Esquire, 58, 278
ethnicity, 3, 4, 29, 118, 121
    ethnic neighborhoods, 117, 127,
        129–132
eugenics, 123–124
Evergood, Philip, 52, 63
Ewen, Stuart, 345–46, 349

family, 201–202, 209–210, 212,
    216–217, 299
fashion, 28, 34, 40, 43–44
    intermediaries, 28, 43, 44
    men's, 277–280
    predictions, 31
    shows, 238–241, *242*, 243–244
Federal Art Project, 51, 53–54, 57
The Feminine Mystique, 296, 298
femininity, 230
Fields, Mamie Garvin, 147–150
film, 85, 240, 243, 302, 306–314
Fiske, Haley, 209–210, 216
Ford Motor Company, 97–*98*,
    100–103, 202, 257, *258*
Ford, Henry, 29, 100
forecasting, 38, 41, 44
formalism, 59, 65
Fortune, 27–28, 279, 281, 284–286,
    300
Foster and Kleiser Company, 254, 262
The Fountainhead, 321, 330
Frederick, Christine, 354
Friedan, Betty, 296, 298
functionalism, 51, 56, 59–61, 63, 65
Futurism, 104, 257

Garvey, Amy Jacque, 160, 162
Garvey, Marcus, 144, 158, 159,
    160–163
gender, 3, 4, 75, 151, 160, 173, 176,
    184, 186, 212, 214, 216, 230,
    234, 278, 281–282, 287, 289,
    303–304
    discrimination, 145
    roles in workplace, 296–97
General Electric, 31, 58, 85, 255
General Motors Company, 27, 29–30,
    34, 38–39, 43–44, 58; *see under*
    specific divisions

gift exchange, 22
Gilbert, A.C., 186–189
Gimbel's Department Store, 179, 235
Good Housekeeping, 81, 127, 295,
    303, 106
government, 262, 321–322,
    327–329, 335
Grant, Madison, 121, 123–125, 131
Greenberg, Clement, 91–93, 95,
    103–104, 108
Gropius, Walter, 57, 65

half-tone screen process, 75–77
Harper's Bazaar, 62, 81
Hepburn, Katharine, 296, 308, 310
Hiller, Lejaren à, 3, 76, 80–86
Hitchcock, Alfred, 279–280
home, 22–23, 212, 348
home ownership, 217
Hoover, Herbert, 41, 123
hybridization, 9

illumination, electrical, 252–254
illustration, 3, 10–13, 15–16, 19,
    21–22, 55, 86, 131–132
    advertising, 75–76, 78
    botanical, 3, 12
    commercial, 3, 79–85
immigrants, 4, 117–119, 122, 125–133,
    173, 213–214
immigration, 118–119, 122–124, 127
industrial arts, 31–32, 40, 42–44
industrial design, 53–56, 60, 231, 267
industry, 18–21, 28, 40
    culture industries, 51, 61, 345
installments (sales), 27, 30
insurance business, 199–217
interior design, 4, 22–23, 230–233
International Ladies Garment Workers'
    Union, 143, 158
intimate apparel trade, 229–246

Japonisme, 11, 81
Johnson, James Weldon, 121–122
Johnson, Kathryn, 149–150

Kallen, Horace, 287, 290
Kant, Immanuel, 92–93
Kemp, Maida Springer, 143, 158
Ketchum, Howard, 40–45
Ku Klux Klan, 122, 124

labor, 51–52, 56, 256, 347–348,
 351, 354
 domestic, 143–146
 labor movement, 59, 66, 143–144,
  157–158, 346, 348
 mental labor, 321–322, 324,
  332–336
Laboratory School of Industrial Design,
 see Design Laboratory
Ladies' Home Journal, 76, 85, 106,
 301, 304
LeBrun, Napoleon, 203–205, 215
leisure, 21, 126, 144–45, 173, 231, 353
leftist politics, 52, 57, 59, 91, 345, 348
Levy, Jacques, 54, 58, 59
Lewis, Sinclair, 252
life insurance business, 199–217
lingerie trade, 229–246
Loewy, Raymond, 55, 56, 58, 267
Look, 284, 290, 291, 305

Macy, R.H., Company, 176, *180*, 181
Mailer, Norman, 349–352, 354–357
Main Street, 252
magazines, 76, 298, 305, 306, *see under*
 specific titles
Malone, Annie, 148–49, 153–54, 158
The Man in the Gray Flannel Suit (film),
 280
The Man in the Gray Flannel Suit
 (novel), 277, 280–283, 287–288
marginalism (economics), 347, 349,
 351–352
market, 3, 5, 21, 28–29, 39, 56, 176,
 178, 186, 251, 268, 325, 344, 356
 segmentation, 32, 266
marketing, 2–4, 9, 15, 19, 21, 55, 67,
 127–128, 155, 159, 175, 178,
 184–186, 231, 264, 352–353
Marshall Field's Department Store, 177,
 181, 184, *185*, 233, *236*
Marx, Karl, 347, 349
Marxism, 91, 348, 354, 357
masculinity, 160, 173–76, 179, 181,
 183–186, 189
mass production, 1, 2, 37, 40, 59, 125,
 171, 229
material culture, 5, 56, 65, 230
McCausland, Elizabeth, 57–59, 63

Metropolitan Life Insurance Company, 4,
 199–217
Metropolitan Museum of Art, 125, 133,
 134
middle classes, 22, 29, 75, 117, 127,
 129, 132, 173–174, 179, 186,
 278, 283, 285–291, 296–301,
 321–324, 326, 330–332, 336
Mills, C. Wright, 281, 283–290,
 324–328, 330, 332, 334, 336
Model T Ford, 29, 36
modernism, 3, 4, 29, 31, 39, 51–53,
 59, 64–66, 91–109, 259
modernity, 37, 56, 60, 144–145, 216
Mumford, Lewis, 54, 108, 267
Munsell Color System, 31, 39, 42, 43
Museum of Modern Art, 52, 59, 60,
 63–65

National Association of Colored
 Women, 147–148, 150–154, 156
National Auto Show, 36–37
nativism, 122, 127, 186
nature, 9, 13–15, 23–24
Negro World, 159, 160–163
New York World's Fair (1939–1940),
 58, 60
nitrocellulose, 29, 32
"normality," 278, 291

Oakland Motor Car Company, 29, *30*
offices, 199–217, 281–282, 290
The Organization Man, 283–290, 311,
 321–322, 324
Osborn, Henry Fairfield, 123–125
outdoor advertising, 251–268
Outdoor Advertising Association of
 America, 253, 259, 262, 267
Outerbridge, Paul, 92, 94, 95, *96*,
 97, 109

packaging, 9, 15, 18–19
Packard, Vance, 291, 349
Paepcke, Walter, 52, 66
Pan-Africanism, 159
patriotism, 185, 217
Peck, Gregory, 280, 303
Pereira, Irene Rice, 54, 63, 65
philanthropy, 152–153

photography, 3, 4, 75–86, 91–109, 128, 131, 208, 215–216
pictorialism, 81–82, 84–85
planned obsolescence, 55
play, 188–89
Playthings, 171, *172*, 173–174, 177–179, 181, 183–184
Pontiac, 34, 39
Popular Front, 3, 51–54, 57, 59–61, 64–67
Pratt Institute, 34, 54, 65, 66
Printer's Ink, 82, 84, 188
printmaking, 10, 15
production (as phase of industry), 1–2, 5, 19, 21, 29, 56–57, 59, 66, 75, *see also* mass production
property, 322, 325, 331–335
  intellectual, 322, 331, 333, 335
psychology, 75, 79
public health, 210, 216–217
publishing, 61, 67

race, 3, 4, 118, 123–125, 128, 130–131, 134, 143–163, 289
radicalism, 51–52, 56, 59, 64–65, 158
railroads, 325, 327, 329
Rand School of Social Science, 120, 122
Rand, Ayn, 5, 321–336
Rand, Paul, 58, 60, 63, 66
Randolph, Asa Philip, 156–158
Randolph, Lucille Campbell Green, 156–158
realism, 75, 76, 79–80
representation, 4–5, 52, 56, 126, 128
  architectural, 201–202, 216
  defined, 1–2
  graphic, 10–13, 21
  photographic, 77, 79, 81
retail commerce, 28, 75, 230–235, 243–246, 252, 254, 351, 356
Riesman, David, 330, 349
Riis, Jacob, 131–132
Robinson, J.W., Co., 255–256

sales, 1, 22, 27, 29, 76
Saturday Evening Post, 76, *78*, 82, *83*, *85*, 127, 145, 304
Schamberg, Morton, 98–99
Scientific American, 206, *207*, 208

scientific management, 34, 212
Scott, Walter Dill, 79, 355
seed trade, 9–24
Selling Mrs. Consumer, 354
sexuality, 23–232, 240–242, 243, 246
Sheeler, Charles, 92, 96, 97, *98*, 99–104, 109
Sloan, Alfred, Jr., 29, 38
Smith, Adam, 343–344, 356–357
socialism, 121, 157, 158
Standard Oil, 260, 264
Steichen, Edward, 84, 92, 100, 104, *105*, 106–109, 215
Steiglitz, Alfred, 84, 93, 94, 99, 107, 208
Stewart, Adina, 143–144, 158
Strand, Paul, 94, 99
streamlining, 55–56, 59–60, 65, 259
strip development, 251, 253, 257, 260–263
suburbia, 256, 259, 284, 289

taste, 28, 39, 44, 57, 59, 66
"taxpayers," 204, 260, 264
Teague, Walter Dorwin, 55, 85, 260
technology, 29, 43, 201
  architectural, 206
  office, 212–213
  photographic, 76
  print, 9, 15, 21
television, 296–298, 312
Terrell, Mary Church, 147, 150, 152
time, 346–353, 357, 358
tourism, 4, 117–118, 125–134
Towle, H. Ledyard, 27–28, 34–41, 43–45
toy trade, 171–189
Toys and Novelties, 178, 182
Tracy, Spencer, 296, 308, 310
trade shows, 241–243
True Blue, 29, *30*, 39, 44, *see also*, Duco Finish
Truman, Harry S., 278–279, 299
Tuskegee Institute, 149, 151

unions, 61, 62, 66–67, 334, 356–357, *see under* specific names
United American Artists, 52, 61, 63, 65

Universal Negro Improvement
    Association, 144, 158–163
urban sprawl, 251, 259, 266

Vanity Fair (magazine), 95, 100, 101,
    106, 107
Veblen, Thorstein, 54, 349
Vogue, 100, 104, 106, 107, 108

Walker, Madam C.J., 146–148, 149,
    152–157, 161–163
Wanamaker's Department Store, 64, 176,
    179, 181–182, 230, 235, 239, 240
Washington, Booker T., 149, 153, 159
welfare, 210, 212–213, 216–217
Westinghouse Corporation, 55, 66
White Collar, 283–290
White, Clarence, 84, 94–96, 100
wholesale commerce, 229, 230–232,
    237–238, 241, 243–246
Whyte, William, 283–290, 311,
    321–322

Wilson, Sloan, 277, 280–283,
    285–286, 287
A Woman of Distinction, 310–311
Women's Home Companion, 303, 305
Women's Wear Daily, 233–234
work, 296–297, 347, 357
    blue-collar work, 321
    white-collar work, 64, 212–215, 278,
        281, 286–290, 330–334
    women at work, 298–306
    see also, offices
working classes, 51, 202, 216, 283,
    288, 330
Works Progress Administration,
    54, 57
World War I, 31, 34, 42, 118, 148, 159,
    177
World War II, 278, 280–281, 298

Yale, 54, 66

zoning, 120, 133